ELEMENTS

OF

NATURAL PHILOSOPHY,

By E. S. FISCHER,

HONORARY MEMBER OF THE ACADEMY OF SCIENCES OF BERLIN, PROFESSOR OF MATHEMATICS AND NATURAL PHILOSOPHY IN ONE OF THE COLLEGES OF THE SAME CITY, &c. &c.

TRANSLATED INTO FRENCH

WITH

NOTES AND ADDITIONS,

By M. BIOT,

OF THE INSTITUTE OF FRANCE,

AND NOW

TRANSLATED FROM THE FRENCH INTO ENGLISH

FOR THE

USE OF COLLEGES AND SCHOOLS

IN THE

UNITED STATES.

EDITED

BY JOHN FARRAR,

PROFESSOR OF MATHEMATICS AND NATURAL PHILOSOPHY IN THE UNIVERSITY AT CAMBRIDGE, NEW ENGLAND.

◆

BOSTON:

HILLIARD, GRAY, LITTLE, AND WILKINS.

1827.

DISTRICT OF MASSACHUSETTS, TO WIT.

District Clerk's Office.

BE it remembered, that on the twenty-fourth day of November, 1827, in the fifty-second year of the Independence of the United States of America, Hilliard, Gray, & Co., of the said district, have deposited in this office the title of a book, the right whereof they claim as proprietors, in the words following, viz:

"Elements of Natural Philosophy, by E. S. Fischer, honorary Member of the Academy of Sciences of Berlin, Professor of Mathematics and Natural Philosophy in one of the Colleges of the same city, &c. &c. Translated into French, with Notes and Additions, by M. Biot, of the Institute of France; and now translated from the French into English for the use of Colleges and Schools in the United States. Edited by John Farrar, Professor of Mathematics and Natural Philosophy in the University at Cambridge, New England."

In conformity to the act of the Congress of the United States, entitled "An act for the encouragement of learning, by securing the copies of maps, charts, and books, to the authors and proprietors of such copies, during the times therein mentioned;" and also to an act, entitled, "An act supplementary to an act, entitled, 'An act for the encouragement of learning, by securing the copies of maps, charts, and books, to the authors and proprietors of such copies, during the times therein mentioned,' and extending the benefits thereof to the arts of designing, engraving, and etching, historical and other prints."

JNO. W. DAVIS,
Clerk of the District of Massachusetts

CAMBRIDGE.
Hilliard, Metcalf, and Company
Printers to the University.

ADVERTISEMENT.

The comprehensive and elementary outline of Natural Philosophy by E. S. Fischer, of which the following is a translation, has been much used and highly approved in the German and French schools. It was selected by Biot, himself the author of two very valuable works upon the same subject, as best suited to a certain class of students, whose want of leisure, or of previous preparation, might preclude them from more ample and elaborate treatises. A few alterations and additions have been made for the purpose of adapting it to the use of learners in the public and private seminaries of the United States. The alterations consist principally in converting the French weights, measures, degrees, &c. into the corresponding English denominations. The additions are distinguished by being in brackets.

Cambridge, November, 1827.

CONTENTS.

SECTION I.
OF BODIES IN GENERAL.

CHAP. I.—*General Considerations respecting the Properties which belong to all Bodies* 1
CHAP. II.—*State of Aggregation of Bodies* . . . 3
CHAP. III.—*Great Variety of Material Properties in Bodies* 5
CHAP. IV.—*Different Modes of Considering Bodies* . . 8
    Atomic System . . . . ib.
    Dynamic System . . . . . . ib.
    Empirical Considerations 9
CHAP. V.—*Mathematical Laws of Motion* 10
CHAP. VI.—*Physical Laws of Motion, or Investigation of Moving Forces* 12
CHAP. VII.—*Historical View of what is known respecting Gravity* 15

SECTION II.
SOLID BODIES.

CHAP. VIII.—*General Properties of Solid Bodies* . . 18
CHAP. IX.—*The Interior Construction of Solid Bodies* . 21
CHAP. X.—*Equilibrium of Solid Bodies, or Fundamental Principles of Statics* 23
    Equilibrium of Free Bodies . . . . ib.
    Equilibrium of Bodies which move about a Fixed Axis 24
CHAP. XI.—*Centre of Gravity of Bodies* . . . 25
CHAP. XII.—*Free Descent of Heavy Bodies.—Laws of Motion uniformly accelerated* 27
    Motion down Inclined Planes . . . 32
CHAP. XIII.—*Free Curvilinear Motion* 34
    (1.) *Projectiles* . . . . . . ib.
    (2.) *Central Forces.* 35

Contents.

Chap. XIV.—*Motion in given Lines*	37
(1.) *Curvilinear Motions*	ib.
(2.) *Oscillations of the Pendulum*	38
(3.) *Application of the Pendulum*	42
Chap. XV.—*Communication of Motion by Impulse*	47
Chap. XVI.—*Vibratory Motions, and the Sounds which they produce; or the first Principles of Acoustics*	52

SECTION III.
HEAT.

Chap. XVII.—*Heat in general; its expansive Force; Thermometer and Pyrometer*	57
Addition	67
Chap. XVIII.—*Changes produced by Heat in the State of Aggregation of Bodies*	68
Chap. XIX.—*The Propagation of Heat*	73
The Calorimeter	75
Chap. XX.—*Production of Heat and Cold*	79
Artificial Cold	81

SECTION IV.
LIQUID BODIES.

Chap. XXI.—*Liquids in General*	83
Water	ib.
Mercury	85
Alcohol	86
Ether	87
General Remarks upon Liquids	ib.
Chap. XXII.—*The Specific Gravity of Solids and Liquids*	88
Chap. XXIII.—*Equilibrium of Liquids, or First Principles of Hydrostatics*	94
Pressure of a Liquid against the Bottom and Sides of a Vessel	96
Pressure of a Liquid upon Solid Bodies immersed in it	97
Floating Bodies	98
Chap. XXIV.—*Hydrostatic Balance and Hydrometer*	99
Areometer or Hydrometer	101
Chap. XXV.—*Influence of Adhesion and Cohesion upon Hydrostatic Phenomena*	103

Contents.

Chap. XXVI.—*Motions of Liquids, or First Principles of Hydraulics* 111
    Hydraulic Experiments confirming the preceding Theory 114
    Influence of Forces different from Gravity upon Hydraulic Motions . . . . . . ib.
    The Motions of Solid Bodies in Liquids . 117

SECTION V.

AERIFORM BODIES.

Chap. XXVII.—*Elastic Fluids in General* . . . 119
    Atmospheric Air . . . . . . ib.
    Oxygen 121
    Azote 122
    Hydrogen 123
    Carbonic Acid Gas . . . . . ib.
    Elastic Vapours 124

Chap. XXVIII.—*Water in Atmospheric Air, or First Principles of Hygrometry* 125
    Addition relative to Hygrometry . . . 128
    General Remarks upon Hygrometry . . 133
    Addition 134

Chap. XXIX.—*Barometer and Air-Pump* . . . 137
    Barometer . . . . ib.
    Air-Pump 141
    Condensing Pump 143
    Mechanical Properties of Air . . . 144
    Dilatability of the Air . . . . . ib.
    Pressure of the Air 146
    Gravity of the Air 148
    Specific Gravity of other Gases . . . 149

Chap. XXX.—*Equilibrium of Air, or First Principles of Aerostatics* . . . . ib.
    Law of Mariotte; or Ratio of the Pressure and Elasticity to the Density or Specific Gravity 150
    Law by which the Density of the Air decreases as we ascend into the Atmosphere . . . 153
    More exact Estimate of the Influence which Heat has upon the Mechanical Properties of a Dilatable Fluid 155

viii *Contents.*

Measurement of Heights by the Barometer . 156
Height of the Atmosphere 158
CHAP. XXXI.—*Motions of Elastic Fluids* . . 159

SECTION VI.
ELECTRICITY.

CHAP. XXXII.—*Electrical Machine, and General Phenomena of Electricity* 164
CHAP. XXXIII.—*Opposite Electricities* . . . 171
Electrical Phenomena in the Dark and in Rarefied Air 173
Hypothesis of Franklin 175
Hypothesis of Symmer 176
Addition.—The Electric Balance . . . 177
CHAP. XXXIV.—*Striking Distance, Sphere of Activity, Accumulated Electricity* 179
Sphere of Activity 180
Accumulated Electricity 184
CHAP. XXXV.—*Electrophorus and Condenser* . . 190
Electrophorus . . . . . . ib.
Condenser 193
CHAP. XXXVI.—*Electricity excited by other Means beside Friction* 194
Galvanism 196
Voltaic Pile, or Galvanic Battery . . 198
Relations of Electricity and Galvanism . 201
Addition . . . . ib.

SECTION VII.
MAGNETISM.

CHAP. XXXVII.—*General Properties of the Magnet* . 211
Relation between the Magnet and Unmagnetized Iron 212
Properties of the Magnet 213
The Reciprocal Action of Magnets . . 214
Communication of Magnetism . . . ib.
Distribution of Magnetism, and Sphere of Magnetic Activity 215
CHAP. XXXVIII.—*More Particular Examination of the Phenomena of the Magnetized Needle* . . . 217

Declination Needle 217
Dipping Needle 219
Terrestrial Magnetism 221
Excitation of Natural Magnetism . . . **222**
Addition . . . . ib.

SECTION VIII.

OPTICS.

CHAP. XXXIX.—*Of Light in General; particularly the Phenomena which depend upon its Motion in a Right Line; or First Principles of Optics* 225
    Mechanical Phenomena of Direct Light . . **227**
CHAP. XL.—*Vision* 233
CHAP. XLI.—*Reflection of Light by Mirrors, or First Principles of Catoptrics* 239
    Fundamental Law of Catoptrics . . . 240
    Plane Mirrors 241
    Spherical Mirrors 242
    Phenomena produced by Concave Mirrors . ib.
    Phenomena produced by Convex Mirrors . 245
    Mathematical Additions 247
CHAP. XLII.—*Refraction of Light in Transparent Bodies; or First Principles of Dioptrics* 253
    Law of Dioptrics 254
    General Phenomena which depend upon the Refraction of Light 257
    Particular Phenomena which are produced by means of Polished Glasses 258
    Plane Glasses with Parallel Faces . . . ib.
    Spherical Glasses or Lenses . . . 259
    Phenomena produced by Converging Glasses 261
    Phenomena produced by Diverging Glasses . 267
    Mathematical Additions 268
CHAP. XLIII.—*Compound Optical Instruments* . . 275
    A. *Refracting Telescope* . . . . ib.
    Phenomena produced by means of Converging Glasses when the Object is behind the Glass 277
    Phenomena produced by means of Diverging Glasses, when the Object is behind the Glass . 278

Contents.

B. *The most Important Kinds of Refracting Telescopes* 278
C. *Compound Microscope* 281

CHAP. XLIV.—*Theory of Dioptric Colours, or the Decomposition of Light* 283
    The Glass Prism . . . . . ib.
    Colours produced by Thin Laminæ . . 289
    General Observations upon Newton's Theory of Colours 290
    Effects of the Dispersion of Colours in Optical Glasses 291

CHAP. XLV.—*Reflecting Telescope and Achromatic Lenses* 292
    State of Optics before Newton's Time . . ib.
    Errors of Newton in the Theory of Colours . 293
    Reflecting Telescope 294
    Ingenious Researches of Euler; his Errors.—Dollond.—Klingenstiern . . . 296
    Mathematical Additions 299

APPENDIX TO OPTICS.

Coloured Rings 306
Another Explanation of the Coloured Rings on the Hypothesis of Undulations.—Dr Young's Principle of Interferences 314
Diffraction of Light 321
Double Refraction 324
Polarisation of Light 336

SECTION I.

OF BODIES IN GENERAL.

CHAPTER I.

General Considerations respecting the Properties which belong to all Bodies.

1. ALL the knowledge with which our senses furnish us, is either of material substances denominated *bodies*, or of the changes which take place in them. But there are only two of the senses that are capable of convincing us immediately of the existence of other bodies; these are the sight and touch; and the latter only is capable of determining with certainty whether an appearance is a body or not. Thus a body is properly a *palpable thing*.

2. There are certain properties which are *general*, that is, common to all bodies; and we are assured of their *generality*, either because we could not perceive bodies without them, or because experience has proved that they are found in all bodies.

3. One of the first of these properties is *extension*, with all its modifications. Every body has a determinate *form*, although, in liquid and aeriform bodies, it varies with the form of the enclosures which confine them. Every body has a determinate magnitude, or fills a certain space, which we call its *bulk* or *volume*. Every body is *divisible*; and we must distinguish between *geometrical* and *physical divisibility*. The former is unlimited; and we are ignorant whether the last be also unlimited, or whether there be some point at which it ceases; experience, however, teaches us that by means of natural and artificial forces, bodies may be divided into particles so small as to become imperceptible to the senses.

4. Another general property is *impenetrability*. By this we mean that no body can coexist with another body, in identically the same portion of space. It is by impenetrability that bodies become palpa-

ble; it must, therefore, belong to whatever we call *body*. Nevertheless we might doubt, at first, whether it exists in all bodies in an absolute manner, that is, under all circumstances.

5. The property in question certainly exists; 1. Between two bodies perfectly homogeneous, of whatever kind, solid, liquid, or aeriform. 2. Between two solid bodies, even heterogeneous, so long as they continue in the state of solids. 3. Between a solid and a fluid body, so long as the first retains its solid state. Hence it is evident that it exists between our own bodies and all other perceptible bodies.

But this property appears to be doubtful when two fluids, whether liquid or aeriform, are mixed together; or when a solid body is dissolved in a fluid; or lastly, when two bodies form a *combination* perfectly homogeneous, which is to be distinguished from a *mixture* however perfect. It would seem, however, from a more intimate knowledge of natural phenomena, that impenetrability exists as well in these cases as in the other.

6. A necessary consequence of impenetrability is *coercibility*; so that the words *impenetrable*, *palpable*, and *coercible*, signify the same thing.

7. *Gravity* and *mobility* are not really necessary conditions of perceptibility; still experience teaches that they belong to all perceptible bodies without exception; but as these two properties are the most essential, considered with reference to mechanical philosophy, we shall treat of them at length hereafter.

8. Most philosophers reckon, also, among the general properties of bodies, *porosity*, *compressibility*, and *elasticity*; but the reasons for the opinion that these qualities belong to all bodies, are not conclusive.

9. The preceding observations apply only to perceptible bodies; but the farther we advance in the knowledge of nature, the more we find ourselves constrained to acknowledge the existence of imperceptible substances. Among modern philosophers there are many who incline, for good reasons, to deny the existence of gravity and impenetrability in imperceptible substances, and to allow them only extension and mobility. Others ascribe to them the two first properties, but in a degree imperceptible to our senses. All agree in denominating them *imponderable* or *incoercible substances*.*

---

* If there really exist substances which are not perceptible, as many phenomena tend to show, the ideas which we are to form of

CHAPTER II.

State of Aggregation of Bodies.

10. ALL natural bodies are either *solid* or *fluid*. Solid bodies are those whose particles naturally adhere to each other, so that they cannot be separated, or change their relative position, without the action of some external force; which circumstance gives to these bodies a particular and determinate form. In fluid bodies, on the contrary, the particles adhere so little to each other, that they may be easily separated, and still more easily change their relative position. For this reason, these bodies cannot preserve any particular and determinate form. Among fluid bodies, there is a very remarkable difference. Some naturally preserve their volume, without making a continual effort to extend it; these are called *liquids*. In others, the particles tend continually to separate from each other; these are denominated *elastic* or *aeriform fluids*. The three states of aggregation are called *solid*, *liquid*, and *aeriform* or *gaseous*.

11. Many bodies are capable of passing successively into the three states of aggregation, by means of natural or artificial causes, without experiencing any internal change. Water, for example, mercury, and most of the easily fusible metals, have this property; and can be successively rendered solid, liquid, and aeriform. Others appear under two of these states only; of this description are the metals which cannot be fused without great difficulty; also certain liquids and elastic fluids, as alcohol and many other substances. Lastly, there are many bodies which appear only in one state, as the simple earths, infusible metals, and most of the gases.

12. There are two methods of changing the state of aggregation of bodies. The first is by heat. Water, for instance, in temperate climates is for the most part a liquid. Below a certain temperature it is solid; and above a certain temperature it is aeriform. The

---

their nature and intimate constitution, can only be deduced from the actual properties, manifested by their phenomena; which may be termed the abstract expression of the principle of all their effects. To this degree of abstraction we have attained in the consideration of electricity and magnetism.

second method is by chemical combination. When two bodies combine very intimately together, one often communicates to the other its state of aggregation. Often also the compound takes a state of aggregation different from that of the component parts. For instance, salt becomes liquid in water; water itself becomes an elastic fluid in air. Siliceous earth passes to the state of a gas in fluoric acid. Muriatic acid gas and ammoniacal gas form the solid muriate of ammonia. Hydrogen and oxygen gases compose water in a liquid state, &c. If, as is very probable, heat be the effect of an imperceptible substance capable of combining with other substances, these two methods are confounded together.*

13. The changes in the states of aggregation depend, according to all appearances, upon the opposition of two forces, one attractive and the other repulsive. The first is a property inherent in the particles of bodies. The second is produced by the caloric which combines with them. The body is solid when the attractive force exceeds the repulsive; liquid, when both are in equilibrium; and aeriform, when the repulsive force exceeds the attractive.

14. The state of aggregation of bodies has a great influence upon all natural phenomena; and particularly upon the laws of motion and equilibrium. It is this which determines the divisions of mechanical philosophy.†

---

* The hypothesis here referred to is far from being well established. We know in fact, nothing at all of the principle of heat. Many phenomena are very well explained by supposing it to be a material radiating substance, capable of forming combinations. There are others which are less easily explained upon this hypothesis than upon that of undulations excited in an elastic medium.—[See *Cam. Optics*, p. 293, et seq.]

† Aristotle's opinion respecting the four supposed elements, fire, air, earth, and water, has an evident, though erroneous reference to the different states of aggregation.

CHAPTER III.

Great Variety of Material Properties in Bodies.

15. EXPERIENCE shows that bodies act differently upon one another. In this consists the *material variety of bodies.*

16. Hitherto almost the only hypothesis for explaining this phenomenon, has been the supposition that the small particles of bodies may have the same material nature, and that they differ only in magnitude, shape, and relative position, in different bodies; but this hypothesis is neither sufficient nor probable.

17. Experience is the only sure guide in natural philosophy; and although the light which it throws upon this subject, belongs to chemistry, it is nevertheless necessary, in order to convey a just idea of natural phenomena, to give here a brief view of the results of chemical analysis.

18. Almost all bodies in nature are composed of heterogeneous substances; thus, for example, cinnabar is composed of sulphur and oxide of mercury; these substances are called the *constituent principles*, to distinguish them from the *integrant particles* which are simply the homogeneous fragments of a body. Often the constituent principles of a body may themselves be decomposed into other *remote constituent principles;* for example, the oxide of mercury is composed of mercury and oxygen. But the chemist finally arrives, in all cases, at substances which he cannot decompose, either because they are really in a simple undecomposable state, or because he wants the means of carrying the decomposition farther.

19. In 1804, chemists reckoned 42 of these ponderable and undecomposable substances, of which all bodies are formed. In 1818, the number exceeded 50.* Every elementary work on chemistry

---

* This number increases in such a manner, as chemical researches are multiplied, that it would be absolutely useless to attempt to fix it with precision. We now find, for example, in rough platina no less than 11 simple or undecompounded metals; and who can say that more will not still be found? This multiplicity is probably the effect of the little advancement yet made in mineral chemistry; for it cannot be presumed that these substances are all strictly incapable of being reduced one to another. But in the present state of the

contains a list of these substances, which varies every year. It now comprehends four elastic substances, and 48 solid ones. Of these last, four are inflammable, and all the rest are metals. To give greater clearness to this subject, we shall consider some chemical phenomena more particularly.

20. For example, a pure salt, such as sulphate of soda, saltpetre, or common salt, becomes perfectly dissolved in pure water, and forms with it a single liquid perfectly homogeneous. We cannot discover, by the best microscope, a particle of salt in this solution. This phenomenon seems to contradict the laws of gravity, if we suppose that the particles of salt only float in the water, infinitely divided. We are rather to believe that they have themselves become fluid, and are distributed equally among all the particles of the water. Hence we perceive the great difference there is between a *combination* and a *mixture*. The solution of a salt is a compound body, whose constituent principles are salt and water.

21. If we expose such a solution to a proper heat, the water evaporates; but the salt resumes its state. Here is an example of chemical *separation* or *decomposition*.

22. Sulphate of soda itself may be decomposed into sulphuric acid and soda. These substances are, therefore, the *remote constituent principles* of the saline solution, and the *immediate constituent* principles of sulphate of soda itself. But sulphuric acid may be decomposed into sulphur and oxygen. Thus, these two last are, with respect to the sulphate of soda, remote constituent principles. The sulphur, oxigen, and soda, are simple substances, or as yet undecomposed.*

23. If we mix one part by bulk of oxygen gas, called also *vital air*, with two parts of hydrogen gas, or inflammable air, the result is a gaseous mixture entirely homogeneous, called *detonating gas*. If

---

science it is absolutely necessary to regard as distinct, all substances which resist our means of decomposition; and this is the reason why the number has increased rapidly, as chemistry has been extended.

* Since this work appeared, Sir H. Davy has discovered that potash and soda are metallic oxides. He arrived at this result by causing the electric current of a powerful voltaic battery to act upon these alkalies. MM. Guy Lussac and Thénard have given this fine discovery an important place in chemistry, by decomposing the alkaline oxides by the mere force of affinities.—[On this subject, see *Cam. Electricity*, p. 165.]

in a thick glass vessel, so tightly closed that no ponderable substance can enter or pass out, we place about a fifth part of what it is capable of containing of detonating gas, and then communicate to it the electric spark, the enclosed mass of air becomes ignited; all the gas instantly disappears and the interior surface of the vessel is covered with a watery vapour. By repeating the experiment, a sufficient quantity of this may be produced, to convince us that the product is really water.

24. Water is, therefore, itself a compound body, and its constituent principles are oxygen and hydrogen; but as in the above experiment, nothing perceptible, except the electric spark, was admitted into the vessel or suffered to escape, and yet the detonating gas underwent so remarkable a change, we are obliged to admit either that the electric spark separates from the gas, some imperceptible substance, which cannot be prevented from traversing the body of the vessel, or that it introduces some substance into it.*

25. In all the chemical phenomena above described, it is certain that nothing takes place but a combination or a decomposition; and the same is true of all chemical phenomena. This explication of the material varieties of bodies, to which we are led by experiment, consists, therefore, in the idea that there does not exist a great number of simple substances; but that those which are such, are essentially different, and form, by their infinite combinations, all the material differences which are observed in bodies.

26. The mixture of two substances is, without doubt, the consequence of an attraction, a tendency to unite, or rather to penetrate mutually into the void interstices, which exist among their material particles. This is what is meant by the *affinity* of substances; and this property is considered as a natural force which is exerted at each point of contact of heterogeneous bodies, although often it does

---

* The author undoubtedly refers to the heat which is disengaged from the mixture, when the two gases which compose it, enter into combination and form water. I have proved by direct experiment, that the transmission of the electric spark is not necessary for the formation of water. Enclose the two gases in a gun barrel and compress them rapidly, and the mere heat thus disengaged will enflame them and determine their combination. Caution is necessary in this experiment, for the tube often bursts by the force of the explosion.

not produce any combination between them, but only a slight adhesion, since a more powerful force acts in a contrary direction and prevents their combination.

CHAPTER IV.

Different Modes of Considering Bodies.

27. THE dynamic system prevails at the present time in Germany, and the atomic system in France. We must not, therefore, neglect to give a brief exposition of these systems by which human reason has attempted to represent as far as possible, the intimate essence of bodies.

Atomic System.

28. THE advocates of this system suppose each body to be composed of indivisible and impenetrable particles, which they call *atoms*. They are almost infinitely small, void spaces being interposed being them, and thus porosity is rendered a necessary property of bodies. These atoms do not touch each other, but are kept at a distance by certain attractive and repulsive forces which are exerted between them. Hence it follows that there is much more void space than matter in any body. According to this theory, the material varieties of bodies may be explained either by supposing a material difference of atoms; or a difference in their form, magnitude, position, and distance. When two substances enter into chemical combination, the atoms of one penetrate the interstices of the other, and the atoms of the two substances combine so perfectly, that they become as it were, a new kind of constituent principles, except that they are not simple, but compound.

Dynamic System.

29. ACCORDING to this system every body is considered as a space filled with continuous matter. Porosity then becomes an accidental property of matter; but compressibility and dilatability are essential properties. The state of a body depends simply upon certain forces

attractive or repulsive; and its volume must change as soon as the ratios of these forces cease to be the same. According to this theory the material varieties of bodies are explained, by supposing the existence of certain primitive substances, the different combinations of which produce all bodies. When two substances enter into chemical combination, the advocates of this system are compelled to admit that each absolutely penetrates the intimate essence of the other.

Empirical Considerations.

30. The history of science teaches us that considerations purely speculative have always been productive of error. The true philosopher will not, therefore, yield implicit faith either to the atomic or dynamic system. The intimate nature of bodies will always be concealed from us. What we know of them externally, we owe entirely to an attentive observation and careful use of what is furnished by our senses. Mathematics itself leads us astray, when it has for its foundation only ingenious hypotheses and not principles established upon facts. The philosopher ought, therefore, to take nothing for truth but what has been proved by experiment. Still he is allowed and obliged to make use of hypotheses; he must not fail, however, to bring them to the test of observation. Every hypothesis which cannot be confirmed or refuted by experiment, is nothing but a conceit or subtilty. Nevertheless hypotheses of this kind may sometimes be employed as means of representing real things, but then it must always be remembered that they are only fictions accommodated to the feebleness of our intellect.

This mode of studying nature is called *empirical*;* and it is regarded as the only exact means of advancing in natural science.

---

* [It is more frequently called in English the *inductive method*, and Lord Bacon is considered as the first who distinctly recognised it.]

CHAPTER V.

Mathematical Laws of Motion.

31. If we conceive all bodies to be annihilated, there still remains the idea of an unlimited extension in every direction; this is what we mean by *infinite* or *absolute space*. Every portion of this space which we conceive to be terminated in any way, or which is occupied by any part of the material universe, is called *limited* or *relative space*. Absolute space is immoveable, but we can conceive of the motion of all relative space.

32. That portion of space which is occupied by a body, is called its *place*. *Motion* is change of place; *rest* is continuance in the same place. Both are termed *relative* or *absolute*, according as they are referred to absolute or relative space.

33. When all the parts of a body have a common motion, the line through which any one of its points passes is called the *trajectory* of the body. The motion is *rectilinear* or *curvilinear*, according as the line described is straight or curved. The motion is *uniform*, when the body passes through equal spaces in equal times. That which is not uniform is called *varied motion*. Motion is *accelerated*, when the spaces passed through in the same intervals of time, become larger and larger. It is *retarded*, when the spaces passed through in the same intervals of time, become smaller and smaller.

34. The space which a body, moving uniformly, passes through in a unit of time, a second, for example, is called its *velocity*. In the case of motion which is not uniform, the velocity changes each instant; and this velocity, in a given instant, is equal to the space which the body would describe in a unit of time, if it were uniformly to preserve the velocity which it then had.

35. In the case of uniform motion the space described is proportional to the time. We ascertain the velocity, therefore, by dividing the space by the time employed in describing it.*

---

* Let S denote the space described by a body moving uniformly in the time T. If we designate the velocity by V, we shall have $V = \dfrac{S}{T}$. This fundamental formula of all mechanics serves also for

36. With respect to absolute space, a body can have only one motion at the same time; but with respect to relative space, it may have an indefinite number; for if a body has a motion with respect to a relative space, this space may have a second motion with respect to another relative space, which may itself have a third motion with respect to the body and the first space; and so on.

37. *If a body situated in* A, (fig. 1) *have two uniform motions in the directions* AB *and* AC, *and if* AB *and* AC *represent the spaces which would be described in equal times, by virtue of these separate motions, the body, by virtue of the two combined, will describe in the same time, and with a uniform motion, the diagonal* AD *of the parallelogram* ABCD, *which is constructed upon the lines* AB *and* AC.

According to the preceding article there is only one way of causing the body, placed at A, to take two motions at the same time; and that is by giving it a motion in relative space, and then giving another motion to this relative space itself, together with the body. Let AC, therefore, be the line which the body, moving uniformly, describes in a given time, in the relative space in which it moves; and at the same time, let AC itself be moved uniformly in the direction AB, in such a manner that at the expiration of the given time, it shall occupy the situation BD. It is easy to conceive that the body, by the combination of these two uninterrupted motions, will describe the diagonal AD, and that it will describe it with a uniform motion.*

If we cause the body to move in the direction AB, and the line

---

infinitely small motions, provided S and T be regarded as *infinitely small*.

In this equation S does not represent a line, but the number of linear units, feet for example, which have been described; and in the same manner T represents the number of units of time, as seconds for example, employed in describing them. Accordingly S and T and their quotient V, are abstract numbers. In general, we cannot bring heterogeneous quantities, as space and time, into direct comparison. Each must first be reduced to units of its own kind, and then we have only to compare abstract numbers. The same is true in all cases when physical data are introduced into calculation.

* These two propositions are capable of being rigorously demonstrated, according to the mathematical principles of mechanics; that is, we deduce them from the abstract idea of forces.—[See *Cam. Mech.* art. 35, et seq.]

AB to pass to the situation *CD*, the consequence will be the same.

38. We call the motions *AB* and *AC* *simple* or *lateral motions*, and *AD* the *mean* or *compound motion*. This very important proposition is called the *theorem of the composition of motion*.

39. It makes no difference whether we say the body has the two motions *AB* and *AC*, or only the single motion *AD*. We may compound the two motions in one, and reciprocally we may decompose each motion *AD*, into two others *AB* and *AC*, in directions taken at pleasure.

40. By repeating the application of the theorem, any number whatever of motions may be compounded into one; or a single motion may be decomposed into any number of motions in directions taken at pleasure.

41. This theorem may even be applied to motions in curved lines and to those which are not uniform, if we represent by *AB* and *AC*, infinitely small spaces, which may be described in infinitely small times. This proposition may, therefore, be extended to all sorts of motions which can be imagined.

42. Every absolute motion may be considered as relative, if we refer it to a limited space. Every relative motion may be considered as absolute, if we regard the relative space as at rest. It is, therefore, of no importance to us, for any physical purpose, to know whether a body in motion or at rest, is so absolutely or relatively.

CHAPTER VI.

Physical Laws of Motion, or Investigation of Moving Forces.

43. Every motion, and every change produced in the velocity or direction of a motion, must have a cause, like any other change of state in bodies. That principle, whatever it is, which we recognise as the immediate cause of a change in the state of rest or motion of a body, is called a *moving force*.

44. All natural moving forces may be comprised under the following divisions.

(1.) The volition of animated beings is capable of producing motion by means of the muscles of the body. This is the only kind of moving force which we recognise immediately by sensation.

(2.) The mobility of all bodies, taken in connexion with their impenetrability, results in a moving force; for if two impenetrable bodies impinge against one another, a change must necessarily take place in their respective states; that is, they exert opposite forces against each other.

(3.) Moving forces also exist in the particular properties of many bodies; among others, in the elasticity of solid bodies, and the dilatability of aeriform bodies.

(4.) There are many motions of which we do not know the cause, or only know it very imperfectly. This is the case with the motions produced by gravity, magnetism, heat, electricity, &c.*

45. In reality, it is impossible to withdraw a body physically from the influence of all moving forces. But we can imagine it thus withdrawn; and this is necessary in order to apply the theory. Then there will remain only the idea of an inert mass, deprived of all force, and incapable of changing its state. This being supposed, the first law to which Newton reduced the theory of motion was the following: *A body at rest continues in a state of rest, and a body put in motion, continues in a state of motion, uniformly and in a straight line, until some moving force changes the state supposed.* This indifference to motion and rest, is regarded as a general property of bodies, and is called the *force of inertia.*

46. The *mass* of a body is the quantity of matter which it contains. This must not be confounded with its *bulk* or *volume.* In the chapter on gravity, we shall see that the *weight* of a body is the measure of its mass.

47. The quantity of motion depends in part upon the mass of the body put in motion, and in part upon its velocity. If the masses are equal, the quantities of motion are proportional to the velocities; if the velocities are equal, to the masses. Hence it follows that generally the quantity of motion is as the product of the mass into the velocity.†

---

* The motions imparted to material bodies by the electric and magnetic forces, are now perfectly explained in all their details.

† Let the masses of the two bodies in motion be M and m; their respective velocities V and v; and their respective quantities of motion B and b. If then we suppose another body which has the

48. Since we have little or no knowledge of moving forces, considered in themselves, we must be equally ignorant of the immediate measure of these forces; but we can measure them by their effects; that is, by the amount of the motions which they produce; and we know that the force employed must be proportional to it. *A force is therefore measured by the product of the mass into the velocity of the body in motion* (47.) Such, in substance, is Newton's fundamental law of motion.*

49. It is obvious from this, in what manner moving forces may be represented by numbers or lines. The latter method is particularly convenient, when two or more forces act upon the same body; then the lines which express the ratios of the forces, represent at the same time their directions, the ratios of the velocities which they tend to communicate to the body, and lastly, the ratio of the spaces which the body would have described, if it had been moved by each of the forces separately.

50. The third fundamental law of motion, discovered by Newton, is the following. *When two bodies act one upon the other, their actions and reactions are always equal;* that is, if the motion of a body becomes itself a moving force, by the pressure or impulse which it produces upon the other body, the two bodies experience an equal but opposite effect. What one gains in motion the other loses, since the force must be equal to its effect (46.)

---

same mass M as the one, and the same velocity v as the other; and call its quantity of motion β; we shall have the proportion

$$B : \beta :: V : v;$$

whence, multiplying the two proportions together, we have

$$B : b :: MV : mv.$$

* This proportionality is in itself neither evident nor necessary. We can conceive of an infinite number of mechanical laws of motion; in which the velocity will not be proportional to the moving force. But the phenomena which must result from them in the composition of motion, would differ from those which the present state of the universe presents to us; and the latter take place as if the velocity were proportional to the force. This law, therefore, is the only one which ought to be physically admitted; though it is obvious that its truth is contingent.—See La Place's *Système du Monde* and *Mécanique Céleste*.

CHAPTER VII.

Historical View of what is known respecting Gravity.

51. GRAVITY, considered with respect to its effects, is by far the most important of natural mechanical forces. Its cause is entirely unknown. But we know the laws by which it operates more exactly than those of any other natural force. As the illustration of its effects is one of the principal objects of mechanical philosophy, it is proper that they should be described in all their details. Most of these effects, however, can only be stated here in a historical manner; for some of the methods by which philosophers have determined the laws of gravity, must necessarily be deferred till the reader is further advanced; and the rest do not belong to the present subject, but to astronomy.

52. The first effect of gravity which we have to consider is the pressure directed towards the earth, which each body exerts upon those which are placed beneath it. This pressure, the determinate intensity of which is called the *weight* of a body, may be very exactly measured by means of a balance. It is invariable, whatever changes take place in the form, position, extension, and chemical properties of a body, provided that no ponderable matter is added or taken away. This circumstance justifies the conclusion that the weight of a body depends solely upon the quantity of ponderable matter which it contains, and consequently that the mass must be in the same proportion.*

53. Experience teaches us that when several bodies are *homogeneous*, that is, absolutely identical as to their nature and constitution, the weights of these bodies are to each other as their bulks. But this proportionality does not hold with respect to bodies which are *heterogeneous*, either by nature, or in consequence of the circumstances in which they are placed. Hence arises what is termed the

---

* In order that nothing may enter into the definition of the mass, which depends upon the constitution of bodies, we are to understand by material points equal in mass, those, which, having equal and opposite velocities, would be an equilibrium. The same definition extends also to equal masses. For example, this equality takes place with respect to the masses which are in equilibrium in the two scales of a balance, the arms of which are equal.

density, or, in other words, the *specific* or *proper gravity* of a body. Specific gravity, then, is the ratio of the absolute weight of one body to that of another, the latter being taken for unity.

54. In estimating the specific gravity in numbers, we employ two kinds of units. For solids and liquids, the weight of pure water is taken for unity; we weigh a body of a given bulk, and determine the weight of the same bulk of water. We divide the first weight by the second, and thus obtain the specific gravity of the body.* This estimate has the advantage of being independent of all differences of weights and measures. There are many means of estimating the specific gravities of bodies. The most exact and best methods will be explained, when we come to treat of hydrostatics.

55. In the case of aeriform bodies, we commonly take the weight of a cubic inch of the gas itself and compare it with the same bulk of atmospheric air. But this mode of estimating is subject to variation on account of a difference in the weights and measures employed. We shall speak of the methods made use of under the head of areometry.

56. When a heavy body is not sustained, it falls with an accelerated motion, the laws of which we shall soon undertake to investigate. The direction of the descent is called a *vertical*. A line or surface to which this direction is perpendicular is called a *horizontal line* or *surface*. This is the direction always assumed by the surface of liquids in a tranquil state.

57. When we compare the directions of gravity in places very near each other, they appear to be absolutely parallel; but a more exact knowledge of the terrestrial globe has taught us that they are everywhere so directed as to meet at points near the centre of the earth.

58. *In a vacuum, or space void of air, all bodies fall with the same velocity.* This law is well confirmed by the theory of the pendulum, and furnishes a rigorous demonstration that the masses of bodies are proportional to their weights. A body falling without obstruction

---

* Let W be the absolute weight of a body, expressed in units of a determinate kind, as ounces; let A be the absolute weight of an equal bulk of water, expressed in the same manner. If we call S the specific gravity of the body, we shall have the proportion

$$A : W :: 1 : S; \text{ whence } S = \frac{W}{A}.$$

describes in the first second a space equal to 16,1 feet. This also is ascertained by the theory of the pendulum.

59. In the same place gravity is invariable. Observations on the pendulum have confirmed the position of Newton, that gravity cannot be the same at every point of the earth's surface, and that its intensity is less at the equator than at the poles. This variation necessarily results from the circumstance, that the earth is not exactly spherical. But as the quantity by which its figure varies from a sphere is very inconsiderable, the inequality thus produced in gravity, is likewise very small.

60. Gravity has been found to be a little less on very high mountains than on plains. This observation would naturally have led us to the inference that gravity decreases as we remove from the surface of the earth, if Newton had not already made the discovery in another way.

61. Newton, by a profound knowledge of the general laws of motion, and availing himself of what the researches and observations of two thousand years had taught respecting the motions of the heavenly bodies, demonstrated that a reciprocal attraction exists between all bodies in nature, and that it is in the direct ratio of the mass of the attracting body, and in the inverse ratio of the square of of its distance. Then, comparing, by means of the calculus, the force which retains the moon in its orbit, with the force which causes bodies here to fall towards the surface of the earth, he proved that this last gravity is nothing else than a particular case of that attraction, common to all bodies, which he called, for this reason, *universal gravitation*.

62. Newton has shown, that the force of gravity takes place in some of the most important phenomena of the universe. It is this which binds together all the several parts of a body, in such a manner, that no ponderable particle can ever be lost. It is this which unites in one vast whole all the bodies of which the planetary system is composed, imparting a perpetual order and harmony to their motions. If the Creator were to break this invisible chain, all nature would return to a state of chaos.

SECTION II.

SOLID BODIES.

CHAPTER VIII.

General Properties of Solid Bodies.

63. The parts of a solid body adhere together in such a manner that an effort is required to separate them, or even to change their respective positions. On this account a solid body has a particular determinate form. The force which connects its different parts, is called the *force of cohesion*. Musschenbroek, Buffon, and some others, have made numerous experiments upon this force.

Musschenbroek caused bars of metal to be formed 0,17 of an inch square, and suspended by them different weights in succession until he broke them. The following is the result of his experiments upon different metals;

	lb.
For German Iron	1930
Fine Silver	1156
Swedish Copper	1054
Fine Gold	578
English Tin	150
Malacca Tin	91
English Lead	25

Similar experiments, made with rods of wood 0,28 of an inch square, gave the following results;

	lb.
For Beech	1250
Oak	1150
Linden	1000
Fir	600
Pine	550

The force of cohesion in ductile metals is increased by moderate hammering; but too heavy blows diminish it. It is diminished by heat and increased by cold. In general, cohesion is a variable force, capable of being altered by a great many chemical and mechanical means.

64. The property which particles have of changing their relative positions without being disunited, is not always proportional to their susceptibility of being separated. This distinction gives rise to the various qualities of solid bodies, which we designate by the somewhat vague terms, *hard, soft, tenacious, friable, stiff, flexible*, &c.

65. The force of cohesion still manifests itself when bodies are divided into small fragments. It appears that all bodies when placed in contact, have a tendency to attach themselves to one another; unless the contact is very imperfect, or the weight of the bodies renders the effect insensible. This property is called *adhesion*. It is distinguished from cohesion, because it exerts itself as well upon heterogeneous as upon homogeneous bodies; whereas cohesion, properly speaking, only takes place between homogeneous bodies.*

66. The attraction which exists between two homogeneous bodies, is properly called *affinity*. Adhesion is not, therefore, a distinct force, but may be considered as a feeble cohesion or a feeble affinity.

67. We now know three sorts of attractions which act upon all bodies. These are, gravity, cohesion, and affinity. The cause of these attractions is entirely unknown; we are even ignorant whether they depend upon one or several causes. But the phenomena which they produce are so different, that we are obliged to attribute them to different causes until it is ascertained that they act according to one single law.**

---

* Adhesion and cohesion ought not to be regarded as distinct forces, but rather as modifications, or simply as analogous effects of that affinity which attracts particles towards each other.

** It is very probable that the laws of chemical affinity differ from the law of gravity. This last is reciprocally proportional to the square of the distance; and without knowing the nature of affinity, it will be seen that its action decreases much more rapidly, so that it ceases to be sensible at very small distances. It is true that a force reciprocally proportional to the square of the distance, when it acts upon the different points of the body, may produce results depending on its figure, and decreasing very rapidly in intensity. It is thus

68. *Compressibility* seems to be a property common to all solid bodies. But the effect of compression is so feeble in very solid bodies, that we may most generally regard it as nothing. Still even in this case we can conceive of its existence.

69. Some bodies preserve, after the pressure ceases, the form which they have thus received; others tend to recover their primitive figure and to fill their primitive space, the moment the pressure is removed. These last are called *elastic*. Elasticity has a great influence upon the phenomena of motion, and we ought, for this reason, to give a more precise idea of it.

70. An elastic body always tends to recover its form and bulk. If it is pressed in one part, it distends itself in another, where it can act freely. If it is enlarged in one part, it contracts in another. If it is bent and then left to itself, it returns at once to its former disposition.

71. There appear to be no bodies perfectly elastic or perfectly unelastic. Every solid possesses this property to a greater or less degree. Among the most elastic bodies, we may reckon tempered steel, bell-metal, ivory, bone, dry wood, gum elastic, &c. Among the least elastic, on the contrary, may be mentioned the softer metals, tin, lead, gold, silver, soft clay, &c. This property of solid bodies must not be confounded with the *dilatability* of aeriform bodies, which is also sometimes called elasticity.*

72. It is obvious from mere inspection that many solid bodies are porous; others are ascertained to be so from experiment; but there are also many solid bodies, such as glass, well cast metals, &c., the porosity of which cannot be demonstrated either by the magnifying-glass, or any other physical means. Moreover, in many bodies there are phenomena which seem absolutely to contradict the idea of po-

---

that the precession of the equinoxes, produced by the attraction of the sun and moon upon the oblate spheroid of the earth, decreases as the cube of the distance increases; that is, it would be eight times smaller if these bodies were twice as far apart. But it is difficult to suppose that there exists no other essential difference than that of figure, between particles of such different properties, as those which compose bodies.

* The phenomena of elasticity have been the subject of very valuable experiments made by s'Gravesande, and afterwards by Coulomb.

rosity.* Accordingly, the dynamic theory does not suppose porosity necessary to the explanation of the different densities of bodies.

CHAPTER IX.

The Interior Construction of Solid Bodies.

73. MOST, if not all solid bodies, appear to form a certain regular assemblage of small parts. The regularity of the fragments of many minerals, the superposition of the laminæ in transparent crystals, the facility with which many bodies are broken or cleft in certain directions rather than in others, the breaking of unannealed glass drops, present phenomena which confirm this remark.

74. The discoveries of M. Haüy give us the most exact idea of the structure of crystals. This idea is the more important because crystallization appears to be a general law of nature. Crystallization consists in this, that in the passage from the fluid to the solid state, each body takes a regular and determinate form.

75. According to the researches of M. Haüy, every crystal, formed naturally or artificially, admits of being cleft and subdivided, according to the direction of certain planes, with more facility than in any other way. This operation is different for different crystals. If it be continued in all the directions where it is possible, the laminæ which result from it being successively removed, until none of the exterior surface remains, we obtain a *nucleus*, which ordinarily has a different form from that of the entire crystal, and subsequent divisions of it would only diminish, without changing the direction of the planes which terminate it. M. Haüy calls the form of the entire crystal, the *secondary form*, that of the nucleus the *primitive form*. The nucleus itself may be divided into corpuscles of the same form, which he calls *integrant particles*. The detached laminæ are also composed of similar particles as their cleavage proves, and consequently the entire crystal is formed of them. M. Haüy supposes

---

* It is probable the author speaks here only of what *appears*, and not of what *is in reality* the case; for I cannot believe that there are any phenomena which are not, in reality, strictly reconcilable with the idea of porosity.

that these integrant particles are themselves small crystals, the configuration of which is determined by the combination of the elementary particles which constitute the rudiments of the entire crystal. As yet there has been no experiment to verify this supposition.

76. Hitherto, M. Haüy has found only three form of integrant particles; the triangular pyramid, the triedral prism, and the quadrangular prism. He has ascertained only six primitive forms; the parallelopiped, octaedron, tetraedron, hexaedral prism, rhomboidal dodecaedron, and triangular dodecaedron. The secondary forms vary without end, by the regular aggregation of the primitive forms.

77. It is extremely remarkable that crystals of the same substance have a nucleus and integrant particles of the same forms, while on the contrary, their exterior figure admits of an endless variety, as is often realized to a great degree in the productions of nature.*

78. The regular form of crystals and the property of being easily divided in certain directions, indicate that the force of cohesion does not exert its power to the same degree in all the points of their particles; and that these particles have certain poles of attraction, which, according to their greater attractive force, determine the position of these particles.**

79. When, by artificial means, we cause fluid bodies to pass to the state of solids, they always form themselves into regular crystals; only these crystals are sometimes so small, that a microscrope is necessary to enable us to perceive them. If, as is by no means improbable, all solid bodies have first passed through the fluid state, we are induced to believe, that an exact and most minute division would make known a similar regularity in their interior structure.

For a better understanding of the theory of crystallization, the reader is referred to the Mineralogy of M. Haüy.

---

* Arragonite appears to form an exception to this rule. Its crystallization differs from that of calcareous spar, though its chemical principles appear to be the same.

** There is a certain number of crystals whose cleavage is equally easy or difficult in all directions where it is possible; if, moreover, the faces of cleavage are equally smooth and of a similar aspect, we regard this equality as the indication of a symmetry in the corresponding faces of the primitive particle. In general, the direction of the planes of cleavage and the characters of the faces, compose what is called the crystalline system, and constitute indications to which the integrant particle is conformed.

CHAPTER X.

Equilibrium of Solid Bodies, or Fundamental Principles of Statics.

80. We have here two cases to examine; 1. That in which the forces act upon a free body, that is, one which is not obstructed in any way. 2. That in which they act upon a body which is not free, but so confined as to move about a certain point or about an axis.

Equilibrium of Free Bodies.

81. When a material point is acted upon at the same time by two equal but directly opposite forces, as *AB, AC*, (*fig.* 2.) this point cannot obey either. In this case, the state of rest which results from the mutual destruction of the two forces, is called *equilibrium*. If the opposite forces are unequal, there results a motion in the direction of the greater.

82. When two forces, *AB* and *AC*, (*fig.* 3.) act in different directions upon the body *A*, it cannot obey both at the same time, except by describing the diagonal *AD*, of the parallelogram *ABCD*. The two forces, therefore, have exactly the same effect as the single force *AD* would have.

83. Upon this is founded the *composition* and *decomposition* of moving forces. Instead of the two forces *AB* and *AC*, we may find the single force *AD*, which is equivalent to them. *AB* and *AC* are called the *simple forces* or *components*; and *AD* the *resultant*. Reciprocally, we can decompose each simple force *AD*, into two forces *AB* and *AC*, taken in any given directions, and acting precisely as this force. Hence the phrase *parallelogram of forces*. It is easy to perceive how two or more forces may be resolved into one, and how one may be decomposed into two or more.

84. If three forces, *AB, AC, AE*, (*fig.* 3.) keep the body *A* in equilibrium, the third, *AE*, must be in the direction of the diagonal *AD produced*; and it must have with respect to the other two, the same magnitude as the diagonal *AD* has with respect to the two lateral lines *AB* and *AC*. From this proposition it will be easily perceived in what manner a single force may be found equivalent to any number of given forces.

Equilibrium of Bodies which move about a Fixed Axis.

85. Let LM (*fig.* 4.) be a body without gravity, turning about a fixed point C to which it is attached. If this body is acted upon by a single force AC, the direction of which passes through the point C, an equilibrium takes place; whether this force tends toward the point C or in an opposite direction. For in these two cases, its effect is equally destroyed by the resistance of the fixed point. But every force, the direction of which does not pass through this point, will produce a motion of rotation.

86. Let there be two forces P and Q, applied at another point A of the body, and acting in the directions AP and AQ. Let us suppose also that the plane of the two lines AP, AQ, contains the fixed point C. At the point C let the parallelogram $ABCD$ be formed. It will be easily seen, that there will then be an equilibrium, if we have the proportion $P : Q : : AB : AD$.

87. If we draw from the point E, the lines CE and CF, perpendicular to the directions of the forces, it may be demonstrated by geometry, that $AB : AD : : CE : CF$. Consequently,

$$P : Q : : CE : CF.*$$

88. There would also be an equilibrium if the two forces P, Q, applied at the point A, were in other directions, for example, towards G' and H'; provided that their ratio remained the same, and their plane passed always through the fixed point C. Indeed, if these conditions were fulfilled, it would be immaterial whether the point A were placed within or without the body LM; and if A were without the body, the distance at which it might be situated would make no difference. It might, therefore, be at an infinite distance; that is, AP and AQ might be parallel.

In all cases, without exception, there is an equilibrium, when $P : Q : : CE : CF$, provided the plane of the two forces contains the fixed point.

89. From this proportion, taking the product of the means and extremes, we have $P \cdot CF = Q \cdot CE$.

---

* In the triangles BCF, DCE, F and E are right angles, and the angle B is equal to D, each being equal to BAD; consequently, these triangles are similar, and we have $DC : BC : : CE : CF$; whence $AB : AD : : CE : CF$.

The perpendiculars *CE*, *CF*, are called the *distances of the forces*; and the product of a force by its distance, is called the *statical moment* or simply the *moment* of this force. Accordingly, we may express the condition of equilibrium in the following manner. *Two forces, P and Q, will keep a body, moveable about a fixed point C, in equilibrium, when their moments are equal.**

90. If more than two forces act upon the body *LM*, we consider separately the forces which tend to turn the body one way, and those which tend to turn it the other. *An equilibrium takes place when the sum of the moments of the forces which tend to turn the body in one direction, is equal to the sum of the moments of the forces which tend to turn it in the opposite direction.*

On these propositions (85—90) is founded the entire theory of pullies, wheels, and levers. But its detailed exposition belongs to the science of machines.

CHAPTER XI.

Centre of Gravity of Bodies.

91. THE gravity of each of the particles of a solid body may be considered as a force which acts upon it in a vertical direction. If we attempt to place a body *AB* (*fig.* 5) upon a support *CD*, which has a sharp point, it is evident, from what has just been said of equilibrium, that there must be in the body a point, which being supported, the whole body will be kept in equilibrium.

This conclusion is always correct, in whatever position the body is placed on the support. If we make this experiment in three directions perpendicular to each other, we shall determine the only point,

---

* If the body actually moved about the point *C*, the velocities of rotation of the points *F* and *E* would be as *FC* to *EC*. If we call *V* the velocity of the point *F*, and V' the velocity of the point *E*, we shall have $V : V' :: FC : EC$. Consequently, $P : Q :: V' : V$ and $P \times V = Q \times V'$. The product PV, QV', of each force by its *virtual velocity*, is called the mechanical moment of this force. Accordingly, we say there will be an equilibrium, when the mechanical moments of the forces *P* and *Q* are equal.

which being sustained, the whole body will be kept in equilibrium. This point is called the *centre of gravity* of the body.

92. When the centre of gravity is sustained, the whole weight of the body is sustained, in the same manner as if it were all concentrated in this single point. This supposition is true with respect to equilibrium, but it is not always applicable to a state of motion.

93. We must not confound the centre of gravity with the centre of figure. They coincide only in bodies of a uniform density; but in bodies of unequal density the centre of gravity is always nearer the denser part; it is even true that the centre of gravity is not always in the interior of the body. In rings, for example, and many other figures, it is exterior to the body.

94. The centre of gravity may be sustained in two ways; from above, if the body is suspended; or from beneath, if it is placed upon some support. When a body is suspended by a thread, the centre of gravity is always in the direction of the thread produced. In this manner we can find the centre of gravity of a body more readily, than by the method above given. We have only to attach a thread to two points in the body, and suspend it successively in the two corresponding directions.

95. When a body is placed upon a support, its situation is the less secure, according as the surface sustained is smaller, and the centre of gravity more distant from the middle of this surface.

96. When the form of a body is variable, as is the case with the bodies of men and animals, the centre of gravity is also variable, When a man stands erect and lets his hands fall equally on each side, the centre of gravity is in the lower part of the abdomen, nearly between the hips. It may be inferred from what precedes, that the position of this point is of the utmost importance as it respects the stability of the body; and hence the almost involuntary efforts which are made to keep it in its place and thus prevent a fall.

97. There are many physical phenomena the explanation of which depends upon the centre of gravity. As they are instructive, they merit some attention. Of this description are the cylinder rolling up an inclined plane; the double cone which seems to rise against the effort of gravity; the little vaulter, &c. The difficult art of rope-dancing refers itself also to this theory. But what is of particular importance, is the application of the centre of gravity to the theory of balances.—[See *Cam. Mech.* p. 161.]

CHAPTER XII.

Free Descent of Heavy Bodies.—Laws of Motion uniformly accelerated.

98. When a body falls freely by the mere action of terrestrial gravity, its velocity increases at each instant, because gravity acts upon it constantly during its descent; but as gravity at the same place, and for small distances from the surface of the earth, may be considered as an invariable force, the velocity of a falling body must increase just as much in one instant as in another. Hence we may say that a falling body has a *motion uniformly accelerated.*

99. The descent of a body is much too rapid to permit the laws of its motion to be ascertained by direct observation. But the machine invented by Atwood* furnishes a convenient method of retarding the descent, so that without altering the essential laws of the motion, we can observe its phenomena from one second to another.

100. By means of this machine we learn,

(1.) *That in every uniformly accelerated motion the spaces described are as the squares of the times.* If, therefore, we call g the space described during the first second, however great or small it may be, and if we designate by S the space described in T seconds, we shall have $S = g\,T^2$.

(2.) *That the velocities are to each other as the times, and that the velocity which the body has at the end of each second, is found by multiplying double the space described during the first second, by the time.* If then we call V the velocity which the body acquires in T seconds, we have $V = 2g\,T$.

(3.) From these two propositions we deduce the following; *The spaces described are as the squares of the velocities.*†

---

* [A description of Atwood's machine may be found in Adams's Lectures on Natural Philosophy, vol. iii. p. 125.]

† Let S be the space passed over by a heavy body during the time T, in virtue of the action of gravity; let us conceive the time T, to be divided into a certain number n, of intervals t, equal among themselves; whence we shall have $T = nt$. We can compare the motion sought with that of a body without weight which receives at the end of each of the instants t, $2t$, $3t$, an impulse capable of making

101. In order to express, by numbers, all the circumstances of a motion uniformly accelerated, it is only necessary to know g; that is, the space described in the first second. It is ascertained by means of the apparatus above referred to, that when a body falls

---

it describe uniformly the space v in a unit of time; this comparison will approach the nearer to the truth as the intervals t, which separate the successive impulses of the force become smaller, and finally the error will disappear entirely in the results which are independent of the absolute value of these instants. Let us follow then the consequences of our supposition, and analyze the effects which the successive impulses will have produced at the end of the time T upon the moving body.

The instant 0 is the time of commencement. The moveable body then receives an impulse capable of making it describe the space v in a unit of time. This first impulse acts upon it during the time T; it causes it then to describe, in this interval, the space Tv.

At the instant following t the moving body receives an additional impulse equal to the preceding, but this impulse acts only during the time $T - t$; it causes it then to describe the space $(T - t)v$.

By examining, in this way, the spaces which the successive impulses cause the body to describe, to the end of the time T, it will be seen that these spaces form the decreasing arithmetical progression,

$$Tv\,;\ (T-t)v\,;\ (T-2t)v\,;\ \ldots tv.$$

Then the number of terms is equal to the number of instants t, that is, equal to n. By substituting for T its value nt, this progression will become

$$ntv\,;\ (n-1)tv\,;\ (n-2)tv\,;\ \ldots tv.$$

The sum of these partial spaces is the whole space really passed over by the moving body. Now this sum is

$$(ntv + tv) \times \frac{n}{2} = \frac{n \times (n+1)\,tv}{2}.$$

We have represented this space by S; we have then

$$S = \frac{n \times (n+1) \times tv}{2};$$

or substituting for n its value $\frac{T}{t}$,

$$S = \frac{T(T+t)}{2} \times \frac{v}{t}.$$

freely and without obstruction, it describes 16,1 feet in the first second, and acquires a velocity equal to 32,2. This being known, we can easily calculate the space described and the velocity acquired, after any determinate time; and generally, knowing one of these three things, the time, space, or velocity, we can find the other two.

Let us designate by g the space passed over, in this manner, by the moving body in a unit of time, and suppose T commensurable with this unit. We can, in like manner, divide the unit of time into a number n' of intervals equal among themselves and each equal to t; and by resuming the reasoning, in the same manner, for this second case, we shall find

$$g = \frac{1 \times (1 + t)}{2} \times \frac{v}{t};$$

whence we deduce

$$\frac{S}{g} = T \times \frac{(T + t)}{1 + t};$$

or, what amounts to the same thing,

$$\frac{S}{g} = T^2 - \frac{T(T-1)t}{1+t}.$$

The smaller t becomes, the more the factor $\frac{1}{1+t}$ will be diminished, and consequently the nearer the ratio $\frac{S}{g}$ will approach to an equality with T^2. Now, by supposition, t is the interval of time which elapses between the successive impulses of the force, and this interval is entirely imperceptible to our senses, in the case of gravity. So that we must here suppose $t = 0$, which gives

$$S = g\, T^2,$$

that is, in uniformly accelerated motion, the spaces passed over are proportional to the squares of the times.

Net us now examine the value of the acquired velocity after the time T. Let V be this velocity; it will be equal to the sum of all the impulses given to the moving body, during the time T. Now, since $T = nt$, it is clear that the moving body receives a number n of impulses in this interval; and as each one of them gives to it the velocity v, their sum will be nv or $T \times \frac{v}{t}$; we shall then have

$$V = \times T\frac{v}{t}.$$

We can, in like manner, determine all the circumstances of every other motion uniformly accelerated, when we know the corresponding value of *g*. This value, therefore, is the measure of all motions of this kind; and is hence called the *measure of acceleration*, or the *accelerating force*.*

Now, by calling *g* the space passed over in a unit of time, we have seen that

$$g = \frac{(1+t)}{2} \frac{v}{t};$$

dividing these equations, member by member, they become

$$\frac{V}{g} = \frac{2T}{1+t}, \quad \text{or} \quad \frac{V}{g} = 2T - \frac{2Tt}{1+t}.$$

The more *t* diminishes, the nearer the ratio $\frac{V}{g}$ approaches to an equality with $2T$; in the case of gravity we must make $t = 0$, and we have rigorously

$$V = 2gT,$$

that is, the velocity is proportional to the time.

We have supposed that the time *T* is commensurable with the unit of time. If this condition be not fulfilled, we should render it exact by adding to the time *T*, a portion of the interval *t*; and then we should commit an error the extent of which would depend on the space described by the moving body during this small interval. But, as we afterward make *t* nothing, it is evident that the error will, in like manner, become nothing. This shows that the preceding results are independent of the hypothesis of the commensurability which has helped us to discover them.

* The two formulas, developed in the preceding note, $V = 2gT$, and $S = gT^2$, are the fundamental propositions by which all questions in uniformly accelerated motion are solved. By supposing that *g* is given, it will be readily perceived that by means of it, whenever one of these quantities *T*, *S*, *V*, is given, the two others can be determined; for if it is T which is given, the two preceding equations immediately give *V* and *S*; if *V* is given, we deduce

$$T = \frac{V}{2g}, \text{ and } \quad S = gT^2 = \frac{V^2}{4g^2};$$

and lastly, if *S* is given, from the equation $S = gT^2$, we obtain

102. When a body is projected upwards in a vertical direction, it is clear that gravity uniformly diminishes the velocity, in precisely the same ratio as it increases the velocity on its descent. The body, therefore, ascends until the continued action of gravity has destroyed all the velocity communicated by the first impulse. Then it descends, and it is plain that it must recover at each point of its descent the same velocity it had at this same point in ascending. This remark enables us to determine the height which a body will attain, when we know the velocity with which it is projected.*

103. The foregoing propositions are only rigorously true when bodies fall in a space void of air. In the air, on the contrary, their cannot be an exactly uniform acceleration, because the body, at each instant must displace a quantity of air, and must lose all the motion which it communicates to the air. If, therefore, a falling body has a small mass and large bulk, its motion must evidently be very much retarded by the resistance of the air; and this is conformable to experience. Reciprocally the resistance of the air is less sensible in proportion as the falling body has a large mass and small bulk.

$$T = \sqrt{\frac{S}{g}}, \text{ and hence } V = 2g T = 2g \sqrt{\frac{S}{g}} = 2\sqrt{gS}.$$

If the question is concerning the free descent of bodies produced by the action of gravity, it is only necessary to substitute for g 16,1 feet. If the inquiry relates to any other uniformly accelerated motion we must substitute for g the value which belongs to it.

* Let U be the velocity of projection given to a body at the moment it is propelled upward, and count the time T from this epoch. The body will cease to ascend when the repeated impulses of gravity to make it descend have amounted to the sum of the velocities or a total velocity V equal to U. Now designating by T the time after which this will happen, we shall have $V = 2gT$, according to the laws of gravity; it is necessary then that this product $2gT$ should be equal to U, which gives $T = \dfrac{U}{2g}$; this is the time at which the moving body stops; afterwards it begins to descend. When in the space S which it will then have described, it will be found equal to gT^2 or $\dfrac{U^2}{4g}$; an expression which may be easily reduced to numbers when the initial velocity U is given.

Motion down Inclined Planes.

104. If a heavy body D (*fig.* 6) be placed upon an inclined plane AB, it rolls or slides toward the bottom, but with less force than it would have in a free vertical descent. The magnitude of this force may be determined in the following manner. Let D be the centre of gravity of the body, and draw from the centre D to the inclined plane, the vertical DE, representing the absolute force of gravity, or the weight of the body; that is, the force that would be exerted in the case of a free descent. Then draw the two lines DF, DG, the first perpendicular and the second parallel to AB. The force DE may be considered as decomposed into two others, one, DF, perpendicular, the other, DG, parallel to AB. The first can produce no motion, being counteracted by the resistance of the plane.

The second, DG, on the contrary, acts in the direction in which the body moves, and produces all the motion it has. The vertical force, therefore, that is, the weight of the body, is to the force with which it moves down the inclined plane, as DE is to DG. If from the points A and B, taken at pleasure, on the inclined surface, we draw the vertical line AC and the horizontal line BC, we have the triangle ABC, similar to the triangle DEG; and

$$DE : DG :: AB : AC;$$

that is, the vertical force is to the oblique force as the length of the inclined plane is to its height. There is a particular instrument called the *inclined plane*, intended to verify this proportion.

105. At whatever point of the inclined surface the body is situated, the accelerating force will always be the same; this motion, therefore, is uniformly accelerated. In the case of free vertical descent, we have called this force g, which is equal to 16,1 feet; and the proportion $AB : AC :: g : \frac{AC}{BC} g$, enables us to determine all the circumstances of motion down an inclined plane.*

---

* Galileo, who first developed accurately the laws which govern the motion of falling bodies, made use of the inclined plane to verify the result.

106. One circumstance, very important in its consequences, is, that the body in descending from A to B, acquires exactly the same velocity as if it had fallen freely from A to C; for the velocities at each point are to each other as AB to AC, that is, as the lengths of the planes.*

107. If we suppose two bodies, of which one falls vertically from A to C, and the other obliquely from A to B, but both having in A the same determinate velocity, it is clear that they will also have the same velocity in C and B. Let $ABCD$ (*fig.* 7) then be a plane, interrupted at pleasure by the angles B, C, &c. If we draw through A and D the vertical lines AK and DE, and through A, B, C, D, the horizontal lines AE, FG, HI, KD; it is evident that a body sliding down the broken plane will have at A, B, C, the same velocities as the body falling vertically from A will have at F, H, K, or one from E, in G, I, D.

108. As the number, magnitude, and situation of the interruptions, are perfectly arbitrary, this proposition is likewise true of a curved line AB (*fig.* 8). If we draw at pleasure the horizontal line AC and the vertical line CB, we can determine the velocity of a body moving along AB, at any points D, F, by drawing through these points the horizontal lines DE and FG. It will be exactly the same as if the body had fallen freely from C to F or G. Hence we deduce the following remarkable proposition; *When a body passes from one inclined surface to another, it acquires the same velocity, whatever course it takes.* In reality, however, the resistance of the air may cause a difference.

---

* If we represent by g the accelerating force belonging to a vertical descent, that which urges a body down an inclined plane will be found by the proportion

$$AB : AC :: g : \frac{AC}{AB} g.$$

Let V be the velocity acquired by a body descending freely from A to C, and V' the velocity belonging to an oblique fall from A to B, we shall have, according to note to article 101,

$$V = 2\sqrt{g \times AC}, \text{ and } V' = 2\sqrt{\frac{AC}{AB} g \times AB} = 2\sqrt{g \times AC},$$

that is, exactly equal to the preceding.

Elem.

CHAPTER XIII.

Free Curvilinear Motion.

(1.) *Projectiles.*

109. When a heavy body receives an impulse in a direction oblique to the vertical, it describes a curve, the form of which may be found in the following manner;

From the point *A* (*fig.* 9), where the motion commences, draw the vertical line *A* 25; take *A* 1 for unity; then beginning from *A*, set off, according to this unity, the distances 4, 9, 16, 25, according to the progression of square numbers. If then *A* 1 represents the space described by a heavy body in the first second of descent, it is evident that the points 4, 9, 16, 25, are the places at which it will be found, at the end of the 2d, 3d, 4th, 5th, seconds. At the instant when the body begins to fall, let us suppose that it receives an impulse in the direction *AF*, such that if the body had no weight and yielded entirely to this impulse, it would describe *AB* in the first second, and in the following seconds, the spaces *BC*, *CD*, *DE*, *EF*, equal to the first.

Now the only case in which a body can have two motions at once, is when it moves in a space which is also in motion. In the case before us, the motion produced by gravity takes place in the line *A* 25, and to represent the motion communicated by the impulse, we must suppose this line to move together with the body in a direction always parallel to itself, and with a velocity equal to the velocity of projection. Accordingly, at the end of the 2d, 3d, 4th, 5th seconds, the line *A* 25 will occupy the positions *B* β, *C* γ, *D* δ, *E* ϵ, *F* φ. If then we draw 1 *b*, 4 *c*, 9 *d*, 16 *e*, 25 *f*, parallel to *AF*, it is evident that the body will be in *b*, at the end of the first second, in *c* at the end of the 2d, and so on. And if these points are connected by the curve line *A b c d e f*, this line will represent the path of the body.

110. It may be shown that this curve belongs to the species called *parabolas*.—[See *Cam. Math. Trig.* art. 172; also *Cam. Mech.* art. 303.]

111. Here experiment differs very widely from theory, on account of the resistance of the air; and although it would be very difficult to calculate this resistance, it is obvious that its effect would

be to make the part Gf, which theoretically has the same curvature as the part AG, increase very rapidly in its curvature, as we remove from the point A of departure.

(2.) *Central Forces.*

112. From what precedes, we may conclude that in order to produce a curvilinear motion, at least two forces are requisite; and that one at least of these must be an accelerating force, while the other may be an instantaneous impulse. Among the endless variety of cases of this kind, there is no one more interesting to the student of natural science, than that in which a force continually draws a body towards a certain centre, while the body has received an exterior impulse from another force. These combinations of forces are called *central forces*, and the motions which they produce *central motions*.

113. Let C (*fig.* 10) be the point towards which a body situated in A is constantly urged, but let us suppose that the body receives at the same time a motion in the direction AD. Although the central force acts constantly and without interruption, we shall for a moment suppose, for the convenience of illustration, that it acts by separate impulses, and that it repeats its action in very small but equal portions of time, which we call *instants*. In the first instant, the central force tends to move the body from A to B, and the lateral force from A to D; it will therefore describe the diagonal AE of the parallelogram $ABDE$. Produce AE till $EG = AE$, and EG will be the path which would be described in the second instant, if the body were free; but at the beginning of this instant, the central force will tend to move it from E to F; it will, therefore, describe the diagonal EH, and so on. It is obvious that, according to the preceding supposition, the body would describe a broken line $AEHL$. But as the central force does not act by separate impulses, it is certain that the true path of the body will be a curved line, the form of which may be infinitely varied, either by the difference of intensity and direction of the lateral force, or by difference of the power and the laws of the central force.

114. Many writers call the force which urges the body towards C, a *centripetal* force, to which a contrary force is opposed, called *centrifugal*. But some confusion exists as to what constitutes this

last; and a more precise limitation of the term is rendered necessary; especially as the terms centripetal and centrifugal are in very common use. Huygens, first used the term centrifugal force, and the meaning he affixed to it we shall now explain. The action of the forces by which the body in question is made to describe the diagonal AE, may be represented in a manner somewhat different from that above stated. Let BA be produced till $AM = AB$, and draw DM; $AEDM$ is a parallelogram, and we may consider the force AD as decomposed into two others AM, AE, the first of which, AM, is equal and opposite to the centripetal force; these two forces, therefore, destroy each other, and the body can only be acted upon by the force DM or its equal AE. This force AM is what Huygens calls the centrifugal force; it will be readily seen, that in all cases, it is equal and opposite to the centripetal force. Instead of using the term in this sense, many call the lateral force AD the centrifugal force; but it would be better to call it the *tangential* force, since it always tends to impel the body in the direction of a tangent to the curve which it describes.

115. It is by the effect of the centrifugal force that the strings of a sling are felt to be stretched when we whirl it; and it is by the effect of the tangential force, that the stone flies off in the direction of a tangent, when let loose from the sling. It is also by the effect of the tangential force, that water dashes over the sides of a vessel, when made to revolve rapidly. An ingenious machine has been invented called the *whirling table*, for the purpose of illustrating all the laws of central motion. A description of it may be found in [*Enfield's Institutes*, &c. and *Adams's Lectures on Nat. Phil.*]

A ball suspended by a thread furnishes a very easy and simple method of observing the formation of central motions. As this ball can only be at rest when situated in a vertical line below the point of suspension, it always returns to this position when made to diverge from it; and thus the effect of gravity here represents a central force. If we give the ball an impulse in a direction oblique to the vertical, it takes a curvilinear motion about the central point. This motion may be elliptical or circular, according to the difference of direction and force of the impulse.

116. It is upon this simple action of central forces, that the wonderful motions of the heavenly bodies depend. Kepler first discovered the principal laws of these motions; but he did not deduce them from the laws of mechanics; he ascertained them only by

great industry and acuteness of observation. Newton laid the foundation of the theory of these motions, and discovered the simple laws of universal gravitation, by which the harmony of all these bodies is preserved and perpetuated.

CHAPTER XIV.

Motion in given Lines.

117. A BODY may in various ways be made to take a different motion from that which it would have taken, by the free action of the forces exerted upon it. Hence in mechanics we distinguish between a *free motion* and a *motion in given lines*. We shall here examine only two of the latter kind of motions; namely, curvilinear motions, and the oscillation of a pendulum.

(1.) *Curvilinear Motions.*

118. When a free solid body receives an impulse which does not pass through its centre of gravity, it takes a motion compounded of two others. 1. A uniform motion of translation in space, common to all its particles. 2. A motion of rotation, also uniform, about an axis passing through the centre of gravity, but the direction of which may be variable or constant in the interior of the body. In all bodies we may draw through the centre of gravity three lines at right angles to each other, which are permanent axes of rotation; that is, if the rotation has once commenced about one of these axes, it will always continue to take place about this same axis, provided that the body experiences no resistance or impulse to disturb the freedom which we have supposed in its motions. This appears to be the case with the heavenly bodies. All these results are demonstrated in treatises on mechanics.

119. Let us consider in particular the case of a uniform motion of rotation about a permanent axis, passing through the centre of gravity. Let this centre be represented by C (*fig.* 11), and let the axis of rotation be perpendicular to the plane of the figure. In this case every point of the body will describe about the axis of rotation

the circumference of a circle; the point A, for example, will describe the circumference $AEKD$. During this motion of rotation, the force of cohesion, by which the particles of the body are united, will perform the part of a centripetal force. But however great may be its effect, considered in this relation, it does not depend at all upon its proper intensity, but simply upon the motion and form of the body moved. To be easily convinced of this, let AG be the arc which the point A describes in an infinitely small interval of time. Draw the tangent AB, and complete the parallelogram $AFGH$. Now, if AF represents the force with which A tends to follow its tangential motion AF, AH is the central force by which it is drawn towards C; and this evidently does not depend at all upon the physical properties of the body, but upon the velocity of the point A, and its distance from the axis of rotation C. Thus, in the rotation of a solid body, there must always be produced at the surface of the body a centripetal force, which is necessary to prevent the particles from escaping. Such a force must also exist in each point of a revolving body, and it is the more intense according as this point is farther distant from the axis of rotation C, that is, as the velocity is greater. Now as the velocity of rotation is unlimited, we may always conceive it to be so great that the centrifugal force shall exceed the force of cohesion; in which case the particle A must yield to its tangential force AF and be detached from the body. When the point of the body where the particle is, arrives at G, the particle itself will be in F; and consequently, compared with the place where it was, will be farther, reckoned from the centre C, by the space GF; which is a manifest effect of the centrifugal force.

120. The effects of the centrifugal force, combined with those of a central force, reciprocally proportional to the square of the distance, completely explain the slightly oblate form of the planets, and the diminution of gravity at their equators. The principle of a centrifugal force enables us to account also for a variety of phenomena in curvilinear motions, which present themselves every day.

(2.) *Oscillations of the Pendulum.*

121. When a heavy body is attached to a fixed point, about which alone it can turn, it cannot remain in equilibrium, unless its centre of gravity is sustained; that is, unless it is in the vertical plane passing through the axis of suspension.

If a body, placed in equilibrium in this manner, is made to vibrate by a lateral impulse, its motion will not be uniform. It may be put in motion by gravity alone, without an impulse, by removing it more or less from the position of equilibrium, so that the centre of gravity be not in the vertical line passing through the point of suspension. If then we leave the body to itself, *oscillations* will take place; and this species of motion is of great importance.

122. Every body AC (*fig.* 12), whatever be its form, is called a *physical* or *compound pendulum*, when its centre of gravity B does not coincide with the point of suspension A. A *simple* or *geometrical pendulum* is a single straight line AB (*fig.* 13), turning about A, and having all its weight concentrated in the single extreme point B. Strictly speaking, no such pendulum exists; but a small body B (*fig.* 14), of a compact mass, suspended by a fine wire AB, sufficiently represents it. The *length* of such a pendulum, considered as simple, is the distance from the point of suspension A to the centre of gravity B of the body.

123. If a simple pendulum AB (*fig.* 15) be drawn into the position AC, and then abandoned to itself, the material point B, is forced to describe the arc of a circle CB. It describes it with an increasing velocity, since gravity acts continually upon it at each point of its course; but as the direction of this force becomes more and more oblique to its motion, the acceleration will not be *uniform*, but will become less and less continually. The velocity increases from C to B, where it is at its maximum, the accelerating force becoming nothing. Accordingly, the body will not remain at B, but will continue to describe the arc BH, by virtue of its force of inertia. It is obvious, however, that since gravity now acts in a contrary direction, its velocity must decrease just as fast as it before increased; so that it will have in G, for example, the same velocity that it had in E, at the same height. If we draw from the point C, where the motion commenced, the horizontal line CH, it is evident that the body must rise to H; but at H it will be in the same state as at C, and will, therefore, return from A to C, and thus continue to oscillate between these two points. Some writers understand by the word *oscillation*, a single passage through the arc of vibration; others apply it to two passages, one backward the other forward. We shall use it in the former sense.

124. It is evident that these oscillations would continue in the same manner without end, if there were no obstacle to the motion;

but the resistance of the air, and the force, however inconsiderable, which is necessary to bend the wire at A, destroy every instant some portion of the velocity. For this reason the length of the arc diminished continually, until at length the pendulum ceases to vibrate. But the obstacles to the motion may be so far reduced, that these oscillations will continue several hours in succession.*

125. Though it is very easy to explain the manner in which the motions of the pendulum are produced, it is very difficult, without the aid of the calculus, to present an exact and entire theory of the instrument. We shall, therefore, content ourselves with stating the mathematical results deduced from experiment.

(1.) The most remarkable property of this species of motion is the perfect equality, or, as it is technically called, *isochronism* of the oscillations. The duration of an oscillation is very little affected by the magnitude of the arc CB; and as the arc is generally one of a few degrees, in experiments, where the pendulum is employed, the oscillations are to our own senses perfectly isochronous.†

(2.) In equal arcs of oscillation, when they are described in a vacuum, the weight, the magnitude, the form, and the quantity of matter of the body, have no effect upon the duration of an oscillation.

(3.) The time of an oscillation changes with the length of the pendulum, and is proportional to the square root of its length.‡

---

* In the experiments upon the length of the pendulum, made at the observatory at Paris, with the apparatus of Borda, the motion was perceptible, by means of a microscope, after an interval of 24 hours.

† The time of an oscillation increases somewhat with the magnitude of the arc BC, or the angle BAC; and by comparing it with that of an infinitely small oscillation, which is always sensibly the same, the increase will be as follows;

If $CAB = 30°$ the increase will be	0,01675
15° " "	0,00426
10° " "	0,00190
5° " "	0,00012
$2\frac{1}{2}°$ " "	0,00003.

The time of an infinitely small oscillation is here taken for unity, and in an arc of $2\frac{1}{2}°$ the difference is extremely small. These results are obtained from the formula in the following note.

‡ The most important, but at the same time the most difficult problem in the theory of the pendulum, is that which relates to the de-

126. It may be inferred from these laws that the time of oscillation of the simple pendulum, is purely the effect of gravity, independently of the influence of every other force. And it is for this reason that we stated in Chapter VII., that the pendulum is perfectly fitted for the most exact researches respecting gravity.

(4.) From this consideration we deduce the fourth law; viz. that the time of oscillation must vary, other things being the same, when

---

termination of the time employed by the pendulum in making any part of an oscillation. It is very easy, however, to determine the velocity of a body at each point; if for example, the body passes from C to E, it has the velocity which it would have acquired by falling freely from D to F. The complete determination of the time cannot be obtained except by a complicated integration, of which we shall give simply the result. Let L be the length of the pendulum, T the time of an oscillation through the arc CBH, V the versed sine of the angle CAB, g the force of gravity, or the space described by a heavy body in the first second of its fall, and π the semicircumference of a circle whose radius is 1, or 3,1415926, we shall have

$$T = \pi \sqrt{\frac{L}{2g}} \left(1 + \frac{1}{8} V + \frac{9}{256} V^2, \&c. \right)$$

The quantity comprehended within the parentheses, forms in fact an infinite series; but it converges so fast that in very small arcs the first term is always sufficient, so that we can take

$$T = \pi \sqrt{\frac{L}{2g}}.$$

In greater arcs we have occasion to employ the second and sometimes even the third term. It will be seen that g and L will be both expressed in the same kind of measure, which is the unit of length, and the time T is given in seconds, since g answers to the free vertical descent during a second of time.

This formula serves as the foundation of the whole theory of the pendulum. We shall deduce only one theorem from it. If we raise to the square the approximate value of T and multiply it by $2g$, we obtain

$$2g T^2 = \pi^2 L.$$

This formula may be employed when one of the three quantities T, g, and L, is given, to find the third. It is of great importance in the theory of gravity.—[See *Cam. Mech.* art. 243, et seq.]

gravity itself varies. The time will be longer if gravity diminishes, and shorter if it increases.—[See note to page 40.]

127. The theory of the compound pendulum presents a still greater difficulty. We shall only speak of two things, viz. the *length* of such a pendulum, and its *centre of oscillation*.

If we suspend by the side of a compound pendulum AC (*fig.* 12), a simple pendulum AB (*fig.* 14) we can lengthen or shorten them, so as to cause them to vibrate in equal times. If then we take the length AB of the simple pendulum, and apply it to the compound pendulum, so that AD (*fig.* 12) $= AB$ (*fig.* 14), we shall find that D is always below the centre of gravity B of the compound pendulum. There are even cases in which D falls entirely without the body AC. This point D is called the *centre of oscillation;* and AD is called the *length* of the compound pendulum. As soon as we have determined with sufficient exactness, the centre of oscillation of a compound pendulum, it may, in all respects, take the place of a simple pendulum.

(3.) *Application of the Pendulum.*

128. The pendulum, on account of the isochronism of its oscillations, affords the best means of measuring time, and consequently is best adapted to the purpose of regulating clocks and watches. Huygens was the first who applied it in this way. There is one inconvenience attending this use of the pendulum arising from the effect of heat and cold in varying its length; but there are means of correcting this defect.*

---

* It is known that all bodies are expanded by heat and contracted by cold. In the first case, the lengthening of the pendulum lowers the centre of oscillation, and the oscillations become slower. In the second case, the contraction shortens the pendulum, and, the centre of oscillation being raised, the oscillations are more rapid. Means have been devised to make this cause of irregularity correct itself. [The expansion of iron and brass being to each other as three to five, if we make the rod FB (*fig.* 15) of iron, and the rod AO of brass in the proportion of 5 to 3; they being connected at the lower extremities, and the weight being attached at O, the rod AO will expand upward just as much as the rod FB expands downward, and the

129. The application of the pendulum to researches respecting gravity, is still more important for the progress of science. Under this head we remark;

(1.) That the invariable isochronism of the oscillations in the same place, demonstrates the constancy of gravity itself.

(2.) It is proved by the pendulum, not indeed in so striking a manner as by experiments in a vacuum, but with still greater exactness, that all bodies acquire, by gravity, the same velocity in their fall; for a body that would fall more slowly than another, would, if suspended in the manner of a pendulum, perform its oscillations with less velocity.

(3.) The simple seconds pendulum furnishes a method of determining the space described by a heavy body in the first second of its fall, with greater precision than Atwood's machine. Indeed it is obvious without a precise demonstration, that a determinate ratio must always exist between the length of the simple seconds pendulum and the space through which a body falls in a second; since both depend simply upon gravity.

---

point O where the weight is applied, will consequently remain, amid all changes of temperature, at the same distance from F, the point of suspension. A number of rods of each kind is usually employed, as represented in figure 16, where the rod which supports the weight, is attached at F, and free at D, D', the brass rods expanding upward and the iron ones downward, as before; so that if the proper proportion as to length be observed, a compensation for the effect of temperature will be obtained. Other means have been invented for accomplishing the same purpose. Of these we shall mention only one which has been attended with great success. The weight AB (*fig.* 17) is made to consist of a glass tube about two inches in diameter, and from 4 to 5 inches long, filled with mercury. As the rod of the pendulum supporting the weight, expands downward, the mercury expands upward, as in the contrivance first mentioned, and the quantity may be increased or diminished till a compensation is effected. A clock, provided with a pendulum of this construction, made by T. Hardy of London, for the Royal Observatory at Greenwich, was found, after two years' trial, to vary only $\frac{1}{5}$ of a second in 24 hours from its mean rate of going. A clock of the same construction, owned by W. C. Bond of Boston, though much less costly, has been found, by careful observation, to go with nearly the same accuracy.]

(4.) The opinion of Newton respecting the diminution of gravity at the equator is perfectly confirmed by observations on the pendulum. A pendulum that exactly beats seconds here, oscillates more slowly at the equator and more rapidly at the poles. The same pendulum, therefore, must be shortened at the equator and lengthened at the poles, in order to beat seconds exactly. Among numerous observations to this effect we select the following;

[Place of Observation.	North Latitude.	Length of the Seconds Pend:
St. Thomas	0° 24' 41''	39,02074
Trinidad	10 38 56	39,01884
New York	40 42 48	39,10168
Hemmerfest	70 40 05	39,19519
Spitsbergen	79 49 58	39,21469.]

[It is evident from what precedes, that the value of g answering to different latitudes, may be exactly obtained from the length of the pendulum in these latitudes, and these values must be considered as the proper measures of gravity in the places where the observations are made. The difference in the value of g at the equator, compared with that at the highest latitude yet attained, amounts only to about one inch. It may be easily shown, moreover, that the length of the seconds pendulum, is to the space described by a body falling freely in one second, as 1 to 4,93480;* so that one of these results may be readily deduced from the other, by a simple proportion. Now in the latitude of London, at the level of the sea and at the temperature of 60° the length of the seconds pendulum is found to be 39,1386 inches; hence we deduce the value of $g = 193,14$ inches, or 16,1 feet, nearly.]

(5.) On very high mountains the oscillations of the pendulum are a little slower than on the general level of the earth's surface. Bouguer found that a pendulum which made 98770 oscillations in 24 hours, at the level of the sea, made in the same time on the Pichincha, only 98720. Gravity, therefore, diminishes as we remove from the surface of the earth.

(6.) The pendulum, when at rest, indicates the direction of gravi-

---

* [In the formula $2 g T^2 = \pi^2 L$, of a preceding note, if we make T equal to 1, we shall have $2 g = \pi^2 L$, which gives $1 : \frac{1}{2} \pi^2 :: L : g$, which is the proportion given in the text.]

ty in the most exact manner. In the neighbourhood of vast chains of mountains, it has been found that its direction deviates a little from the vertical towards the mountain; this is a manifest proof of the existence of an attractive force in the mountain, which is exerted upon the body of the pendulum.* The most exact observations of this kind were made in Scotland in 1774, by the English astronomer, Dr Maskelyne. He calculated the attractive force of the mountain by means of the small angle through which the plumb line deviated from a vertical direction; and compared it with the attractive force of the earth, as ascertained by the effect of gravity. This enabled him to compare the mass of the mountain with the entire mass of the earth; and the result of this important but delicate inquiry was, that the mass of the earth is about $4\frac{1}{2}$ times as great as the mass of a globe of water of the same bulk. This result contradicts the opinion of those who think that the interior of the earth is filled with water. Thus it is to the pendulum that we are indebted for some important inferences respecting the nature, or at least the density of the bodies composing the interior of our globe.†

(7.) Finally, the pendulum may be applied to various experiments upon the motions of bodies; because we can easily produce by means of it, motions of a determinate magnitude, direction, and velocity. It may be demonstrated by geometry, that the velocity of the pendulum at the point B (*fig.* 18), when it falls from different heights, is as the chord of the arc passed through; that is, the velocity of the pendulum in B, when it has commenced its motion in C, is to the velocity in B, when it has commenced its motion in E, as the arc CB is to the arc EB. Now it is easy to divide the arc BC in such a manner that the chords, reckoned from B, shall be to

---

* This deviation is proved and measured by observing the meridion distances of the same star from the zenith, on both sides of the mountain. As these distances are reckoned from the vertical, determined by the plumb line, we can ascertain whether they are the same or different. For the attraction of the mountain tends to augment the one and diminish the other.

† Cavendish arrived at the same result by a very simple experiment. This was to render sensible the attraction exerted by two large globes of metal upon the extremities of a horizontal lever, suspended at its centre by a wire susceptible of torsion.—See the *Mécanique* of M. Poisson, vol. ii. p. 34.

each other as the numbers 1, 2, 3, 4, and 5. If then at one time we raise the pendulum to 12, and at another to 5, the velocities in *B* will be as 12 to 5, &c. An arc thus divided may be called a *scale of velocity*.*

In these circumstances the unit of velocity is not determined, and the scale only gives the ratio of velocity; but we can dispose the apparatus in such a manner that the scale shall indicate in inches the absolute velocity acquired by the pendulum.†

---

* Let V, V', be the velocities which the pendulum acquires by its fall through the arcs CB and EB; these velocities are the same that a body acquires by a free descent through the vertical lines DB and FB (108.) We have then $V^2 : V'^2 :: DB : FB$ (100.) Now by a known property of the circle [*Leg. Geom.* art. 213,]

$$2 AB : BC :: BC : BD; \text{ also } 2 AB : BE :: BE : BF.$$

Here BC, BE, designate the chords of the two arcs. Consequently,

$$BD = \frac{BC^2}{2 AB}, \text{ and } BF = \frac{BE^2}{2 AB}.$$

Hence $V^2 : V'^2 :: BC^2 : BE^2$; or $V : V' :: BC : BE$; that is, the the velocities are proportional to the chords of the arcs through which the pendulum falls.

† The question is to find the angle BAC, through which it is necessary to raise the pendulum, in order that it shall arrive at B with a velocity V. From what has been shown, note to art. 101, we have

$$DB = \frac{V^2}{4g},$$

when the pendulum is to have in B the velocity V. Now the radius of the described arc $AB = L$; then

$$AD = L - \frac{V^2}{4g}.$$

But in the triangle CDA, we have $AC : AD :: 1 : \cos BAC$; whence

$$\cos BAC = \frac{AD}{AC} = 1 - \frac{V^2}{4gL};$$

from which the angle BAC may be obtained by the trigonometrical tables. If in this formula we express g and L in inches, and take successively for V, the natural numbers 1, 2, 3, 4, &c., we shall have a series of angles which will indicate how high the pendulum must be raised in order to have in C, 1, 2, 3, 4, &c., inches of velocity.

CHAPTER XV.

Communication of Motion by Impulse.

130. Since on the surface of the earth no place is to be found absolutely void of all impenetrable matter, every body in motion is continually impinging against others. Consequently, we cannot appreciate any motion with perfect exactness, if we are unacquainted with the laws according to which bodies communicate their motions to each other by impulse.

131. An apparatus is made use of to ascertain the effects of impulse. The essential parts of it are two pendulums *AB* and *AC*, (*fig*. 19.) of equal length, and suspended in such a manner that the heavy bodies *B* and *D* which terminate them are exactly in contact. Behind them, attached to the same support, are scales of velocity constructed in the manner prescribed in the preceding chapter. These scales may be traced upon the arcs described from the points *A* and *C* as centres, or more conveniently upon a right line *EF*; so that if we raise one of the pendulums to a certain point *G*, the number at *G* will indicate the velocity which the pendulum will have at the lowest point of its arc, where it will impinge against the mass *D* of the other pendulum. We may thus cause one pendulum to impinge against the other, or both to impinge at the same time, and observe the phenomena which thence result in their motions.

By means, therefore, of these angles, we may form on the arc *BC*, a scale of absolute velocities.

The isochronism of the circular pendulum is only approximate; it is true only for very small arcs, and we have seen that the oscillations become less rapid as the arcs are longer. It might be proposed to find what kind of curve would make the isochronism exact in all the arcs. Geometers have determined this to be a *cycloid*, so called, because it may be generated by a point of a circle rolling on a plane. This curve is such, that the gravity decomposed according to each of its elements, is always exactly proportional to the arc which remains to be described before reaching the lowest point; hence arises the isochronism. Attempts have been made to apply this curve to timekeepers; but they have been abandoned on account of the difficulty attending its rigorous construction.

Another appendage consists of a series of balls arranged one after the other, the object of which is to show in what manner the motion of one or several is transmitted to all the rest.

A third consists of two pendulums so arranged as to be capable of impinging at the same time against a third body. There is still another appendage to percussion machines, by which heavy bodies are made to fall from a determinate height upon a hard or soft body, for the purpose of observing the effects of such collision.

132. According to Newton's third law of motion, in every case of the collision of two bodies, a transmission of motion takes place from one to the other; but we cannot determine generally the quantity of motion transmitted, because this depends upon a great variety of circumstances, such as the direction, form, mass, velocity, cohesive force, elasticity, state of aggregation, &c., of the bodies put in motion. Since it is necessary to take into view all these circumstances, the theory of collision must be of great extent, and in some particulars of no small difficulty. We must, therefore, confine ourselves to the most remarkable cases; and chiefly to the central and direct impulses of elastic and unelastic bodies. The impulse is called *central* when the bodies move before collision in the straight line passing through their centres of gravity, and when the collision takes place in this line. It is called *direct*, when the surfaces are perpendicular to the direction of the motion, at the place of collision.

133. The only case which we intend to examine particularly, is that of the collision of unelastic bodies, because this is the basis of the whole theory. When two bodies of this description impinge against one another, the moving body communicates to the body which is at rest, or moving in an opposite direction, the quantity of motion necessary to give both an equal velocity. The same is true of two bodies, of which one moves faster than the other. When they have acquired the same velocity, the effect of collision ceases, because no pressure can take place between them, and they pursue their course together and with an equal velocity, as if they formed one body.

The case which most frequently occurs, and which is also most easily determined, is when the body impinged is at rest. It is evident, independently of calculation, that in this case the velocity after collision must be greatly altered, and must depend principally upon the ratios of the masses. The smaller the mass of the body impinged, compared with that of the impinging body, the less will be the force necessary to put it in motion, and the less will the velocity of the impinging body be changed.

On the contrary, the greater this mass is, the less will be the velocity after collision. If the mass of the impinged body is much greater than that of the impinging body, the motion, after collision, will never be strictly nothing, but may be absolutely inappreciable by our senses, as when a hammer is struck against a wall, or a stone is suffered to fall upon the earth.*

Among the circumstances which modify the effects of collision, we shall speak first of the force of cohesion. The impulse exerts an immediate action only upon the parts in contact, and from these it is propagated to the other parts. This is done more rapidly in proportion as the bodies are more hard and inflexible; and

---

* When the masses and velocities of the bodies before collision are known, it is very easy to find by calculation the velocity after collision. Let m be the mass and v the velocity of the impinging body, and m' the mass and v' the velocity of the body impinged. We remark that v' is to be taken positively when the bodies move in the same direction, and negatively when they move in opposite directions. This being supposed, the sum of the quantities of motion before collision will be $mv + m'v'$. After collision, the two bodies have the same velocity which we call x; and the mass put in motion is $m + m'$; consequently, the quantity of motion is $(m + m')x$. These two being equal, we have

$$(m + m')x = mv + m'v', \text{ or } x = \frac{mv + m'v'}{m + m'}.$$

The results stated in the text are deduced rigorously from this formula. If m' is at rest before collision, $v' = 0$, and $x = \frac{mv}{m + m'}$. If v' is not equal to zero, but m' is infinitely small compared with m,

$$x = \frac{mv}{m} = v;$$

that is, the body loses only an infinitely small part of its velocity. If m, on the contrary, is infinitely small compared with m',

$$x = \frac{m'v'}{m'} = v';$$

that is, the impinged body neither gains nor loses by collision, or at least loses only an infinitely small part of its velocity.

more slowly in proportion as their particles are more yielding. In this last case the bodies are compressed and their form is changed; or else, if the force of the cohesion is less than the force of collision, they break into fragments more or less numerous. Lastly, the effects are variously modified, according as the bodies are hard or soft, tenacious or friable, &c.

134. Elasticity, in particular, has a great influence upon the effect of collision. As the particles of elastic bodies yield, the bodies are compressed as long as the velocities are unequal. Hence the effect of collision does not cease in this case, as in that of unelastic bodies, the moment the velocity becomes equal in the two; but they afterwards separate from one another because they are forced to resume their form; and if they were perfectly elastic they would do it with exactly the same force as that with which they were first compressed.

Thus the impinging body loses, and the impinged body gains, just double the motion which they would have had, if they had been unelastic. Finally, if the bodies are imperfectly elastic, the loss and augmentation of motion, though greater than for unelastic bodies, are not in the double ratio, as is the case with perfectly elastic bodies.*

---

* Let m be the mass of the impinging body, v its velocity before collision, and u its velocity after; let m' be the mass of the impinged body, v' its velocity before collision, and u' its velocity after. If the two bodies were unelastic, their common velocity after collision would be (133)

$$x = \frac{mv + m'v'}{m + m'},$$

and m would have lost in velocity $v - x$. This loss would be double in bodies perfectly elastic, that is, $2(v - x)$, and somewhat larger than $v - x$ in bodies imperfectly elastic. Let n be a number between 1 and 2. Then the loss of velocity expressed generally will be $n(v - x)$; so that after collision there remains $u = v - n(v - x)$. In like manner, the body m', if not elastic, will gain $x - v'$, by collision; if perfectly elastic, $2(x - v')$; and generally $n(x - v')$. Its velocity after collision will, therefore, be $u' = v' + n(x - v')$. If in the values of u and u' we substitute for x its value, found above, we shall have, by a simple transformation,

$$u = v - n\left(\frac{v - v'}{m + m'}\right)m', \text{ and } u' = v' + n\left(\frac{v - v'}{m + m'}\right)m.$$

These two formulas are of very general use; if we suppose $n = 2$,

135. The variations depending upon the direction of the impulse are still more numerous. We shall only state this single law, that at each *eccentric* impulse there is always produced a circular motion about the centre of gravity, which, in most cases, renders the mathematical estimation of the effect very difficult. The law, at the same time, is so general, that when two bodies are connected together by a visible line, or even by an invisible attractive force, no partial motion of one body is possible, without being felt by the other; and if one of them is put in motion, both begin to turn about their common centre of gravity. Thus the moon and earth move about their common centre of gravity. In like manner the planets do not, strictly speaking, move simply round the sun, but both the sun and planets move together about the centre of gravity of the solar system.

136. We shall here state only a single case of *oblique collision*. If an elastic ball A, (*fig.* 20) is thrown in a direction BA against an elastic wall, experience teaches that it rebounds in a direction AH, under an equal angle. To explain this effect let BA represent the force of collision. Decompose this into two others, one FA, parallel to the wall CD, and the other EA perpendicular to it. The only effect of EA, if it acted alone, would be to make the body rebound with an equal force AE, in the direction AE. But the other force FA, having no obstacle, would, if it acted alone, impel the body in the direction AG. Now since these two act at the same time upon the body, it must describe the diagonal AH. In general, the oblique and the eccentric impulse reduce themselves by means of the decomposition of forces to the laws of central and direct impulses.

137. We have also mentioned the state of aggregation of bodies, among the circumstances which modify the effect of collision. If a solid body moves in a fluid, or if one fluid moves in another, these bodies are in constant collision with respect to each other. But as this difficult branch of the theory of collision belongs to the examination of liquid and aeriform bodies, we shall only remark here, that the equality of action and reaction which constitutes Newton's third law of motion, is still observed in these motions; for in conformity with this principle, the body put in motion loses just as much motion

---

they are applicable to perfectly elastic bodies. If we put $n = 1$, they answer for unelastic bodies. Finally, if the bodies have an imperfect elasticity, n has an intermediate value which may be ascertained by experiment.

as it communicates to the fluid medium. Regard must be paid to this law, if we would judge properly of any motion which takes place in the air or in the water.*

CHAPTER XVI.

Vibratory Motions, and the Sounds which they produce; or the first Principles of Acoustics.

138. ALL we know respecting the production of sound is derived from the observation of solid sonorous bodies. This is the reason why we treat of acoustics in this place, and not as is generally done, under the head of air.

139. If an elastic wire chord stretched between AB (*fig.* 21) be drawn out of its rectilinear direction and then left to itself, it does not on its return remain in this direction, but like a pendulum moved out of the vertical line, it passes beyond its natural position at rest, then back again, taking first the position ADB, then ACB on the opposite side. This motion, performed with great rapidity, is called an *oscillation* or *vibration*. The theory of these motions is a difficult one. For this reason we shall give a simple statement of the laws confirming them by experiment.†

140. The vibrations of a chord have this in common with the oscillations of a pendulum, that they are almost exactly isochronous. The time of a vibration depends entirely upon the *length, weight,* and *tension* of the chord.‡

141. When the vibrations are very quick, we hear a determinate

---

* [For a more complete analysis of the laws of collision, see *Cam. Mech.* art. 292, &c.]

† Some writers apply the term *vibration* to the internal motion of the smallest particles of a body, by which they actually change their respective situations, though in a manner imperceptible to our senses. Undoubtedly there are such motions, but they never produce any sound.

‡ Let T be the time of a vibration; g the force of gravity; l the length of the chord; w its weight; and f the force with which it is stretched. We shall have

sound, which is more or less *grave* or *acute*, according to the velocity of the vibrations.

142. There is a very convenient instrument for illustrating the laws of these vibrations called a *monochord*. It consists of one or a small number of chords stretched over a wooden table in such a manner that their length and tension may be varied at pleasure. In making experiments with this instrument, the following principle, capable of being demonstrated by the calculus, must be admitted. *The times of oscillation of the same chord, other things being the same, are proportional to its length.*

143. By means of the monochord it is shown that there is a particular musical interval answering to each ratio in the oscillations or lengths of the chord. These are denominated as follows;

For the ratio ...
$$\begin{cases} 1:2 & \text{octave,} \\ 2:3 & \text{fifth,} \\ 3:4 & \text{fourth,} \\ 4:5 & \text{major third,} \\ 5:6 & \text{minor third,} \\ 6:7 & \text{superfluous second,} \\ 7:8 & \text{second,} \\ \left.\begin{matrix} 8:9 \\ 9:10 \\ 10:11 \end{matrix}\right\} & \text{entire tone,} \\ \left.\begin{matrix} 11:12 \\ 12:13 \\ 13:14 \\ 14:15 \\ 15:16 \end{matrix}\right\} & \text{semitone.} \end{cases}$$

$$T = \sqrt{\frac{lw}{2gf}}.$$

This formula serves generally for all kinds of chords.

Let us suppose a cylindrical chord of the same thickness and elasticity through its whole length. Let r be half the diameter, and δ the specific gravity of the substance. If we call π the semicircumference of a circle whose radius is 1, the bulk of the chord will be $\pi r^2 l$, and its weight $w = \pi r^2 l \delta$. If we substitute this value in the formula above given, we shall have

$$T = \sqrt{\frac{\pi r^2 l^2 \delta}{2gf}} = rl\sqrt{\frac{\pi \delta}{2gf}}.$$

This formula is as general as the preceding, and is more convenient for chords which are homogeneous throughout.

The ratios expressed by more compound numbers are of little use in music. The 5 first, together with the ratio of 3 : 5 which gives the sixth, are called *concords* or *consonant intervals*. The others are called *discords*.

144. A chord renders the tone which is proper to it, either by striking it or passing over it the bow of a violin. In the first case, a practised ear perceives, besides the fundamental tone of the chord, a variety of relative tones. If we call 1 the time of vibration of the fundamental tone, $\frac{1}{2}$ will be the time of vibration of the nearest relative tone, and the following will be $\frac{1}{3}, \frac{1}{4}, \frac{1}{5}, \frac{1}{6}, \frac{1}{7}$, &c. These relative tones are thus accounted for. While the entire chord performs one oscillation (*fig.* 21), its half (*fig.* 22), its third (*fig.* 23), its fourth (*fig.* 24), vibrate also, which renders the compound motion of the chord very complicated. When we pass a bow over the chord it is not apparent that such relative tones are produced. The points G (*fig.* 22); K, L, (*fig.* 23); O, P, Q, (*fig.* 24); in which the direction of the vibration changes, are called *nodes of oscillation*. We can, by a certain address, produce only relative tones.

145. It is possible, by means of a bow, to obtain tones not only from chords but from all bodies however little elastic. Chladni, to whom we are indebted for so many valuable discoveries in acoustics, has given a method of rendering almost visible the oscillations of plates and many other bodies, by sprinkling sand of equal thickness over them.

146. Next to the monochord, nothing is more convenient for experiments upon sound, than the vibrations of elastic bars, fixed at one of their extremities. They may be taken long enough to enable us to count the vibrations. By this means the following law may be demonstrated; *that the times of oscillation decrease as the squares of the lengths*. By diminishing the thickness, we are enabled to produce oscillations so rapid as to give a sound sensible to the ear. We may consequently determine, by means of the calculus, the times of oscillation which escape observation. Finally, by taking this in connexion with the monochord, we may confirm all the results of the theory of sound.

147. It is demonstrated, by experiments of this kind, that the lowest appreciable tone is that which is produced by a chord performing about 32 vibrations in a second. Each of the octaves to this sound corresponds to a number of vibrations, double that which precedes it; whence we obtain the following series;

Lowest tone	32	oscillations in a second
1st octave	64	" "
2d "	128	" "
3d "	256	" "
4th "	512	" "
5th "	1024	" "
6th "	2048	" "

There is also as to acuteness a limit to appreciable tones. The 9th octave above the lowest tone, is considered as the highest tone which can be sensible to the ear.

148. Although this is not the place to speak of the properties of the air, we must remark that this fluid possesses a high degree of elasticity; that is, it is capable of great compression, and when the pressure ceases, of a correspondent dilatation. It will, therefore, be easily seen, that the vibrations of a sonorous body must necessarily produce a similar vibratory motion in the air, which will propagate itself to a great distance from the sonorous body. Thus when a chord AB (*fig.* 25) begins to vibrate, it is obvious that there will be produced about the chord strata of compressed air AcB, AdB, AeB, AfB, &c., which will alternate with the strata of rarefied air. These alternate compressions and rarefactions, which are called *pulses* or *undulations*, succeed each other with great rapidity near the chord, without causing the separate particles of air which compose them sensibly to change their place. This motion has a striking resemblance to the circular undulations produced by throwing a stone into a tranquil body of water. The motion of the air being propagated to the ear, we have the sensation of sound.

149. Experience teaches us that all sounds are propagated with the same velocity, whatever be the rapidity of the vibrations. In atmospheric air, this velocity, according to the most exact computations, is 1142 feet in a second; but sound propagates itself also through water and solid bodies, and with a still greater velocity, as is proved by experiment.

150. As to the force of sound, it is proved by observation, that it diminishes as the air is more rarefied, and increases as the air becomes denser. It decreases also with the distance, and probably in the inverse ratio of the square of the distance.

151. It is difficult to determine by experiment whether sound is propagated in a straight line only, or whether it is also propagated in

curvilinear directions, since the judgments which our senses form, respecting the direction of sound, are attended with great uncertainty. The reflection of sound produced by solid bodies, according to the laws of collision of elastic bodies, renders the first opinion probable. It is to this reflection or reverberation that we are to ascribe the phenomena of echos, the speaking trumpet, whispering galleries, &c.

152. In wind instruments, it is not the solid substance of the instrument, but the column of confined air which forms the sonorous body. But the particular properties of these vibrations are not yet sufficiently explained.

153. There are many modifications of sound besides what we call high and low, loud and soft, concerning which little can be said with certainty, although the ear distinguishes them with great accuracy. Among these modifications may be mentioned the peculiarity in the sound of different instruments, and of different voices. Articulate sounds, uttered by the human organs, are particularly remarkable. They are called *vowels* and *consonants*.

SECTION III.

HEAT.

CHAPTER XVII.

Heat in general; its expansive Force; Thermometer and Pyrometer.

154. HEAT, the presence of which is always known by a particular sensation, and the principal gradations of which are expressed by the words, *heat, warmth, cold,* acts a very important part in nature. By its diminution almost all liquid substances, and even many aeriform bodies, become solid. By its increase almost all liquid bodies and many solids become aeriform. Without heat there would be no life or organization. Indeed the use of heat in providing for our natural and artificial wants, is so various and important, that if it were withdrawn, we should return to a level with the brute creation. For these reasons it may well be regarded as one of the most important subjects of philosophical inquiry.

155. The cause of heat is beyond the reach of our senses. Some philosophers are inclined to ascribe it to an internal motion of the smallest particles of bodies. Chemists are unanimous in ascribing it to the existence of a peculiar substance, which they call *caloric*. We shall find hereafter, if not decisive proofs, at least strong reasons in support of this opinion. In the mean time we shall employ the word *caloric* as a convenient mode of expression.

156. The first effect of heat which we shall notice, is that it causes all bodies to expand; solids little,* liquids more,† and aeriform bodies most of all.‡

---

* The expansion of solid bodies may be proved by a very simple experiment. Let there be a solid body *AB*, (*fig.* 26) which, when cold, exactly passes between the two vertical columns *CD, EF*. If we heat this bar without heating the apparatus *CDEF*, it will no longer be contained between the vertical columns, but will take the oblique position represented in the figure.

† If we fill a vessel *AB*, (*fig.* 27) with a liquid, and insert a tube *CD*, open at both ends, taking care to close entirely the orifice *F*, upon the application of heat, the water will rise and fill the tube.

‡ If we only put a sufficient quantity of water in the vessel to

157. This circumstance suggests a very natural and simple method of measuring with great precision the increase and diminution of heat. Instruments used for this purpose are called *thermometers*. The first person who contrived an instrument of this kind was Drebbel of Holland, but it was very imperfect. This was toward the end of the 16th century. In the 17th century the academicians of Florence improved its construction. Finally, in the 18th, Fahrenheit, at Dantzick, and Reaumur in France, discovered at the same time the exact principles upon which these instruments are constructed.

158. The apparatus most in use at present, is that which is with good reason called *Deluc's thermometer*, his ingenious researches having greatly contributed to its perfection. The following is a description of its essential parts. The lower end of a hollow glass tube (*fig.* 28), is blown into a round bulb. This bulb is then heated, in order to dilate the enclosed air, the upper orifice being left open. This being done, the tube is inverted and the open end immersed in mercury. As the enclosed air cools and condenses, the mercury is forced into the tube by the hydrostatic pressure of the external air, as we shall show hereafter. When the tube and a part of the bulb are filled with mercury, the position is reversed, and the bulb is plunged into boiling water. The mercury immediately rises to a certain fixed point E, called the *boiling point*, and remains there as long as the bulb continues in boiling water. In the next place the bulb is surrounded with melting ice. The mercury now descends to a point G, where it remains invariably fixed, as long as the bulb is surrounded with ice. This is called the *freezing point*. The distance between the two points thus determined, is called the *fundamental interval*. The tube is then attached to a small frame or scale, on which the divisions are marked. The fundamental interval is divided into 80 parts in Reaumur's thermometer; and the divisions are continued above E and below G, as far as the tube ex-

---

cover the lower opening of the tube, and heat the enclosed air, the water will rise very sensibly in the tube. A still better way is to leave nothing but air in the vessel, and after having closed with great care the orifice between the tube and the mouth of the vessel, to insert into the tube a drop of coloured liquid. The least cooling of the enclosed air will cause the drop to descend and precipitate itself on the bottom of the vessel. On the contrary, the least additional heat will cause it to ascend and escape from the tube.

tends. The point G is marked zero, and from this point we count in both directions.

159. If we divide GE into 180 parts and place zero at the point K, 32 divisions below G, and then count each way from this point, the point G will be marked 32, and E 212. This is the thermometer of Fahrenheit. Reaumur's thermometer is usually filled with alcohol instead of mercury. The new French scale is the same as the Swedish scale of Celsius, in which the fundamental interval is divided into a hundred parts, zero being placed at the freezing point.*

---

* This method supposes that the bore of the tube is exactly cylindrical, so that equal quantities of mercury correspond to equal divisions. But in reality this is never the case, whatever care be taken in the choice of the tubes. And hence there are few, if any, perfectly accurate thermometers. Gay-Lussac, who has made many valuable experiments on the dilatation of gases, had occasion for the most perfect thermometers, and the method he used was the following.

Take a glass tube open at both ends, and introduce a little mercury; this will form a small column in the interior of the tube. Mark on the glass the extreme points where the column ends, and apply this distance successively throughout the whole length of the tube, beginning at one extremity. We shall thus have a first scale of equal parts, the length of one of which we call l.

Then take out a portion of the mercury before introduced; for instance, a little less than half. The remaining column, placed at one end of the tube will not fill up one of the first divisions l, but will exceed half of it. Mark the point where it terminates. Let the column now be placed so that one of its extremities shall coincide with the mark of the first division. The other will not reach the mouth of the tube, but as before, will take up more than half of l; mark the point where it terminates. This point and the preceding will be equally distant from the middle of the interval l. Accordingly, we may obtain the middle by bisecting the space which separates them; for, if we have taken out nearly half the mercury first introduced, and if the tube is not very unequal, the distance between the two points must be very small, and for so small an extent the tube may safely be considered as cylindrical. We repeat this process for each of the first divisions, and thus obtain a second scale, containing twice as many intervals as the first. Each of these second intervals

160. The air thermometer consists of a tube ABC, (*fig.* 29) recurved at B, and terminated by a bulb C. The bulb is partly filled with air; the rest of the space contains mercury, which rises nearly to the middle of the long branch of the tube. When the air is heated at C, it expands and the mercury rises; when cooled, it contracts, and the mercury descends. If the points of freezing and boiling are determined as above, and the fundamental interval divided into 370 parts, we shall have the thermometer of Lambert.*

---

is to be again divided as before into two, and these again into two others, and so on until we have the number of divisions required.

This being done, let a bulb be formed at the end of the tube, and introduce the mercury as pure and dry as it can be obtained. The mercury is to be boiled in the tube itself; after which the thermometer is completed in the ordinary way, by marking the points at which ice begins to melt and water to boil. The number of divisions found between these points will indicate the scale of the thermometer; which being constructed upon these principles will be perfectly accurate.

It is easy to reduce these degrees to those of Reaumur or Fahrenheit, or any other proposed scale; for let n be the number of divisions of the fundamental interval; it is obvious that each degree of this scale will be equal to $\frac{80}{n}$ of Reaumur, $\frac{180}{n}$ of Fahrenheit, and $\frac{100}{n}$ of the centesimal scale.

In fixing the boiling point, care should be taken at the same time to note the height of the barometer, which measures the weight of the atmosphere. For when the barometer is low, water boils at a less heat than when it is high, as will be seen in the following chapter. We have been thus particular respecting the thermometer, because it is an instrument of such extensive use.

* When we wish to measure with great exactness very small changes of temperature, we employ another sort of *air thermometer*. We take, as before, a glass tube terminated by a hollow bulb; but instead of introducing mercury, we make use of the air which the tube contains, and measure variations of temperature by the changes of its bulk. For this purpose we separate this portion of air from the air without, which is done by heating the air in the bulb, holding it in the hand. The warmth of the hand expands the internal air and expels a portion from the tube. Then we put a small

161. In constructing the thermometer, mercury has the following advantages. 1. It supports, before boiling, more heat than any other fluid; and by employing it we may extend the scale beyond the point of boiling water to 252 of Deluc, and 600 of Fahrenheit. Below the above point it may be extended to 32 of Deluc, and — 40 of Fahrenheit. At this point the mercury becomes solid. 2. Mercury may be obtained perfectly pure and similar in its properties more easily than any other fluid; and hence the results given by different thermometers may be more safely compared with each other. 3. Mercury is more sensible to the action of heat than any other fluid, that is, it indicates more promptly the effects of heat and cold. 4. But its essential superiority arises from the fact, that its dilatation is nearly proportional to the actual increase of heat; at least between the freezing and boiling points. Deluc demonstrated this fact by a series of very exact experiments.*

---

drop of coloured spirits of wine into the orifice of the tube, and suffer the air within to cool and contract; in consequence of which the drop descends into the tube; and afterwards rises or falls with the smallest change of temperature. The sensibility of this apparatus depends upon the ratio of the tube and ball, and may be estimated according to the known laws of dilatation. But, on account of this extreme sensibility, it can only be employed within very narrow limits; for if the cooling is very considerable, the drop falls into the ball; and if it is much heated it is expelled from the tube.

If two balls be thus formed, one at each extremity, and a coloured drop be introduced through a small perforation afterwards closed, the drop will be influenced only by the difference of temperature of the two masses which it separates. This instrument, which is used in many delicate experiments, is called the *Thermoscope* or *Differential Thermometer*.

* When we mix two portions of water of equal weight, but of different temperatures, a thermometer plunged into the mixture, ought to indicate the degree exactly intermediate between the two degrees of heat, provided its expansion is exactly proportional to the degree of heat. On this fact is founded the method employed by Deluc, in comparing the range of a mercurial thermometer with that of heat. This experiment is very difficult, because in order to be accurate, it is necessary that the bodies operated upon, should be completely insulated from all foreign bodies. But it being a truth of great import-

Pyrometer.

162. Various instruments have been invented for measuring very high degrees of heat. These are called *pyrometers*. Most of them are founded upon the dilatation of solid bodies, and principally of

---

ance, many efforts have been made to establish it. Gay-Lussac at length succeeded.

The reason why the dilatation of a body is not proportional to the heat, is, that when this body changes its state, its capacity for heat also changes, so that a greater or less quantity is requisite now than before the change, in order to alter its temperature an equal number of degrees. It is true, we can avoid the extremes of freezing and boiling at which bodies pass entirely from one state to another; but we cannot avoid approaching these; and it is a well known fact that bodies are prepared for these changes by imperceptible degrees, and anticipate, as it were, the properties which these changes develope. For this reason doubts may be entertained whether the progressive dilatation of the mercury between 32° and 212° is proportional to the progressive increase of heat, although this last point is still very far short of that at which mercury boils. But we may, without hesitation, admit the existence of this proportionality with respect to air and other aeriform bodies which cannot be made to change their state by any physical means. Accordingly, by observing in a great number of experiments, the range of the mercurial and air thermometers, Gay-Lassac found that it is exactly the same in both; so that between these extremes the mercurial thermometer may be considered as indicating with great accuracy a corresponding increase of heat. Since that time MM. Petit and Dulong have ascertained that this property results from the inequalities of dilatation of the mercury, and of the glass which contains it. They found that each of these dilatations, measured separately, and in an absolute manner, increases in proportion as the temperature rises, when we compare it with that of dry air. But the mercurial thermometer only shows the difference of these increments, which is insensible between 32° and 212°; and hence it is that these indications appear to be perfectly exact within these limits. Nevertheless they are not so, and the error increases with the temperature, but always in consequence of the difference of dilatation of the mercury and glass; so that when the mercurial thermometer, for example, indicates 572°, the air thermometer indicates only 559°,4, which shows an error of only 12,6°.

metals. All these instruments are yet very imperfect. The best is the one invented by Wedgewood. Its principle is as follows. Pure clay and all pottery, the chief ingredient of which is clay, form an apparent exception to the law of the dilatation of bodies by heat. Fragments of clay which have not been baked, but only dried in the air, contract under the influence of heat, and in proportion to its intensity; and when they are cooled, they do not recover their former dimensions. The reason is, that dried clay still contains a certain quantity of water which is gradually expelled by heat. Having observed this, Wedgewood prepared tubes of clay of precisely determinate dimensions, and then exposed them to the action of the heat which he wished to measure. For instance, he placed them in a crucible with silver in fusion; after remaining there for some time he took them out, and by means of a very simple apparatus measured the diminution of their diameter. Hence he deduced the degree of heat. To determine this degree, he made use of a particular scale, but one which may be easily compared with that of Deluc or Fahrenheit. New experiments, however, have shown that the indications, given by this instrument, are very uncertain.*

---

* I have myself suggested a method which appears to be very exact, for measuring the highest temperatures. It is founded upon the following property which I have demonstrated from experiment; viz. when a metallic bar exposed in a tranquil air, is plunged at one of its extremities into a source of constant temperature, the elevations of temperature at each point decrease in geometrical progression, when the distances from the focus are in arithmetical progression. Accordingly, when we have ascertained by experiment the propagation of heat in a bar, it is sufficient to observe the temperature at one of its points, and the distance of this point from the constant source of heat, in order to determine the temperature of this last. I have employed this method in determining the temperature of melting tin and lead. The last I found to be $375°,5$. The diminution of heat with the distance is so rapid, that it would be impossible by heating one extremity of a bar of iron six feet long and 1 inch square, to raise the temperature of the extremity one degree; for the heat necessary for this would be so great as to melt the iron.

Some Remarkable Points in Thermometric and Pyrometric Scales.

Degrees of the Thermometer.	Deluc.	Fahrenheit.	Wedge-wood.
Mercury freezes	— 32	— 40	
A mixture of equal parts of snow and ammonia	— 14$\frac{2}{9}$	∓ 0	
Water freezes	+ 0	+ 32	
Deep caverns, mild heat of spring	+ 10	+ 54	
Moderate heat of summer . . .	+ 14	+ 64	
Phosphorus takes fire	+ 20	+ 77	
Temperature of human blood . .	+ 30	+ 99	
Wax melts	+ 48	+ 140	
Alcohol boils	+ 63	+ 174	
Sulphur boils	+ 90	+ 234	
Zinc melts	+ 164	+ 400	
Bismuth melts	+ 190	+ 460	
Lead melts	+ 209	+ 502	
Mercury boils	+ 252	+ 600	
Iron appears red by day . . .	+ 464	+ 1077	0
Copper melts	+ 2024	+ 4587	27
Silver melts	+ 2082	+ 4717	28
Gold melts	+ 2315	+ 5237	32
Heat necessary to weld bars of iron	+ 5953	+ 13427	95
Extreme heat of a forge	+ 7687	+ 17327	125
Cast iron melts	+ 7976	+ 17977	130

Since the highest degrees of the thermometer can be observed in like manner by the pyrometer, it is evident that the two scales may be compared together, although the thermometer cannot be used above 600°. Many other points are mentioned in Lambert's Pyrometry.*

---

* With respect to the above table it is proper to remark, that the temperature of the earth is not the same in every part, as the author would seem to intimate. In the sands of the tropics the thermometer rises very high. At the bottom of Joseph's well in Egypt, 200 feet deep, it stands at 77° of Fahrenheit. In the vaults of the Paris Observatory at 54°. In Siberia there are places, it is said, where the earth never thaws, so that the temperature of caves is never above 32°. Hence it appears that the temperature of the exterior strata of the earth goes on diminishing from the equator toward the poles.

163. Among the instruments made use of to measure heat there is no one which follows precisely the same gradations as heat itself, and which may be employed under all temperatures. Still, in order to have a general measure, at least ideally, we suppose a mercurial thermometer, the variations of which are exactly proportional to those of heat, and which will therefore serve for all temperatures. This ideal measure agrees sufficiently well with the real measure of the mercurial thermometer between the boiling and freezing points. Above the boiling point, the real gradations are more rapid; below the freezing point more slow. But we may compare this ideal measure with the indications of the pyrometer for very high temperatures, and for degrees below the freezing point, perhaps a comparison with the alcohol thermometer would be more suitable. It is therefore possible, in fact, to measure all degrees of temperature, although the estimate of the extremes of heat and cold must be subject to much uncertainty. We shall close this chapter by stating the results of some experiments made upon the dilatation of different bodies by heat.

164. Bodies of different kinds, whether solid or liquid, are unequally dilated by heat. The gradations of dilatation are even different in the same body, according to the different degrees of heat to which we expose it. Indeed, we find, with a few exceptions, that bodies dilate more as they approach the point at which they are to change their state of aggregation. But hitherto the course of dilatation has not been sufficiently observed in any body, with the exception perhaps of mercury, to determine precisely the amount at each temperature.* The usual practice has been to fix the dilatation between the freezing and boiling points, and from this to deduce it proportionally for each degree of the thermometer. The following table contains the *linear dilatations* of several substances from 0 to 80° of Deluc, or from 32° to 212° of Fahrenheit. By *linear dilatation* we understand that which is measured in the direction of one and the same dimension of the heated body, that, for instance, which takes place in the length of a rule, which at zero of Deluc or 32° of Fahrenheit, is supposed to be equal to unity.†

---

* Since this was written, the determination of which the author speaks has been completely effected by MM. Petit and Dulong.

† The dilatations of glass and solid metals, stated in this table, are those ascertained by MM. Lavoisier and La Place.

Steel not tempered	0,0010791
Fine silver	0,0019097
Copper	0,0017173
Brass	0,0018782
Falmouth tin	0,0021730
Soft forged iron	0,0012205
Iron wire	0,0012350
Mercury	0,0061592
English flint glass	0,0008117
Pure gold	0,0014661
Paris standard gold	0,0015515
Platina	0,0008565
Lead	0,0028484
Glass of Saint Gobin	0,0008909

165. Two skilful observers, Dalton at Manchester, and Gay-Lussac at Paris, have lately made at the same time very accurate experiments upon the dilatation of elastic fluids, both vapours and permanent gases; and each has found that *all elastic fluids under equal pressures, are equally dilated by heat.* According to Gay-Lussac, this dilatation from 32° to 212° is 0,375 of the primitive volume, represented at 32° by unity. According to Dalton it is 0,398. The first appears to be the most accurate, because it accords perfectly with very accurate experiments made upon atmospheric air before this time, by the celebrated astronomer, Mayer. Hence we are authorized to conclude that the dilatation of the gases is a simple effect produced by heat alone, but that the dilatation of other bodies is the compound result of several forces. The dilatation of the gases is exactly proportional to the intensity of the heat, which affords ground for hoping that we may one day be able to measure heat exactly by means of this property.

The preceding table expresses only the dilatation of bodies in one single dimension; if we would have the dilatation of the volume we must triple the numbers expressed in the table.

For example, the dilatation of mercury from 32° to 212° of Fahrenheit is expressed by 0,0061591; taking the one hundred and eightieth part of this we have the linear dilatation for a degree of Fahrenheit's scale, equal to 0,00003422 of the primitive length at 32°; tripling this number, we have the cubic dilatation equal to 0,00010266, or a ten thousandth nearly of the primitive bulk at 32°, as appears from the experiments of MM. Lavoisier and Laplace.

This rule is founded upon a very simple theorem in geometry. Let us suppose a homogeneous volume V, which being dilated by heat, becomes equal to V'; it will preserve a similar form in these two states. Now the volumes of similar bodies are to each other as the cubes of their homologous sides; for instance, as the cubes of their lengths l, l', measured in the same direction. We have, therefore, the equation

$$\frac{V'}{V} = \frac{l'^3}{l^3},$$

whence

$$\frac{V'-V}{V} = \frac{l'^3 - l^3}{l^3} = \frac{(l'^2 + l l' + l^2)(l' - l)}{l^3}.$$

If the linear dilatation $l' - l$ is very small compared with l, the dilatation $V' - V$ of the bulk will also be very small compared with V; thus considering these dilatations so small that we may without material error confine ourselves to the first power of the fractions which represent them, we shall see that in the factor $l'^2 + l l' + l^2$, we may neglect them, and suppose $l = l'$; but then this expression becomes $3\,l^2$, and the numerator as well as the denominator of the second member becomes divisible by l^2; performing this division, we have

$$\frac{V'-V}{V} = \frac{3(l'-l)}{l};$$

that is, by tripling the linear dilation $\frac{l'-l}{l}$, which is given by the table, we have the dilatation of the bulk $\frac{V'-V}{V}$, as before stated.

Addition.

Many phenomena relative to the dilatation of bodies which were wanting at the time the author composed this work, have since been determined with great precision by MM. Petit and Dulong. Some of the most important are the following.

(1.) By comparing the absolute dilatation of dry air with the apparent dilatation of mercury in glass, these philosophers found the latter to increase, though by an inconsiderable quantity. The mercurial thermometer indicated 300° (centesimal), when the air thermometer, corrected for the dilatation of the glass, indicated 292,70. At the boiling point of mercury the first indicated 360°, the second 350°. The error, therefore, was only 10°. The two scales began at the freezing point of water.

This small difference was owing, as before observed, to a compensation produced by the likewise increasing dilatation of the glass envelope; for the authors, having by a particular method observed the absolute dilatation of mercury, compared with that of air, found that it increased more rapidly; indeed from 0 to 100 it was $\frac{1}{5550}$ of the volume for a centesimal degree; from 0 to 200 $\frac{1}{5525}$, from 0 to 300 $\frac{1}{5300}$. The temperatures were estimated by the dilatation of air, so that a thermometer founded upon the absolute dilatation of mercury, would have indicated at these different temperatures 0; 100°; 204°,61; 314°,15; and thus for the last there would have been an error of 14°,15, which would have been reduced to only 10°, if we had made use of the apparent dilatation in the glass.

MM. Petit and Dulong having also compared the dilatation of air with that of solids, found the latter to be likewise increasing, even at temperatures very far from that of fusion. Thus at the points 100°, 200°, 300°, measured by the absolute dilatation of air, a thermometer, constructed according to the dilatation of a plate of glass, supposed to be uniform, will indicate 100°, 213°,2, 352°,9; with iron we should have for the two extremes 100°, 372°,6; with copper 100°, 328°,8; with platina 100°, 311°,6. These results, which are very remarkable, are sufficient to enable us to correct the temperatures which had been calculated according to the supposition, till then very probable, of a dilatation sensibly uniform.—See *Annales de Chimie*, for 1818.

CHAPTER XVIII.

Changes produced by Heat in the State of Aggregation of Bodies.

166. ONE very remarkable effect of caloric is the change in the state of aggregation which it occasions in many bodies. We shall consider several bodies under this point of view.

167. Water is liquid as long as its temperature is between 32° and 212° of Fahrenheit. Being reduced to 32° it takes a solid state and

becomes ice. During the cooling, its dilatation diminishes till it is at about 39°, when it is at its greatest density. Below this point it dilates anew, and at 32° it fills nearly the same space it did at 46°. But at the instant it becomes ice it undergoes a much greater dilatation, which even acts with such a force as often to break the most solid vessels. After congelation the dilatation still increases, until the ice is about $\frac{1}{8}$ rarer than water; afterwards it contracts with an increase of cold like all other solid bodies.

168. When water is heated gradually, its dilatation increases in proportion to the intensity of the heat. When it reaches 212° its volume is about $\frac{1}{23}$ greater than at 32°, but at 212° bubbles begin to rise, and a particular motion takes place, called *ebullition* or *boiling*. By making the experiment in an apparatus for distilling, we find that the bubbles which rise are not formed of air, but of water rendered elastic, which resumes its liquid state when cooled. Its bulk is so much augmented by passing into the elastic state, that a cubic inch of water is thus made to fill the space of a cubic foot; that is, it is dilated about 1728 times. Hence we may easily conceive of the prodigious effects produced by steam in the *steam-engine, æolipyle*, &c.

169. The dilatation of mercury varies also by cooling, but in a manner much more uniform than that of water; there is no sensible change before congelation, which takes place at about — 40° of Fahrenheit; but we observe a very great contraction at the instant the mercury assumes the solid state. If it is heated to 600° it begins to take the elastic form; that is, it enters into the state of ebullition.*

170. Very pure alcohol begins to boil at 176°. When mixed with water it supports a much greater heat before changing its state. Hence in Reaumur's thermometer the alcohol must be considerably diluted with water, and yet the point of ebullition is always too low by several degrees. Before ebullition the alcohol expands with an increasing force, and its vapour possesses a high degree of elasticity.† The dilatation of alcohol diminishes by cooling, and perhaps for considerable degrees of cold, it has a range more exactly conformable to

---

* From 32° to 212° the absolute dilatation of mercury is 0,018477.

† The absolute dilatation of the purest alcohol is $\frac{1}{8}$ from 32° to 212°.

that of heat than mercury. We know no degree of cold at which it becomes solid.* For this reason the alcohol thermometer is better adapted to measuring extreme degrees of cold than the mercurial thermometer.

171. Heat produces the same phenomena in many other bodies. All fusible metals become liquid at a determinate degree of heat, and elastic at one still higher. The same is true of all fusible bodies. But in many bodies the passage from the solid to the liquid state does not take place immediately. The gross oils, for example, cannot pass to the state of elastic vapour, without some change in their chemical constitution. There are also solid bodies upon which the highest degree of heat produces no effect, and elastic fluids of which the greatest cold cannot change the state of aggregation. It is on this account that we distinguish elastic vapours from permanent gases. This distinction however, is not very essential.

172. It remains for us to speak of a very remarkable phenomenon produced by a change in the state of aggregation. When we mix a pound of water at 167° with a pound at 32°, the result is two pounds at $\frac{167° + 32°}{2} = 99\frac{1}{2}°$. But if we pour a pound of water at 167° upon a pound of ice at 32°, we obtain two pounds of water at the temperature of 32°. The whole heat, therefore, of the water used is employed in melting the ice, without raising its temperature at all. We call this heat, which thus eludes the senses and the thermometer, *latent heat* or *combined caloric*, because we consider the liquid water as an intimate combination of caloric with the matter of ice.

173. So far as observations extend it appears that a similar phenomenon always takes place when a body melts by the simple effect of heat. Hence the doctrine that this change always takes place at a determinate temperature, which remains invariable during the change, because the heat which is added is all taken up in melting the body.

174. When water passes to the elastic state at 212°, experience proves that no heat can increase its temperature; and even the vapour which rises above the water does not indicate, so long as it is free, a temperature above that of ebullition, although this vapour might be heated to a much greater degree if it were confined. Here

---

* [Mr Hutton states that he succeeded in solidifying it at a temperature of — 110°.—See *Edinburgh Encyclopædia*, art. Cold.]

then it is evident that there must be combined caloric, and that all the caloric which is added is employed in changing the water into an elastic fluid; consequently, while the change is going on there can be no increase of temperature. The quantity of heat which disappears or is combined in this case, is so great, that, according to the experiments of Watt, a temperature of 975° would be produced, if the vapour were to return to the state of water. Still the point of boiling water cannot be fixed at any perfectly constant temperature, because it varies with the pressure of the air. The more the water is compressed, the more it may be heated before boiling. Accordingly, in *Papin's Digester*, it takes a heat much higher than 212°. On the contrary, under the receiver of an air pump accurately exhausted, water boils at the temperature of about 167°. The boiling point of the thermometer should be determined according to some fixed state of the barometer, as when the mercury is at 30 inches, for example.

175. According to the best observations precisely similar phenomena take place in the ebullition of all other fluids. Hence the following is laid down as a general law. *At the instant of passing either from the solid to the liquid, or from the liquid to the aeriform state, a certain quantity of heat disappears so far as the senses or the thermometer is concerned; that is, it becomes combined.*

176. In returning from the aeriform to the liquid, or from the liquid to the solid state, the heat which had before disappeared, reappears and becomes free. This is especially observable in the following phenomenon, which sometimes takes place during the congelation of water. Fahrenheit first observed that tranquil water may be cooled considerably below the point of freezing without ceasing to be liquid; and more recent observations have proved that it will sometimes remain in this state even at 5°. But if we disturb it, a part immediately takes the form of ice, and a thermometer, plunged into the fluid, immediately mounts up to 32°. This is evidently a consequence of the action of the combined heat, which becomes free at the moment the water takes the solid state. Thus the most common phenomena of congelation must exhibit the same effects, if we observe them with sufficient attention.

177. In passing from the elastic to the liquid state, the disengagement of caloric heats the vessel much more than would be expected from the quantity and temperature of the vapour precipitated. It is thus that water is heated in a condenser, and that a considerable quan-

tity of cold water is made to boil by being exposed to the effect of a small quantity of elastic vapour rising from boiling water.

178. As similar phenomena are observed to take place in other fluids, when passing from a denser to a rarer state of aggregation, the following may be regarded as a general law. *In passing from the elastic to the liquid state, and from this to the solid, a certain quantity of heat is always disengaged and set free.*

179. If such experiments do not absolutely prove the existence of a material caloric, it cannot be denied that they render it very probable. This confirms also the opinion of those chemists who consider the liquid and elastic fluids as chemical combinations of a solid substance with certain quantities of caloric.

180. We have already remarked, that the state of aggregation of a body does not depend solely upon the free heat which acts upon it, but also upon its chemical combination with other substances. The phenomena of the absorption and disengagement of caloric, explained above, depend also upon the nature of the combinations and the state in which they are found. Among many experiments relating to this subject we state the following.

When we moisten the ball of a thermometer with ether, the liquor of the thermometer descends during the evaporation. When we pour water upon quick lime a part of the water becomes solid, and the mixture is heated considerably. When we dissolve in warm water as much sulphate of soda as it can dissolve, and expose this solution to a very great cold, it continues clear and fluid as long as it is at rest; but if we throw into this solution, already much cooled, a crystal of the sulphate of soda, or if we only agitate it, a certain portion of the salt becomes instantaneously crystallized, and a thermometer, immersed in the fluid, rises several degrees.

We shall see in the following chapter, why the changes of temperature, produced by chemical combinations, are not always governed by the principles stated in articles 174 and 177.

CHAPTER XIX.

The Propagation of Heat.

181. WHEN bodies in which the thermometer indicates unequal degrees of heat are brought into contact, a transmission of heat takes place from the warmer to the colder, till the thermometer indicates the same in both.

182. This communication cannot in any way be prevented. Heat is, therefore, something which cannot be hindered from penetrating bodies. Still it propagates itself more readily and more rapidly in some bodies than in others. The best conductors of heat are the metals and water. The worst are earthy substances, ashes, wood, charcoal, wool, linen cloth, furs, &c. The conducting power of a body may be estimated by strongly heating one of its extremities and observing the time which it takes for the heat to propagate itself to the other.

183. In atmospheric air there are two kinds of propagation. The first is the one just described, and considered in this view air must be classed with the bad conductors. By the other kind of propagation, heat passes off instantaneously in straight lines from the heated body, and appears only to traverse the air without combining with it. This is denominated *radiant heat*. Scheele first observed it accidentally before the open door of an oven. Many bodies reflect it after the manner of rays of light, particularly the metals, in so much that it may be concentrated at the focus of a metallic mirror. Other bodies absorb it entirely or partially. In exact experiments upon heat this distinction in the modes of propagation must be carefully attended to.

184. One of the most important discoveries respecting heat is due to Wilke, a Swedish philosopher, who in the year 1772 proved, *that different substances which indicate equal temperatures by the thermometer, may nevertheless contain very unequal quantities of heat.* The experiments which led him to this result were made in the following manner. If we mix a pound of water at 32° with a pound of water at some other temperature, as 113°, we obtain a a mixture at 73°, consequently at the mean temperature. But if we immerse a pound of metal at 113°, in a pound of water at 32°,

we find, when the equilibrium is established, a much lower temperature. If, for example, the body immersed be a mass of iron, the water and iron will have only a temperature of 41°. Now if great precaution have been taken to prevent the heat from escaping or penetrating the sides of the vessel, it is evident that the water must receive just as much heat as the iron loses; accordingly this quantity of heat, the loss of which has lowered the temperature of the iron 72°, has raised that of the water only 9°; whence it follows that 8 times as much heat is required to change the temperature of water one degree, as is required to produce the same effect in an equal mass of iron.

185. The quantity of heat required to change, one degree, the temperature of a determinate weight of a body, is called its *specific heat*, or its *capacity for caloric*. This property may be estimated by experiments similar to the above. If we take for unity the quantity of heat necessary to change one degree the temperature of a pound of water, it is obvious *that the specific heat of a body may be represented by a fraction, of which the numerator is the number of degrees by which the temperature of water has changed, and the denominator the number of degrees by which the temperature of the immersed body has changed, the masses being equal.* Thus in the experiment above described, the specific heat of the body would be

$$\frac{9}{72} = \frac{1}{8} = 0,125.*$$

---

* If we call 1 the specific heat of water, that is, the quantity of heat necessary to change one degree the temperature of a pound of water, a will represent the heat necessary to change this temperature a degrees. Let x be the specific heat of the immersed body, that is, the quantity of heat necessary to change its temperature 1°; then bx will be the quantity necessary to change it b degrees. But in our experiment the heat which the water receives, is just as great as that which the immersed body loses. We have then $a = bx$; whence $x = \frac{a}{b}$. If the weight of the water is not equal to that which is taken for unity, but equal to A, and that of the body immersed equal to B, we have by similar reasoning, $x = \frac{Aa}{Bb}$; for Aa is the quantity of heat acquired by the water, and Bbx the quantity lost by the body, and these are equal.

The Calorimeter.

186. Wilke, Black, Crawford, and many other philosophers, have determined, in this way, the specific heat of a variety of bodies. There are, however, many circumstances in which this method cannot be employed; moreover, its results are rather uncertain, since the conductibility of vessels and of the air, render precise experiments almost impossible. Lavoisier and La Place, therefore, rendered a great service to science by inventing the *calorimeter*. A complete description of this instrument may be found in the *Antiphlogistic System of Chemistry by Lavoisier*. We shall only observe in this place, that the instrument is constructed upon the principle that a determinate quantity of heat is necessary to melt a determinate mass of ice. By means of the calorimeter we are enabled to measure the heat which a body contains above 32°, or that which is developed by any chemical process, since we can find with exactness how much ice this heat is capable of melting. For this purpose, we place the body to be examined in a space filled on every side with ice broken into small pieces, and brought to the temperature of 32° by exposure for some time in a free air, supposed to be above this temperature. We leave the body thus enclosed till its own temperature becomes 32°; then we collect with care all the water which has become liquid, and the weight of this water gives the measure of the heat employed for its liquefaction.

187. When we wish to determine, with the calorimeter, the specific heat of a body, it is done by the following very simple process. We put into the calorimeter a determinate weight of this body, at a known temperature, 132° for example, and suffer it to melt as much ice as it is capable of melting. If we suppose this to amount to $\frac{1}{15}$ of a pound of water, there has been as much heat employed as would be necessary to raise $\frac{1}{15}$ of a pound of water from 32° to 167° (172); or to change 1° the temperature of 135 times as much water; that is, $\frac{135}{15}$ or 9 pounds. Now, as we have represented by 1 the heat required to change the temperature of a unit of weight of water one degree, the whole quantity of heat above 32° which the body had before the experiment must be represented by $\frac{135}{15}$ or 9. But this heat had raised the temperature of the body in question 100°; consequently, the 100th part would be necessary to change it 1°; that is, its specific heat is $\frac{9}{100} = \frac{1}{11}$. Finally, to

comprehend this in a few words, *it is necessary to take 135 times the weight of the melted ice, and divide the product by the number of degrees above 32° to which the body was raised before the experiment, in order to ascertain the specific heat which belongs to it.**

188. The calorimeter has over the method of mixtures the essential advantage of giving the specific heat of all solid and liquid substances without exception. The inventors attempted to apply it also to aeriform substances; but here the results of all methods must be very uncertain.

The utility of the calorimeter is not confined to researches of this kind. It may be employed in measuring the quantity of heat which is disengaged or absorbed in chemical combinations. Our limits however will not allow us to describe the method of making these experiments.

189. We proceed to state the specific heat of several bodies, as determined by Lavoisier and La Place by means of this instrument.

1. Common water 1,
2. Tin 0,1100
3. Crown glass, or glass without lead . . 0,1929
4. Mercury 0,0290
5. Quick-lime 0,2169
6. Water and quick-lime in the ratio of 9 : 16 0,4391
7. Sulphuric acid of the specific gravity of 1,87058 0,3346
8. Sulphuric acid and water in the ratio of 4 : 3 0,6032
9. Sulphuric acid and water in the ratio of 4 : 5 0,6631

The following are results given by different observers.

10. Ice 0,900
11. Mercury 0,033
12. Iron 0,125
13. Zinc 0,067
14. Lead 0,050

190. We shall now explain what the above table signifies.

---

* The weight of the body being p, its temperature before the experiment $t°$, the weight of the melted ice a, and the specific heat of the body x, we have $x = \dfrac{167\,a}{t\,p}$.

(1.) If we take for unity the quantity of heat necessary to change 1° the temperature of a determinate weight of water, the number 0,125, for example, which stands against iron, signifies that the same weight of iron would require only $\frac{125}{1000}$, that is, $\frac{1}{8}$ of this heat, to change its temperature 1°.

(2.) So far as we can suppose that the degrees of the thermometer increase and decrease in the same proportion as the heat, we may attribute another sense to the numbers of the table. They show the ratio of the actual heat which two bodies of equal weight acquire from 32° to the same given temperature. Thus the numbers 0,033 and 0,125, placed against the numbers 11 and 12, indicate that the quantities of heat above 32°, which mercury and iron contain at the same temperature, are as 0,033 to 0,125, or as 33 to 125. If this ratio were invariable under all temperatures, these numbers would express also the ratios of the absolute quantities of heat. But we cannot rely upon this result farther than between the temperatures of 32° and 212°, and we can only apply it to the quantity of heat over and above that contained in the body at the temperature of freezing.*

191. From this it will be easily seen in what manner we calculate the quantity of heat which actually exists in a given combination. If we mix 4 pounds of sulphuric acid and 5 pounds of water at the same temperature, this mixture must contain besides its proper heat at 32°, 4 times 0,3346 + 5 times 1, that is 6,3384 of heat; each pound, which is the 9th part of the combination, will therefore contain 0,7043. This number might seem to represent the specific heat of the combination; but according to the estimate given in article 189, it is only 0,6631. If we examine other combinations in the same manner, for instance, a combination of water and lime, we find a similar deviation.

---

* At a temperature of t° above congelation every body contains besides its primitive heat at 0°, t times as much heat as is necessary to change its temperature 1°. Thus, if we multiply all the numbers of the table by t, we have the excess of heat which the body contains at t° above freezing. But as the ratios of numbers are not changed when we multiply them by the same factor, the numbers of the table may be employed for this purpose at each temperature without being previously multiplied.

192. It appears, then, that in such combinations of heterogeneous bodies, internal changes of specific heat take place, so as to render it impossible to determine *a priori*, by any calculation, the specific heat of the combination. This remarkable phenomenon is so general that perhaps no two substances can be found whose capacity for caloric does not undergo some alteration by their chemical combination.

193. It is by this fact that we explain the important phenomenon of the production of heat or cold which often appears in the chemical combination of two substances. We observe it in the solution of salts. The muriate of lime, well dried, produces heat when it is dissolved in water; crystallized it produces cold. Calcined magnesia, thrown into concentrated sulphuric acid becomes strongly heated. The same is true of lime or sulphuric acid, when mixed with water.

Thus, when the heat which should be contained in a combination, according to the estimate of article 191, is greater than the actual specific heat, the inference is, that this combination contains less heat than its constituent parts would have at the same temperature; that is, some part of the heat must have been set free since the combination. If, on the contrary, the actual heat is greater than the specific heat, deduced from calculation, cold must have been produced by the combination.

This explains also the reason why, in the changes of the state of aggregation, by chemical combinations, the phenomena are not always conformable to the principles laid down, article 175, &c.*

---

* By very exact experiments, made upon different solid and liquid substances, MM. Petit and Dulong have discovered that their *capacities for caloric* are variable as well as their dilatations. The following table contains their results.

Names of the Substances	Mean capacities between 0° and 100° centes.	Mean capacities between 0° and 300°.
Antimony	0,0507	0,0549
Silver	0,0557	0,0611
Copper	0,0949	0,1013
Iron	0,1008	0,1255
Mercury	0,0330	0,0350
Platina	0,0335	0,0355
Glass	0,1770	0,0190
Zinc	0,0927	0,1015

In these results the capacity of water for caloric is taken for unity.

CHAPTER XX.

Production of Heat and Cold.

194. WE have seen how heat and cold may be produced by means of chemical combinations. We remark also, that all known means of producing these phenomena are referred to such combinations.

195. The best means of obtaining heat, as is well known, is by the combustion of charcoal, wood, peat, &c. We should encroach upon the province of the chemist if we were to attempt to analyze the theory of combustion. Still as a knowledge of the best means of producing heat is important, we shall give the following short explanation. It has been known for about 40 years that combustion properly consists in a chemical combination of bodies called *combustible* with a certain constituent part of atmospheric air, of which we have already spoken under the name of oxygen. This combination is accompanied with a disengagement of heat much greater than takes place in any other chemical combination. At the moment the two substances combine, the disengagement of heat is such as to produce a red colour; hence what is denominated flame. The products of this combination are nearly all volatile; hence the disappearance of the body burned. If the combustible body is composed wholly or partly of substances which become aeriform at an elevated temperature, these parts rise under the form of vapour when the temperature has attained the degree necessary for inflammation; and at the moment they become red by combining with oxygen they form flame.

196. Combustion is favoured and the heat increased by the action of a strong current of atmospheric air; hence the use of bellows. When we employ a current of oxygen gas instead of atmospheric air, we have the greatest heat which is known.

It might perhaps be difficult to account for the heat produced by combustion, if we consider it merely as a change of specific heat; but the uncertainty which prevails respecting the specific heat of gases, makes it impossible to form any definite opinion on this subject.

197. A second very powerful means of producing heat is by the solar rays. Their action is more intense; 1. According as their

direction is more vertical; hence the difference in their effect in different parts of the earth and at different seasons. 2. According as they are more concentrated; hence the excessive heat produced by concave mirrors and burning glasses. When these instruments are of sufficient magnitude their effects are in no respect inferior to the heat produced by oxygen gas, and they may even surpass it. 3. The effect of the solar rays depends upon certain material properties peculiar to each body. Thus it appears that transparent bodies are not immediately heated by them; and among opake bodies those of a light colour are heated much less than those of a deep colour, especially black.*

198. There are also many other circumstances, not well explained, attending this mode of procuring heat. Formerly the sun was regarded as a real mass of fire, and consequently its heat was not supposed to differ essentially from the radiant heat of our terrestial fires. More recently this hypothesis has been called in question, and philosophers have regarded the sun as a body in itself dark, and only surrounded by a luminous atmosphere. They have not allowed to the solar rays any proper heat, but only a force of impulsion capable of exciting the caloric contained in bodies. But what we have said respecting caloric seems to show that an elevation of temperature cannot be produced but by an augmentation of the caloric itself, or a diminution of the capacity of bodies for caloric; and neither of these causes is consistent with the above hypothesis. The celebrated Herschel very recently made experiments which tend to prove that the sun not only sends rays of light, but also rays of a peculiar heat, the laws of which do not agree with those of our radiant heat. The experiments of Herschel are very remarkable and deserve great attention.

199. There is also a third means of obtaining heat and cold, founded upon the principle, *that the compression of bodies is attended with a developement of heat, and their dilatation with the opposite effect.* Many phenomena, a long time insulated, are referred to this law. The heat produced by friction is without doubt a conse-

---

* I have seen in the valley of Chamouni among the Alps, a species of schistus or blackish earth, which the inhabitants of the country spread over the ground in the spring, in case the snow lies late or comes unexpectedly. If there is only one or two feet of snow, a day is sufficient to melt it when covered with this black earth.

quence of compression thus occasioned. The intensity of the heat is in proportion to the degree of compression. It has also for a long time been observed that the condensation of air produces heat, and its rarefaction cold. An experiment recently made at Lyons has shown that this effect is much greater than was formerly believed, since a small mass of air condensed, by a violent blow, to about $\frac{1}{12}$ of the space naturally occupied by it, developes so much heat, that we can not only inflame phosphorus, but also tinder and other combustible substances.

200. Berthollet has established a principle by which many phenomena are easily explained. *Heat produces an elevation of temperature, so long as there are any obstacles to oppose the dilatation of bodies.* The phenomena which take place in the changes of the state of aggregation, the uniform dilatation of all the elastic fluids, as well as the phenomenon mentioned above, appear to be necessary consequences of this principle.

Artificial Cold.

201. There are methods of producing a greater or less degree of cold; but they may all be referred to the law relating to the passage of bodies from a denser to a rarer state of aggregation.

Among these means we first distinguish evaporation, which is always attended with a greater or less depression of temperature according to its rapidity. Ether and alcohol, for this reason, produce the most powerful effects. The evaporation of water also, in phenomena of daily occurrence, produces a considerable degree of cold. And in the East Indies this method is even employed to procure quantities of ice.

The second method is by a dissolution of most of the salts in water, and probably of all, provided they contain all their water of crystallization. This dissolution changes the salt from a solid into a fluid. Most of the salts, however, produce only a feeble degree of cold. On the contrary, a salt which is deprived of its water of crystallization gives heat instead of cold, because the salt first attracts the water and puts it into a solid state before being itself dissolved.

The solution of crystallized salts, when it takes place in sulphuric and nitric acid, produces a still greater effect, particularly that of the crystals of sulphate of soda, which contain much water in a solid state.* But the most energetic effects are produced by mixtures of crystallized salts with snow or pounded ice, in which the two constituent parts pass at once to the liquid state. No salt has yet been discovered whose effects are more powerful in this respect than the muriate of lime, when it contains all its water of crystallization. As a great quantity of this crystal may be obtained, it is not now difficult to freeze considerable portions of mercury.

---

* Sulphate of soda mixed with a little nitric or sulphuric acid concentrated, produces cold; but when mixed with a great quantity of these acids, it produces heat.

SECTION IV.

LIQUID BODIES.

CHAPTER XXI.

Liquids in General.

202. There are few substances which are liquid naturally and in their simple state; nevertheless, besides water and mercury, we may always consider alcohol, ether, and the fluid oils, as possessing this property. But these liquids, and particularly water, have the power of dissolving so great a number of solid, liquid, and even aeriform substances, that we find an infinite variety of liquids, if we consider all solutions as belonging to this class.

Water.

203. The influence which water exerts, as well upon inorganic as organic bodies, and the multiplied uses which are made of it, cannot escape the most inattentive observer.

204. In its pure state water is perfectly transparent, without colour, odour, or sensible taste. But it can only be obtained in this state by repeated distillations. Nature, however, furnishes it almost pure in rain and snow. The water of seas, rivers, fountains, and wells, always contains foreign substances in solution, particularly saline substances, and even organic substances, of which hitherto little notice has been taken. These different modifications render the waters in question more or less appropriate to our use.

205. The force of affinity which water possesses gives it the power, not only of dissolving many bodies, but also of combining with many solid and fluid substances, and with all aeriform sub-

stances. In combinations of this kind it often becomes solid or elastic, and then it entirely eludes our senses.

206. The action of water upon a pure salt separated from every foreign admixture is particularly worthy of notice. According as the quantity of water or salt preponderates, the salt is rendered fluid by the water, or the water is rendered solid by the salt; this is the reason why every salt contains a certain quantity of solid water, called *water of crystallization*, because it was supposed that the salts were incapable of crystallization without this water. Some salts attract water so powerfully that they dissolve in the air; others, on the contrary, are so easily deprived of their water by the air that they become decomposed and crumble into powder. The first species comprehends the dried salts which are artificially deprived of their water of crystallization. The most remarkable of this kind are potash and muriate of lime.

207. We have shown in the preceding section how water is modified by heat. We have seen also, that water is not a simple substance, as was once supposed, but a compound of oxygen and hydrogen. Some, however, have lately undertaken to deny the decomposition of water. It has been pretended that water changes to a permanent gas by a mere combination with caloric or with some other imponderable substance; and that from this state it may be reduced to water by a contrary process. But this opinion rests upon a very uncertain foundation.

208. Among the mechanical properties of water its weight is particularly important. [A cubic foot of water at the temperature of 50°, weighs 1000 avoirdupois ounces. It is usual in experiments upon specific gravities to refer to the temperature of 60° at which a cubic foot of water weighs 62,353 lb., or a little less than 1000 ounces. In the more accurate experiments, however, upon this subject the absolute weight is first ascertained, and the cubic inch is taken as the measure, this bulk of distilled water at the temperature of 60° being estimated at 252,525 grains.]

209. It has been proved by experiment that *compressibility*,* *dilatability*, and *elasticity* belong to water; but it is only when a very considerable force is applied that any such effect is produced.

[* The phenomena of the transmission of sound through water and other liquids had long indicated that they were capable of being compressed. Canton, an English philosopher, clearly detected this

210. It is not proved in a decisive manner, either by experiment or theory, that water in *porous*. It appears to our senses like a perfectly continuous mass; and experiment shows that it is perfectly impenetrable to the most subtle gases, provided no chemical affinity exerts its influence in effecting a combination.*

Mercury.

211. Since extensive use is made of mercury in physical experiments some account ought to be given of this substance. It is a true and perfect metal, approaching even in its chemical properties to the precious metals. In its solid state, it has all the appearance of a metal. The purest is that which is obtained from red lead. Its specific gravity is 13,586, water being unity. With respect to its chemical properties, it is to be observed that it easily dissolves all metals except iron. Its combination with other metals is called an

---

property by observing the volume occupied respectively by oil, water, and mercury, first placed in a vacuum, and afterwards exposed to the pressure of the atmosphere; but the results which he obtained, though exact in themselves, were, however, liable to be affected by the accidental variations of form and temperature to which the apparatus was subject. M. Oersted completely removed these difficulties by plunging the liquid to be compressed, together with the vessel containing it, into another liquid to which the pressure was applied, and through which it was made to pass to the interior liquid without changing the form of the vessel, since it acted equally within and without. M. Oersted found, likewise, that a pressure equal to the weight of the atmosphere produces in pure water a diminution of volume equal to 0,000045 of its original volume. The experiments of Canton gave 0,000044. M. Oersted found, by varying the pressure from $\frac{1}{2}$ of the weight of the atmosphere to 6 atmospheres, a change of volume sensibly proportional to the pressure. Later experiments, made by Mr Perkins, seem to show that this proportionality continues when the pressure amounts to 2000 atmospheres. Before the water, however, is entirely freed from air, the diminution of volume, produced by the pressure, is at first somewhat greater than the above ratio would indicate.]

* I believe it would be impossible to find any circumstances or disposition of apparatus, in which this difficulty would not exist.

Alcohol.

amalgam. In making experiments it is necessary, on account of this property, to avoid bringing it in contact with any metal, except iron. It may be kept in vessels of glass, earth, or wood.

Alcohol.

212. All soft juicy vegetables are susceptible of vinous fermentation. While this process is going on, a part of the saccharine substance which they contain, changes into an inflammable liquid called *alcohol.* By distilling this alcohol with a gentle heat it may be separated from the other constituent principles or vegetable juices, by reason of its great volatility. It is impossible, however, to prevent a considerable quantity of water from mixing with it. By a new distillation it becomes more purified, and is then called *aqua vitæ.* The distillation being repeated several times, it becomes more and more separated from water, and takes the name of *rectified alcohol*, It cannot, however, be so far purified by simple distillations, as not to contain about $\frac{1}{4}$ of its weight of water. If we wish to rectify it farther it must be distilled over a salt deprived of its water of crystallization and perfectly dry. It is believed that this operation disengages it entirely from all the water it contained, and it is then called *pure alcohol.*

213. Pure alcohol is therefore a liquid which is derived immediately from organic nature. It is perfectly transparent and without colour, of a burning taste and agreeable odour. It burns with a bluish flame and produces no smoke, no soot, nor any kind of residuum. Its specific gravity, when pure, is 0,792, water being 1. It mixes with water in all proportions, and appears to produce an internal heat. The combination of the two substances occupies less space than the two filled separately. In the third section, we have already considered it in its relation to heat. It dissolves many bodies, particularly resins, by combining with which it forms what is called *varnish.* It dissolves many salts and has no effect upon others. In its pure state, alcohol is exempt from all fermentation and corruption, and preserves bodies which are immersed in it.

Ether.

214. Ether is properly an alcohol in which the proportions of the constituent principles are changed. Ordinarily they are prepared for this new combination by distilling a mixture of alcohol and sulphuric acid with a gentle heat. The product is then called *sulphuric ether*. It is without colour, of a very penetrating and agreeable odour, and a burning taste; it is extremely volatile, and becomes inflamed not only by contact with a burning body like alcohol, but even by the near approach of one. It burns in the same manner as alcohol, but deposites a small residuum. It dissolves many bodies, particularly the resins; and for that which is called *gum elastic*, or *India rubber*, it is the only known solvent which does not destroy its elasticity. It is the lightest of all known liquids. The specific gravity of ether, carefully prepared, is only 0,745; and according to Lowitz, it is capable of being purified still more. If we mix it with nearly an equal quantity of water, the two substances do not form a homogeneous combination; but when the mixture becomes tranquil, we distinguish two liquids, of which the upper is composed mostly of ether with a very little water, and the lower mostly of water with a very little ether. It does not, therefore, combine with water in all proportions.

General Remarks upon Liquids.

215. It is proved by experiment that all liquids, with the exception perhaps of the grosser oils, take the elastic state when exposed in small quantities in a vacuum. From this phenomenon we necessarily infer, that for all liquids in which it occurs, the liquid state is not so much the consequence of an internal attraction, as of an external pressure, arising in part from the gravity of the liquid itself, and in part from the external air; a hypothesis which accords perfectly with that of article 13. For, since the liquid state supposes an absolute equilibrium between the attractive force of the matter and the force of the caloric which tends to dilate it, it is reasonable to suppose that throughout the natural world, where we do not find any exact equilibrium, there does not perhaps exist a body which could

preserve its liquid state by means of its internal forces alone. The perpetual instability of the action of heat would also be an obstacle to this equilibrium. But, on the contrary, there may be many bodies in which one or the other only of these forces preponderates. Thick and viscous substances appear to owe their state to a feeble preponderance of the force of cohesion. In other substances the slight excess of the expansive force is kept in equilibrium by external pressure. This was essentially the opinion of Lavoisier; only he seems to have paid too little attention to the proper gravity of the fluid matter.*

CHAPTER XXII.

The Specific Gravity of Solids and Liquids.

216. ALTHOUGH the ordinary methods of estimating specific gravity belong to hydrostatics, there is one which can be here completely explained. It is the method of Klaproth, and it is the more deserving of being made known, inasmuch as it has never to my knowledge been described, though in most cases it ought to have the preference over other methods, on account of its simplicity, convenience, and exactness. The whole apparatus required consists of a correct balance, and one or more glass vessels shutting air tight.

217. *To find the specific gravity of a liquid.* First weigh an empty phial; that is, *balance it by weights.* Then weigh it filled with distilled water, taking care to stop it accurately. Next fill it with the liquid to be examined, and divide this weight by that of

---

* All liquids vaporize in a vacuum, even the gross oils; and the elastic force which they exhibit is greater, according as their ebullition takes place at a lower temperature. Thus ether, which boils at 100°, has at the temperature of 66°, a considerable elasticity, which becomes manifest in a vacuum; water, which boils at 212° would have at 66° an elasticity much less; and the gross oils which boil only at high temperatures would have one still less; for at the boiling temperature they only have a force sufficient to counterbalance the weight of the atmosphere; and it is not strange, therefore, that they have a very feeble one at low temperatures. We shall resume this subject when we come to treat of evaporation.

the first; the quotient will be the specific gravity sought. If, for example, the phial contain 864 grains of distilled water, and only 673 grains of ether, the specific gravity of the ether is $\frac{673}{864} = 0{,}779$.

The accuracy of this process is evident from what has been said respecting specific gravities (53.)

218. *To find the specific gravity of solid bodies which do not dissolve in water.* To estimate the specific gravity of a solid body, it is only necessary that the body should be introduced into the vessel; but it is not necessary that it be a single fragment; it may even consist of fine dust. We may, however, for more bulky substances procure vessels with an opening sufficiently large to receive them. The most simple manner of performing the experiment is the following;

First weigh the vessel exactly filled with distilled water. Then place the body to be examined in the same scale with the vessel; and put in the other scale a weight sufficient to balance it. We thus ascertain the weight of the body. Then take away the body and the vessel, and introduce the body into the vessel filled with water. The vessel is then to be closed, and great care must be taken that no bubble of air be left in the interior. Having wiped the exterior dry, it is to be placed in the scale where it was before. This will then be lighter than the other, and as much weight must be added to it as is necessary to establish the equilibrium. This weight which is added, indicates how much water the body displaced from the vessel. Divide the weight of the body by the weight of the water displaced, and the quotient will be the specific gravity sought. If, for example, the body weighs 523 grains, and the water displaced 84 grains, the specific gravity of the body will be $= \frac{523}{84} = 6{,}226$.*

---

* In order that a balance may be rigorously exact, its two arms must be perfectly equal, and the same weight placed in either scale must equally produce an equilibrium, the body weighed being the same. But it is almost impossible to attain to such perfection; and if we would take the trouble to subject those balances which pass for the most exact to an examination of this kind, we should scarcely find one that would bear the test. But we can dispense with this degree of perfection; and, provided the balance is sensible, determine the weight of a body as well as if the two arms were exactly equal. We have only to weigh in the same scale both the body and the weight with which we compare it. In the first place, we put in one scale the body to be weighed, and counterbalance it with some heavy substance; when the equilibrium is established, we take the

219. There are bodies which imbibe water, without being dissolved or decomposed. With respect to these, the determination of the specific gravity seems to present an ambiguity. In case of freestone, for example, we may wish to ascertain its specific gravity abstracted from the interstices which it contains; that is, we may seek what would be the specific gravity of the same weight and volume of this stone, provided it had no sensible interstices. Or we may seek the specific gravity of the proper mass of the body. In these two cases we proceed as follows. We first weigh the body in the air. Suppose it weighs 1000 grains. We then immerse it in water until it has imbibed all that it will, and ascertain how much its weight is augmented. Suppose this augmentation to be 50 grains. We then introduce this body into the vessel, and see how much water it displaces; suppose this to be 240 grains. Now if we wish to determine the specific gravity in the first sense, we divide 1000 by 240, and find it to be 4,167. If we would determine it in the second sense, we must consider that the proper mass of the body has not displaced 240 grains of water, but $240 - 50 = 190$ grains. Its specific gravity is therefore $\frac{1000}{190} = 5,263$.

When bodies become decomposed in water, as is the case with most argillaceous substances, this double signification still holds. Only in the first sense, when we consider the body as a continuous mass, the specific gravity must be uncertain in itself, since a body of this kind may have a very different density on account of the solution of the continuity of its parts. In this case we can only form an approximate estimate. We obtain it by the same process as in article 218, observing only to close the vessel before the body is decomposed. If, on the contrary, we wish to know the specific gravity in the second sense, we have but to crumble the body as fine as possible, and then to proceed as in article 218.

220. *To find the specific gravity of bodies which dissolve in water.* When we wish to know the specific gravity of a salt, or any other body which dissolves in water, we make choice of another liquid, as alcohol or oil, in which it does not dissolve. We first determine, as in article 217, the specific gravity of this liquid compared with water.

---

body away and substitute weights till the equilibrium is restored. It is evident that these weights represent exactly the weight of the body whose place they take, independently of any inequalities in the balance. This method of *double weighing* was suggested by Borda.

Suppose it be 0,866. We then determine the specific gravity of the salt with reference to this liquid, as in article 218. Suppose it be 3,278. Lastly, we multiply these two numbers together, and their product 2,829748, expresses the specific gravity of the body.*

221. We shall here present a short list of specific gravities.

Platina	20,722	Klaproth.
Gold	19,258	Brisson.
Mercury	13,586	Fischer.
Lead	11,352	————
Silver	10,784	Klaproth.
Bismuth	9,070	Brisson.
Copper	8,876	————
Brass	8,395	————
Iron	7,800	Bergman.
Steel	7,767	Musschenbroek.

---

* The specific gravity of water being 1, let that of the liquid be a, and that of the body b. Let the vessel contain p of the water and q of the other liquid. Let the weight of the salt be r, and that of the liquid displaced by it s. We shall have

$$1 : a :: p : q,$$
$$a : b :: r : s;$$

multiplying the two proportions, term by term, and omitting the common factor, we obtain

$$1 : b :: pr : qs.$$

Whence $b = \dfrac{qs}{pr} = \dfrac{q}{p} \times \dfrac{s}{r}$, which is the rule given above.

In all the preceding operations it is necessary, if we would obtain the utmost accuracy, to know the weight of the air which the vessel contains; and this is deduced from its capacity; for since bodies lose in the air a part of their weight equal to that of the fluid displaced, this weight forms a quantity to be added to all the results; and it is evident that if we neglect it, our results are not strictly accurate. For the same reason it is necessary to observe the barometer and thermometer during the experiment; for the weight of the volume of water displaced will be affected by the state of the air as indicated by these instruments. Care must also be taken to remove all the air contained in the interior of the liquids.

Tin	7,264	Bergman.
Zinc	6,862	——
Chalk	2,25 to 2,32.	
Carrara marble	2,716	Brisson.
Compact gypsum	1,87 to 2,29.	
Heavy spar	4,3 to 4,4.	
Clay	1,8 to 2,0.	
Rock crystal	2,653	Brisson.
Silex	2,58 to 2,67.	
Fluor spar	2,44 to 2,60.	
Pumice stone	0,914	Brisson.
Free Stone	2,11 to 2,56.	
Common green glass	2,5 to 2,6.	
White glass	2,4 to 2,5.	
Flint Glass	3,329	Brisson.
Saltpetre	1,900	Musschenbroek.
Common salt	1,918	——
Ammonia	1,420	——
Pure alcohol	0,791	Lowitz.
Sulphuric ether	0,716 to 0,745.	
Wax	0,954 to 0,960.	
Olive oil	0,913	Musschenbroek.
Oil of turpentine	0,792	——
Green oak wood	0,93	——
Dry ——————	1,67	——
Beech	0,85	——
Fir	0,55	——
Cork	0,24	——

222. One remarkable circumstance in the chemical combination of two bodies is that the specific gravity of the combination cannot any more than the specific heat be determined *a priori*, because the combination always has a different density from that of the constituent elements. If, for example, we mix equal volumes of distilled water and alcohol of the specific gravity of 0,824, we might suppose that the specific gravity of the mixture would be the mean between 1,000 and 0,824, or 0,912; but if we make the experiment we find it to be from 0,930 to 0,940; so that the liquid is more dense after the combination, and occupies a smaller space than the constituent elements did.

223. As heat dilates all bodies and consequently diminishes their specific gravity, the experiments should be made at a determinate temperature where accuracy is required. We usually take the temperature of 60° of Fahrenheit, because both in summer and winter this is the most common temperature of rooms which are occupied, and a difference of one or two degrees is not very important.*

224. *To find the capacity of a vessel or of any other body.* The exact determination of the weight of water, and of the specific gravity of bodies, has among other advantages, that of furnishing an easy method of ascertaining by weight the capacity of all bodies with much greater accuracy than by geometrical measurement. If we wish to find the capacity of a vessel, we fill it with water and find the weight of the water it contains. This weight expressed in grains and divided by 252,525, gives the capacity of the vessel in inches. If we aim at great accuracy it is necessary to reduce the weight to the temperature of 39°, according to the known dilatation of water.

225. If we multiply the specific gravity of a body by 252,525, we find how much a cubic inch of the substance of this body weighs in grains; and if we know the absolute weight of the body, we determine its capacity in cubic inches by dividing the whole weight by the weight of a cubic inch. Such is the general utility of this method of determining specific gravities.†

---

* It would sometimes be very difficult to obtain artificially this mean temperature of 60°, and it would be attended with much trouble to preserve it; but by a short calculation we may avoid this inconvenience; for if we know the dilatations of the bodies on which we operate, which is indispensable, it is easy, by observing the temperature at which the experiment is made, to reduce all the weights to the temperature required and thus find their ratios.

† Let V be the material capacity or volume of a body, S its specific gravity, p its absolute weight in grains, and $252{,}525\,S$ the weight of a cubic inch of the body. Then

$$V = \frac{p}{252{,}525\,S}.$$

If two of the three quantities $V, p, S,$ are given, we easily find the third; for

$$p = 252{,}525\,SV, \text{ and } S = \frac{p}{252{,}525\,V}.$$

CHAPTER XXIII.

Equilibrium of Liquids, or First Principles of Hydrostatics.

226. THE essential mechanical character of a liquid is the perfect freedom with which the parts move among themselves. Hence we deduce the following principle, which may be considered as the foundation of the theory of the equilibrium and motion of liquids. *Every pressure which is exerted upon a liquid, not only acts in its proper direction, but propagates itself uniformly in all directions to every part of the liquid.**

In a heavy liquid each particle situated below the surface, for example, in A (*fig.* 30) is pressed by the weight of the column of liquid AB which is above it. This particle presses with the same force and in all directions, the rest of the liquid with which it is surrounded.

If we cause a horizontal plane CD to pass through A, every other particle E, which is situated in this plane, must be pressed with the same force, if no motion takes place. Hence we deduce the principle theorem of Hydrostatics, *that the surface of a heavy liquid must be horizontal, in order that the liquid may be in equilibrium.*

This theorem supposes the directions of the forces to be perfectly parallel. If we suppose a celestial body formed solely of water and in a state of rest, its surface must be spherical; but on the contrary, if it moves about its axis, it will take an oblate form in consequence of the centrifugal force which tends to make its particles separate

---

* This principle of the equality of pressure in all directions may be presented in a manner still more simple, from the consideration of equilibrium. The most certain fact with which we are acquainted as to the constitution of liquids is their extreme mobility. If, therefore, their particles are in equilibrium, each one must be equally pressed on all sides; if not, since it is perfectly moveable, it would yield to the superior pressure. It is understood that in estimating the forces which act upon a liquid, we comprehend the impenetrability of the particles, which causes them to resist one another; and also the impenetrability of the sides of the vessel which support the same pressure as the contiguous particles of water.

from the body at the equator; and this form will be the more flattened according as it turns with greater velocity. See articles 119, 120.

227. The theorem is true, whatever be the form of the vessel, and in whatever manner its interior is divided, provided only that the portions of the liquids in the different compartments have a communication with each other. If, for example, the line EF represent a thin partition, separating the liquid through the whole extent of the vessel; according to the third law of Newton, this surface will resist just as much as it is pressed; that is, it will act precisely as the particles of the liquid would do if they were in its place. Such a partition, therefore, will not destroy the equilibrium. We may accordingly introduce into the vessel as many partitions of this kind as we please, and it is obvious that in all the compartments which communicate with each other, the liquid will always rise to the same height. Consequently liquids must always rise to the same height in recurved tubes, whatever be their form, curvature, and dimensions.*

228. The banks of rivers are rarely formed of substances impenetrable to water. It is on this account that we always find subterranean water in their neighbourhood. It is evident from the preceding theorem that this water must have the same height with the water in the river, though a sudden increase or diminution of the latter may produce a temporary difference. The subterranean water does not proceed wholly from the river, but also from rain and snow; and consequently, according to circumstances, it may furnish water to the river or take water from it. Local circumstances determine to what distance and to what depth this influence may extend.

It is a singular fact that the existence of subterranean waters, which is a thing so well known to practical engineers, is not mentioned in any work on physical science with which I am acquainted. Still it affords the most simple and natural explanation of the production and support of fountains and rivers, the explanation of which has often been attempted upon the wildest hypotheses.

---

* There is one exception to be made for the case in which the tubes are very narrow or capillary, for there the fluids do not take an exact level. But this is owing to the action of an attractive force peculiar to the material particles which compose the tube and the fluid; and for the present this force is left out of consideration. It will be explained in another place.

Pressure of a Liquid against the Bottom and Sides of a Vessel.

229. Since the intensity of the pressure which each point of a liquid supports and exerts is determined by article 226, we may also determine without difficulty the pressure which any given surface pressed by a liquid, exerts and supports.

When the surface is horizontal it supports precisely the weight of a column of the liquid which has for its base the surface pressed, and for its altitude the height of the water above the surface. If, for example, in the four vessels A, B, E, F, (*figs.* 31, 32, 33, 34,) the bottom AB is of the same magnitude, and the liquid surface EF of the same height above the bottom, this bottom will support the same pressure in the vessels; and the force of this pressure is determined by the weight of a column of fluid, $ABCD$ raised vertically above the bottom. If we know the extent of the base AB, and the altitude AC, we easily find the space occupied by the column; and if the weight of a cubic inch or a cubic foot of this liquid is known, we know at the same time the weight of the column. Figure 34 represents an instrument by means of which the force of pressure is rendered sensible.

230. The parts of an oblique side AB (*fig.* 35) support an unequal pressure answering to the distance of each point below the surface of the liquid. If this side have the form of a rectangle, it is evident that the pressure which it supports is equal to the weight of a prism of water, which has for its base half the square of the altitude BF of the water, and for its altitude the breadth of the surface pressed. The total pressure is the same upon a vertical as upon an oblique side.*

231. When two or more liquids which do not mix, as mercury, oil, and water, are put into the same vessel, they will take their places one above the other according to their specific gravities. But the surfaces which separate them must be horizontal in a state of equilibrium.

---

* Let us suppose that having produced the line CA, we draw BF perpendicular to its prolongation. Then take $AE = BF$. Now if we take a point G in the side, and draw through it the horizontal line HI, BI is the altitude of the column of water which presses upon G.

232. If we introduce into a recurved tube *ABC*, (*fig.* 36) a very heavy liquid, as mercury, for example, and pour into one of the branches of the same tube another lighter liquid, water for example, their surfaces will be horizontal; but the surface *C* of the lighter liquid will stand much higher than the surface *A* of the heavier. If we draw through *H* where the two liquids separate, the horizontal line *DE*, the pressure in order that an equilibrium may take place, must be equal at *D* and *E*; now this can take place only when the altitudes of the two columns which exert a pressure upon *DE*, are in the inverse ratio of the specific gravities.

Pressure of a Liquid upon Solid Bodies immersed in it.

233. Let us suppose in a body of tranquil water *BCD* (*fig.* 37) a mass of water *A* of a form and magnitude taken at pleasure, but circumscribed within a space entirely geometrical and distinct from the rest of the fluid. It is evident that the sum of the pressures exerted upon it by the surrounding water must produce an upward pressure just as great as the weight of the insulated mass; since otherwise this mass would not remain in equilibrium. If now we suppose this mass annihilated, and its place filled by a solid body of the same form and magnitude every point of its surface will be equally pressed by the surrounding water, and will exert a pressure as great as the water of which it takes the place.

But as the triangles *BAF*, *BGI*, are similar, as well as *BAE*, *BGH*, we shall have *AE* : *GH* :: *BF* : *BI*, since the ratio *BA* : *BG* is common to both triangles. But since in this proportion *AE* = *BF*, *GH* must be equal to *BI*. Consequently, *GH* represents the pressure which the point *G* supports. The same may be proved of every point; hence we conclude that the triangle *BAE* represents the pressure upon the whole line *AB*. Now if the side *AB* is a rectangle, each line parallel to the section *AB* supports the same pressure. Consequently, the pressure upon the whole plane *AB* is the weight of a prism of water which has *ABE* for its base, and the length of the plane *AB* for its altitude. But the triangle *ABE* has its base and its altitude equal to each other and to the line *BF*. Thus its surface is equal to half the square of the line *BF*.

Under these circumstances the body is acted upon by two forces, one of which is exerted upward, and is equal to the weight of the water displaced, and the other is the weight of the body itself acting in an opposite direction. Hence we deduce the following theorem. *A body immersed in a liquid loses just so much of its weight as is equal to the weight of the liquid displaced.*

234. If the body *A* were just as heavy as the water displaced, it would, like the mass of water itself, float freely in the water. If it were heavier than the mass of water, it would descend, not with the whole force of its weight, but with that of its excess over the weight of the water displaced. If it were lighter, it would rise towards the surface with a force equal to the excess of the weight of water displaced over its own weight.

Floating Bodies.

235. In the last case where the body immersed is lighter than the fluid, it rises till some portion passes the surface of the water. By the effect of this ascent the quantity of water displaced is diminished, and consequently the force which raises it; there must be a time, therefore, when the weight of the water displaced is equal to the weight of the body; then the body is in a condition to float upon the liquid.

236. But experience proves that a body cannot float in all situations, although it is immersed to a suitable depth. To understand the cause of this, and in general to assign a reason for all the phenomena of floating bodies, two points are to be particularly attended to. 1. The centre of gravity of the body in which we may suppose all the weight concentrated. 2. The centre of gravity of the water displaced, in which we may suppose to be concentrated all the force which tends to raise the body. The first of these points remains always in the same place in the body; but the second changes its situation according to the changes which take place in the form and situation of the parts of the body which are immersed. If these two points are not in the same vertical line, the body cannot float on the surface of the liquid. If the first point is placed vertically above the second, still the body does not float in a stable manner. It is also necessary that the circumstances of the body be such, that if its position be changed by an infinitely small quantity, it will naturally return to it

by a series of oscillations. If the centre of gravity is vertically below that of the water displaced, the body must necessarily float and in a stable manner. This condition should be carefully attended to in lading and managing a vessel. [On this subject see *Cam. Mech.* art. 437, &c.

CHAPTER XXIV.

Hydrostatic Balance and Hydrometer.

237. A BALANCE fitted to weigh bodies under water, is called a *hydrostatic balance*. To effect this object it is only necessary to fasten small hooks below a common but accurate balance. The body to be weighed is attached to a very fine thread or hair, the weight of which is so inconsiderable compared with the entire mass of the body that it may be neglected. This is suspended under one of the scales in such a manner, that it can be weighed in the air or water at pleasure.

238. *To find the volume of a solid body.* We first weigh it in air with the hydrostatic balance to which it is attached by a fine thread or hair. Then, without detaching it, we immerse it in water; and as it loses a part of its weight, we add to the scale below which it is suspended, the weight necessary to restore the equilibrium. We thus ascertain how much water the body has displaced; and this additional weight, expressed in grains and divided by 252,525, will give the volume of the body in cubic inches.

239. *To find the specific gravity of water.* When the volume of the body immersed is known, the weight added indicates how much water is displaced. This is the method by which the specific gravity of water is ordinarily determined.

240. *To find the specific gravity of a solid.* We first weigh it in air, and then see how much weight it loses in water. The first divided by the last gives its specific gravity. But it is taken for granted that the body is heavier than water, and of such a nature that water neither dissolves nor decomposes it. This method is therefore, particularly applicable when the body is too large to be introduced into a vessel.*

---

* We might even in this case make use of the method of Klaproth by substituting a cylindrical vessel, closed air-tight, instead of one

241. *When a body is mechanically composed of two known substances to find by means of the hydrostatic balance, how much it contains of each.* Archimedes, who may be regarded as the inventor of hydrostatics, found that 18 pounds of gold being weighed under water, lost one pound; 18 pounds of silver lost $1\frac{1}{2}$; and a crown weighing 18 pounds, which was composed of silver covered with a thick gold leaf, lost $1\frac{1}{3}$. Hence he concluded, by the rule of fellowship, that the quantity of silver was to that of the gold as the differences of the three numbers 1, $1\frac{1}{3}$, $1\frac{1}{2}$, that is, as 2 to 1; and that consequently the crown was composed of $\frac{1}{3}$ gold and $\frac{2}{3}$ silver. This method can be employed only when the two substances are mechanically mixed, and not when they are chemically combined. In the latter case it would give erroneous results.*

---

of an indeterminate form. When this vessel is filled with water, we close it by passing horizontally over its orifice, a plate of ground glass, which excludes all the water that does not make a part of its capacity. In this way the cylinder may be very exactly closed, and all the water be removed which may have adhered to its surface.

* Suppose a mass B, whose weight is p, composed of two substances A, C; let x be the quantity of A; then $p - x$ will be the quantity of C. We find, by experiment, that the weight p, when it consists only of the substance A, loses a in water; that the weight p of the compound body loses b, and that the weight p of the substance C loses c. The question is to find x. We have the proportion $p : x :: a : \frac{ax}{p}$; that is, if the weight p of the body A loses a, the weight x loses $\frac{ax}{p}$. Also, $p : p - x :: C : \frac{C(p-x)}{p}$; that is, the weight $p - x$ of the body C loses $\frac{C(p-x)}{p}$. The compound body, therefore, loses in all $\frac{ax}{p} + \frac{C(p-x)}{p} = b$; whence we easily obtain the value $x = \frac{p(b-c')}{a-c'}$. This formula leads precisely to the rule given in the text; for we have $p - x = \frac{p(a-b)}{a-c}$; and consequently $a - b : b - c :: p - x : x$.

Areometer or Hydrometer.

242. A glass vessel AB, of the form represented in figure 38, may be sufficiently light, not only to float on the water, but also to sustain itself there, when it has at its lower extremity B, a weight of lead or mercury. By means of this weight, the centre of gravity may be carried so near the bottom as to make the instrument float with stability in a vertical position. Now we have seen that a floating body always displaces a weight of liquid equal to its own weight. It is evident, therefore, that such an instrument will be immersed to a greater depth in a light liquid than in a heavy one; hence it will be seen that the instrument may be disposed in such a manner as to indicate the specific gravity of the liquid by the depth to which it sinks. For this purpose we introduce into the tube AC a paper containing a scale which indicates immediately the specific gravity. This instrument is called a *areometer* or *hydrometer*.

243. The use of the hydrometer in estimating the specific gravity of liquids, will appear, from what has already been said, to be superfluous. But we commonly employ it for a different purpose. For example, in liquid mixtures, such as beer, wine, brandy, saline solutions, &c., the specific gravity changes with the proportion of the constituent principles; and it is often very important for scientific, economical, and mercantile purposes, to know how much such a liquid contains of each of its constituent principles. To make this estimate, we commonly have recourse to the hydrometer. But it is evident that there must be a different scale and arrangement for each particular application. Hence the instrument has different names; as *alcoholometer*, *vinometer*, &c. It is also called *assay-instrument*, *gravimeter*, and *pèse-liqueur*.

244. The description of one of these instruments will suffice for all. We shall take the alcoholometer, and confine ourselves to a general description of its construction. Suppose the instrument immersed first in distilled water and then in alcohol. In the first it sinks to zero; in the second to 100. We then form mixtures containing 10 parts of alcohol and 90 of water; 20 of alcohol and 80 of water, and so on to 90 of alcohol and 10 of water. We immerse the instrument in each of these mixtures, and having observed how low it sinks, we mark on the scale the numbers 10, 20, 30, &c. The intervals will be unequal; but as they only increase slowly we

may still divide each of them into 10 equal parts, and we shall thus have an instrument which will indicate immediately how many parts of alcohol are contained in a mixture of water and alcohol. In order to render the degrees larger and more conspicuous two instruments are often employed, one ranging from 0 to 50°, and the other from 50° to 100°.

245. What we have said will convey a general idea of instruments of this kind. They serve to point out the proportion of one of the constituent principles, as salt, acid, &c. As to hydrometers for wine and spirit, they only represent arbitrary degrees of goodness. Even the areometers of Baumé indicate nothing more; since their scales have equal parts, and only the two extreme points are determined with precision by weighing; whence these areometers will at least agree among themselves.

246. There is still another kind of areometer without a scale, called *Fahrenheit's*. It differs from the preceding in having only one mark, which indicates the depth to which the instrument sinks in the lightest liquid, and in having above the tube a small trencher to receive the weights. In fluids where it does not sink to the above mark, we force it to take this situation by means of weights placed upon the trencher. This simple apparatus furnishes a very convenient method of comparing the specific gravities of liquids. We first weigh the instrument itself. Suppose it weighs 460 grains. Then we immerse it in distilled water, and add weights till it sinks to the mark. Suppose it requires 104 grains. Then we know that the instrument displaces 460 + 104 or 564 grains of water. If we find it necessary to add 160 grains for another liquid, we know that the instrument displaces 460 + 160 or 620 grains of this liquid. 620 grains, therefore, of this liquid fill the same space as 564 of the other. Consequently its specific gravity is $\frac{620}{564} = 1,099$.

Nicholson has lately made an ingenious change in this areometer, and thus rendered it a convenient instrument for estimating exactly the specific gravity of solid bodies.

247. In using all these instruments great attention must be paid to the temperature, as has been before observed.

CHAPTER XXV.

Influence of Adhesion and Cohesion upon Hydrostatic Phenomena.

248. If we suspend plates of glass, marble, or metal, horizontally from a hydrostatic balance; and having balanced them by means of weights, if we cause the plates to touch the surface of a liquid, we find that it requires new weights to make them separate from this liquid. The solid body, therefore, attaches itself to the surface of the liquid, which is undoubtedly the effect of an affinity exerted between them. But it follows also from this experiment, that the particles of the liquid adhere together with a certain force, since otherwise the solid body would always take away a part of the liquid with it, and since in order to effect the separation, it would be necessary to add just as much weight as that of the liquid separated. But the result of the experiment is entirely different. Glass, marble, and wood, actually take away a portion of water, of alcohol, and of most liquids with which they are put in contact; that is, they are moistened, but the weight of the liquid removed, is much less than that employed to effect the separation. Mercury does not even wet these bodies, and yet it requires a considerable weight to detach them from its surface.

249. From the universality of this phenomenon, we conclude that there exists a reciprocal attraction or affinity between the particles of all solid bodies and liquids. In like manner the property which the particles of each liquid possesses, of adhering together with a certain force, is the consequence of an interior cohesion, or simply of an exterior pressure. We shall call this phenomenon *attraction*, but without intending to designate by the word any thing more than the fact itself.

*250. In what we have hitherto said respecting the general conditions of the equilibrium of liquids, we have had regard to gravity alone. But the attractive forces of which we have spoken, introduce modifications into these phenomena, which we are now to consider. As they are very various in their details, although they all depend upon the same general cause, philosophers have sought to explain them in many different ways. But Laplace is the first who made known the real cause, and submitted the whole to rigorous calculation. Not having room to trace here the whole course of this profound analysis,

---

* The remainder of this chapter was added by Biot.

we shall endeavour to lay down the fundamental principles and state the most important results.

251. If in a mass of tranquil water the surface of which is horizontal, we immerse vertically a tube of glass of a very small bore called *capillary*, the water immediately rises in the interior of the tube, and supports itself there above its proper level. This elevation is greater in proportion as the diameter of the tube is smaller, and follows exactly the inverse ratio of this diameter. This is the result of experiment, and it is the most simple effect of capillary attraction. We cannot suppose that this phenomenon is owing to the action of the air, for the same takes place under the receiver of an air-pump. We are obliged, therefore, to regard it as the result of the attractive forces either of the water or of the glass, or of both these bodies; and such was also the idea of Newton. But this great man did not state precisely in what this attraction consisted, nor how it operated. It is even evident from what he has said of the ascent of water between glass plates, and of the motion of a drop of orange oil between two planes slightly inclined to each other, that he did not know the true cause of these effects. Clairaut is the only geometer who has since occupied himself with this problem. In his fine work on *The Figure of the Earth*, he treated it as a true question of hydrostatics, and analyzed in a very exact manner the different forces of attraction or gravity, which combine to determine the ascent of the liquid. But it seems that his ingenious mind was led astray by the false idea that the attractive action of the tube might extend even to the centre of the liquid column raised by capillary attraction. Now this is not in fact the case; for the liquid always mounts to the same height in a tube of the same substance and the same diameter, whether we choose a thick or a thin one; so that the strata of glass which are at a sensible distance from the interior surface produce no appreciable affect. This fact which is abundantly verified, shows, therefore, that the attractive force of the glass, or generally of the substance of the tube, decreases very rapidly, as the distance increases; so that its effect is sensible only very near the point of contact, and becomes nothing upon the particles at an infinitely small distance. In this respect the force in question is precisely similar to what the chemists term *affinity*. This idea, founded on experiment, is the basis of the theory of Laplace.

252. By admitting it, we see at once, that the small liquid column, which occupies the axis of a capillary tube cannot be thus sustained

above its level by the attraction of the sides; for this tube, though capillary, having still a magnitude sensible to our eyes, the affinity of the substance composing it cannot extend so far. We must conclude then that this column is thus elevated by the action of the water upon itself. The question then is, how can this action produce such an effect. The answer to this question constitutes the discovery of Laplace. In order to understand it, let us consider the manner in which a precisely analogous action is produced, that of bodies upon light. A luminous particle, when it is at a sensible distance from a body, does not experience any appreciable action; but when it approaches to a contact, the affinity begins to manifest itself. The particle becomes more and more attracted towards the surface of the body, by the action of the matter of which it is composed. At length enters and penetrates the interior. This action of bodies upon light becomes very evident in the phenomenon called *refraction*. Setting out from these principles, we determine with the utmost accuracy by calculation alone, the march of the refracted ray. Now this attraction at small distances is not only exerted upon the particles of light, but also in the same manner, upon all material particles which come in contact with the surface of bodies. It acts, therefore, upon the particles which compose this surface.

253. Accordingly, when a tranquil liquid naturally takes a horizontal surface, we must suppose that this liquid exerts a particular action upon itself, independently of terrestrial gravity. This action tends to make the particles of the surface enter into the interior of the fluid, and would actually produce this effect were it not for the resistance which results from impenetrability. Now when water rises in a capillary tube, it does not present a plane surface, but that of a concave meniscus, nearly approaching to a hemisphere. In this state it still exerts upon the particles of its surface a perpendicular action from without inward. But is this action equal to that which would result from a plane surface? This we must ascertain before we can determine the conditions of equilibrium, and this accordingly was the point first examined by Laplace.

The method employed is that described in his *Mécanique Céleste* for calculating the attractions of spheriods. He first proved that a body terminated by a sphere, or by any portion of a sphere of sensible extent, exerts, from without inward, upon the particles of its surface an action different from that of a plane surface. This action is more feeble if the surface is concave, as when water rises in glass tubes; and stronger when it is convex, as when mercury is depressed in a tube which is not perfectly dry. The difference of these forces is the same in both cases. It is reciprocally proportional to the radius of the sphere, and always very small compared with the action of the plane. In order to form an idea of the cause which produces it, we may represent the column terminated by a concave surface, as a body terminated by a plane, plus a concave meniscus at its upper extremity; and the column terminated by a convex meniscus, as a body terminated by a plane minus a concave meniscus turned downward. Now the attraction of this additional meniscus is always the same, and always tends to elevate the fluid column, in whatever direction its concavity turns. But in the first case it is necessary to subtract its effect from that of the plane, in order to have the action of the fluid upon itself from without inward and from above downward; whereas in the second case, we must add it to the action of the plane upon itself, since, not being occupied by the fluid, there results a diminution in the ascensional force, and consequently an augmentation in the attractive force of the fluid for itself, the latter being opposed to the former. If the surface is not spherical, its action upon itself is still made up of two terms, one of which represents the action of the plane, and the other, according as it is negative or positive, that of the concave or convex meniscus. This second term, always very small with respect to the first, is half the sum of the actions of two spheres, having for their radii the greatest and least osculating radii of the surface at the point in question. From this law, Laplace easily determined the partial differential equation, which expresses the nature of the surface; and by an approximate integration suited to each circumstance, he deduced the form of this surface, and the action of the fluid upon itself. It follows from this analysis, that the term which expresses the action of the meniscus upon the fluid column, placed at the centre of a capillary tube, is reciprocally proportional to the diameter of the tube.

254. Setting out from the results furnished by the calculus, we are able to give a satisfactory explanation of the phenomena of capillary tubes. Beginning with the case in which the fluid is elevated above the natural level, and which requires the upper extremity of the fluid column to be concave, we suppose an infinitely small filament of fluid extending from the lowest point of the meniscus along the axis of the tube, and then returning in any manner through the

mass of the liquid to the free surface. The fluid being in a state of equilibrium, this filament will be in a state of equilibrium. But it is pressed downward at the two extremities with unequal forces. The force exerted at the free surface is the action of a body terminated by a plane surface; the other in the interior of the tube is the action of the same body terminated by a concave surface, or one in which there is a contrary attraction upward, the little annulus cut off by a horizontal plane passing through the lowest point of the meniscus, and which is supported by the attraction of the glass, exerting an upward force. It is necessary, therefore, in order that an equilibrium may take place that the fluid should rise in the tube till the weight of the column thus elevated above the natural level, should compensate for this difference in the downward pressures exerted at the two extremities of the filament. This difference is in the inverse ratio of the diameter of the tube; the height of the small column must accordingly be in the same ratio; and this is conformable to the results of our observation.

255. If the fluid surface were convex instead of being concave, the results would be contrary. In this case, Laplace has demonstrated that its action would be greater than that of the plane, always in the inverse ratio of the diameter of the tube. Consequently, if we suppose a liquid to take this form in a capillary tube, by repeating the above reasoning with this simple modification, we shall see that the small curvilinear filament is still pressed unequally at its two extremities, more at the convex surface, and less at the horizontal. Hence it follows that in order to an equilibrium, the fluid must be depressed in the tube where the action is strongest, until it produces a difference of level, which will compensate for the weakness of the opposite force. The depression of the fluid will therefore be as the difference of the two forces, that is, reciprocally proportional to the diameter of the tube; and this is what actually takes place, when the fluid does not wet the tube, and attach itself to its sides, as when we immerse a glass tube in water, after having put a thin coat of oil over its interior surface; or when we immerse in mercury a glass tube not perfectly dry. Under these circumstances the surface of the fluid within the tube takes a convex form, and the fluid is depressed below its level, exactly in the inverse ratio of the diameter of the tube. But if we remove the obstacle which prevents the glass and the liquid from adhering to each other, then the latter will take the concave form and ascend in the tube above its level. This

happens even in the case of mercury, when it is well dried, and when the tube has been deprived of all moisture by long boiling. Such, for example, are those barometric tubes, from which all air and vapour has been removed by the repeated boiling of mercury in them. This leads us to remark that a single boiling is not sufficient for this purpose; and ordinary barometers prove it; since the mercury always preserves in them a convex form.

256. The peculiar character of this theory consists in this, that it makes every thing depend upon the form of the surface. The nature of the solid body and that of the fluid determine simply the direction of the first elements, where the fluid touches the solid, for it is at this point only that their mutual attraction is sensibly exerted. These directions being given, they become the same always for the same fluid and the same solid substance, whatever be the figure of the body itself which is composed of this substance. But beyond the first elements and beyond the sphere of action of the solid, the direction of the elements and the form of the surface are determined simply by the action of the fluid upon itself.

All the causes, therefore, which by acting upon the surface of the glass, can change the direction of the first elements, must change also the curvature of the liquid surface, and consequently the elevation of the fluid. This explains the depression of water in tubes coated on the interior with an oily substance, the elevation of mercury in dry tubes, and its depression in moist ones. Friction may also produce analogous effects, and Laplace has cited examples of this kind. These effects are easily explained by his theory, and instead of being irregular and anomalous, as they appear at first, they are, on the contrary, subjected to fixed laws, and may be exactly predicted.

257. Capillary phenomena are not confined to tubes, but take place also in plane spaces. Water rises and mercury falls between two glass plates, placed at a small distance from each other. The law of these phenomena is the same as in the case of tubes. The elevations and depressions are reciprocally proportional to the distances of the plates. But there is this singular difference, remarked by Newton, that the absolute effect is half of what it is in tubes; that is, between plates at the distance of $\frac{1}{30}$ of an inch, for example, the water rises to precisely the same height as in a tube of $\frac{1}{15}$. Newton merely stated this result in the queries placed at the end of his Optics; and although it is very remarkable, it does not appear

to have arrested the attention of philosophers till Laplace took up the subject; probably because they confined themselves to the capillary effects perceived in tubes, without suspecting they had so intimate a connexion with those of plates. This singular relation is easily deduced from the theory of Laplace. We have seen that in the case of tubes the action of the concave or convex surface upon the column raised is half the action of two spheres which would have for their radii the greatest and least osculating radii to the surface at the lowest point. If the tube is flattened in one direction, the corresponding radius of curvature augments; and finally becomes infinite when the tube is changed into two parallel planes; the part of the attraction of the surface which was reciprocally proportional to this radius, diappears, therefore, by the effect of this change, and there remains only the term depending on the other osculating radius. The attractive action is thus reduced one half. Such is the simple and rigorous result furnished by the theory of Laplace.

258. This theory explains also, with the same simplicity, all other capillary phenomena. Thus, the ascension of water in concentric cylinders or conical tubes, the curvature which it takes when it adheres to a glass plane, the spherical form which liquid drops naturally take, the motion of a drop between two glass plates slightly inclined, the force which brings together bodies floating near each other on the surface of water, the adhesion of plane discs to the surface of liquids, sometimes so strong, that it requires a considerable force to separate them, &c.; all these various effects are deduced from the same formula, not in a vague and conjectural manner, but with numerical exactness; and they thus acquire relations not before known. For example, we see clearly from this theory, why two parallel glass plates, immersed in water at a small distance from one another, tend to approach each other even when the water rises between them. For if we conceive between these two plates, and in the axis of the column raised, a small vertical filament recurved horizontally at its lower extremity, and terminating perpendicularly to the interior surface of one of the plates, this filament will be pressed differently at its two extremities. In the first place it will be pressed horizontally and from without inward, by the action resulting from the liquid in contact with the plane surface of the glass. Secondly, at the superior extremity it will be pressed from above downward, by the action of the plane minus that of the meniscus, and moreover by the weight of the small column of water, which is

elevated in the vertical branch above the point in question. Thus if we subtract the force of the plane which presses the other extremity, there still remains for the pressure from without inward, the action of the meniscus, minus the liquid column raised. These two actions exactly compensate each other if the point in question is at the natural level of the fluid; but equilibrium does not take place above this point. As we rise above it, the distance from the surface becoming smaller, the weight of the liquid column cannot compensate the attractive action of the meniscus, and the two plates, being attracted towards the top by this force, tend necessarily to approach each other. Those who will take the trouble to compare these results with the numerous explanations given by philosophers, and with those of Newton himself, will perceive the advantage of a mathematical theory over simple conjecture.

259. Laplace subjected his theory to the most rigorous proof by comparing it with experiments. For this purpose, he selected those which were made by Hauksbee, under the inspection of Newton, to which he also added others still more accurate, made by Gay-Lussac at his request. Though the formulas were only approximate, the agreement between them and the results of these formulas is truly wonderful; and it is obvious that this precise numerical determination of the results is the true touchstone of the theory.

There are no discoveries in the sciences which have not sooner or later some useful application. The effects of capillary attraction are perceived in barometric tubes; and as the surface of the mercury is convex, there must result a slight depression in the height of this column, which then does not exactly indicate the weight of the atmosphere. This effect is nothing in barometers with two branches, because the two forces resulting from the convexity of the fluid counterbalance each other. But it exists in simple barometers, and may become appreciable in exact researches. Laplace has indicated a very easy process for determining by experiment the corrections to be made on this account at all observed heights; and he has moreover calculated a table in which the value of these corrections is expressed numerically according to the diameter of the tube.

260. It is obvious also from the preceding remarks, that the heights must be reckoned from the summit of the convexity of the mercury, and not, as some observers do, from the point where this convexity begins. Proceeding according to this second method, the observed heights of the mercury are all too small by a quantity equal to the

radius of the meniscus, which being augmented proportionally to the difference of the weight of the mercury and air, may produce considerable errors in estimating the elevations of objects.

CHAPTER XXVI.

Motions of Liquids, or First Principles of Hydraulics.

261. WATER is subjected to many different motions, the consideration of which is of great interest to reflecting men, because these effects have an important influence upon the wants of social life. These motions are either natural or artificial. Springs, brooks, torrents, rain, all the agitations of the sea, especially the tides, as well as constant and variable currents, are examples of the first kind. Among the artificial motions, we distinguish particularly those of water in canals and in those ingenious hydraulic machines, which are found to be of such great utility. It belongs to mechanical philosophy to establish and confirm the principles of these different motions. But with respect to their application, that part which relates to the natural motions belongs to physical geography, and the other to the science of machines.

262. Detached masses of liquid observe exactly the same laws as solid bodies, when all their parts move with an equal velocity and in the same direction. Thus the motion of a drop of water which falls with the conditions which we have assigned, is absolutely the same as that of a solid mass under similar circumstances. But the essential mobility of all the particles of a liquid, with respect to one another, renders it almost impossible for them to have motions directed the same way and with the same velocity. Interior motions take place, which it is difficult to observe, and still more difficult to calculate. These interior motions embarrass the theory. Hydraulic experiments have also in themselves a peculiar difficulty, arising from the fact that we cannot withdraw the motions of liquids from the influence of all foreign forces, so easily as we can those of solids; and that we cannot without great trouble, determine exactly by the calculus what must be the effect of each of these forces.

263. The principal problem to be solved in hydraulics, relates to the velocity with which a liquid passes out through an opening made

in the bottom or sides of a vessel. Let *ABCD* (*fig.* 41) and *EFGH* (*fig.* 42), be two vessels of different heights *AC*, *EG*, which we suppose to be filled with a certain liquid and to be kept full by a constant influx. In the bottom *CD* and *GH* of both, are apertures *IK*, *LM*, of the same dimensions, but very small compared with the extent of the vessels.

If then we suppose the liquid to be acted upon by gravity alone, we can very easily determine by the general laws of motion, the *ratios of the velocities* of the masses of water which flow through the two apertures. For supposing, as we have done, that the height of the liquid remains invariable in the two vessels, it is evident that the velocities in each will be uniform. The quantities which run out in equal times, are then as the velocities, whatever these times may be. Since in general, the quantity of each motion is measured by the product of the mass into the velocity, and since here the masses are proportional to the velocities, it is evident that the quantity of motion produced in any given time, is as the square of the velocity. But the ratio of the quantities of motion is also the ratio of the moving forces. In the cases we are examining, these moving forces are the weight of the two columns of liquid which are situated vertically above the apertures. Since, their bases are the same, these columns are as their altitudes *AC* and *EG*. The square of the velocity in *IK* must therefore be to the square of the velocity in *LM*, as *AC* is to *EG*; that is, *the velocities are as the square roots of the heights of pressure.*

This is the most important principle of hydraulics.

264. It may also be demonstrated by the laws of accelerated motion, that *the absolute velocity of a liquid flowing out by the mere force of gravity, is equal to the velocity which a heavy body would acquire by falling from the superior surface of the liquid down to the aperture.**

---

* In order to demonstrate the truth of this law, we observe that the total velocity of the liquid flowing out, as well as all other velocities resulting from pressure, are not produced instantaneously, but observe an *acceleration* beginning from zero. This acceleration is uniform in the present case, since we have supposed the height of pressure to remain the same. Our problem is, therefore, to be solved by the laws of uniformly accelerated motion. Now let *PQIK*, (*fig.* 41) denote the pressing column; *NOIK* a small part of this

265. A change in the magnitude of the aperture cannot change this velocity; for if we double the aperture, the weight of the pressing column will also be doubled, it is true, but at the same time, the mass to be moved will be doubled in like manner.

It follows from this that the ratio of the magnitude of the aperture to the extent of the vessel, has no immediate influence upon this velocity. For if the aperture were equal to the bottom of the vessel, the inferior stratum CD would fall at the instant the opening was made, with the acceleration determined in the preceding article; but if the vessel were to remain full, the velocity of the water flowing in would be a new force, to which regard is had in the fundamental principle. It is for this reason that we have supposed the opening extremely small compared with the extent of the vessel, in order to diminish the effect of this foreign force.

266. These laws do not depend at all upon the specific gravity of the fluid. If one vessel contain mercury and the other water, both being at the same height, the pressure of the mercury for equal openings will be, it is true, 14 times greater; but the mass being as many times more difficult to be moved, the velocity will not be altered.

267. If the vessel is not pierced at the bottom, but on the side, as at EF (*fig.* 43), the particles of water do not flow out with an equal acceleration through all the points of the opening. Yet if the open-

---

column taken at pleasure. If the mass $NOIK$ falls by its own weight, it must have, after describing the path NI, a velocity $c = \sqrt{4g\ NI}$. But here the velocity which we shall call x, must be greater, since its acceleration is produced by the weight of the whole column $PQIK$. The acceleration of free descent, therefore, the measure of which is g, must be to the acceleration in the present case, as the weight of $NOIK$ is to the weight of $PQIK$. The acceleration sought is, then, the fourth proportional to NI, PI, and g; that is, $\dfrac{g \times PI}{NI}$; so that to find x, we have only to substitute this value in the place of g in the above formula, and we have

$$x = \sqrt{4g \cdot \frac{PI}{NI} NI} = \sqrt{4g \cdot PI}.$$

It will of course be seen that this velocity is the same as that of a heavy body falling freely, after having described the space PI or AC.

ing is small, and the point G be in the middle of it, we may, without material error consider the mean velocity of the liquid as that which belongs to the altitude BG.

268. If the opening is made in the upper surface of a horizontal projection, as GH (*fig.* 44) the water spouts out with a primitive velocity perfectly answering to the principles which we have established.

Hydraulic Experiments confirming the preceding Theory.

269. For these experiments we commonly make use of prismatic or cylindrical vessels; the greater they are, the better. The experiments are most frequently made with water. The bottoms and sides of the vessels have openings of different forms and magnitudes; and we also employ cylindrical and conical tubes of all dimensions suited to the apertures. The vessels are always kept full during the experiment, by a constant flowing in of water; or else the opening is so small compared with the dimensions of the vessel, that the water may flow out for several seconds without perceptibly lowering the water.

270. With such an apparatus we can determine by experiment the velocity with which the water flows in each case. We suffer the water to flow during 10 seconds, for example. The weight of this water, expressed in grains, being divided by 252,525, the weight of a cubic inch, will give the number of cubic inches in the mass; and this being again divided by 10, the number of seconds, will give the solidity of the mass which runs out in a second. This mass forms a column the base of which is the aperture, and the altitude the space described in a second or the velocity. If then we divide this column by the superficial dimensions of the aperture, we have the velocity with which the water flows.

Influence of Forces different from Gravity upon Hydraulic Motions.

271. The theory here presented, rests upon principles so incontestible, and the proofs of it are so simple, that we cannot doubt its correctness. Yet if we compare the results of this theory with experiment, we do not find them to be completely verified. The first

principle of article 262 is well confirmed by fact, since the velocities of water flowing from different heights, are in reality as the square roots of the altitudes of pressure, provided the apertures are of equal dimensions. But what relates to the absolute velocity is never conformable to the law expressed in article 264. In most cases this velocity is less, which may be easily accounted for by the obstacles which oppose it. But there are also cases in which it is greater; indeed this augmentation is sometimes more than one half. Moreover, with the same height of pressure, we find a change of velocity in every case when we give the aperture a different disposition; when, for example, we form it alternately by a simple orifice made in a thin plate, and by longer or shorter tubes, cylindrical or conical, and, in this last case, made larger at the interior or exterior extremity. Hitherto we have not been able to reduce this difference to simple principles. Yet these experiments themselves prove that the deviations are not occasioned by gravity, but depend entirely upon foreign circumstances. They do not, therefore, prove any thing contrary to the theory proposed; but only show that we have not yet been able to subject the influence of these forces to mathematical laws.

272. The forces and circumstances which modify the primitive velocity of a liquid, originally acted upon by gravity alone, may be comprised in what follows.

(1.) Flowing water has to conquer the resistence of the air, which diminishes its velocity.

(2.) The motions which take place in the interior of each liquid when flowing, are an important cause of modification. It is difficult to observe these forces, and still more difficult to subject them to exact laws. When a jet of water issues through the opening EF, (*fig.* 45) from the vessel $ABCD$, it is not merely the vertical column above EF which falls; but all the water in the vessel, if it is not very large, has a motion of descent. If this vessel be of glass, and we distribute small fragments of some light substance, as sealing-wax, for example, through the water, this motion becomes visible. Towards the top the whole liquid mass falls with sufficient uniformity, if the vessel be of equal magnitude. Lower down the motion does not continue either uniform or rectilinear; but the particles of water take nearly the directions represented in figure 45. The water flows, therefore, from all parts towards the aperture, and as its motions are partly opposed to each other they must produce a considerable retardation in the velocity.

The interior motions become still more varied, and the diminution of velocity still more considerable, if the vessel is not of the same dimensions throughout, especially if it is of an irregular form, and still more if it consists of a tube several times recurved.

Particular attention should be paid to the form of the jet as modified by these interior motions. If the aperture is simply pierced in a thin plate, the jet immediately below it has the form of a truncated cone inverted, as *EFGH* (*fig.* 45); but in such a manner that the sides *EG*, *FH*, are curved inward. The dimensions of this cone are very constant in the circumstances supposed. The smallest diameter of the jet *GH* is 0,8 of the diameter *EF* of the aperture; now the surfaces of circles being proportional to the squares of their radii, the section of the fluid column is 0,64, or about two thirds that of the orifice. Below *GH* the fluid column dilates. The distance between *GH* and *EF* is only equal to half the diameter of the aperture *EF*. This phenomenon is called the *contraction of the jets*. The velocity of the water increases very rapidly between *EF* and *GH*; since in *GH* it must be greater by one half than in *EF*; for, in equal times, the same quantity of water passes through *EF* and *GH*; and since these two sections are to each other as 3 to 2; the velocities in each must be in the inverse ratio, that is, as 2 to 3. Experiments prove that the velocity of water in *GH* approaches nearly to the velocity which belongs to the altitude of descent *AC*. It appears, therefore, that in the section *EG* the effect of all the foreign forces has disappeared, and that the water has then recovered the velocity which it ought to have from the effect of gravity alone. This is a very striking proof of the exactness of the theory we have stated.

(3.) Lastly, the greater or less adhesion which take place between the vessel and the liquid, and that which always exists between the particles of the liquid, have a much greater influence upon the velocity of the issuing water than we should at first imagine.

It is undoubtedly to this influence that we are to ascribe the different velocities we observe, according as we give different forms to the orifice. It is evident that these adhesions are obstacles to the motion in most cases; and when the aperture is very small, all motion may be prevented by them. Yet it appears that under certain circumstances these forces do not diminish the motion, but, on the contrary, augment it. The most remarkable effect of this kind takes place when we apply to the aperture a tube in the form of an inverted cone, which has the dimensions of the contracted jet, and when we add below this another conical tube which spreads insensibly.

273. When water spouts upward, it meets a particular obstacle besides those already described. Every drop rises with a retarded motion. The velocity is, therefore, less in the higher parts of the jet than in the lower. Accordingly the more elevated portion of the water exerts a pressure upon that which is below, and retards its motion. For this reason the jet never attains the height due to the primitive velocity of the water. Moreover the water which rises is retarded still more by that which falls, and sometimes it is crowded back into the orifice from which it issues. On this account water rises higher when it does not issue in an exactly vertical line. As to the disposition of the aperture, experience has shown that the one best adapted to give the jet a great elevation, is also the most simple; that is, a small orifice pierced in a thin plate.

274. It is a general law for all cases, that when a liquid issues from a vessel the vessel itself suffers a pressure in the opposite direction. This pressure may even give the vessel, if it be sufficiently moveable a motion, in a contrary direction. This pressure still exists when the aperture EF (*fig* 43) is closed; and its intensity may be estimated from what was said, article 230.

But whatever be its force, it cannot in this last case produce any motion, because in the opposite side AC there is always a part HK, the length and breadth of which exactly correspond to EF, and which suffers an equal and opposite pressure. But if EF is open, and water issues from it, the pressure upon HK has no longer a counterpoise, and hence it may give the vessel a contrary motion, if it be easy to be moved.

The Motions of Solid Bodies in Liquids.

275. A solid body cannot move in a liquid without putting a certain quantity of its mass in motion. But it loses just as much of its own motion as it communicates to the liquid, as is evident from what has been said.

We consider this loss as the effect of a force which the liquid opposes to the body put in motion, and call it the *resistance of the liquid*. The efforts of the greatest mathematicians have not yet been able to reduce the theory of this resistance to simple and exact laws. Since the time of Newton it has been generally admitted that this resistance is proportional to the product of three factors, which are the square of the velocity of the body in motion, the extent of the surface which resists this velocity, and lastly, the density of the liquid, supposing all other circumstances the same in each case. But a great number of experiments made since the middle of the last century, principally in France, have proved that all these principles are uncertain. It is only in case of mean velocities that they agree tolerably with experiment. When the velocities are very great or very small, they deviate very widely. What has been said of the resistance of a liquid at rest may also be applied to the impulse of a liquid in motion against a solid body, and also to the case in which both have motions contrary to each other.

276. We come now to consider a case which is attended with no difficulty; that is, the vertical descent and elevation of solid bodies in water.

If a body which weighs 8 grains displaces only 7 grains of water, it sinks. Yet as its mass of 8 grains is put in motion by a force of only one grain, it would fall in truth with a velocity uniformly accelerated, if the water made no resistance; but its motion would be like the force which acts upon it, 8 times less than in a vacuum; moreover, as the water resists it in its descent, its acceleration will be weakened at each moment; and the resistance increasing nearly as the square of the velocity, the acceleration will diminish very rapidly, and will soon become nothing. In fact, there must be an instant when the resistance of the water takes from the body just as much velocity as the accelerating force of gravity communicates. After this moment the body falls with a perfectly uniform motion. This moment arrives the sooner in proportion as the specific gravity of the body differs less from that of water.

Exactly the same may be said of a light body rising in water. If the liquid made no resistance it would ascend with a uniformly accelerated motion, since the force which raises it is constant. But the resistance of the water produces precisely the same effect as in the last case.

In a transparent vessel these two kinds of motion may be rendered visible by means of bodies only a little lighter or a little heavier than water.

277. The limits of an elementary work do not permit us to present any thing more than the fundamental principles of hydraulics. The application of these principles to the great variety of hydraulic engines belongs to the science of machines.

SECTION V.

AERIFORM BODIES.

CHAPTER XXVII.

Elastic Fluids in General.

278. It was formerly supposed that atmospheric air was the only elastic fluid in nature. Modern chemistry has taught us that there are many of these fluids to which we give the name of *airs* or *gases*. The examination of gases evidently belongs to chemical philosophy; and accordingly we shall only present those views of the subject which are indispensable to the student of mechanical philosophy.

Atmospheric Air.

279. It is principally from an exact observation of what takes place in combustion, that we learn that air is not a simple substance, as was formerly believed; but a mixture of two gases, oxygen and azote, nearly in the ratio of 1 to 3.* These are at least the essen-

---

* More exactly a volume of atmospheric air equal to 1 contains 0,21 of oxygen; the rest is a mixture not yet exactly known, of azote and carbonic acid, perhaps also of some other gases. The most probable estimates give 0,785 of azote, and 0,005 of carbonic acid; so that azote is much the most abundant. It does not contain hydrogen in sensible quantities; that is, we cannot admit more than 2 or 3 thousandths of it. These proportions of atmospheric air are exactly the same in every part of the earth, at least with respect to the oxygen it contains. Such are the results obtained by chemists, and principally by MM. Humboldt and Gay-Lussac.

tial ingredients of atmospheric air; but we should be deceived if we were to suppose that it contains nothing but these substances. Atmospheric air has the very active property, though not yet sufficiently observed, of dissolving most of the fluids, as well as a great number of solids, and of communicating its elastic state to portions of these bodies more or less considerable. A little attention to the phenomena which occur every day will leave no doubt on this point. Thus every body which diffuses an odour must be in fact dissolved by air. Of this nature are most metals, lime, moistened clay, &c. But air combines also with many inodorous bodies; and water presents a very striking proof of this.* Moreover, observation proves that all kinds of gas, especially carbonic acid and hydrogen, are naturally produced by chemical operations, in the interior of the earth, or at its surface, and that most gases combine without changing their state of aggregation. It is farther evident, that millions of organized beings live and die in atmospheric air; that during their life there continually takes place between them and the air an exchange of aliment and secretions, most of which are in the aeriform state; and that, during the decomposition of these beings, their constituent principles change into simple substances more or less elastic. These different considerations are sufficient to convince us that atmospheric air, principally in the lower regions, is a combination of an infinite number of elastic fluids, many of which elude not only our senses, but also the most delicate chemical agents, on account of the smallness of their quantity. In the upper regions of the atmosphere, the air appears to be more simple and pure. Yet various phenomena, such as the aurora borealis, falling stars, meteors, &c., which the simple combination of

---

* The reasons advanced by the author are by no means so strong as he thinks. It appears from the experiments of Saussure and Dalton, that the evaporation of water and other liquids does not require for its production the action of a dissolving force, for it takes place with equal rapidity in a vacuum. It is probable that this evaporation is the simple effect of the elastic force which all liquids possess in virtue of the combined caloric; and air by its material presence and pressure, far from favouring evaporation, rather presents a mechanical obstacle, and forces it to take place more slowly. Perhaps many other phenomena of the same kind, in which bodies are reduced to vapour, belong also to internal causes, and not to the dissolving force of air or the gases. But it is not necessary to pursue this subject.

the two essential principles of air could not produce, prove the influence of other substances of which we do not perhaps suspect the existence in these elevated regions.*

We shall treat in separate chapters of the relations of air to water and of its mechanical properties.

Oxygen.

280. When we heat strongly the oxyde of manganese or saltpetre, in a retort exactly closed, there is disengaged, especially from the first of these substances, a considerable quantity of air, which is almost pure oxygen. We find in works on chemistry the means of obtaining it in a state of absolute purity. This substance, for the discovery of which we are indebted to Scheele and Priestley, and for the exact analysis to Lavoisier, is of such importance in nature, that the knowledge of it is almost the sole cause of the revolution which has taken place in chemistry within the last 30 years. Without oxygen, life cannot be supported; hence it is sometimes called *vital air.* It is necessary to combustion; hence Scheele calls it *air of fire.* It enters into the composition of most of the substances which chemists call *acids,* and on this account Lavoisier has given it the name of *oxygen,* that is, *generator of acids.* The term *dephlogisticated air,* employed before the time of Lavoisier was derived from a false theory, and ought to be abandoned. Oxygen combines not only with organic inflammable substances and with most saline matter, but also with many inorganic bodies, and particularly with the metals. By this combination it takes away their metallic properties, and changes them into earthy or vitreous substances of various colours, called *metallic oxydes, metallic earths, metallic calces.* The oxyde of manganese, of which we have already spoken, and the sub-

---

* M. Gay-Lussac in his aerostatic voyage brought air from the higher regions of the atmosphere; and this air presented precisely the same constituent principles, as that at the surface of the earth; so that as yet there is nothing to prove that the atmosphere is not throughout of the same nature; for the phenomena which we do not yet know how to explain, are not a sufficient reason for admitting the existence of certain substances which direct experiment does not indicate.

stances so well known under the names of *rust, verdegris, white lead, tin, white arsenic,* &c., belong to this class. Although oxygen is one of the principal parts of water, since it makes 0,88 of its mass, water absorbs only a little of this gas.*

Instruments have been invented, called *eudiometers,* to determine how much oxygen atmospheric air contains; and it appears that this quantity is constant. The construction, as well as use of these instruments belongs entirely to chemistry.

Azote.

281. When we burn a sufficient quantity of phosphorus in the midst of a certain volume of atmospheric air completely enclosed, about a quarter of this volume disappears, and what remains is *azote,* a gaseous substance not respirable, and incapable of supporting combustion. Although azote does not appear to enter into so many various combinations as oxygen, it is nevertheless a substance of extreme importance, since we find that it is one of the constituent principles of all living organic bodies. Some German philosophers call it *saltpeterstoff* (substance of saltpetre) because, being combined in certain proportions with oxygen, it produces nitric acid, and by combining this acid with potash, we obtain saltpetre. The former denomination of *dephlogisticated air* is to be rejected entirely. For further particulars respecting this substance, the reader must consult the books on chemistry.†

---

* This is generally true; but by presenting oxygen to water at the moment when it is disengaged from certain combinations, Thenard succeeded in making it absorb more than 200 times its volume of this gas, with a degree of combination so intimate that even the removal of the atmospheric pressure did not effect its disengagement.

† It is a singular fact that almost the only characteristics by which azote can be known, are negative; that is, we only know that it does not produce such and such effects. The only exception to this is the property discovered by Cavendish, which consists in the power which azote possesses of forming nitric acid, when we combine it with oxygen by means of the electric spark. But this operation is too difficult to be employed as a common test; so that if there exist in azote, as is very possible, several distinct substances which agree in their negative properties, they may easily be confounded.

Hydrogen.

282. Since the invention of balloons, the term *inflammable air* has been applied generally to this kind of *gas*, which in a pure state is 12 or 13 times lighter than atmospheric air of the same elasticity. The older chemists called it *inflammable spirit*,* but they did not carefully examine its nature. It is irrespirable. No combustion can take place in it, although it becomes itself combustible when combined with oxygen. When we mix two parts of this gas (measured by bulk and not by weight) with one part of oxygen or four of atmospheric air, we obtain what is called *detonating gas*. We have before seen that the inflammation of detonating gas produces water. On account of this property Lavoisier gave it the name of *hydrogen*. A mass of water is composed of 0,88 by weight of oxygen, and 0,12 of hydrogen. This gas has a very slight affinity for water. We obtain it in its pure state by causing the vapour of water to pass through an iron tube heated to redness. The oxygen of the water combines with the iron, and the hydrogen passes off. We obtain it still more easily by dissolving iron or zinc in diluted muriatic or sulphuric acid. Then the water is decomposed. The oxygen combines with the metal and the hydrogen is liberated.

Carbonic Acid Gas.

283. This gas was formerly called *fixed air*, because it was originally recognised as a constituent principle of many solid bodies, especially of calcareous compounds. It forms nearly half the weight of calcareous spar, marble, limestone, &c. This gas is disengaged from these substances by pouring upon them a quantity of diluted sulphuric or other acid. It has since been discovered that this air is the same as that which is produced by the combustion of charcoal, and which has all the properties of an acid; hence it has received the name of *carbonic acid*. It issues in great quantities from the interior of the earth in many countries, and especially in the neighbourhood of volcanoes. As it is heavier than atmospheric

---

* In German this is called *brennbarer Geist*. The author observes, that perhaps this may be the derivation of the word *gas*.

air, and only mixes very slowly with it, it forms in some places a stratum of air several feet thick, in which no animal can live, because it is absolutely irrespirable. The *Grotto del Cane*, near Naples, presents a phenomenon of this kind. If we mix this gas with water and agitate it strongly, it will take into combination a volume nearly equal to its own. This gas will even hold a considerable quantity of water in solution.* It communicates to water an agreeable, lively, and acid taste; and by combining with it in different proportions it forms the essential principle of mineral waters. Lime water, which is made by dissolving quick lime or calcareous earth in water, furnishes a convenient method of discovering its presence in water. When we pour a small quantity of such a liquid into lime water, the latter becomes turbid, because the carbonic acid combines with the lime, and this combination is insoluble in water.

284. Chemists are acquainted with many other gases, and new ones are discovered from time to time; but being most frequently employed for their chemical properties alone, they are of less importance to the student of mechanical philosophy than those above considered. All these substances are *permanent* gases; that is, they retain their aeriform state at all known temperatures. Gravity and elasticity are mechanical properties common to them all, and they differ in different gases only in intensity.

Elastic Vapours.

285. We have already seen in the section on Heat, that liquids may be made to pass into the elastic state either by the action of heat, or by the dissolving force of other gases. While they are in this state, their mechanical properties do not differ essentially from those of the permanent gases; and they are subject to the same laws of equilibrium and motion. Perhaps even the difference which exists between vapours and gases is as little essential as that which is found to take place between liquid mercury and the solid metals.

---

* Since this was written the experiments of Dalton, confirmed by other chemists, prove that in a given volume of carbonic acid there does not arise a greater quantity of water in a state of vapour than in any other gas.

CHAPTER XXVIII.

Water in Atmospheric Air, or First Principles of Hygrometry.

286. The mechanical philosopher must necessarily be acquainted with the reciprocal effects of air and water, since otherwise we should be led to false conclusions in many circumstances; for example in the experiment of the dilatation of gases by heat.

Even the driest air always contains a quantity of water; and many instruments, under the name of *hygrometers,* have been invented to measure this quantity; but it is impossible to judge exactly of the construction and use of these instruments, unless we know the laws according to which water distributes itself in a system of bodies, all having an affinity for it. We must, therefore, explain these laws, though they belong rather to chemistry than mechanics.

287. Water may be contained in the air in two ways. It may float in it, only divided into very small bubbles, without actually taking the elastic state; or it may be perfectly dissolved in it, and actually have the aeriform state.

288. The visible vapour which rises from heated liquids is formed of small bubbles which may be discovered by the microscope. These drops would fall to the earth in perfectly tranquil air. But it is difficult to find a mass of air perfectly at rest, and the slightest motion is sufficient to raise a great quantity of these drops. If only a few are found in the air they do not affect its transparency; but still they may occasion some errors in the results of experiments, because at the least elevation of temperature they may pass into the elastic state. If they exist in considerable quantities they form visible vapour. Hence the origin of fog and clouds. Still we must not conclude, reciprocally, that all visible vapours consist of bubbles of water. Not only may all other liquids form visible vapours, but solid bodies may also do it, when they are divided into portions sufficiently attenuated. The vapour or smoke of flame is formed solely of charcoal, minutely divided; and the white vapour produced by burning phosphorus is phosphoric acid, originally solid, but now in a state of minute division.

289. When we put water into an open vessel and expose it to free air, it gradually diminishes and at length disappears, because it is dissolved in air. If this evaporation takes place in a mass of air

which is accurately enclosed and deprived of water, its volume increases, and its elasticity and specific gravity are changed. This is a proof that the evaporated water is not only mixed mechanically with air, but that it is also chemically combined with it, and consequently that it has passed to the elastic state. Not only atmospheric air, but perhaps also all other gases without exception, may combine in this manner with a greater or less quantity of water. Air does not lose its transparency on account of the water dissolved in it; but while in this state it may even appear to our senses very dry. This effect is reciprocal between air and water; and the parts of water which are not yet vapourized, always combine with some particles of air to which they communicate their state of aggregation, that is, cause them to pass to the liquid state.

290. The dissolving force of air is not equally great under all circumstances; heat and condensation augment it; cold and dilatation diminish it.* Thus when a mass of air has absorbed as much water as it can contain, if it is cooled or dilated, a part of the water rendered elastic takes again the liquid state and appears in bubbles of vapour. It is on this account that the receiver of an air-pump is often covered with vapour when the air becomes rarefied; and it is for the same reason, that cold bodies become moist on their surface when brought into hot air.

In these circumstances the water is said to be *precipitated*. On the contrary, the bubbles of vapour dissolve or change into elastic vapour when the air in which they float, becomes heated or compressed.

291. Many bodies, independently of air, have a great affinity for water. When a body of this kind is placed in a mass of air containing water in solution, it takes from this air a part of its water. The more water it has already attracted, the less strongly it continues to attract; and on the contrary, the more water the air has lost, the greater is the force with which it retains the rest. There

---

* Air in condensing disengages heat, in dilating absorbs it. Accordingly the effects of condensation and dilatation of air on vapours are to be referred to changes of temperature. When the primitive temperature is restored, the quantity of vapour capable of existing in a given space, becomes exactly the same, whatever be the dilatation or condensation of the air contained in this space. [See additional note at the end of the chapter.]

must, therefore, necessarily be a moment when both bodies retain the water with equal force; then the effect ceases. This state of rest is called *hygrometric equilibrium*. If a mass of air containing water is in contact with different bodies of this kind, each of them takes from it a part of its water, some more and others less, according to their affinity for water; on the contrary, if bodies which have absorbed water, are exposed to air which contains less water than is required to establish the hygrometric equilibrium, it will take water from them till this equilibrium is effected.

292. There probably exists no body which has not some affinity for water; but in many this affinity is insensible. Those which show the greatest affinity for this liquid are called *hygrometric bodies*. To this class belong all bodies which are derived from organic nature, as wood, bone, ivory, hair, paper, parchment, the epidermis which covers the internal and external parts of the bodies of animals, musical strings made of it, the tubular part of feathers, silk, &c. There are also many inorganic bodies which are hygrometric. For example, all soluble salts remain hygrometric even in the liquid state, and when the solution is saturated. Most of the acids, and especially sulphuric acid, possess this property; also slate, argil, and other minerals which adhere to the tongue. We may also reckon in this class bodies which are too compact to imbibe water, but the surface of which becomes covered with it when exposed to a warm and moist air, such are glasses, metals, &c.

293. As the temperature and density of the atmosphere are continually changing, there must also be a continual exchange of water between the air and the bodies with which it is in contact.

294. Such are the observations and principles upon which is founded *hygrometry*, or the estimation of the quantity of water contained in the atmosphere. From these principles it will be easily inferred that water in distributing itself through a system of bodies, in order to establish the hygrometric equilibrium, observes laws analogous to those by which heat is propagated in order to produce the thermometric equilibrium. Moreover we are taught by chemistry, that the various chemical affinities act according to the same laws, which are general for all substances. This is a decisive reason for admitting the materiality of heat.

Addition Relative to Hygrometry.

295. All that the author has said in this chapter respecting the manner in which the hygrometric equilibrium is established between different substances having an affinity for water, is perfectly just; but the evaporation of water in air and most of the gases, does not appear to depend upon this cause; for experiments prove that it takes place independently of affinity; or at least as if the effect of affinity were entirely insensible.

To prove the truth of this assertion, we must call to mind an important fact which Saussure, and after him, Volta and Dalton, have established by very exact experiments, which is, that the *maximum* of elastic vapour which can arise in a given space, depends solely upon the temperature, and continues invariable when the temperature remains the same; whether the space be filled with air of any density, or be a vacuum. Dalton has even extended this fact to all the gases which have not a very great affinity for water; such as oxygen, azote, and hydrogen. Some restriction is perhaps necessary for carbonic acid, muriatic acid, and ammoniacal gas; but for the rest, and especially for oxygen and azote, which are the elements of atmospheric air, it appears very evident that their affinity for water does not produce evaporation; for then this affinity would be the same for all, which is hardly probable; and a vacuum would act upon water with an equal force of affinity, which is absurd. Besides, this property is not peculiar to the vapour of water; it is common to all evaporable liquids, as alcohol, ether, ammonia, muriatic acid, &c. Each of these liquids sends off a determinate quantity of vapour in a given space, when the temperature is the same, whether this space be a vacuum or be filled with air or any gas whatever, with the exception of those cases in which there is a very great affinity.

296. According to this single principle, which is founded upon exact and rigorous experiments, the whole theory of hygrometry becomes exceedingly simple, so far as evaporation is concerned. If a liquid is exposed freely in a void space, or one which is filled with air, a certain quantity will evaporate, depending upon the dimensions of this space and upon the temperature. This quantity may be measured by its weight, and by the pressure which its elastic force produces upon the mercury of the barometer. If the space is indefinite the liquid will be entirely evaporated; this is what takes place in the

open air. If it is limited the evaporation will be limited also. It will cease at a certain limit, depending upon the dimensions of the space and the temperature; but this limit will be the same, whether the space be void or full of air. Only in the first case the evaporation will be instantaneous, because nothing opposes it; in the second it will be progressive and will require a certain interval of time, on account of the mechanical obstruction which the air, by its presence, offers to the dissemination of the particles of the liquid; and in these two cases, after a greater or less interval, the barometer introduced into this space will indicate the same increase of pressure.

This is what takes place with respect to a liquid which is not subjected to any foreign force, and which yields solely to the repulsive action of the caloric interposed between its particles, which is the determining cause of evaporation. But if the liquid is retained by a solid body, which has an affinity for it, it will be continually acted upon by two contrary forces, which according to circumstances may be equal or unequal. If the space in which the body is placed be deprived of vapour, the elastic action will have all its energy, and a part of the liquid will separate from the solid body, taking the aeriform state. But even by this effect the preponderance of the elastic force will be found to be diminished; for the tendency to evaporation will become less; and on the contrary, the action of the solid body upon the water which remains will increase in proportion to what it has already lost. Hence results a *state of hygrometric equilibrium;* but this state will be disturbed by a change of temperature. If the temperature be raised the elastic force will preponderate, and a new quantity of liquid will evaporate. If it be lowered, the affinity of the body will preponderate, and a portion of the vapour being absorbed will return to the liquid state. These constant changes are sufficiently sensible with respect to certain bodies, as hair, feathers, cords, to vary their dimensions; and we may thus observe all their successions. It is upon this property that the instruments called *hygrometers* are founded; and it is obvious that the action of these instruments admits of an easy explanation upon the principles above stated, without supposing in the air a dissolving force which is not indicated by any experiments. The whole depends upon the simple fact of the *moveable equilibrium* between the affinity of the solid body for water and the elastic force of heat.

It is proper to observe that the results here stated were not generally known when the work of M. Fischer was published; otherwise this judicious author would unquestionably have adopted them. He was only able to state in a note some results of Dalton which came to his knowledge while the work was in the press.

To supply this omission, so far as is practicable in a work where correct ideas of physical phenomena are rather to be stated than carried out into detail, I have inserted a table of the elastic force of aqueous vapour at different temperatures from 20° below zero of the centesimal scale to 130° above. This table is deduced, by interpolation, from a multitude of experiments made by MM. Dalton and Gay-Lussac.

Elastic Force of Aqueous Vapour estimated in Millimetres for each Degree of the Centesimal Thermometer.

Degrees.	Tension.	Degrees.	Tension.	Degrees.	Tension.	Degrees.	Tension.
−20	1,333	18	15,353	56	119,39	94	611,18
−19	1,429	19	16,288	57	125,31	95	634,27
−18	1,531	20	17,314	58	131,50	96	658,05
−17	1,638	21	18,317	59	137,94	97	682,59
−16	1,755	22	19,417	60	144,66	98	707,63
−15	1,879	23	20,577	61	151,70	99	733,46
−14	2,011	24	21,805	62	158,96	100	760,00
−13	2,152	25	23,090	63	166,56	101	787,27
−12	2,302	26	24,452	64	174,47	102	815,26
−11	2,461	27	25,881	65	182,71	103	843,98
−10	2,631	28	27,390	66	191,27	104	873,44
−9	2,812	29	29,045	67	200,18	105	903,64
−8	3,005	30	30,643	68	209,44	106	934,81
−7	3,210	31	32,410	69	219,06	107	966,31
−6	3,428	32	34,261	70	229,07	108	994,79
−5	3,660	33	36,188	71	239,45	109	1032,04
−4	3,907	34	38,254	72	250,23	110	1066,06
−3	4,170	35	40,404	73	261,43	111	1100,87
−2	4,448	36	42,743	74	273,03	112	1136,43
−1	4,745	37	45,038	75	285,07	113	1172,78
0	5,059	38	47,579	76	297,57	114	1209,90
1	5,393	39	50,147	77	310,49	115	1247,81
2	5,748	40	52,998	78	323,89	116	1286,51
3	6,123	41	55,772	79	337,76	117	1325,98
4	6,523	42	58,792	80	352,08	118	1366,22
5	6,947	43	61,958	81	367,00	119	1407,24
6	7,396	44	65,627	82	382,38	120	1448,83
7	7,871	45	68,751	83	393,28	121	1491,58
8	8,375	46	72,393	84	414,73	122	1534,89
9	8,909	47	76,205	85	431,71	123	1578,96
10	9,475	48	80,195	86	449,26	124	1623,67
11	10,074	49	84,370	87	467,38	125	1669,31
12	10,707	50	88,742	88	486,09	126	1715,58
13	11,378	51	93,301	89	505,38	127	1762,56
14	12,087	52	98,075	90	525,28	128	1810,25
15	12,837	53	103,06	91	545,80	129	1858,63
16	13,630	54	108,27	92	566,95	130	1907,67
17	14,468	55	113,71	93	588,74		

297. Trusting to our senses, we judge as erroneously of humidity as of heat. We consider air or any other substance as moist, when it deposites moisture upon our bodies. We judge that it is dry when it takes away moisture. The same mass of air may, therefore, appear dry to one observer and moist to another. For this reason philosophers directed their attention long ago to the construction of an instrument which should indicate the humidity of the atmosphere with greater certainty than the sense of touch. We have not room to describe the numerous attempts of this kind that have been made. The first instruments were extremely defective, and even the best at the present day are far from approaching the accuracy of the thermometer. It is a singular fact that we are much better able to measure a substance that is imperceptible to our senses, than one which we can directly observe.

298. We shall only remark with respect to the earliest hygrometers, that the best of them are founded upon the hygrometric properties of cat-gut cords, which untwist by the effect of the humidity which they acquire, and thus become shorter since they augment in size.

299. Among the instruments of this kind lately invented, there are only two which deserve the name of hygrometers; that of Saussure, and still more recently that of Deluc. We shall only speak of the first, which is most in use. The hygrometric body employed by Saussure, is a hair, deprived of all oily substance by being boiled in a weak solution of potash. The hair, thus prepared, contracts by dryness, and is lengthened by humidity. It is firmly attached at one of its extremities; the other end is fixed to an index very easily moved, which is turned one way by the hair, and the other by a small weight. This index by its movement on a graduated arc, indicates the contractions or elongations which the hair undergoes in consequence of the variations of humidity in the surrounding air.

300. The essential advantage of this hygrometer consists in this, that we determine by experiment two fixed points, those of extreme dryness and extreme moisture, that serve as the limits of scales which admit of being compared with one another. Lambert had already conceived the idea of this instrument, but he did not succeed in the execution of it so well as Saussure and Deluc.

301. We determine the *point of extreme dryness* by placing the instrument under a large glass receiver together with calcined salts,

and letting it remain in this situation as long as we can perceive that the hair continues to contract.

202. We determine *the point of extreme humidity* by suspending the instrument under a receiver, the sides of which are wet with water. The receiver itself is placed on a shelf covered with water to prevent the introduction of external air. The apparatus thus disposed is suffered to remain as long as the hair continues to lengthen, and we note the point on the graduated arc at which this limit takes place.

The distance between these two fixed points are divided into 100 parts called degrees.

General Remarks upon Hygrometry.

303. It may be asked what a hygrometer properly indicates. According to the theory explained above, the elongation of the hair indicates that it has received water from the air; and the shortening that it has parted with water to the air; and a state of rest, that the hair and the atmosphere are in a state of hygrometric equilibrium. Consequently, if the forces with which the air and hygrometric bodies attract water were in constant ratios to each other, the motion of the index would be affected only by the augmentation or diminution of water contained in the atmosphere, and there would be no difficulty in determining in what ratios it existed for each degree of the hygrometer. But as the elastic force of the aqueous vapour increases when the temperature is raised, and decreases when it is lowered, the index of the hygrometer must move, although the absolute quantity of vapour does not change whenever a change of temperature occurs. Moreover, as the air may contain, independently of water, a mixture of many other substances, all of which act upon the water with a particular force, it is evident that the indication given by a hygrometer, is a complicated result of many forces. It happens also that liquid water suspended in the air, and the bubbles of vapour which float in it, act conjointly upon the hygrometer, without our being able to distinguish them. These facts hardly permit us to cherish the hope of giving to these instruments that degree of accuracy which is desirable.

304. Another defect of almost all the hygrometers hitherto invented, consists in this, that the hygrometric substance is of organic origin. It is true, bodies of this kind are for the most part very

sensible to moisture; but it is a general law that every body produced by an organic force, must, after this force is destroyed, change its chemical constitution by being exposed to the air, to moisture, and to multiplied variations of temperature. These hygrometric substances must, therefore, in time become unfit to be employed, since in changing their material properties they change also their attractive force with respect to water. This is a circumstance to which no attention seems hitherto to have been paid.

305. As there is no probability that we can ever obtain a hygrometer the scale of which shall indicate immediately how many parts of water are contained in the air, there remains no other means of making this estimate exactly, than by chemical decompositions. Calcined salts furnish a method sufficiently convenient and precise for this purpose. It is necessary to put the air to be examined in a vessel of a capacity accurately known, and expose it thus for a long time to the action of calcined salts; taking great care to prevent every approach of moisture. The increase of weight in the salt, determined by a very delicate balance, will express the quantity of water contained in the air; only this estimate will be a little too small, since it is evident from the theory we have described, that no body can take from the air all the water which it contains.

Addition.

306. Since the publication of this work, M. Gay-Lussac has found out a very simple process for measuring the actual quantities of aqueous vapour corresponding to the indications of Saussure's hygrometer. This process consists in enclosing the hygrometer in a large glass vessel partly filled with water, or a known saline solution, and the tension of which in the barometer at a known temperature has been previously estimated. After having carefully closed all communication between the interior of the vessel and the external air, the apparatus is left to itself for several days. The liquid at length saturates as far as its force of emission admits, the interior of the vessel with aqueous vapour, and the hygrometer being placed in equilibrium with it, at length stops at a certain degree of its division. We thus learn that this degree corresponds to the known tension of the liquid, and consequently to the quantity of vapour with which we know this tension must fill the space. By repeating the experiment with various liquids of different tensions, from pure water

which produces complete saturation, to a drying liquid such as sulphuric acid, which produces extreme dryness, we obtain a succession of results which being interpolated, express the general law applicable to the intermediate degrees. In this manner the following table was formed from the results obtained by M. Gay-Lussac, and kindly communicated to me.

Hygrometric Table, constructed for the temperature of 10 centesimal degrees, from the experiments of M. Gay-Lussac.

Tension of the Vapour.	Degrees of the Hair Hygrometer.	Tension of the Vapour.	Degrees of the Hair Hygrometer.	Tension of the Vapour.	Degrees of the Hair Hygrometer.	Tension of the Vapour.	Degrees of the Hair Hygrometer.
0	0,00	26	47,55	52	73,68	78	89,51
1	2,19	27	48,86	53	74,41	79	90,03
2	4,37	28	50,18	54	75,14	80	90,55
3	6,56	29	51,49	55	75,87	81	91,05
4	8,75	30	52,81	56	76,54	82	91,55
5	10,94	31	53,96	57	77,21	83	92,05
6	12,93	32	55,11	58	77,88	84	92,54
7	14,92	33	56,27	59	78,55	85	93,04
8	16,92	34	57,42	60	79,22	86	93,52
9	18,91	35	58,58	61	79,84	87	94,00
10	20,91	36	59,61	62	80,46	88	94,48
11	22,81	37	60,64	63	81,08	89	94,95
12	24,71	38	61,66	64	81,70	90	95,43
13	26,61	39	62,69	65	82,32	91	95,90
14	28,51	40	63,72	66	82,90	92	96,36
15	30,41	41	64,63	67	83,48	93	96,82
16	32,08	42	65,53	68	84,06	94	97,29
17	33,76	43	66,43	69	84,64	95	97,75
18	35,43	44	67,34	70	85,22	96	98,20
19	37,11	45	68,24	71	85,77	97	98,69
20	38,78	46	69,03	72	86,31	98	99,10
21	40,27	47	69,83	73	86,86	99	99,55
22	41,76	48	70,62	74	87,41	100	100,00
23	43,26	49	71,42	75	87,95		
24	44,75	50	72,21	76	88,47		
25	46,24	51	72,94	77	88,99		

This table is constructed for the purpose of giving the degrees of the hair hygrometer when the tension of aqueous vapour, actually existing in the air, is known. The tension of aqueous vapour for the state of complete saturation, is represented by 100, and the other smaller tensions are expressed in centesimal parts of this unit. Consequently, if we observe them under another form, for example, in millimetres, it is necessary, in order to apply them to our table, to multiply by 100 and to divide by 9,475 millimetres, which, from the table of page 131, expresses the total tension of vapour in millimetres at the temperature of 10° centesimal.

Hygrometric Table, constructed for the Temperature of 10 *centesimal degrees, from the experiments of M. Gay-Lussac.*

Degrees of the Hair Hygrometer.	Tension.	Degrees of the Hair Hygrometer.	Tension.	Degrees of the Hair Hygrometer.	Tension.	Degrees of the Hair Hygrometer.	Tension.
0	0,00	26	12,59	52	29,38	78	58,24
1	0,45	27	13,14	53	30,17	79	59,73
2	0,90	28	13,69	54	30,97	80	61,22
3	1,35	29	14,23	55	31,76	81	62,89
4	1,80	30	14,78	56	32,66	82	64,57
5	2,25	31	15,36	57	33,57	83	66,24
6	2,71	32	15,94	58	34,47	84	67,92
7	3,18	33	16,52	59	35,37	85	69,59
8	3,64	34	17,10	60	36,28	86	71,49
9	4,10	35	17,68	61	37,31	87	73,39
10	4,57	36	18,30	62	38,34	88	75,29
11	5,05	37	18,92	63	39,36	89	77,19
12	5,52	38	19,54	64	40,39	90	79,09
13	6,00	39	20,16	65	41,42	91	81,09
14	6,48	40	20,78	66	42,58	92	83,08
15	6,96	41	21,45	67	43,73	93	85,08
16	7,46	42	22,12	68	44,89	94	87,07
17	7,95	43	22,79	69	46,04	95	89,06
18	8,45	44	23,46	70	47,19	96	91,25
19	8,95	45	24,13	71	48,51	97	93,44
20	9,45	46	24,86	72	49,82	98	95,63
21	9,97	47	25,59	73	51,14	99	97,81
22	10,49	48	26,32	74	52,45	100	100,00
23	11,01	49	27,06	75	53,76		
24	11,53	50	27,79	76	55,25		
25	12,05	51	28,58	77	56,74		

This table is constructed for the purpose of giving the tensions of vapour answering to the degrees of the hygrometer. These tensions are, as in the preceding table, expressed in centesimal parts of the total tension. Consequently, if we would express them in millimetres, when the degree of the hygrometer should have indicated them, it is necessary to multiply them by 9,475 millimetres, and to take the hundredth part of the product.

CHAPTER XXIX.

Barometer and Air-Pump.

307. We now proceed to examine more particularly the mechanical properties of air. For this purpose we must first be made acquainted with two instruments, which are of great importance in natural science, and the proper design of which is to make known the mechanical properties of the air, that is, its gravity and dilatability. These instruments are called the *barometer* and *air-pump*.

Barometer.

308. We fill with mercury a glass tube AB (*fig.* 46), the length of which should exceed 30 inches, and the diameter of the bore be at least $\frac{1}{10}$ of an inch, one of its extremities A being hermetically sealed. We then close with the finger the orifice B of the tube, invert it, and immerse this extremity in a vessel of mercury CD, taking care that no air enters. Then, if we remove the finger which closes the orifice, the mercury will descend in the tube; but not to the level CD of the vessel; it will remain at an elevation EF of about 30 inches. If the surface of the mercury CD were not exposed to any pressure, it would descend to E, according to the laws of hydrostatics. The column of mercury, therefore, can only be sustained by the pressure of the atmosphere upon the free surface CD of the mercury. This experiment, which Torricelli first made at Florence, in 1644, not only serves to prove that the air exerts a pressure, but also indicates the exact measure of this pressure; for we see that it is just equivalent to that of a column of mercury of the height EF. When the operation is performed with proper care there is in the tube above the point F a space entirely void of air. This is called the *Torricellian vacuum*. The entire apparatus is called the *Torricellian tube*, and when it is furnished with a scale to measure the height EF, it takes the name of *barometer*.

309. Various experiments have been made for the purpose of ascertaining the best form to be given to the tube. The most simple and advantageous arrangements are represented in figures 47, 48, 49. Figure 47 represents a *bason barometer.* GBH is a vessel

of wood or glass attached to the tube *BH*. There may be at this place a small opening to facilitate the passage of the air into the interior of the vessel, though it penetrates very easily even through compact wood. Figure 48, represents the *phial barometer*, so called from the form of the tube. Figure 49, represents a barometer consisting of a single tube *ABG* of a magnitude as uniform as possible; it is called the *syphon barometer*. This last is the instrument most used for experiments.* It is very obvious that the scale divided into inches, which is annexed to each of these barometers to measure the height of the column *EF*, must be made with very great accuracy. One general condition of every good barometer, is, that the space *AF* should be free of air, and moreover, that the interior diameter of the tube should be at least one tenth of an inch; for where it is less, the mercury remains too low, even when there is a complete vacuum, on account of the capillary attraction.†

310. Soon after the invention of the barometer, it was observed that the pressure of the air is variable, and that the mercury rises or falls about one inch above and below its mean height at *F*. It was also observed that there is a certain relation between the state of the barometer and the state of the weather; since, in fact, when the mercury in the barometer is high, the weather is ordinarily serene; and it becomes variable when the mercury is low. But this rule is not certain, though it is verified more frequently than it fails. A more particular explanation of this must be sought in physical geography.

---

* Its principle advantage consists in being independent of the effects of capillary attraction. If the tube is sensibly of a uniform bore in its two branches, the convexity of the surface of the mercury produces an equal action in both, which does not disturb the equilibrium, and the weight of the atmosphere is exactly represented by the difference of height of the two columns.

† This is true for ordinary barometers; but the interior of the tube may be so well dried by repeated boiling, that the surface of the mercury will be plane, and even concave. Then the liquid will be above the level and not below it. This remark is simply theoretical; for, in practice, if the surface of the mercury were concave instead of being convex, there would be an opposite inconvenience. In general it is best to avoid having narrow tubes, on account of capillary attraction.

The ordinary barometers of the shops, intended only to indicate the state of the atmosphere, without a scale graduated in inches, are unfit for a scientific observer. They serve well the purpose to which they are applied, which is to indicate the variations of atmospheric pressure. Indeed, if we take for the point of departure the mean height of the barometer at the place where it is used; when it is above this height the weather is commonly serene and constant; and when below, it is almost always variable.

But the variations in the state of the barometer are not the same throughout the earth. At the equator and on high mountains the variations are very small. Its changes become more considerable as we approach the poles, and particularly in low countries. Illustrations of this phenomenon belong to physical geography.

311. Shortly after the invention of the barometer it was observed that the mercury descends when the instrument is carried to a more elevated situation. Indeed it descends about one tenth of an inch for 87 feet. From this observation we may compare the gravity of the air with that of mercury or water; for one tenth of an inch of mercury exerts the same pressure as 87 feet of air; and as 87 feet $=$ 10440 tenths of an inch, it will be seen how many times mercury is heavier than air. If we divide this number by 13,57, the specific gravity of mercury, the quotient 769 indicates how many times water is heavier than air.* This observation has also given rise to the ingenious idea of measuring altitudes by the barometer. The principle upon which this problem depends and the manner of performing it, will be explained hereafter.

312. We may determine exactly by the barometer the pressure which the air exerts upon a given surface. The following calculation furnishes an estimate, which may, at the same time, show how a more exact one is to be obtained. When the barometer is at 30 inches, the air presses upon the surface of a square inch as much as a column of mercury, having a square inch for its base, and 30 inches for its altitude. This column comprehends, therefore, 30 cubic inches. Now as a cubic inch of water is equal to 252,525 grains, 30 cubic inches of water $= 30 \times 252,525$ grains, or 15,78 troy ounces. Whence mercury being 13,57 times heavier than water, 30 cubic inches of mercury $= 15,78 \times 13,57$ or 214,12 troy

---

* M. Arago and myself found, by careful experiment, that at the temperature of melting ice and under the pressure 29,92 inches, the weight of the air is to that of water as 1 to 770.

ounces. This is equal to 234,7 ounces avoirdupois, or to 14,7 lb. We infer, therefore, that the pressure of the air amounts to nearly 15 lb. upon every square inch, or to about one ton upon every square foot.

313. If we would construct a barometer with water instead of mercury, it would be necessary to have it nearly 14 times as long; that is, between 33 and 34 feet. But for other reasons, a water barometer would be a very inconvenient instrument. Still it is important to know to what height water may be raised by the pressure of the air; and hence it will be seen why the exhausting part of all kinds of pumps must not be more than 33 feet in height.

314. For very exact barometric observations, it is necessary to apply a small correction on account of heat; for since heat dilates the mercury, it is manifest that, the pressure remaining the same, if the mercury is heated the column will be lengthened, and its highest point will be elevated in the tube which sustains it. We should have no need of any correction if it were possible always to preserve the mercury at the same temperature, for example at 32°; but since this is impossible, it is necessary to reduce the different elevations to the same temperature by calculation. We commonly select for this purpose the temperature of 32°. According to the best observations mercury expands $\frac{1}{9742}$, or 0,0001 nearly for 1° of Fahrenheit's thermometer. Thus to reduce a given height of the mercury to the temperature of 32°, we must subtract for each degree above 32° 0,0001 of the whole height of the column, and add as much for each degree below 32°. To have the temperature of the mercury as precisely as possible, we attach a thermometer to the frame work of the barometer.*

---

* Strictly speaking, when the temperature of the mercury is t degrees above 32°, we ought, in order to reduce it to 32°, to subtract, not $\frac{1}{9742}$, but $\frac{1}{9742 + t}$ of its length, for each degree; and when the temperature is t degrees below 32°, we should add $\frac{1}{9742 - t}$ for each degree. For let l be the length of the column at 32°, and l' its length at t degrees; we have

$$l\left(1 + \frac{t}{9742}\right) = l',$$

whence
$$l = \frac{l'}{1 + \frac{t}{9742}} = l' - \frac{l' t}{9742 + t}.$$

Air-Pump.

315. In the year 1650, Guericke, of Magdeburg, invented one of the most important instruments that is known in philosophy, the *air-pump*, by means of which we can remove the air from the interior of a vessel, or at least rarify it to a very great degree. We have not room for a description of its original construction, and the changes which it has undergone. We shall only indicate here the essential parts of the most simple apparatus of this kind. *ABCD* (*fig.* 50) is a hollow cylinder of metal, the interior of which must be made with great exactness. The *piston EF* admits of being raised and depressed in the interior of the cylinder, by means of the rod *G*, without suffering the air to enter. The piston is pierced in the middle *HI*, by an aperture. A piece of gummed taffeta is stretched over the orifice at *H*, and confined at its two extremities; so that the air which comes from below through *HI*, will raise it and escape; but the air from above presses it against the opening and closes the passage. This apparatus attached to the piston is called a *valve*. In the bottom of the cylinder is a second valve of this kind, which allows the air to pass from below into the cylinder, but does not permit it to return. The aperture to this valve corresponds with the tube *KLMN*; and at the extremity *N* of this tube is fixed a plate of ground glass *OP*. But the opening of the tube *N* is a little above this plate, and has a stop-cock by which it may be at any time closed.

In most experiments we place on the plate a glass receiver *Q*, the bottom of which is ground with emery in order that it may be fitted exactly to the glass plate, and exclude the air. It is sufficient to press the receiver a little when we place it upon the plate, in order to make it adhere. Lastly, at some place *L* in the tube is a *stop-cock*, fitting the tube exactly, so as to establish or cut off at pleasure, the communication between the tube and the external air.

Sometimes, instead of two valves, there is simply a stop-cock placed in the tube *KL* immediately below the cylinder. This is pierced in such a manner as to open at pleasure a communication between the cylinder and the tube, the cylinder and the external air, or the external air and the tube. This arrangement has some inconveniences, but it has also many advantages.

316. Suppose the receiver placed on the plate, the opening at *L* closed, and the piston lowered to the bottom of the cylinder. If this piston be raised a vacuum is produced below it; the air in the receiver and tube, therefore, has no counter pressure above the valve *K*, of course it will open this valve and expand into the cylinder. In this manner the enclosed mass of air becomes already rarefied. If the piston be thrust down again, the air which had entered the cylinder cannot return into the tube, but escapes through the valve of the piston. If the piston be made to rise and fall successively, at every ascent some portion of the air in the receiver passes into the cylinder; and at every descent the air which had passed into the cylinder is expelled through the valve of the piston. Thus the air becomes more and more rarefied. But it is impossible to create a perfect vacuum, because after a certain time, we reach a limit at which we can no longer produce any effect. This takes place when the air is so much rarefied that its elastic force is not sufficient to raise the valve *K*. When we wish to introduce the exterior air into the receiver, we turn the stop-cock at *L*.*

317. One appendage to the air-pump, which is very necessary in exact experiments, is a small syphon barometer called a *guage*. It consists of a recurved tube, *ABC* (*fig.* 51), of which one of the branches *A* is closed, and the other *B* open. The space *ABF* is filled with mercury; and as the whole instrument is only about 6 or 7 inches high, the pressure of the air in the open branch will cause the mercury to rise to the top of the other. This tube is attached to a small support, in such a manner that we can place it upon the plate of the machine, and cover it with the receiver. Between the two branches of the tube is a scale *DE*, which is divided into inches and tenths. When we place this apparatus under the receiver, and be-

---

* It is obvious from this, that all the changes which tend to render the valve more sensible, or even to supply its place altogether, as may be done, for example, by polished plates sliding upon one another, must be so many improvements in the machine, giving it a greater power of exhaustion. In this view nothing can be more complete than the air-pumps constructed by Fortin at Paris. They create a vacuum so nearly perfect, that the tension indicated by the instrument attached for this purpose never exceeds what is inevitably produced by the vapour of the water which is always disengaged from the sides of the vessels to which it adheres.

gin the exhaustion, we soon perceive that the air does not press the mercury with sufficient force to make it rise to A. It therefore descends in this tube and rises in the other, so that we can see at each stroke the altitude of the column reduced to an equilibrium with the rarefied air.

This instrument indicates properly the pressure which the rarefied air exerts by the force of its elasticity; but we shall see in the following chapter that this is proportional to its density. If we compare the column of mercury which is supported by the pressure of the rarefied air, with the height of the barometer, we shall have the ratio of the rarefaction. Suppose the barometer to be at 30 inches, and that the guage placed under the receiver indicates $\frac{1}{2}$ an inch; we conclude that the air is rarefied in the ratio of $\frac{1}{2}$ to 30, or of 1 to 60. Those are considered as very good pumps, in which the mercury can be reduced to an elevation of $1\frac{1}{2}$ or 2 tenths of an inch. Ordinarily we are satisfied if the air, at its greatest rarefaction, does not exert a pressure equivalent to more than half an inch of mercury.

318. Instead of placing this guage under the receiver, it is still better to attach it to the pump itself. For this purpose, the open branch of the tube should be longer than the other, and be furnished with a stop-cock. This branch should communicate by some means or other with the tube LM (*fig*. 50) in which the air is rarefied to the same degree as in the receiver. Such a disposition has the advantage of showing the rarefaction in any vessel whatever, which may be substituted in place of the receiver.

319. It has been objected to the use of the guage, that it does not afford any exact result, because the humidity always adhering to the glass plate and the sides of the receiver, produces elastic vapour while the exhaustion is going on; and consequently, that what we observe is not the simple effect of rarefaction. But Laplace has deduced a formula from the experiments of Dalton which enables us to estimate this quantity; and Smeaton has invented a guage against which this objection cannot be urged.

Condensing Pump.

320. We can only rarefy the air by means of the apparatus above described. The instrument for condensing the air is still more simple.

The piston *EF* is without a valve. It is sufficient that the air can enter the cylinder by a small opening in the side immediately below the highest point to which the piston can rise. The valve *K* must be disposed in such a manner that the air can pass from the cylinder into the tube *KL*, without being allowed to return. If we wish to condense the air in a receiver, it is necessary to confine this receiver very firmly to the plate; otherwise the force of the condensed air will remove it. Very strong vessels also are necessary, because they are exposed to great pressure outward. To ascertain the degree of condensation, we adapt to the receiver a barometer much longer than those which serve to measure the ordinary pressure of the atmosphere.

Mechanical Properties of Air.

321. The mechanical properties of air, which, like itself, are imperceptible to our senses, are manifested by their effects; and these are ascertained by means of the barometer and air-pump. The mechanical properties of any gas may be reduced to two; *gravity* and *dilatability*. The existence and nature of the first have been already considered. We proceed, therefore, to treat of the dilatability of air.

1. *Dilatability of Air.*

322. The dilatability of air consists in this, that every portion of air enclosed shows a tendency to dilate itself and to occupy a greater space. As each liquid by the mere force of its gravity exerts a pressure against the sides of the vessel which contains it, so every portion of air, however small, by the mere force of its dilatability presses all the sides of the vessel which confines it. This force is greater in proportion as the volume is more condensed. A liquid needs only to be confined at the bottom and sides; an aeriform fluid must be confined on every part. The smallest mass of air expands when there is room, and fills all the space left to it. Even at the state of the greatest rarefaction which we can produce, the air still exerts a certain pressure against the sides of the vessel containing it, which may be measured by the guage. Reciprocally, every portion

of air may be compressed into a less space than that which it occupies; only its pressure against the sides of the vessel becomes greater, the more it is condensed.

No direct experiment can decide what are the limits of this condensation and rarefaction, or whether there be any. The law which governs the ratios of the density and dilatability will be considered in the next chapter. But the mutual dependence of the pressure and dilatability is self-evident. In the state of equilibrium they must be in equal ratios; for, if we suppose the air condensed in a cylinder by means of a piston, in order that the piston may be at rest, the force of pressure must be just as great as the force which the dilatable air opposes to it. Consequently, if the air is confined on all sides by solid walls, these walls, according to the third law of Newton, must resist with a force equal to that which the dilatable air exerts against them; if their force of cohesion is too weak for this they will burst.

Since the pressure which a mass of air exerts may be measured by the barometer, we have at the same time, in this manner, a measure of the dilatability.

323. The dilatability of the air may also be rendered evident, without the use of the air-pump, by means of very simple but instructive experiments, which I proceed to describe. Into a glass flask AB (*fig.* 52) having a long and narrow neck, we introduce so much water that when inverted as represented in the figure, the water shall rise to about half the length of the neck. We mark this place with a thread, and having exactly closed the orifice B of the flask AB with the finger, we immerse it under water in a larger vessel DEF. If we immerse it to the thread, the water will be at the same height within and without the flask, for the interior air is then of the same density that it was before being closed. It is, therefore, in equilibrium with the external air; and notwithstanding the smallness of its mass, it exerts by its dilatability the same pressure upon the water contained in the neck of the flask, as the exterior air, by its gravity, exerts upon the water without the neck. If we immerse the flask AB lower, for example, so that the thread shall be at G, the pressure of the external air is added to that of the column of water CG; and the interior air by virtue of its dilatability, which renders it compressible, must rise above the thread. On the contrary, if we raise the flask AB so that the thread shall be at H, for example, the air, by its dilatability, must expand so that its

pressure, added to that of the column of water in the neck of the flask which is now above C, shall counterbalance the external pressure of the air.

Hence we see how easy it is to give a mass of inclosed air a dilatability equal to the pressure of the external air. The different gases act in the same manner as atmospheric air under similar circumstances.

324. By means of the air-pump we can observe the dilatability of the air in more than one way, and with very considerable rarefactions and condensations.

(1.) The operation of rarefaction and condensation, of itself demonstrates the dilatability of the air.

(2.) A bladder apparently exhausted of air, is distended when exposed in the vacuum of an air-pump.

(3.) Figure 53 represents a Heron's fountain. This consists of a closed vessel AB, of any form, about half filled with water, to which is applied a tube CD, the inferior orifice of which nearly touches the bottom, and the upper orifice of which is terminated by a pretty sharp point. The mouth OO of the vessel is accurately closed, except where the tube passes. If in such an apparatus the air is first condensed above the water by means of a bellows or a condensing pump, when we let it return to its natural state, the water is forced through the opening D, and jets out with more or less force, according as the air is more or less condensed. If we put such an apparatus with the air not condensed, under the receiver of an air-pump, and rarefy the external air, the same effects are produced.

(4.) The force of compressed air is exemplified in a very striking manner in the air-gun.

Pressure of the Air.

325. Since the pressure and dilatability of the air are always in equal ratios, it is immaterial whether we say that the pressure which the air exerts upon a given surface is the effect of the gravity of the atmosphere, or that it is produced by the dilatability of the air. The air which surrounds us is pressed by the whole weight of the atmosphere; and it thus acquires at each point a dilatability equal to the weight which compresses it. This force of dilatation must be always the same at equal heights. Consequently, at equal heights above the surface of the earth, the mercury in the barometer must

also rise to the same degree, whether in free air or in inclosed spaces, provided that these have the smallest communication with the external air, and provided the places of observation are not too remote from each other. The force of this pressure has already been determined.

326. By means of the air-pump we may observe this pressure in different ways.

(1.) If we place on the plate of the air-pump a metallic cylinder open at both ends, and attach a bladder to the upper orifice; when we exhaust the air from beneath it, the bladder will at first be strongly pressed and will at length break. A glass plate attached to the cylinder by wax will break still more easily.

(2.) If we place on the plate a glass cylinder open at both ends, and close the upper orifice with a wooden vessel disposed for the purpose and filled with water, when we exhaust the air below, the water, pressed by the weight of the external air, will penetrate through the wood and fall in drops. In some circumstances mercury will do the same, and fall like a fine shower of silver.

(3.) The phenomenon presented by the Magdeburg hemispheres is to be referred to this cause. Two hemispheres of metal are disposed in such a manner that their edges are exactly fitted to each other. To the one is attached a ring, and to the other a stop-cock and pipe which may be screwed to the air-pump. The edges are covered with tallow to prevent the admission of air. So long as the internal air has the same dilatability as the external, the hemispheres are easily separated. But if we exhaust the air from within, they are so strongly pressed together by the external air, that a very great force is required to separate them. We may estimate this force in pounds by multiplying by 47 the square of the diameter of the sphere expressed in inches.*

---

* If the diameter of the sphere is r, the plane of the great circle where the separation must take place, will be $r^2 \pi$, π being the semi-circumference of the circle whose radius is 1. If r is given in inches, πr^2 is the surface expressed in square inches. The pressure of the air upon every square inch is about 15 lb. Consequently, the total pressure is equal to $15 r^2 \pi$; but since $\pi = 3,14$, $15 \pi = 47$. This result is always a little greater than the actual pressure, because it is impossible to exhaust the air completely; but it is augmented somewhat by the cohesion of the hemispheres independently of the action of the air.

Aeriform Bodies.

(4.) The different kinds of syphon barometers exhibit phenomena which can only be explained by the pressure of the air.

Gravity of the Air.

627. If the air is a heavy fluid, every body immersed in it must lose as much of its weight as is equal to the weight of the fluid whose place it occupies. Thus, if we attach to a very delicate balance a light body of considerable volume, for example, a piece of cork, and put it in equilibrium; and then place the balance under the receiver of the air-pump, and produce a vacuum, the body will preponderate because it loses so much the less of its true weight as the surrounding air is more rarefied.

By weighing a body in the air we obtain a result too small, when its density is less than that of the weight opposed to it; but too large in the opposite case; and exact, when the densities of the two are equal.

328. In order to weigh the air accurately, we make use of a glass globe as light as possible, and about 5 or 6 inches in diameter. At an opening is fixed a pipe with a stock-cock, which may be screwed to the plate of the air-pump. The cubic capacity of the globe, after the stop-cock is turned so as to shut it, must be determined in the most exact manner. We then exhaust the air as perfectly as possible, turn the stop-cock, remove the globe, and weight it with a very accurate balance. We then open the globe and let it fill with air; it thus becomes heavier, and we ascertain how much the weight is augmented. The excess is the weight of the air contained in the globe. If we divide this weigh by the capacity of the globe, expressed in cubic inches, we shall have the weigh of a cubic inch of air. If the experiment is to be performed with extreme precision, we make use of a guage to ascertain how many cubic inches of air remain in the globe in order that we may deduct them from its cubic capacity.

Moreover, as the weight of the air varies with the state of the barometer and thermometer, the experiment must be performed at a determinate state of these two instruments, or a reduction must be made by calculation. We ordinarily select for this purpose, the temperature of 60°, and a barometric height of 30 inches. But it is better to have recourse to reductions, for it is almost impossible to combine these two conditions exactly.

Specific Gravity of other Gases.

329. After the globe is weighed, if we introduce some other gas, we can find the weight of it in the manner indicated for air. We can thus ascertain the weight of a cubic inch, and this, as before observed, is the usual method of expressing the specific gravity of the gases.

330. We shall give the specific gravity of some of the gases, as determined by the most careful experiments, made at a barometric height of 30 inches, and at the temperature of 60° of Fahrenheit.

	Water being 1.	At. Air being 1.
Atmospheric air	0,00122	1,0000
Azote	0,00119	0,9722
Oxygen	0,00136	1,1111
Carbonic acid	0,00186	1,5277

CHAPTER XXX.

Equilibrium of Air, or First Principles of Aerostatics.

331. WHILE the air is considered as a heavy fluid the essential laws of hydrostatics must be applied to it.

(1.) Every pressure made in air propagates itself in all directions in the same manner as in liquids.

(2.) In a state of equilibrium the pressure must be equal upon all the points of every horizontal plane; but, on account of the great levity of the air, this pressure must diminish as we ascend much more slowly than in liquids. But the law of this diminution is not the same for air and liquids, as we shall see hereafter.

(3.) The pressure of the air upon a given surface may be determined in the same manner as that of water; that is, it is equal to the weight of a prism of mercury whose base is the surface pressed, and whose altitude is the height of the mercury in the barometer. But on account of the slow diminution of the pressure of the air, we do not perceive any difference whether the plane be horizontal, vertical, or oblique, unless it be one of great magnitude. Neither does it make any difference whether the pressure proceeds from free air or from air inclosed, provided the latter have the same dilatability as the external air. We have already explained the method of estimating this pressure.

(4.) Any body immersed in the air loses a portion of its weight equal to that of the air displaced by it, as we have seen in the case of liquids.

(5.) A body which is lighter than the same volume of atmospheric air, rises until it is in equilibrium with the surrounding fluid, which, as we shall see hereafter, always becomes rarer as we ascend. On this is founded the theory of *balloons;* as well those in which the air is rarefied, according to the method of Montgolfier, as those which are filled with hydrogen gas, according to the method of M. Charles.

Law of Mariotte; or Ratio of the Pressure and Elasticity to the Density or Specific Gravity.

332. The effects of dilatability constitute a fundamental difference between elastic fluids and liquids. Among these effects we notice particularly the diminution of density depending upon the height. The inferior strata of the air are pressed by the whole weight of the atmosphere. In the higher regions the weight becomes more and more feeble, and consequently the density of the air diminishes. But in order to determine the law according to which the density diminishes, we must first determine by experiment what is in general the ratio of the pressure and density in a mass of air.

333. The following law which is extremely simple is abundantly confirmed by experiment.

The density of a mass of air increases and decreases in the same ratio as the pressure, unless some change takes place in the temperature, or in the chemical combination of the parts.

As the pressure and dilatability are always equal, and as the density and specific gravity are synonymous terms, the following is only a different enunciation of the same law.

The dilatability of a mass of air is proportional to its specific gravity, as long as its temperature and chemical combination remain the same.

This important principle of aerostatics is called *the law of Mariotte*, although it was discovered in England by Sir Robert Boyle and his disciple, Townley, a short time before Mariotte recognised it in France. The experiments which serve to show the exactness of this law, are briefly as follows;

In order to measure the condensation of air by pressure, we employ a tube of glass that is recurved like a syphon barometer (*fig.* 49), with this difference, that the short branch is closed at G, and the long branch open at A. It is also convenient to give this last a length of several feet. The air enclosed between G and CD will be compressed at the same time by the column of mercury EF, and by the external air, since A is open. This last pressure is equal to that of the barometric column. If then we gradually fill the long branch with mercury, and always measure the space which the enclosed air occupies, it will be easily seen how the pressure and density may be compared; for the density is in the inverse ratio of the space CG, occupied by the air. In order to measure the rarefaction of the air produced by a diminution of pressure, we employ a straight barometric tube, open at its lower extremity, and provided with a stop-cock at the other. This stop-cock being open, we immerse the lower end of the tube in a vessel filled with mercury, until there remains only an inch or two of air in the tube; we then turn the stop-cock, and gradually raise the tube. In proportion as we raise it, the enclosed air dilates; but a column of mercury rises under it, above the surface of the exterior mercury. We measure from time to time, the space occupied by the enclosed air, and the height of the mercurial column in the tube. The force with which the enclosed air is pressed is always equal to that of the barometric column, minus the column which rises in the tube. The pressure and density may thus be compared under these circumstances, as in the preceding experiment.

In order to perform experiments of this kind upon a small scale, we employ a pretty long barometric tube AB (*fig.* 54), which is open at A and closed at B, and whose interior diameter is about $\frac{1}{2}$ line. This tube must be of a uniform size, especially from A to half its length. To this is added a scale divided into inches and parts. Into this tube we introduce a column of mercury of about 5 or 6 inches in length, which is done by expelling a portion of the air by heat. Let us suppose that the column of mercury is nearly in the middle of the tube. If we hold this in a vertical position, with the open extremity A upward, the pressure supported by the enclosed air BD, will be equal to the pressure of the column of mercury CD, added to that of the barometric column. If, on the contrary, we invert the tube, the open extremity being downward, the pressure supported by the enclosed air becomes equal to that of the barometric column, minus the column CD. In the horizontal position it is just equal to that of the barometric column. We can, therefore, in these three cases, compare the pressure with the space occupied by the enclosed air. Such an instrument resembles in its essential parts the *manometer* of *Varignon* or of *Wolf*.

334. The importance of the law of Mariotte requires that we should know exactly what are its limits and conditions.

(1.) For atmospheric air it has been found to be exact to an octuple condensation, and beyond a centuple rarefaction. We cannot decide *whether it is exact for all imaginable condensations and rarefactions*. The advocates for the atomic theory must deny it. On the contrary, those who maintain the dynamic theory, must support the affirmative. So far as practice is concerned, it is sufficient to know that this law is applicable to all experiments we have occasion to make.

(2.) Experiments have been made only at mean temperatures. But it is a necessary consequence of the experiments of Gay-Lussac and Dalton, *that the same law should obtain for all temperatures;* for if in the two masses of air A and B, the chemical properties and mean temperatures of which are the same, the density is proportional to the pressure, the reason of this proportionality must remain the same for all temperatures, since the masses of air are dilated equally by heat.

(3.) These experiments upon pressure were made only with atmospheric air; and it still remains to determine by immediate experiment, *whether the law of Mariotte is exact for all other elastic fluids*. Nevertheless, since in the experiments upon dilatation, which we have before considered, heat acts uniformly upon all these fluids, it is extremely probable that mechanical pressure also acts uniformly upon all. Another fact which renders this opinion extremely probable, is, that all the experiments made with atmospheric air, have always given the same results, although the air employed in the different experiments, may have differed in its chemical composition.

For these different reasons, until the question is perfectly settled, we may admit, as a very probable hypothesis, that the law of Mariotte is applicable to all elastic fluids.

(4.) Hitherto we have considered the application of the law only with respect to an elastic fluid insulated from others. But it may be asked, *whether the density of two masses of air,* A *and* B, *the chemical natures of which are different, is proportional to the pressure indicated by their volumes.* This question must be answered in the negative; for experiment shows that different masses of air, at the same pressure and temperature, have different specific gravities. They require therefore different pressures to give them the same density.

Law by which the Density of the Air decreases as we ascend into the Atmosphere.

335. By certain simple mathematical operations, we can deduce from the law of Mariotte, the principal theorem of aerostatics, which is the following;

In a state of equilibrium the density of the air must decrease, as we ascend, in a geometrical ratio, when the chemical nature and temperature of the column are the same throughout the whole extent.

Thus, if we divide the column of air $ABCD$, (*fig.* 55) into strata of a thickness taken at pleasure, but all equal to each other, $AEFB$, $EGHF$, &c., the density of the air decreases in a geometrical series at the points E, G, I, L, that is, each succeeding one is less than the preceding in the same ratio.*

---

* Let us suppose that the strata of air are taken so thin, that the density of each may be considered as uniform throughout. Let the density of the inferior stratum be A, that of the next B, of the third C, and so on. Moreover, let a be the weight of the whole column of air $ABCD$; b its weight when the inferior stratum is taken away, c its weight when the second is taken away, and so on. Then the weight of the first stratum $= a - b$, that of the second $= b - c$, that of the third $= c - d$, and so on. Now the density of two bodies of the same volume is in general as their weights. Consequently $A : B :: a - b : b - c$. But, according to the law of Mariotte, the density of two masses of air is proportional to the pressure

336. This theorem may be expressed in various ways; particularly in the six following. When a column of air has throughout the same temperature and the same chemical nature, we may consider as decreasing in a geometrical series,

(1.) The density of the air.
(2.) Its specific gravity.
(3.) The weight of the incumbent mass.
(4.) The pressure which the air suffers and exerts.
(5.) The elasticity of the air.
(6.) The barometric height.

Nos. 1, 2, are different expressions for the same thing. Nos. 3. 4, 5, 6, are also different ways of considering what is in itself the same; for the weight of the air above is only the pressure supported by the air below, or exerted by this same air, in a state of equilibrium. Moreover, the pressure which a mass of air exerts is equal to its elasticity, and the barometric height is the measure of the pressure.

Thus, according to the law of Mariotte, nos. 1, 2, on the one hand, and nos. 3, 4, 5, 6, on the other, indicate properties mutually dependent; and consequently the general sense of the theorem is this; *admitting the law of Mariotte, the properties indicated in* 1, 2, *decrease in the same ratio as those indicated in* 3, 4, 5, 6, *and vice versâ.*

337. As the condition of this theorem is that the column of air shall have throughout the same temperature and the same chemical nature, we must not expect, in reality, to find this geometrical de-

---

which they support. Consequently, $A : B :: b : c$. Omitting the common ratio, we have $a - b : b - c :: b : c$; which gives
$$a c - b c = b^2 - b c,$$
or $a c = b$; whence $a : b :: b : c$. In the same manner we obtain $b : c :: c : d$, also $c : d :: d : e$, and so on. The weights a, b, c, d, e, &c., form, therefore, a geometrical series. But as the densities are proportional to these weights, they also form a geometrical series. This demonstration is rigorously true only for strata which are infinitely thin. But it is a property of all geometrical series, that if we take out some of the intermediate members, these members form a new geometrical series, provided there is always an equal number of terms between those taken out. Hence it is evident that this principle is correct, when the altitudes AE, CG, GI, IL, &c., are of a finite magnitude.

crease of density perfectly exact. But yet we must not consider the law of Mariotte and the theorem deduced from it as mere hypotheses to be admitted or rejected at pleasure. We have just as much reason to consider the law of the descent of heavy bodies, as a mere hypothesis, since the resistance of the air occasions deviations from it. All the motions which take place in the atmosphere are only continual efforts which nature makes to restore the equilibrium, which secondary causes are continually disturbing. There must, therefore, be in fact a continual tendency towards this equilibrium. Philosophers cannot reject general laws, or change them at pleasure; but they should endeavour to ascertain, as far as possible, the influence of disturbing forces.

More exact Estimate of the Influence which Heat has upon the Mechanical Properties of a Dilatable Fluid.

338. We have already mentioned the important discovery made at the same time by Dalton and Gay-Lussac; *that all elastic fluids are equally dilated by heat when the pressure is the same. This dilatation between the freezing and boiling point, amounts to 0,375 or $\frac{3}{8}$ of the volume which the mass had at the first temperature.* This remarkable discovery enables us to determine with great exactness the influence which heat has upon the density and elasticity of a mass of air.

339. Since the law of Mariotte is applicable to each mass of elastic fluid; it follows reciprocally,

That in a mass of air perfectly confined and incapable of changing its volume, the elasticity must increase by being heated in the same ratio as its volume would increase, if, the pressure being the same, it had the power of dilatation.

Hence from the freezing to the boiling point the elasticity of a mass of air, perfectly confined, must increase in the ratio of

$$1000 : 1375 \text{ or } 8 : 11.$$

340. If we now divide the fundamental distance of Lambert's air thermometer into 375 parts; placing 1000 at the freezing point, and 1375 at the boiling point; and if we estimate the temperature by the degrees of this thermometer, the comparison of two numbers of this scale will indicate exactly what, under these two temperatures, would be the ratios of dilatation of a mass of air, the pressure

remaining the same, or those of its dilatability, the volume remaining the same.

If we prefer to divide the fundamental distance into 180 parts instead of 375, conformably to Fahrenheit's thermometer, the number standing at the freezing point must be 480 (a fourth proportional to 375, 1000, and 180,) and consequently that at the boiling point, must be 660. The numbers of this scale would also indicate immediately the ratios of which we have spoken.

341. The march of an air thermometer divided into 180 parts, and that of a mercurial thermometer with the same divisions, do not perhaps perfectly conform to each other; but according to the observations of Lambert, they differ very little between the freezing and boiling points.* If then we put 480° in place of 32°, and 660° in place of 180, or what amounts to the same thing, if we add 480 to the temperature indicated by Fahrenheit's thermometer, these numbers will express, in an approximate manner, the ratios determined in the preceding article. Accordingly it might be useful in aerostatics and perhaps in all that relates to thermometry, to introduce universally the use of the air thermometer instead of the mercurial, or at least to determine with precision the ratios of the two scales.†

Measurement of Heights by the Barometer.

342. The method of measuring heights by means of the barometer, is founded upon the preceding theorem. This method is of such extensive use that we cannot omit giving a brief account of it.

[When the altitudes above the surface are taken in arithmetical progression, the corresponding densities, and consequently the incumbent weights of the atmosphere at these heights, form, as we have seen, a geometrical series; in other words, the heights are the logarithms of the corresponding weights of the atmosphere, according to a particular base, which may be determined by experiment.

---

* Gay Lussac has recently proved, by unquestionable experiments, that they are rigorously the same when the air and tubes are perfectly dried.

† This has since been done by Gay-Lussac, and his results have been confirmed by MM. Petit and Dulong.

Distinguishing these logarithms by λ, if we denote any two heights by h, h', and the corresponding weights of the atmosphere, as determined by the barometer, by w, w', we shall have

$$h' - h = \lambda w - \lambda w',$$

or putting $h = 0$, $\qquad h' = \lambda w - \lambda w',$

that is, the difference of level, or height of one of the places in question above the other, is expressed by the difference of the logarithms of the mercurial columns, these logarithms being constructed upon a particular base adapted to this purpose. Now, since logarithms are changed from one system to another by a constant multiplier, we shall have

$$h' = x \,(\log. w - \log. w),$$

log. denoting the common logarithm of the quantity before which it is placed. Hence, by taking an object whose elevation has been previously ascertained by other methods, we readily find, once for all, the value of the multiplier x, thus

$$x = \frac{h'}{\log. w - \log. w'}.$$

Taking the mean of a great number of observations, conducted with the greatest care by M. Raymond, we find x equal to 18336 metres, or 60156 feet, or 10026 English fathoms. This is on the supposition of a temperature of 32°. Now air, by having its temperature raised from 32° to 212°, dilates 0,375, or

$$\frac{0,375}{180} = \tfrac{1}{449} = 0,00223$$

for each degree of Fahrenheit; and, according to the law of Mariotte, if this air be reduced back again to the same bulk, it will have its pressure increased in the same proportion. We can, therefore, change the constant multiplier 10026 to 10000, by supposing the temperature somewhat lower. Thus, 0,00223 : 0,0026 :: 1° : 1°,16. If, therefore, we subtract 1°,16 from 32°, we shall have 30°,84, or 31° nearly, for the temperature at which the constant coefficient is 10000 fathoms.

343. Given the height of the mercury in the barometer at the bottom of a mountain $= 29,37$ inches, and at its summit $= 26,59$ inches, to find the altitude of the mountain, the mean temperature at the two stations being 26°.

$$
\begin{aligned}
29{,}37 &\quad\ldots\quad \log.\quad\ldots\quad 1{,}46790\\
26{,}59 &\quad\ldots\quad \log.\quad\ldots\quad 1{,}42472\\
&\qquad\qquad\text{diff.}\quad\ldots\quad 0{,}04318
\end{aligned}
$$

Approximate height . . . . . = 431,8 fathoms,
Correction 5 × 0,00223 × 431,8 = — 4,8

True height . . . . 427,0 = 2562,0 feet.

344. We have supposed in the above examples that the temperature of the mercurial columns at the two stations is the same. Where the difference is considerable, the result will evidently be affected by it. If the upper station, for instance, be the coldest, which most frequently happens, the mercurial column will be too short, and will consequently indicate too great a height. The contraction being about 10000th part for each degree of cold, or 0,0025 in. in a column of 25 inches, it would require 4° difference of temperature to produce an effect amounting to one division on the scale of a common barometer, where the graduation is to hundredths of an inch.

This correction is combined with the foregoing rule in the following formula, in which t, t', represent the temperature of the air, q, q', that of the mercury, at the two stations respectively,

$$h' = 10000\left(1 + 0{,}00223\left(\frac{t+t'}{2} - 31\right)\right)\log.\frac{w}{w' \times (1 + 0{,}0001(q-q'))}.]$$

Height of the Atmosphere.

345. If the law of Mariotte is exact for all imaginable degrees of rarefaction and condensation, it follows from the fundamental theorem, that the dilatation of the atmosphere is unlimited, since in a decreasing geometrical progression, the terms, however far continued can never become strictly nothing. This statement in itself contains no contradiction. But yet it does not appear to accord with the observations of astronomers, who suppose the planets to move in an unresisting medium. We cannot, therefore, determine absolutely what is the height of the atmosphere. It is however demonstrated by the theory of barometric heights, that at the height of 40,000, about 45 miles, the air must be at least as rare as in the vacuum of our best air-pumps. Hence we usually say the atmosphere extends

45 miles high. Yet if we estimate exactly the height of some meteors, such as the aurora borealis, fire balls, &c., we are compelled to admit that at the height of more than 60 miles, there must not only be atmospheric air, but also many other substances which we should not expect to find at such an elevation.

CHAPTER XXXI.

Motions of Elastic Fluids.

346. In considering the motions of elastic fluids, the inquirer may confine himself almost entirely to the examination of atmospheric air. For the other gases are found in such small quantities, and fill such small spaces, that their motions have rarely any peculiar interest. But, on the contrary, the immense extent and great agitations of the air which envelopes the globe, the continual winds, periodical or accidental, by which it is agitated, are not only remarkable phenomena in themselves, but in many respects of the highest importance to the interests of society; and we can judge of what vast utility the knowledge of the laws of these motions would be, if we could thereby be able to predict them. There are also many artificial motions of the air, the observation of which is important. In many pneumatic or hydraulico-pneumatic machines, the elasticity of the air or steam is the sole cause of motion. It is by the knowledge of these motions, that currents of air have been created in mines, to drive off the unwholesome gases, and so managed in chimnies as to defend us from the inconvenience of smoke.

347. The philosophical mode of treating these motions, is first to develope their fundamental principles, and then to confirm them by experiment. But in treating what is called *pneumatics*, we have not only to contend with all the difficulties which occur in hydraulics, but it is necessary also to have regard to two peculiar and very active causes, which continually embarrass us in our researches. These are dilatability and heat. Besides, this branch of physical science is entirely without fundamental principles demonstrated by rigorous reasoning, and confirmed by experiment. For these reasons we must content ourselves with general remarks on the subject before us.

348. We should be able to explain with sufficient accuracy all the causes of the motions which take place in the atmosphere, if two conditions essential to exact researches, were not in most cases wanting. The first is the accurate measure of the effect produced; the second is a knowledge of all the different circumstances which influence a single phenomenon. We know, for example, the general causes of wind; but we never know, or very rarely, of what force wind is the effect, and to what distance it extends; or what are the particular causes of the wind which blows at any particular time.

349. Instead of the fundamental laws of pneumatics, we can only state the following general principle, which is too evident to need any proof.

Every cause which acts upon a mass of air in opposition to one of the laws of equilibrium, must produce motion.

As we have already stated the conditions of equilibrium, it will be very easy to form a clear idea of the causes of motion in the air.

350. One of the principal is heat. The motions which proceed from this cause, though exceedingly varied, are all produced in the same manner. Heat increases the elasticity of the air; accordingly, when in any region of the atmosphere a mass of air is heated more than that which surrounds it, it dilates and repels in every direction the air which is colder than itself. In this manner the equilibrium is destroyed; and the heated air becoming lighter, must rise according to the laws of hydrostatics; for the surrounding air being colder, is for that reason heavier. Reciprocally, the cold air must descend and press towards the place where the heat acts; the air then accumulates above the heated place, which necessarily produces a current of air, propagating itself in every direction. Heat, therefore, always produces a double current of air, namely, one tending toward the place from below, and one in the opposite direction from above. Cold evidently acts in precisely the opposite manner.

351. According to this general theory, the motions caused by heat and cold may be easily explained, regard being had to the different circumstances which modify each given case.

Thus most of the winds proceed from the heating and cooling of different regions of the atmosphere, particularly the constant and periodical winds observed in the torrid zone.

It is upon the same principles that currents of air act in chimnies, Argand lamps, &c. We may observe, by means of a lighted candle, the two currents of air above mentioned, at the opening of a door of a heated room. A current of air is also produced in mines, by means of a well or a gallery constructed in them, since the temperature of mines is very different from the exterior temperature. If this difference does not produce a sufficient effect, a fire may be made in the mine.

352. Since at the same temperature and pressure every elastic fluid possesses a particular degree of density, every change which takes place in the chemical combination of a mass of air is, like heat and cold, a cause of motion. Every increase of density acts like heat, every diminution like cold. Now changes of this kind are continually taking place in the atmosphere; since, by means of organic and chemical processes, many of which are probably unknown to us, the air sometimes parts with one or more of its constituent principles to other bodies, and sometimes combines with some of theirs. Here then must be an incessant cause of motions, which, however, are rarely violent, because these changes never take place rapidly.

353. Such changes produce motions, not only because they alter the elastic force of the air, but also *because they increase or diminish its mass*. When the mass of air is increased, currents are formed tending from the place in every direction; when it is diminished the contrary effect is produced. The most active cause of this nature is undoubtedly evaporation. It is found that there annually evaporates a stratum of water of about 30 inches in thickness, in the temperate regions of Europe; and this takes place at the rate of about half an inch in the coldest months, and 4 or 5 inches in the warmest. We may hence imagine how much the mass of air incumbent upon the immense surface of seas and oceans continually augments, especially in the torrid zone; and we may attribute to this augmentation a part of the motions which take place in the whole atmosphere.

But much more violent motions must arise from the opposite cause; that is, when this vapour is condensed and falls upon the earth in rain, snow, and hail; these are particularly remarkable in violent showers, when a limited portion of the atmosphere in the course of a few hours, parts with several thousand tons from its mass; which must evidently produce currents tending towards the place from every quarter. Indeed this is what is often perceived, when the course of a shower is attentively observed.

354. The motions also of other bodies, and particularly of water, are communicated to the air. When the air is tranquil, we observe over the surface of each river, the course of which is considerably rapid, a current of air in the same direction, and it only becomes insensible by the effect of a stronger wind. Those who are acquainted with the vast currents which prevail in seas, will easily conceive that they must, in like manner, give rise to considerable motions in the atmosphere. Miners avail themselves of this principle to produce a current of air. In an adit, through which a stream flows, they place, at a small height above the stream, a partition of boards. Below this the air follows the direction of the stream, above it takes the opposite direction.

355. Many mechanical methods have been devised for producing small motions in the air. Of this kind are the common bellows, exhausting-pump, condensing-pump, &c. These instruments are made of different forms and sizes according to the use to which they are applied. Founders employ a large species of bellows, and they might with advantage employ a condensing-pump. Miners sometimes use bellows with a double current of air, and exhausting-pumps.

356. As air is put in motion by other bodies, so also *it may itself put other bodies in motion, both solid and liquid.*

It is well known, that in hurricanes the air has power to tear up trees, destroy houses, and raise the waves of the sea to a fearful height. This force of the air and other elastic fluids has been made use of for various purposes in the arts. The pressure of a moderate wind puts in motion the sails of a windmill. The steam engine is made to exert an enormous power by the force of aqueous vapour; and is employed as an agent in giving motion to all kinds of machinery. In hydraulic engines which act by impulse, a uniform motion is obtained by the condensation of air in a reservoir. In the air-gun, it is the condensation of this fluid which produces the effect. In fire arms the force is derived from the dilatation of gases produced by the inflammation of gunpowder. It is in vain to attempt to enumerate all the different machines which depend upon the moving force of elastic fluids; and posterity will still find ample room for important inventions. Among the machines of this kind which are rather amusing than useful, may be mentioned *Hero's fountain;* of which, however, an important application has been made in mines.

357. As all the motions produced in solids and liquids take place in the air, the theory of the resistance of this fluid, is a very important subject; but yet very difficult to investigate. The principles established by Newton are not so well confirmed by experiment, as his laws of motion in the case of solid bodies.

358. It is the uncertainty of this theory which prevents us from fixing completely *the laws of the descent of bodies in the air*. What is known upon this subject may be comprehended in the following general statement. The descent of bodies in the air, like that of bodies in a liquid, cannot take place with a motion uniformly accelerated; but its acceleration must decrease in the same manner at each instant. Still the motion cannot become uniform as in a liquid, because the density of the air, and consequently its resistance, continually increase. Thus, if we suppose a body to fall in a column of air of sufficient extent, it would first have an increasing velocity, but its acceleration would continually diminish. At a certain point the acceleration would become nothing, and the velocity would be at its *maximum*. Beyond this point, the resistance always increasing, the velocity itself would diminish, till at length this also would become nothing, and the body would remain suspended in the air. This consequence may appear paradoxical to one who has not an exact idea of the increase of the density of the air. It may be shown by the formula for measuring heights by the barometer, that a column of air extending into the interior of the earth to the depth of 700 miles, would be 100000 times more dense than that at the surface, that is, five or six times more dense than platina, so that the heaviest bodies would remain suspended in it, or rather would have an upward motion.

SECTION VI.

ELECTRICITY.

CHAPTER XXXII.

Electrical Machine, and General Phenomena of Electricity.

359. THE term *electricity* is derived from the Greek word *electron*, signifying amber, on account of the property which this substance was known to possess of attracting light substances when rubbed. But the Greeks did not suspect that this phenomenon was the effect of a very remarkable and extensive force in nature. It was not till the 17th century that sulphur, resins, and many other bodies, were known to have the same property; the inventor of the air-pump enriched the apparatus of the philosopher, with a second very important instrument, called the *electrical machine*. The limits of this work will not permit us to give an account of the primitive construction of this machine, or to notice the various improvements it has undergone. We can only mention a few particulars of one of the most improved forms of these machines.

360. The two most essential parts are the *plate* or *body rubbed* and the *rubber*. The body rubbed is usually a circular piece of polished glass; the larger it is, the better. This plate is made to turn on a metallic axis, supported by a wooden frame. Instead of a plate a glass globe or cylinder is sometimes used.

The *rubber* for the most part consists of two or four oblong cushions, pressed by springs against the glass, so as to produce a strong friction when the plate turns. The cushions are of leather filled with hair, and placed upon metal plates. This leather is to be covered with some oily substance, over which should be spread as equally as possible, a dry amalgam of mercury and zinc. To each cushion, and on the side towards which the rotatory motion of the plate is directed, is fitted a strip of gummed taffeta, or oiled silk, which adheres to the glass when the machine is put in motion. The frame which supports the cushions should be of metal; and it should be attached to the supports of the plate, not by metal, but by firm glass columns or tubes. When the machine is in operation a chain should be attached to the metallic part of the cushions at one extremity, the other being suffered to fall upon the wooden frame, or what is still better, upon the ground. This circumstance is of great importance, for the effects are much more powerful when the rubber has a metallic communication with the earth.

361. With the parts of the machine now described, we can exhibit to the senses most of the phenomena, which constitute the science of *electricity*. When we turn the plate, the atmosphere being warm and dry, we observe the following effects.

(1.) We perceive a phosphoric odour.

(2.) By bringing the hand or face gradually near the plate, we feel at a certain distance, a sensation like that produced by the contact of a spider's web.

(3.) If we touch the plate with a metallic ball, a small crackling spark is perceived, and if the hand be applied instead of the ball the spark is accompanied with a tingling sensation.

(4.) In the dark, this phenomenon is much more striking; and as we turn the machine, streams of fire are seen to glance, from beneath the gummed taffeta and run over the plate.*

---

* The light which attends the electric explosion, appears to me to be the simple result of the pressure which the air and vapours experience, when they are traversed by electricity. For, it is well known that simple pressure disengages light from aeriform fluids; and, on the other hand, the powerful explosions produced by electricity, prove that in its passage through bodies, it exerts a very great pressure. It is true that electric light is observed in a vacuum; but what we here call a vacuum, is simply a portion of space occupied by air reduced at most to $\frac{1}{760}$ of its natural density; or the space may be filled with the vapour of water or mercury. If denser air emits light at a less compression, rarer air will emit it when an infinitely greater pressure is applied, like that produced by the rapid passage of electricity. I first suggested this idea in an account of my experiments upon the formation of water by simple pressure.

(5.) When we cease to turn the machine, all these phenomena continue for some time, though with an intensity sensibly decreasing; but we may still observe phenomena in many respects the most important, as those of *electric attraction and repulsion*. The plate in this state attracts all light bodies, retains them an instant, and then repels them. If we bring towards the plate, balls of cork suspended at the end of a thread, the phenomenon becomes very deserving of attention. If the thread is of dry silk, the small ball is attracted, attaches itself for a moment to the plate, and is then repelled. This repulsion is durable; but if we touch the small ball, it is again attracted and repelled. On the contrary, if the thread is of linen, and especially if it be moist; the ball will only be attracted, and not repelled.

362. When a body manifests these phenomena or only the last which we have described, we say the body is *electrified*; and the unknown substance which produces these phenomena is called the *electric matter* or *fluid*.

363. It still remains to speak of an important part of the electric machine, the *conductor*. This is either entirely metallic, or at least covered with a metallic substance, as gold leaf, for example. Its magnitude and form are arbitrary; it is sometimes a ball, commonly however a cylinder, rounded at its two extremities. For a plate of two feet diameter, we make it about three feet in length and about six inches in diameter. It communicates with the plate by means of two rounded branches of metal, which present several points at the distance of about half an inch from the plate, at the part where the electricity accumulates and passes from under the taffeta. Care should be taken that there be no other points or prominent angles. These branches should be disposed in such a manner that we can remove them, and substitute one for the other, for a very important purpose, of which we shall speak hereafter; this consists in making the conductor communicate with the rubber instead of the plate. One essential circumstance is, that the conductor be placed upon glass supports, and have no other communication with the table on which it rests.

364. When we turn the plate the conductor becomes electrified upon its whole surface, which is evinced by all the phenomena mentioned above; only the spark is greater, attended with a louder noise, and is more sensibly felt. Accordingly it may dart to the distance of several inches, especially when the air is very dry. Another very

remarkable difference is, that by one of these sparks the whole electricity of the conductor is taken from it at once, whereas the plate only loses its electricity at the point where we touch it, even when the motion has ceased. If the conductor communicate with the earth or with the foot of the machine, by a brass chain, it does not manifest the least electricity when we turn the plate.

365. These experiments clearly show the different properties of glass and metal with respect to electricity. The glass is electrified by friction. It strongly retains upon its surface the electricity which is accumulated there, and suffers it to be taken away only at the precise place where we touch it. The metal, on the contrary, is not electrified by friction; it receives the electricity instantaneously through its whole extent, when it is placed in contact with the glass; and the electricity abandons it also instantaneously when the finger or some metallic body is presented to it.

Hence we see why the conductor must be supported by glass columns, and why it is not electrified when it communicates with the earth. The metal *conducts* the electric matter, and the glass does not.

366. Glass and metal are not the only substances which exhibit these opposite properties with respect to electricity; they are those in which the properties in question are manifested in the highest degree.*

Under this point of view, therefore, we may divide bodies into two great classes, *non-conductors*, and *conductors of electricity*. To the first class belong; 1. Among inorganic substances, common glass and all vitrifications with their essential constituent principles; earths and metallic oxides, and all natural crystallizations of these substances; consequently, all precious stones, and nearly all rough stones, which are probably only collections of small crystals. Sulphur and atmospheric air belong to this class. Yet the latter always has some conducting power, sometimes weaker, sometimes stronger, according to the quantity of water it contains. 2. Most of the dry animal substances, particularly silk, wool, hair, feathers. 3. Many dry vegetable substances, principally the resins and resinous mixtures, sealing-wax, amber, cotton, paper, sugar, dry wood, especially

---

* The resins and especially gum lac have a still less conducting power than glass; but they cannot be so conveniently employed in machines of considerable dimensions.

when it is dried by the fire; also gross oils. Among these bodies, however, there is no one that does not conduct electricity to a certain degree. The best non-conductors are glass, sulphur, resin, gum lac, silk; the rest are rather to be considered as bad conductors.

The best conductors are, among inorganic bodies, the metals, water, and coal; among organic bodies, living animals and vegetables; and even the vegetable fibre, disengaged from all the oily and resinous parts, appears to be a very good conductor, at least this is the case with a fibre of linen; and wood, cotton, &c., are perhaps bad conductors only on account of the oily and resinous matter which they contain.*

Non-conductors are also called *electrics*, and conductors *non-electrics*; but these denominations are not well chosen.†

367. We say a body is *insulated* when it communicates with other visible bodies only by non-conductors. To *insulate* a body, therefore, we suspend or support it by one of these. The best *insulators* are glass, sealing-wax, silk, and wood dried by the fire.‡

368. If we compare the phenomena of attraction and repulsion with what has been said of the conducting power of bodies, we deduce the following important principle;

Electrified bodies attract those which are not electrified; bodies electrified with the same electricity repel each other.

A cork ball attached to a non-conducting silk thread, and taken in its natural state, is first attracted; but is repelled as soon as it becomes electrified, and this repulsive tendency continues until the ball

---

* It is very desirable, for many reasons, that skilful chemists would occupy themselves more with electricity. What has been said of non-conductors and conductors, affords room for conjecture that there is some connexion between the electric properties and chemical composition of bodies, which mechanical philosophy alone cannot discover.

† In reality the distinction of non-conductors and conductors is not much better. All bodies, even gum lac, can be penetrated by powerful electricity; so that all these distinctions are to be regarded as merely relative, and none as absolute.

‡ Nothing insulates better than a cylinder of gum lac. Coulomb proved that a thread of gum lac, drawn out by the flame of a candle, is nearly a perfect insulator when the quantity of electricity is small.

has lost its electricity by contact with an uninsulated conductor. If, on the contrary, it is suspended by a conducting linen thread, and not insulated, it cannot be saturated with electricity, and for this reason it is constantly attracted.

369. Upon these phenomena of electric attraction and repulsion are founded almost all the instruments which pass under the name of *electroscopes* and *electrometers*. These serve to measure the intensity of electricity, but for the most part they answer their purpose imperfectly. Still they are useful in many experiments, and therefore we shall give a brief description of them. The most simple is the *thread electrometer*. Two small balls of cork or elder pith are attached to the extremities of a linen thread. We suspend them to the conductor or some other electrified body, so that in their natural position they touch each other by the effect of gravity. As soon as they are electrified they diverge, and their divergence is proportional to the intensity. The size of this instrument varies according to the use to which it is to be applied. For minute degrees of electricity they must be very small. Most of the electrometers are only modifications of this. We have not room for particular descriptions; and can only observe that the best are the *jar electrometer* of Cavallo, the *air electrometer* of Saussure, the *gold-leaf electrometer* of Bennet, and the *straw electrometer* of Volta.* We cannot, however, omit the *quadrant electrometer* of Henley, because it is considered as an essential appendage to an electrical machine. A graduated semicircle is attached, by its diameter, to a column of metal or undried wood, so as to be at a small distance from the column, the diameter being parallel to it. To the centre is attached a small and very moveable pendulum, made of a stem of whalebone, and having a small cork ball at its extremity. The column, which is much longer than the pendulum, may be screwed by its lower extremity, perpendicularly to the conductor of the machine; or it may be supported upright by a metallic rod, and be removed at pleasure. This electrometer being placed on the conductor receives its electricity; and as the pendulum and column are electrified in the same way, the pendulum is repelled by the column, and

---

* It is surprising that the author has not mentioned the *electric balance* of Coulomb; the only one which gives the exact measure of electricity. We shall speak of it hereafter.

the height to which it rises on the graduated quadrant, indicates the intensity of the electricity.

370. The conducting power of bodies does not depend upon their material constitution alone, but also on their form. If, while the plate is in motion, we bring a pointed body of any substance whatever, near the conductor, its conducting power becomes obvious at a considerable distance. Metallic points manifest this effect in the highest degree. This conducting power of points is also manifest, when we attach a point to the conductor in such a manner that the sharp part is directed from the conductor into the air. It is then impossible to charge the conductor with a high degree of electricity.

On the contrary, the dispersion of electricity becomes the more difficult, in proportion as the body is larger and rounder. In this case it is necessary to bring the bodies much nearer, and the passage is accompanied by a spark.

371. When this effluent current of electricity leaves the points, a certain motion is always produced in the air, which may be rendered visible by means of the flame of a candle, or some vapour. Upon this motion is founded the *electric mill*, which consists of a strip of copper in the form of an S, and carefully sharpened at both ends, which is made to turn circularly upon a point placed at its centre. When this point is screwed to the conductor, and the machine is put in motion, the wheel turns backward with great velocity. It is important to remark, that the motion of the air is always directed to the sharp part of the point.

372. As we can cause the electricity of the plate to pass to the principal conductor, so also this may be transmitted to a second conductor provided it be insulated. Thus, for example, a man may be electrified when he stands upon an *insulator*, which is usually a stool supported by four glass feet. In this condition his body exhibits all the electric phenomena, without his experiencing any particular sensation, except when sparks are taken from his body.

373. The chemical effects of electricity are extremely remarkable. We shall only mention the inflammation of alcohol and detonating gas* by the electric spark. In the sequel we shall be made acquainted with other phenomena of the same kind. We shall speak, in another place, of the electrical appearances exhibited in the dark and in rarefied air.

---

* That is a mixture of two parts by bulk of hydrogen and one of oxygen.

CHAPTER XXXIII.

Opposite Electricities.

374. In the first half of the last century, Dufay, a French philosopher, discovered that there were two kinds of electricity, which, when considered separately, have the greatest resemblance, but when compared together exhibit opposite phenomena. He named the one *vitreous* and the other *resinous* electricity, because the first was obtained from glass, and the second from resin.* After his death, philosophers seemed to forget this nice distinction, the discovery of which does so much honour to the sagacity of Dufay. At length, in the latter part of the last century the celebrated Franklin continued the investigation, and pointed out so perfectly the difference between the two electricities, that this discovery has since become the key to the most remarkable electrical phenomena. Instead of the names vitreous and resinous, chosen by Dufay, Franklin adopted those of *positive* and *negative ;* whence it has become common to indicate the one by the sign $+ E$, and the other by the sign $- E$. Yet as the denomination of Dufay is founded upon fact, and that of Franklin upon mere hypothesis, and one too which has lost much of its plausibility since his time ; the terms of Dufay are to be preferred.

375. It is now known that the two kinds of electricity may be excited in many ways, and that they are, in fact, both produced at the same time, one in the rubber, and the other in the body rubbed. Thus when the conductor is disposed in the manner described in the preceding chapter, it is as easy to charge it with the resinous as with the vitreous electricity. It is only necessary to insulate the

---

* The definition is not strictly exact. Glass rubbed with wool, takes the electricity called vitreous ; and when rubbed with cat skin, the resinous. I know of no body which may not be made to take both electricities, by changing the rubber, or by some slight modification in the circumstances of the body rubbed. Still the distinction between the two electricities is not the less real, because it rests upon the attractions and repulsions which belong to them, and not upon the nature of the bodies which produce them.

rubber, and make the conductor communicate with it; then to put the plate in communication with the ground, or draw from it continually, by means of points properly placed, the vitreous electricity produced on its surface.

376. When we turn the plate, after having made this change, the conductor which is then in communication with the body rubbed, and which itself makes a part of it, becomes electrified and exhibits all the phenomena mentioned in the preceding chapter. Only the electricity is always much more feeble, which is probably nothing more than an accidental circumstance, arising from this, that the vitreous electricity which passes from the conductor to the plate, and which counteracts the effects of the other, cannot be entirely taken from the plate, as fast as it becomes fixed there.

377. The principal difference between the two electricities, is seen in the phenomena of attraction and repulsion; for two bodies which repel each other when they have the same electricity, attract each other when they have opposite electricities; from which we deduce the following law;

Electricities of the same name repel each other; and electricities of opposite names attract each other.

To be convinced of the exactness of this law, we dispose the apparatus in the manner above described, so as to give resinous electricity to the conductor, the plate always absorbing the vitreous. The latter being a non-conducting body, always retains a small portion of this electricity, in spite of our efforts to remove it. Then we take a cork ball suspended by a silk thread; if we bring this near the conductor, it is attracted by it, and being saturated with resinous electricity is again repelled; but in this state it is attracted by the glass plate; its resinous electricity is destroyed; after which it charges itself with vitreous electricity, and is then repelled by the plate. In this state, it is again attracted by the conductor; and thus a position may be easily found, in which the ball is alternately attracted and repelled by each, so as to keep up a constant vibration.

378. It is evident from this experiment, that one electricity destroys the other. This becomes still more manifest when we dispose the machine so as to produce the vitreous electricity, with the single precaution of insulating the rubber, and causing it to communicate by a chain with the conductor. In this case we do not find the least trace of electricity in the conductor. Generally when we unite unequal degrees of the two electricities, the least intense is always

destroyed, and the most intense diminished. Hence we see why it is always necessary that the plate communicate with the conductor when the machine is fitted up for vitreous electricity; and why it must communicate with the rubber when the machine is intended to produce resinous electricity.*

379. From these relations between the two electricities, we deduce a mode of distinguishing them. The apparatus commonly used for this purpose, consists of a thread electrometer, suspended and insulated, and a stick of sealing-wax. We know from experiment that wax rubbed with wool, leather, and linen, always acquires the resinous electricity. We communicate to the electrometer the electricity which we wish to examine, so that the balls repel each other, and continue some time separated; then we bring the rubbed sealing-wax near them; if the electrometer has resinous electricity, a part of this electricity is disguised by that of the wax, and the threads collapse; if, on the contrary, it has vitreous electricity, they diverge more than before.

Electrical Phenomena in the Dark and in Rarefied Air.

380. In the dark the two electricities are distinguished from each other in a remarkable manner; that is, by a difference in the luminous appearances which are presented when the electricity is taken away by points. If the conductor is charged with vitreous electricity, and a point is brought near it, we see, at a considerable dis-

---

* Generally when two insulated bodies are electrified by their mutual friction, one takes the vitreous and the other the resinous electricity. This happens, therefore, to the plate and rubber, when they are insulated. It takes place also, when the rubber, always insulated, communicates with the conductor. But the effect soon has a limit; for the vitreous electricity which accumulates on the plate, not being able to escape, prevents new quantities of vitreous electricity from flowing there, and consequently from becoming apparent. Whereas if we take away the vitreous electricity by points, as fast as it is produced, then the natural electricity of the conductor is decomposed, and the vitreous electricity is accumulated on the plate without interruption; and reciprocally the conductor is in a durable and increasing state of vitreous electricity.

tance a bright star, at the extremity of the metallic point which becomes more brilliant as the point is brought nearer. If the point be fastened to the conductor, and the hand or some other conducting body be brought near, we no longer see a bright star, but a pencil of diverging rays. On the contrary, if the conductor is charged with resinous electricity, the two phenomena occur in the inverse order.

381. We shall add another experiment, which does not, indeed, show so clearly the difference between the two electricities, but which is remarkable in other respects.

Although dry atmospheric air is a bad conductor of electricity, yet highly rarefied air is capable of being traversed by it; this is evinced by the following experiment. We rarefy the air in a glass vessel having a metallic cover, as the receiver of an air-pump, or a glass tube prepared for the purpose; then, if we make the conductor communicate with one extremity of the vessel, and the other with the ground, it being dark, the passage of the electricity through the rarefied air takes place under the form of a whitish light. This phenomenon, which may be called the *electrical aurora borealis*, continues as long as we turn the plate.

There are many ways of varying this experiment, and most of them exhibit very agreeable luminous appearances. If we place at the two extremities of the vessel two metallic points directed inward, the light escapes from one diverging, and enters the other converging. If the vessel be a receiver, and a metallic rod be transmitted through the upper cover, having at its end metallic radii in the form of a star, placed horizontally, the electric light passes off from each of the points toward the lower plate, producing the appearance of a fountain of fire. By substituting for the star a ring or a body of any other figure, different forms may be given to the current of light.

382. In these experiments the following circumstance is worthy of attention. When we bring the conductor near the vessel in which the electrical light is exhibited, a particular movement takes place in this light at the place to which the conductor is brought. We can then take sparks from the conductor, but they are variable as to their intensity. This observation proves that electric attraction acts even through the glass, though a non-conductor.

We remark, in this connexion, that the phosphorescence, which is exhibited by some barometers, not perfectly deprived of air, when we incline the tube in the dark so as to make the mercury pass from one end to the other, has its cause in this same electrical phenomenon.

383. These luminous appearances are the same, or nearly the same, with respect to both electricities. Franklin and many of his followers believed that there was a difference, consisting in this, that when the conductor is charged with vitreous electricity, the electricity passes always from the conductor; and that when it is charged with resinous electricity, the electric light passes from the ground to the conductor. But this was rather a deduction from the hypothesis than from actual observation; for, with the most exact attention to all the motions of the electric light, it is impossible to determine the directions of this motion, because it takes place so instantaneously. It appears to an attentive eye, sometimes to approach the conductor and sometimes to recede from it, and sometimes to be directed both ways at the same time.

Hypothesis of Franklin.

384. According to Franklin, electric phenomena are the effect of a single substance infinitely subtile, which is diffused through all bodies, by laws analogous to those of caloric. Its particles repel each other, but they are more or less attracted by other bodies. As long as this electric matter is in a state of equilibrium in a system of bodies, no electric phenomenon is exhibited; but when, on the contrary, this matter is accumulated above or diminished below the point of equilibrium, the body is electrified, positively in the first case, negatively in the second; and the electric phenomena are produced by the efforts which the electric matter makes, to restore the equilibrium which has been disturbed.

385. What principally led Franklin to this hypothesis, was the observation that the rubber must not be insulated; for, in fact, we are obliged to admit that the electricity which accumulates on the plate, passes from the rubber. The possibility of charging the conductor successively with the two electricities, is easily explained upon this hypothesis, which indeed affords a solution to a great proportion of electric phenomena. But the subject of attraction and repulsion presents a difficulty. If two bodies, electrified positively, are brought together, according to this hypothesis, their surrounding electric atmospheres, being pressed, force them to recede. If two bodies negatively electrified, are brought near each other, the natural

electricity, placed between their rarefied atmospheres, and thereby rendered more intense, is forced to expand, and thus obliges the bodies to diverge. Lastly, if two bodies, one positively, the other negatively electrified, are brought towards each other, they approach, because the positive atmosphere of the first, is attracted by the negative atmosphere of the second. We shall find several phenomena hereafter which admit of only a forced explanation upon this hypothesis; among others the following may be mentioned; in the passage of electricity through a point, the current of air which it produces is always directed towards the sharp part of the point; and it is still the same when we electrify the conductor negatively, according to the expression of Franklin. For a circumstantial account of this hypothesis, we refer the reader to Franklin's letter on electricity.

Hypothesis of Symmer.

386. Robert Symmer, in the first part of the 51st volume of the *Philosophical Transactions*, published another hypothesis, which has taken the place of that of Franklin, in the minds of most inquirers, because it satisfies the phenomena better. According to Symmer there are two kinds of electric matter which attract each other, while, on the contrary, the particles of each taken separately, repel each other. Their union, which is called *combined electricity*, produces the state of equilibrium; their disunion the electric state. The one taken separately gives the phenomena of vitreous electricity, the other those of resinous electricity. When two bodies have both vitreous, or both resinous electricity, their homogeneous atmospheres repel each other. When one has vitreous and the other resinous, their heterogeneous atmospheres attract each other.

The combined electricity of the rubber is decomposed by friction; the plate attracts the vitreous electricity; the resinous electricity, becoming free, escapes into the earth through the conductor attached to the rubber; new currents of combined electricity flow through this same conductor; and as long as the machine is in motion, this effect continues in an uninterrupted manner. This hypothesis explains also without difficulty, some more complicated phenomena, which will present themselves in the sequel.

387. The earliest hypotheses are entirely inadmissible. Among the more recent, that of Deluc which may be found in his *New Ideas upon Meteorology*, deserves attention.

It may be doubted whether any of these hypotheses is entirely conformable to fact; but that of Symmer is unquestionably entitled to the preference, because it affords the best explanation of electrical phenomena.

Addition.

The Electric Balance.

388. M. Coulomb has greatly improved upon the ideas of Symmer. He is the first who may be said to have reduced them to an exact theory, especially by the discovery which he made of the law of electric attractions and repulsions; for it is not enough that the strict inquirer knows bodies to attract or repel each other in a given manner. If he would adapt an hypothesis to these facts, this hypothesis must be such as will represent them with exactness; that is, such that all the circumstances of the phenomena may be deduced from it by rigorous calculation. This is effected by the discovery of M. Coulomb. In order to render it intelligible, we must describe the instrument with which it was made, and which M. Coulomb called the *electric balance*.

389. To a very fine silver wire fixed, at one of its extremities, to some solid body, we suspend a long and slender needle of gum lac, a substance which strongly resists the passage of electricity. We place this needle in a horizontal position, and adapt to one end a very small circle of gilt paper. This circle is the body to which we communicate electricity; the needle of gum lac serves to insulate it; and the silver wire, by its force of torsion, serves to measure the attractive or repulsive force which is exerted upon it by the electrified bodies presented to it.

It is obvious that only a very small force is necessary if it be determinate and constant, to twist this wire through 360° or 180°, and consequently to derange, to the same degree, the natural state of equilibrium of the needle. Accordingly, the angle described by the paper circle will increase in proportion to the intensity of the attraction or repulsion; and if we know the force of torsion corresponding to different angles of deviation, we may easily determine how the electric action varies with the distance. Now this may be easily done; for M. Coulomb has proved, by very exact experiments, that the force of torsion in a wire of a certain length, is exactly proportional to the angle of torsion; and to avoid the difference which might arise from the irregular form of bodies, we employ for the attracting or repelling body, a copper sphere insulated at the extremity of a cylinder of gum lac. The small gilt circle upon which it is to act, may be considered as a point; the sphere is so placed that in the natural position of equilibrium, it is in contact with the circle; and to avoid the errors produced by agitations in the air, the whole apparatus is inclosed in a glass case, on the outside of which are traced the horizontal divisions, which serve to measure the angles described from the point of contact.

Let us now consider the mode of using this instrument.

390. We take the copper sphere by its handle of gum lac, and communicate to it a certain quantity of electricity from the conductor, after which we replace it in the balance. The gilt paper shares its electricity and is immediately repelled. After a series of oscillations the needle settles down at a determinate angular distance from the sphere, in which position it is evident that the torsion, experienced by the wire, is in equilibrium with the repulsive force, and may thus serve to measure it. In order to be definite, let us suppose that this torsion, or the repulsive force which acts upon the needle, is 36°.

Then if we forcibly twist the wire in a contrary direction, which may be done by means of an index placed at the top of the glass cover, and attached to the wire, the torsion will preponderate and the circle will approach the sphere. Suppose that we turn the index till the needle is only 18° from the sphere, instead of 36°, as it was at first; we find that in order to bring it into this position it is necessary to turn the index 126°. This torsion is evidently to be added to the preceding 36°, and in the second case, the total force of torsion would be 162°, if the small circle were in the same position as before; but as the angular distance of the needle is 18° less, the wire is evidently untwisted by this quantity; the actual torsion is therefore 162° — 18° or 144°.

By comparing these results we find that when the deviations of the needle were 36° and 18°, the forces of torsion required to counterbalance the repulsive force, or in other words, the intensities of this repulsive force, are represented by 36° and 144°; whence it follows that if the deviations of the needle are as 2 to 1, or as 1 to ½, the repulsive forces are as 1 to 4; that is, the repulsive force of the electricity increases as the square of the distance diminishes, or diminishes as the square of the distance increases. In general, *it is inversely proportional to the square of the distance.* Other experiments, made in the same manner, with different intensities, give the same ratio. If we apply the method to electric attractions, we find them subject to the same law.

391. For the sake of greater simplicity we here suppose the distance between the sphere and paper circle to be measured by the arc of the circle which separates them; this is not rigorously exact, for it is the chord which measures the distance. But when the arcs are small, as we suppose them in this example, the difference is inconsiderable; besides, allowance is made for it in nice calculations; and it is only when this correction is made that the preceding law is exact. It is remarkable that it is the same as that of the celestial attractions.

392. By means of what precedes, the theory of the two fluids, as M. Coulomb presents it, may be reduced to this hypothesis.

Electrical phenomena are produced by the reciprocal action of two invisible and imponderable fluids, the properties of which are, that the particles of each repel one another, and attract those of the opposite fluid, in the inverse ratio of the square of the distance.

By this hypothesis we can represent all the phenomena, and subject many of them to a rigorous calculation; but we must not regard it as any thing more than a convenient mode of explanation; we only know that the phenomena take place as if they were produced by two fluids endowed with the above properties; the actual nature of electricity is still unknown.

CHAPTER XXXIV.

Striking Distance, Sphere of Activity, Accumulated Electricity.

393. WHEN we bring a conducting body, not pointed, near the electrified conductor, we have seen that at a certain distance a passage of electricity takes place by means of a spark, and the same sort of

electricity which the conductor possesses, is thus communicated to the body; and the body is said to be electrified by *communication*. If the body which receives the electricity is well insulated, it retains its electricity when the conductor is removed. The space surrounding the electrified body, within which this effect is produced, is called its striking distance; and we say that a conductor gives sparks at 4 or 6 inches, when the passage is effected at these distances. The striking distance is very variable. It depends on the intensity of the electricity, the conducting power of the body, the form of this body, and the qualities of the surrounding air.

Sphere of Activity.

394. The action of electricity is not limited to its striking distance; it manifests itself beyond this distance in a manner less remarkable, it is true, but still perhaps not less worthy of attention. The law of this action is very clearly demonstrated in the following manner.

We take an insulated conductor, a metallic tube, for example, and apply to one of its extremities a sensible electrometer, presenting the other extremity to the conductor of the machine. We then perceive, by the electrometer, that the insulated conductor gives signs of electricity beyond the striking distance, and always of the same electricity with that of the conductor of the machine. But this electricity is distinguished from that communicated by the spark; thus, if we remove the body from the conductor, it diminishes in the same manner as it before increased; whereas the other suffers no diminution by a change of place, except what is inevitably produced by the conducting power of the air. This mode of electrifying a body is called *developement of electricity*. If we again bring the conductor to the point where its shows sensible signs of electricity, and then touch it with the finger, the threads of the electrometer collapse, and all traces of electricity disappear. But if we remove the conductor a little, always keeping it insulated, the threads again diverge, and always in proportion to the distance to which it is removed. This phenomenon, precisely opposite to what happened before we touched the conducting body, indicates that the body has passed to the opposite state of electricity, which indication is confirmed by the trial electrometer.

395. The whole space within which this effect is produced, is called the *sphere of activity;* and the influence of this sphere of activity is one of the most important points in the theory of electricity, because no other shows so clearly the particular laws of electric statics.

396. According to the hypothesis of Symmer, the following is the order of the phenomena in the sphere of activity. If the conductor of the machine is charged with vitreous electricity, the insulated conductor having the two electricities combined, its resinous electricity is attracted by the vitreous electricity of the conductor; it is not by this means taken away, but disguised, so that its influence upon the vitreous electricity of the conducting body is diminished. This last is therefore free to a certain point, and becomes the more so as the body is brought nearer the conductor. If we remove the body, the repulsive effect which the electricity of the conductor produced upon its natural vitreous electricity, is weakened; consequently the two electricities of this body combine more fully, and the effect upon its natural electricity becomes less sensible; finally, when the body is entirely without the sphere of activity of the conductor, it returns to the state of equilibrium in which all the phenomena disappear.

But if we touch the body while near the conductor, we take from it only its vitreous electricity, which is then but imperfectly combined; and its resinous electricity remains, because it is retained and disguised by the vitreous electricity of the conductor. If afterwards we remove the body, what remains of its natural vitreous electricity is not sufficient to disguise its resinous electricity; consequently the latter becomes more and more free, and thus produces its accustomed effect.

We have only to change the expressions vitreous and resinous, and this explanation will apply to the case when the conductor is electrified resinously.

We see that these phenomena are naturally deduced from the hypothesis of Symmer.

397. To explain the formation of the sphere of activity, according to the same hypothesis, it is only necessary to admit that the two electricities act upon each other at a distance, but that this action has no other influence, except to diminish their reciprocal activity, and cannot take away either from the bodies in which they are fixed.

If one of the two, the vitreous electricity, for example, is accumulated in a body, it attracts the resinous electricity contained in the combination of the two electricities of the surrounding air; at the same time it repels the vitreous electricity. By this double influence, it diminishes the mutual action which had hitherto rendered the combination without effect. Hence the vitreous electricity of the nearest stratum of air becomes almost entirely free, and produces a similar, but more feeble effect upon the two electricities of the surrounding strata; and this influence thus propagates itself from stratum to stratum to a greater or less distance, according as the force of the vitreous electricity with which the effect began, is more or less intense. According to this explanation, neither of the two electricities, any where in the sphere of activity, is in its natural state; but one is in a constrained state which is more considerable in proportion as it is nearer the body actually electrified.

When an insulated conductor is placed in the sphere of activity, the resinous electricity of its natural state is combined, to a certain degree, with the vitreous electricity of the sphere of activity, and consequently its vitreous electricity becomes sensible to a certain point.

When, on the contrary, an uninsulated conductor is placed in this sphere of activity, although the same thing takes place, the effect is different, because the vitreous electricity escapes through the conductor which is presented to it, and there remains only the resinous electricity in a combined state.

In this sense we are to understand the expression, that the sphere of activity always tends to excite in the body which is placed in it, an electricity opposite to its own.

398. If the two sides of a thin glass plate are covered with tin foil to within an inch or two round the border of the plate, so that all communication between the two metallic coverings is cut off, when we place the plate in such a manner that these coverings shall continue insulated, and communicate the electricity of the conductor to the upper surface, the lower surface will manifest the same electricity. If we take the electricity from the upper surface, by means of a point directed towards it, the electricity of the lower surface also disappears; yet the electricity, in these circumstances, escapes with greater difficulty than in any other arrangement. If, on the contrary, we take away the electricity of the lower surface by contact, and

then apply a point to the upper surface, the lower surface indicates an increasing but opposite electricity.

399. We cannot fail to perceive, in the essential circumstances of this experiment, a perfect resemblance to that of article 394, when we suppose the electric sphere of the upper surface to extend through the glass to the lower surface. This opinion seems to be perfectly confirmed by the observation of article 382. If the upper surface is charged with vitreous electricity, it neutralizes the natural resinous electricity of the lower surface, and then the vitreous electricity of this becomes free. If we take the vitreous electricity from the upper surface, the resinous electricity of the lower surface becomes again combined with the vitreous electricity of that surface, and the whole is disguised. But if we first touch the lower surface, we take away its free vitreous electricity; then there only remains its resinous electricity, which is neutralized by the vitreous electricity of the upper surface, as long as this remains fixed; but if we take this vitreous electricity from the upper surface; the resinous electricity of the lower surface becomes free.

400. By comparing the two experiments, the essential conditions of the formation of a sphere of activity, are determined with still more exactness by the following enunciation.

A conducting body must be near another electrified body, and be separated from it by a non-conducting medium. We shall see hereafter that the electrified body may as well be a non-conductor as a conductor. In the air, the distance between these two bodies may be very considerable, because then the sphere of activity extends very far. But if the non-conducting medium is dense and compact, as glass, for example, the sphere of activity only extends to small distances; for this reason the glass employed in this experiment must not be too thick. In these circumstances, the conductor brought near, always exhibits the phenomena of the sphere of activity, provided the electricity be not accumulated to such a degree that the conductor comes within the striking distance. This last case, as we shall see hereafter, may take place spontaneously, in consequence of a very great charge, even when the separating medium is glass.

Accumulated Electricity.

401. When we cause the inferior surface of the plate to communicate with the ground, and then electrify the superior, this last receives a much greater quantity of electricity than when both are insulated. A glass plate electrified in this manner is said to be *charged*, and the electricity is said to be *accumulated*, because its effects are strikingly distinguished from those of the ordinary electricity hitherto considered. If we touch only the lower surface, no effect is produced, because its free electricity has passed into the earth; if we touch the upper surface only, we receive its electricity, not like that of the conductor, by a single spark, but by several small sparks, producing a sharp sensation, and succeeding each other rapidly. Finally, if we touch both surfaces at once, we receive the whole electricity of the plate by one strong discharge, which not only produces a painful sensation in the part to which it is directed, but also in both arms, and especially at the elbow joints; it is called the electric *shock*, and is never produced by the feeble degrees of electricity obtained in the ordinary way. This discharge of the glass plate may not only be effected by the hands, but by any other conducting communication between the metallic surfaces. If we continue to charge the plate the electricity always accumulates, till a *spontaneous* discharge takes place, by means of a spark from the upper surface, which traverses the glass to the lower surface, and often breaks the plate. It is also a circumstance worthy of remark, that this accumulated electricity does not, in general, act so strongly upon the electrometer as free electricity. We may be convinced of this by causing a quadrant electrometer to communicate with the upper surface of the plate while it is charging, or what amounts to the same, by attaching it to the conductor.*

402. It is truly surprising to see how easily all these phenomena are explained by the hypothesis of Symmer.

If the conductor furnishes vitreous electricity, this accumulates upon the upper surface of the plate, until its sphere of activity ex-

---

* For, notwithstanding the great quantity of electricity accumulated, the electrometer will only indicate a feeble tension, on account of the attractive action of the opposite electricity, spread over the other surface of the plate.

tends through the glass to the lower surface. Then the lectricity of the upper surface neutralizes the resinous electricity of the lower surface; but as each combination is reciprocal, it is itself neutralized to a certain degree, and thus the upper surface is placed to a certain point in a non-electric state, at least as long as it does not contain more vitreous electricity than it might have received without this combination. But the vitreous electricity becoming free on the lower surface, passes off and gives place to the new combined electricity which comes from the ground. This is decomposed by the vitreous electricity which is accumulated on the upper surface, like that which existed there before, and it will be easily seen that this operation will continue without interruption, so long as the upper surface receives an excess of vitreous electricity. But while the electricity thus accumulates, the striking distance extends farther into the glass; and, if it attains the lower surface, a spontaneous discharge will take place.

If we discharge the plate before this happens, all the electricity accumulated on the upper surface, combines instantaneously with all the electricity accumulated on the lower surface, by the shortest course which is offered to it, and produces the electric shock at the moment of the instantaneous passage through the body.

The diminution of the electricity upon the electrometer arises from this; that the two electricities can only take effect in the free state, and on the plate they exist in a certain state of combination. This combination, however, is not a real union of the two fluids, since this takes place afterward by the discharge. Each of the electricities adheres to the surface to which it is brought; but in their proximity the action of the one represses that of the other.

403. If we cover the upper surface with a substance which conducts electricity badly, for example, with a varnish mixed with metallic powder, the plate becomes charged, but the electricity does not diffuse itself tranquilly over the surface; on the contrary, it darts from the middle towards all the sides in serpentine streaks. If we cause the lower coating to communicate with the edge of the upper by means of a strip of tin foil, it will still be charged; but when the electricity is accumulated to a certain degree a spontaneous discharge takes place through the strip of tin foil, which gives beauty to the phenomenon. Such a plate is called a *magic square*.

404. As the form of the glass plate for this experiment is entirely arbitrary, we ordinarily use, in the production of accumulated electricity, the apparatus called the *Leyden jar*. The arrangement now considered best for this purpose is the following. We coat the interior and exterior surfaces of a glass jar with tin foil, except an inch or two at the top, which is usually covered with sealing-wax dissolved in alcohol, because such a covering insulates better than the glass alone. The interior coating is charged immediately by the conductor; and in order to charge it more conveniently, a small metallic rod is inserted into the jar, reaching three or four inches beyond the mouth, and having the outer extremity terminated with a ball; the lower extremity is attached to a round plate of lead, which adapts itself exactly to the bottom of the jar. This rod is supported at the top of the jar, by passing through a pasteboard cover, covered with sealing-wax, near the place where the interior coating ends.

In order to charge the jar, we take it in the hand, and present the ball to the conductor; or else we place it on the table, and cause the ball to communicate with the conductor by means of a chain.*

405. As it would be dangerous to discharge very great quantities with the hands, we employ for this purpose a particular instrument called a *discharger*. It consists of a curved metallic rod, rounded at the two extremities, and terminated by two balls; sometimes one end has a ring and the other a ball. We place one end in contact with the exterior coating of the jar, and touch the ball of the jar with the other. In this way the whole charge passes through the metallic arc, without creating the least sensation in the hands. The discharger is still more convenient when it consists of two metallic arcs, moveable upon an insulating handle of dry wood coated with sealing-wax; so that we can vary at pleasure the distance between the two extremities; one of which is commonly terminated by a ring, and the other by a ball.

---

* It is asserted in many works, that thick glass is less liable to break than thin. But this is not true. The jars made by Elckner, of Berlin, like all other instruments of this skilful artist, are made with great care; they never break by an artificial discharge, and support almost all spontaneous discharges; and they owe this superiority to being very thin, and of a density as nearly uniform as possible. If the explanation we have given of the sphere of activity be correct, this fact agrees perfectly with the theory.

406. The discovery of accumulated electricity was made in the year 1745, at the same time, by two observers; the prebendary Kleist, at Cammin, and Muschenbroeck at Leyden. Hence the jar is called the *Leyden jar* or *jar of Kleist*, and the experiment itself the *Leyden experiment*.

407. By means of the Leyden jar, a variety of instructive and amusing experiments may be performed. With respect to the first we shall only remark what follows.

The discharge always takes place when we establish a communication between the two coatings of the jar, whatever be the extent of this communication. We may, therefore, give the electric shock to a great number of persons at the same time, if they join hands, the first in the series touching the outer coating of the jar, and the last the ball at the end of the rod.

If electricity be left to pass either through a good or a bad conductor, it takes the former and does not touch the latter. For this reason we may hold the discharger in the hand, without experiencing any shock. When, however, the passage through a bad conductor is much the shorter, the electricity will sometimes follow this instead of the other.

The chain of communication may even be interrupted at one or several places; and, provided the distance is not too great, the discharge takes place, yet with this difference, that at each interruption the passage is attended with a spark which gives a shock.

408. When we wish to augment the effect of the Leyden jar as much as possible, we unite several jars together, and thus form what is called the *electric battery*, a communication taking place between all the exterior coatings, and also between all the interior. The first is easily effected by placing all the jars on the same sheet of tin foil; and the last by joining all the rods or their balls with a metallic rod.

This apparatus is charged from the machine, by causing the conductor to communicate with the interior surface of one of the jars by means of a wire or chain.

We cannot determine, in general, how many times the plate must be turned to obtain a complete charge, since this depends not only upon the size of the machine, but also upon the state and temperature of the air.

As the effects of a charged battery are such as to render it necessary to be on our guard, it is to be regretted that no means have been devised for determining with certainty to what degree the battery is charged. Under these circumstances we must make the best use of the imperfect indications which are in our power. 1. In each case we should count how many times we have turned the plate, in order to obtain a rule from the first experiment to guide us in the next. 2. The quadrant electrometer should always be placed upon the conductor and observed. It rises, indeed, much more slowly by the charge of a battery than by the electricity of a single conductor, or the charge of a single jar; but we may deduce from its state during the first experiment a rule for those which follow; and we may also observe, to a certain degree, the progress of the charge in the first experiment. 3. Before beginning the experiment, we place on the metallic communications which unite the interior surfaces, a metallic rod terminated at the two extremities by a ball about $\frac{1}{4}$ of an inch in diameter, and prolonged to some inches beyond the battery. From time to time we apply the ball of an insulated discharger to one of the extremities of this rod. At a certain distance a spark is obtained, and this distance affords a tolerable indication of the force of the charge. For a battery of 20 or 30 quart jars a distance of half an inch indicates a very powerful charge. 4. If upon observing what passes in the battery we hear a crackling noise, we should hasten to discharge it, for this indicates either that there is one damaged jar, or that a spontaneous discharge is about to take place.

We should carefully avoid a spontaneous discharge, because this almost always breaks one or more jars. The artificial discharge is made in the same manner as for a single jar, by establishing a communication between the two coatings.

409. The effect of the battery increases with the number of jars employed, or rather with the extent of coated surface.

Regard must also be paid to the force of the electrical machine employed. The more feeble it is, the longer is the time required to charge the battery, and the greater is the quantity of electricity lost by contact with the air, which obstructs the charging.

410. The universal discharger of Henley is an almost essential appendage to an electric battery. It is constructed as follows. Upon a small board about 12 inches in length, and 6 or 8 in breadth, are screwed near the extremities, two insulating columns 8 or 10 inches high. Each of them supports a metallic rod placed transversely and terminating at one end in a ring, and at the other in a ball, or in

a point, when the ball is unscrewed. These metallic rods are attached to the column by means of a socket and hinge, in such a manner as to have three kinds of motion. Each rod moves forward and backward in a tube, and turns horizontally and vertically. Between the two columns is a small table of dry wood, which may be raised, depressed, or taken away at pleasure. Upon the small table is also a plate of the same size, fitted with screws so as to form a press.

In order to make use of this apparatus, we attach one of the ends of a metallic chain to the ring of one of the transverse rods, and the other to the exterior coating of the battery. We put the body to be submitted to the shock, upon the small table, or press it between the two plates; then we give to the balls of the two metallic rods a suitable situation and distance with respect to the body; we attach the ring of the common discharger to the ring of the second metallic rod, and touch with the ball of the common discharger, the interior coating of the battery. Then, as will be easily seen, the electric spark is obliged to pass through the body which is placed between the two balls of the universal discharger.

411. Among the innumerable experiments which are made with an electric battery we shall mention only the following. Birds and other small animals are killed instantaneously by the discharge of a battery. To make the experiment upon larger animals, it is necessary to use much caution. Caterpillars appear to form an exception, and are capable of sustaining the discharge of a battery.

The spark from a battery passes through a plate of thin glass, with a great noise, but without shivering it; it only makes a hole almost imperceptible.

It pierces through several folds of paper or pasteboard, a pack of cards, sheets of tin or lead; and it is remarkable that the perforations in the case of paper have a sort of burr projecting each way from the middle. The electric spark renders red hot, melts, or burns fine metallic wires. It is very easy to make this experiment, even with small batteries, if we take a small portion of a very fine wire, for example, one of the smallest steel chords used in pianos.

A leaf of gold or silver, pressed between two plates of glass, forms an incrustation on the glass by the electric spark. A leaf which contains alloy, loses by the operation a part of its colour in several places, which is the effect of an incipient oxydation.

If we apply the two balls of Henley's discharger to the surface of water, at 5 or 6 inches from one another, the discharge takes place with a loud report. If we hold the finger in the water during the discharge we experience a certain sensation. Undoubtedly the vapour above the water favours the discharge.

If we put the balls of the discharger in water, at a small distance from each other, the spark appears in the water between the balls, which gives the water a singular motion.

CHAPTER XXXV.

Electrophorus and Condenser.

412. Alexander Volta of Pavia, has enriched the electrical apparatus with several very remarkable instruments, among which are the electrophorus and condenser. It is the characteristic of the discoveries of this philosopher, that no part is the result of chance; the whole is the fruit of study, and of the application of theoretical principles.

Electrophorus.

413. This instrument consists of a circular plate of tin, surrounded by a border slightly raised. Its size is very variable. Some are only a few inches in diameter, and others are 2 or 3 feet. The border should be raised in proportion to the size, or about $\frac{1}{8}$ of an inch in the smallest, and an inch in the largest. It is filled with resin, sealing-wax, sulphur, or other resinous composition. Care should de taken that the surface be free from cracks and inequalities of every kind.

The third and last essential part is the *cover*. It consists of a circular plate, the diameter of which is smaller by $\frac{1}{8}$ or $\frac{1}{10}$, than that of the part above described. It should be of some conducting substance, and have no angle or prominence. If it is of tin, the border should be rounded; but then it is difficult to preserve it perfectly plane, and without inequalities; for which reason it is better to make it to consist of several pieces of pasteboard placed one upon the other and covered with tin foil. We suspend it by three silk cords, like the scale of a balance, or furnish it with a glass handle. Lastly, it must be capable of being removed separately.

414. We excite the electricity of the resinous plate by rubbing it with cat-skin, or the tail of a fox, perfectly dry, which gives it the resinous electricity.

The properties which distinguish the electrophorus will appear from the following experiments;

(1.) If we place the cover upon the electrified resinous plate, the electricity is preserved there several days, and even weeks. Hence the name *electrophorus* or *bearer of electricity*.

(2.) If we place an electrometer upon the cover, before placing it upon the resinous plate, and then bring it gradually towards the plate, the threads of the electrometer will diverge as it approaches. The cover is, therefore, electrified, and its electricity is the same as that of the resinous plate. But if we remove the cover without touching it, the threads collapse, and in proportion to the distance; so that when it is without the sphere of activity of the plate, all signs of electricity disappear.*

(3.) If we replace the cover, and touch it before taking it away, or what is still better, if we touch at the same time, and with the same hand, the metallic part of the plate and the cover, the finger which touches the cover receives a slight spark, and the threads of the electrometer collapse, so that the cover will seem no longer to possess any electricity. But if we now remove it by the insulating handle, the threads of the electrometer will diverge and remain at a certain distance when it is without the sphere of activity of the plate; the cover is therefore electrified, but with a different electricity from that of the plate. If we again replace the cover, the threads collapse, and all signs of electricity disappear; but if we touch the

---

* When we make this experiment, the cover must not be suffered to remain too long in contact with the resinous plate, or even in its sphere of activity; for, as the natural electricity of the cover is decomposed, and the vitreous part only is retained by the attraction of the plate, while the resinous is repelled, the latter has a tendency to escape. It is this which causes the threads to diverge. Now as the surrounding air never produces a perfect insulation, a part of the electricity escapes in this way; and though the effect is inconsiderable during a short interval of time, yet as it is constantly repeated, the plate will in time be discharged of its resinous electricity, precisely as if we had touched it; and we can perceive its successive diminutions by the gradual collapsing of the threads.

cover before replacing it, we receive a considerable spark, by which all its electricity is taken away.

(4.) We can repeat this experiment as often as we please, and alternately take sparks from the cover, when removed and when replaced, without diminishing the electricity of the plate.

415. After what has been said in the preceding chapter, respecting the sphere of activity, these phenomena require little explanation. The only new circumstance here exhibited, is, that there is no true *communication*, but simply a *separation* of electricity, when we place the cover on the plate. We have already seen that the form of bodies has a great influence upon the communication of electricity; and that the communication is more difficult, in proportion as the body offers fewer points or angles. The electrophorus then teaches us a new law of communication; *between two plane surfaces, one of which is of a conducting nature and the other a non-conductor, there can be no communication.*

416. The electrophorus may supply the place of the electrical machine in a great number of cases; for when it is once electrified, it is, if we may so speak, an inexhaustible source of electricity. By means of it we can even charge Leyden jars, and give them either kind of electricity at pleasure. For this purpose, we place two jars near the electrophorus, and cause the exterior coating of one to communicate with the metallic cover. This jar takes sparks from the cover when it is on the resinous plate, and the other jar takes sparks from it when it is removed. The first is, therefore, charged with resinous electricity, and the second with vitreous. But it takes a long time to obtain powerful charges, unless the electrophorus is very large.

417. We shall here mention an easy method of accumulating electricity on the plate. We charge a jar with electricity by means of the electrophorus or machine, and place it on the plate; this being done, we take it by the knob, and move it over the electrophorus; in this manner all the vitreous electricity of the jar passes gradually into the hand, and the plate as gradually takes all the resinous electricity, which it retains combined, and thus its electricity is augmented.

418. Among the experiments to be performed only with the electrophorus, there is one which consists in producing certain appearances called *Lichtenberg's figures*. We charge two jars with different electricities. We take each of them by the outer coating,

and draw figures on the resinous plate with the knobs, having previously removed all other electricity from the plate, by rubbing it and then wiping it with a linen cloth. This being done, we spread some fine powder over the resinous plate, as sulphur 1, red lead, &c. and the figures traced by one and the other of these electricities, are easily distinguished by means of the particles of powder, which arrange themselves about the outlines of the figures.

Condenser.

419. Great pains have lately been taken to examine the feeble degrees of electricity which are manifested in many cases. It is important, therefore, to be acquainted with the instruments necessary for such investigations. The principle one, besides very sensible electrometers, is the condenser of Volta, by means of which the most feeble quantities of electricity may be detected and observed.

420. The construction of the condenser may be varied in different ways, but it is always extremely simple. The essential parts are the *cover* and the *base*. The cover is disposed like that of the electrophorus, only it is commonly smaller, being from 2 to 5 inches in diameter. It is convenient to have it of metal, the lower surface being polished. The *base* is a plate of a little larger diameter; it should be made of some non-conducting substance, or if we use a conductor, it should be covered with some substance which will not allow the electricity to penetrate it. Commonly it is a polished disc covered with taffeta or a thin layer of varnish. We might also use dry marble, or dry wood varnished, &c.; or, since the air is a bad conductor, we may place three small glass plates upon a table as a support, and put the cover above them; thus making the stratum of air below answer for a base.

421. In the electrophorus the resinous plate is electrified; in the condenser we communicate the feeble quantity of electricity, which is to be examined, directly to the cover while it is on the base. So long as it remains on the base, it shows scarcely any signs of electricity; but if we remove it, it produces a sensible effect upon the electrometer, and even gives sparks. We might make the experiment with the small quantity of electricity which a jar retains after a discharge.

422. From what has already been said, the theory of the condenser presents no difficulty. There is no communication between the cover and the base; consequently the electricity communicated to the cover forms a sphere of activity. If we give the vitreous electricity to the cover, it neutralizes to a certain degree, the natural resinous electricity of the base, and is, of course, itself neutralized to the same degree. In this way, as with the jar, the cover is capable of accumulating more electricity; it therefore absorbs all the electricity of the bodies which are presented to it; but this electricity is entirely or nearly disguised, as long as the cover is placed upon the base; but when removed beyond the sphere of activity of the base, the electricity becomes free and manifests itself in the usual way.

It will be readily seen how this instrument, so useful for measuring small quantities of electricity, may be applied in other cases.

CHAPTER XXXVI.

Electricity Excited by other Means beside Friction.

423. Several philosophers of the last century, and particularly Nollet, Winkler, and Franklin, conceived, about the same time, the idea that lightning was an electrical phenomenon. But the celebrated Franklin not only had the incontestable merit of deciding the question by actual experiment; but he acquired a lasting fame also by the invention of lightning rods. A detailed exposition of the theory of thunder and lightning belongs rather to physical geography than to mechanical philosophy; still we have introduced the subject here, because it furnishes evidence, in a striking manner, that there is in nature the means of exciting a powerful electricity, of which we have yet perhaps no knowledge; for we have not the slightest reason to believe that the electricity which manifests itself in thunder and lightning, is produced by the friction of air against air, or of air against the vapour of water. The following circumstance demands some attention. During a shower, the atmosphere being filled with the vapour of water and drops of rain, has a communication of a conducting nature with the ground, by which a very considerable quantity of electricity is insensibly drawn from the cloud. But, as very powerful discharges take place in the mean time, and are often con-

tinued for several hours, we are compelled to admit, that there is some constant operation in the cloud itself, by which so great a quantity of electricity becomes free, that the conducting power of the air cannot convey it away, or even sensibly diminish it. As to the manner in which this phenomenon takes place, we are unable to offer any satisfactory theory.

424. Friction is undoubtedly the most active means of exciting electricity; and it is certain that electricity is always excited whenever two bodies are rubbed together, especially if they are not homogeneous. It may be that this electricity does not produce a sensible effect, either on account of its feeble intensity, or because it is immediately conveyed off by the conducting media which are presented to it. But we are now acquainted with other means of exciting electricity, besides friction, though only in feeble degrees.

Among these means we should first mention the great influence which heat and cold have upon electrical phenomena. They change the conductibility of bodies. Glass, heated to redness, becomes a conductor; and ice, in a state of extreme cold [below — 13 of Fahrenheit] becomes a non-conductor. Siliceous earth, heated in a crucible, shows an electric attraction for the sides of the vessel. The electrical phenomena presented by a heated tourmaline, are exceedingly curious.

A vast field for research is here open to chemists; for there is reason to believe that in each chemical combination, changes are produced in the electric state of bodies. Indeed traces of electricity are discovered when water passes to a state of vapour; when charcoal is consumed; when sulphur, wax, and resin are melted; and, according to the acute observation of Lavoisier and Laplace, when iron is dissolved in sulphuric acid, &c.

It is exceedingly desirable that chemists should complete the investigation of this subject; for it may lead to the most interesting results. It is obvious how necessary it is in such inquiries to have instruments capable of rendering sensible the slightest degrees of electricity.

Galvanism.

425. The most important discovery that has been made in our time on this subject, is that of the developement of electricity by the simple contact of two metals, one of which takes the vitreous, and the other resinous electricity. This discovery has given rise to new and remarkable results. Means have been discovered of considerably augmenting the electricity obtained in this way, and it is thus found to produce effects which are absolutely peculiar to it; so that some philosophers still question its perfect identity with common electricity.* All that belongs to this new discovery has received the name of *galvanism*, from Galvani, a philosopher of Bologna, who first observed the phenomenon which has led to these researches; yet we owe to the sagacity of Volta, all the most important discoveries connected with the subject.

426. In 1791, Galvani accidentally perceived that the thigh of a frog, separated from the body and skinned, experienced contractions, when made to communicate with two metals, one in contact with the nerve, and the other with the muscle. He afterwards found this phenomenon to take place equally in every part of the animal, but that the irritability of the muscle necessary to produce it, continued only a short time after death. These experiments were soon repeated with various modifications throughout Europe. We shall state the most interesting facts which have been made known by Galvani and others.

(1.) The experiment succeeds with all the metals, and even with some other bodies, as charcoal, plumbago, &c.; but it is best to employ zinc in connexion with gold, silver, or copper.

(2.) Instead of two metals we may employ a kind of galvanic chain of several bodies, one end terminating in a nerve, and the other in a muscle. The effect takes place as soon as the circuit is completed. But it appears that all bodies are not equally adapted to this purpose; and that the distinction between conductors and non-conductors of electricity obtains here also.

---

* This might have been true when the author wrote; but since Volta proposed his ingenious theory, there has been but one opinion among enlighted inquirers on the subject.

(3.) It is not necessary that one end of the chain should terminate in a nerve and the other in a muscle; both may be terminated by a nerve or by the muscular fibres which communicate with the nerve.

(4.) The presence of water appears to be an essential condition of this phenomenon; for when the parts of the animal placed in contact, are not moist, there is no effect, or at most a very feeble one.

(5.) The experiment may be performed upon animals of whatever kind, and even upon the separate parts of the human body. But the irritability continues longer after death in cold-blooded animals, than in the warm-blooded.

(6.) The contact of two metals also produces striking effects upon the living body. If we place two pieces of different metals upon one or two incisions made in any part of the body, we experience a sharp pain, when the two metals are brought into contact.* If we put a piece of zinc under the tongue, and a piece of silver above it, and bring the pieces of metal into contact, we experience a decidedly acid taste. If we change the order of the pieces of metal the taste is different, and according to some, alcaline. If we place one piece of metal against the internal angle of the eye, and the other between the lower lip and the jaw, we see at the moment of contact, a flash nearly resembling distant lightning. Some also pretend they perceive a very subtile difference in the light, when the order of the metals is changed.

427. At first, philosophers differed much in the explanation they gave of these phenomena. Some thought they had discovered a new natural force, which acted only upon the animal organization, and which, therefore, ought to be termed *animal electricity*. Many considered these as purely electrical phenomena, but disagreed in their explanation. Galvani supposed that in the living state, the interior of the nerves contained vitreous electricity; that the muscles or exterior envelope of the nerves contained resinous electricity, and that these experiments were analogous to the discharge of a Leyden jar. Volta, on the contrary, had observed that the simple contact of

---

* This experiment was performed by M. Humboldt; applying pieces of gold to two blisters made on his shoulder, he experienced all the effects here described; and this discovery suggested several important physiological remarks.

two metals, excited in both a feeble degree of electricity, so that resinous electricity could be detected in the one, and vitreous in the other; and he maintained that this property, taken in connexion with the well known susceptibility of the nerve to the action of the feeblest degree of electricity, furnished the true explanation of these phenomena. This opinion appears to be confirmed by all the experiments that have been since made.

Voltaic Pile, or Galvanic Battery.

428. Volta was led by reasoning alone, and not by conjecture, to the discovery of a method, by which this kind of electricity might be wonderfully augmented; this is called the *Voltaic pile*. In order to construct it, we place silver and zinc, or copper and zinc plates, alternately one above the other, and separate each pair by a piece of cloth moistened with water or a saline solution. The order must continue the same throughout the series; thus silver, zinc, water, &c., so that the two extremities of the pile shall terminate with different metals. Each extremity takes the name of *silver* or *zinc pole*, according to the metal which terminates it. In order to observe the effects in a satisfactory manner, the pile should consist of at least 50 pairs. The plates may be about the size of a crown or dollar. We shall speak in particular of the effect of larger plates.

In general, the column is disposed in such a manner as to be completely insulated. We often begin and end the pile by double plates, between which is interposed a thin strip of brass, leaving on one side a small projection, to which wires may be attached in performing the experiments.

429. The most remarkable phenomena exhibited by such a pile are the following:

(1.) If we attach wires to the extremities of the pile, and take one of these in each hand, we experience a painful sensation which is repeated continually, as long as the communication is kept up. This effect is more energetic when the hands are moistened; and still more so, when we take a piece of wet metal in each hand, the wires communicating with these; or when the extremities of the wires are immersed in a vessel of water, and we touch the water with both hands.

The effect of the pile may be produced upon any part of the body, and through a number of persons forming an arc of communication.

(2.) The luminous appearance mentioned in article 426, may easily be produced and varied by means of the pile. For this purpose we have only to take one of the wires in the moist hand, and bring the other to the eye also moistened, or to the tongue. In the last case we experience, moreover, an extremely acrid taste. All the phenomena of articles 425, 426, become more conspicuous and striking by means of the pile.

(3.) When we cause the wires to communicate with two very delicate electrometers, they manifest feeble, but unequivocal signs of electricity. The zinc pole always exhibits vitreous electricity, and the silver or copper pole resinous. These electricities may be observed still better by means of a small condenser.

With this apparatus we can charge small jars, trace the figures of Lichtenberg on the electrophorus, &c.

(4.) If we attach an iron wire to one pole and touch the other pole with the same wire, we perceive a spark.* The experiment is more certain when we envelope the extremity of the iron wire in a thin gold leaf. This leaf is consumed at the place through which the spark passes. By means of gold leaf we can also inflame detonating gas, phosphorus, sulphur, &c.

(5.) The most important experiment performed with the pile belongs to chemistry. But it is so remarkable that we cannot omit noticing it. We refer to the decomposition of water. To effect this, we fill a glass tube with distilled water and close both extremities with cork stoppers. The wires attached to the two poles are made to pass through these stoppers and terminate in the water at the distance of a few lines from each other. The ends of the wires are commonly sharpened, but this is not essential. The wires may be of silver or any grosser metal. In the latter case we observe the following phenomena. The extremity of the wire attached to the silver or copper pole, disengages bubbles from the water, which accumulate in the upper part of the tube. Having collected a sufficient quantity of the gas for examination, we find it to be hydrogen, one

---

* If we attach two very fine wires to the poles, and bring their extremities gradually into contact, an attraction takes place, which retains them together.

of the constituent principles of water. The extremity of the wire connected with the zinc pole, is covered with the oxyde of the metal of which the wire is formed, which proves that oxygen has been disengaged at this wire. Thus we find the two constituent principles of water.

When the two wires are of platina or pure gold, gas is disengaged from each; hydrogen, as before, from that connected with the copper pole, and oxygen from that connected with the zinc. In this case we employ a recurved tube in the form of the letter V, for the purpose of collecting and examining the two gases separately. This decomposition may also be effected by common electricity, but not so conveniently nor so abundantly.

(6.) In general, the electricity of the pile is much more efficient in its chemical effects, than in those which are mechanical. In the pile itself, we not only perceive a decomposition of the water with which the interposed cloths are wet, but also, when a saline solution is used, we perceive a decomposition of the salt, which strongly attacks and oxydates the metallic plates between which the cloths are placed. On this account many have thought that the electricity of the pile is to be attributed rather to this chemical action, than to the contact of the metals; but the principles established by Volta, as well as the experiments themselves, are opposed to such a supposition.

430. From some late experiments, it appears that the intensity of some of its effects is in proportion to the height of the pile or the number of pairs, while that of others depends upon the size of the plates.

The effects produced upon the bodies of animals, vary with the number of pairs; but the greater or less size of the plates seems to have little or no influence. On the contrary, the chemical effects are much more powerful when the plates are 6 or 8 inches in diameter, than when they are only 2 or 3. There is reason to believe that no metal is capable of resisting the heat of the electric pile. Silver, gold, and platina, melt and become oxydated with a beautiful blue light, that is, they burn. But the metal must be reduced to very thin leaves before it is employed for this purpose.

Relations of Electricity and Galvanism.

431. It is remarkable that among the many strong resemblances between electricity and galvanism, we nowhere find a perfect accordance. The sensation produced by the pile, is very different from that produced by the jar. With small plates we obtain only a feeble spark; with large plates, the chemical effects of the spark far exceed those of common electricity. The phenomena of attraction and repulsion, as well as the charging of jars, are produced by the pile with great difficulty; whereas water is decomposed with much greater facility by means of the pile, than by common electricity. Insulation, without which most of the experiments made with common electricity do not succeed, appears to be of little importance in most of the experiments which are performed by means of the pile; yet this condition becomes essential when we wish to produce an effect on the electrometer, or charge a jar or condenser. The presence of water is entirely unnecessary in most electrical experiments; but becomes an essential condition for nearly all galvanic experiments.

Nevertheless, as all these differences result rather from diversities of intensity, than from actual anomalies in what constitutes the phenomena, we cannot doubt the identity of the force which is exerted in the two cases. Indeed, we may easily conceive that there must be a great difference in the effects, when we reflect that almost all the phenomena of common electricity are produced by an instantaneous motion of the electric matter; whereas the phenomena of galvanism are produced simply by a constant current of this matter.

Addition.

432. To complete the view of galvanism presented by the author, and to show its resemblance in all respects to common electricity, I have thought it proper to annex a report made to the French National Institute, on the subject of Volta's experiments.

The first galvanic phenomena consisted in muscular contractions excited by the contact of a metallic arc. Galvani and many others regarded them as the result of a particular kind of electricity, inherent in animals. Volta first showed that the animal arc made use of in these experiments, served only to receive and manifest the galvanic influence. He considered the muscular irritation, which was first thought to be the most important part of the phenomenon, as nothing more than the effect of the electric action produced by the mutual contact of the metals, of which the exciting arc was formed. This opinion which found many advocates and many opposers, led to a variety of experiments intended to support or refute it; and the effect was such as is always witnessed in the infancy of discoveries. A multitude of apparent anomalies presented themselves, which were absolutely inexplicable, on account of the delicate circumstances accompanying them, the influence of which was not yet known.

433. Such was the state of this branch of science when the committee on galvanism made their first report to the Institute. Their aim was to determine accurately the conditions necessary for developing and modifying the galvanic effects. They did not attempt to explain them; but confined themselves to a mere statement of facts, in the order which seemed most proper. At this time the researches by which Volta had endeavoured to connect with his first discovery all the phenomena which galvanism presented, were unknown in France. This distinguished philosopher has since recognised many other facts which he has combined together in an ingenious theory. If there still remains something to be done in order to determine with exactness the laws of this singular action, and subject them to a rigorous calculation, the principal facts which are to serve as a basis, seem to be firmly established.

434. The principal fact from which all the rest are derived, is the following. If two different metals, insulated, and having only their natural quantity of electricity, are brought into contact, and then withdrawn, we find them in different electric states, one being positive and the other negative.

This difference, which is very small at each contact, being successively accumulated in a condenser, becomes sufficient to produce a sensible divergence in the threads of the electrometer. The action is not exerted at a distance, except when different metals are in contact; it continues during the contact, but its intensity is not the same for all metals.

It is sufficient to take, for an example, copper and zinc. By their mutual contact the copper is electrified negatively, and the zinc positively.

After having proved the developement of metallic electricity, independently of every moist conductor, Volta introduced these conductors.

435. If we form a metallic plate, consisting of two pieces, one of zinc and one of copper, soldered end to end, and taking the zinc extremity between the fingers, apply the other extremity, of copper, to the upper plate of the condenser, which is likewise of copper, this will be charged negatively; as is evident from the preceding experiment.

If, on the contrary, we take the copper end between the fingers, and touch the upper or copper plate of the condenser, with the zinc extremity, the plate of the condenser on being separated, will be found not to have acquired any electricity, although the lower plate communicates with the common reservoir.

436. But if we place between the upper plate and the zinc extremity a paper moistened with pure water, or any other moist conductor, the condenser becomes charged with positive electricity. If, under these circumstances, we touch the plate with the copper extremity, it still becomes charged, but negatively. These facts admit of no dispute. The following is Volta's explanation of them.

The metals (says he) and probably all bodies, exert a reciprocal action upon their respective electricities, at the moment of contact. When we take the metallic plate by its copper extremity, a part of its electric fluid passes into the other extremity, which is of zinc; but if this zinc is in immediate contact with the condenser, which is also of copper, the latter tends to discharge its fluid with an equal force, and the zinc cannot transmit any to it; the plate must, therefore, be in its natural state after contact. If, on the contrary, we place a moistened paper between the zinc plate and the copper plate of the condenser, the moving property of the electricity, which exists only in the case of contact, is destroyed between these metals; the water which appears to possess this property only in a very feeble degree, compared with the metals, does not prevent the transmission of the fluid from the zinc to the condenser, and this becomes charged positively. Lastly, when we touch the condenser with the copper extremity, the interposed moist paper, the action of which is very feeble, does not prevent the plate of the condenser from transmitting a part of its positive electricity into the zinc extremity, and thus, upon destroying the contact, the condenser is negatively charged.

437. According to this theory it is easy to explain the voltaic pile. For the sake of greater simplicity, suppose it placed on an insulator; and let unity represent the excess of electricity, which a zinc piece must have over a copper one in immediate contact with it.* If the pile is composed of only two pieces, the lower one of copper, and the other of zinc, the electric state of the first will be represented by $-\frac{1}{2}$, and that of the second by $+\frac{1}{2}$.

If we add a third piece, which must be of copper, it will be necessary in order to effect a transmission of the fluid, to separate it from the zinc piece, by a piece of moistened pasteboard, then it will be in the same electric state with the last; at least if we leave out of consideration the proper action of the water, which appears to be very feeble, and perhaps also a slight resistance which the water, as an imperfect conductor, may oppose to the transmission. The apparatus being insulated, the excess of the upper piece can only be acquired at the expense of the copper piece which is below. Then the respective states of these pieces will no longer be as before.

For the lower piece which is of copper, we shall have $-\frac{2}{3}$.

For the second which touches it, and which is of zinc, $-\frac{2}{3}+1$, or $+\frac{1}{3}$;

The third which is of copper, and separated from the preceding, will have the same quantity of electricity; that is, $+\frac{1}{3}$; and the sum of the quantities of electricity lost by the first piece, and acquired by the two others, will be equal to zero, as in the preceding case of two pieces. If we add a fourth piece which will be of zinc, it must have an unit more than that of the copper, which is immediately under it; and as this excess can only be acquired at the expense of the lower pieces, the pile being insulated, we shall have, for the lower piece which is of copper, -1; for the second, which

---

* The quantities of electricity accumulated in a body beyond its natural state, other things being the same, are proportional to the repulsive force with which the particles of the fluid tend to separate from each other, or to repel a new particle which we endeavour to add to them. This repulsive force, which in free bodies, is counteracted by the resistance of the air, constitutes what we call the *tension* of the fluid; this tension is not proportional to the divergence of the straws in Volta's electrometer, or of the balls in that of Saussure; it can be exactly measured only by means of the electric balance.

is of zinc and in contact with the first, 0; that is, it will be in its natural state.

For the third piece, which is of copper, and which is separated from the preceding, we shall have 0; this also will be in its natural state. For the fourth piece, which is of zinc, and in contact with the preceding, we shall have $+1$.

By pursuing the same reasoning we can find the electric states of each piece of the pile, supposing it insulated and formed of any number of elements. The quantities of electricity will increase for each of them, from the base to the summit of the column, in an arithmetical progression, the sum of which will be zero.

438. If, for greater simplicity, we suppose the number of elements even, it is easy to prove by a simple calculation, that the lower piece which is of copper, and the upper piece which is of zinc, must be equally electrified, one positively, the other negatively; and the same is true of any pieces taken at equal distances from the extremities of the pile.

Before passing from the positive to the negative, the electricities will become nothing; and there will always be two pieces, one of zinc and the other of copper, which will be in their natural state; they will be at the middle of the pile; this we have seen, for example, in the case of four pieces.

Suppose now that we establish the communication between the lower piece and the common reservoir; it is evident that this piece, which is negatively electrified, will tend to recover from the ground what it has lost; but its electric state cannot change without changing that of the pieces above it, since the electrical interval between two successive pieces must always be the same when in a state of equilibrium. It follows, that all the negative quantities of the lower half of the pile, will be neutralized at the expense of the common reservoir. Then the state of the pile will be as follows;

The lower piece which is of copper, will have the electricity of the ground, which we shall call zero.

The second piece which is of zinc, and in immediate contact with the preceding, will have $+1$.

The third which is of copper, and separated from the last by moistened paper, will have the same electricity, namely, $+1$.

The fourth which is of zinc, and in contact with the preceding, will have $+2$.

Thus the quantities of electricity will increase upward in arithmetical progression.

439. Then, if we touch with one hand the summit of the pile, and with the other the base, these excesses of electricity will be discharged through the organs into the common reservoir, and will excite a sensation so much the stronger, as this loss repairs itself at the expense of the ground; and there must result an electric current, the rapidity of which being greater in the interior of the pile, than in the organs which are imperfect conductors, will enable the lower part of the pile to recover a degree of tension, approaching that which it had in the state of equilibrium.

The communication being always established with the common reservoir, if we put the summit of the pile in contact with the upper plate of a condenser, whose base communicates with the ground, the electricity which is found at this extremity of the pile, in a very feeble degree of tension, will pass into the condenser, where the tension may be regarded as nothing; but the pile not being insulated, this loss will be repaired at the expense of the common reservoir; the new quantities of electricity, recovered by the upper plate, will pass into the condenser, like the preceding, and will accumulate there to such a degree, that by separating the collector plate we may obtain from it sensible electrometrical signs, and even sparks. As to the limit of this accumulation, it evidently depends upon the thickness of the small stratum of gum lac, which separates the two plates of the condenser; for in consequence of this thickness, the electricity accumulated in the collector plate, being able to act only at a distance upon that of the lower plate, is always greater than that which puts it in equilibrium in this last; and hence results, in the collector plate, a slight tension, which here has for its limit, the tension existing in the upper part of the pile.

In like manner as the electricity of the column accumulates in the condenser, it will also accumulate in the interior of a Leyden jar, whose exterior surface communicates with the common reservoir; and, since the pile continually recharges itself at the expense of this same reservoir, the jar will be equally charged, whatever be its capacity. But its interior tension can never exceed that which exists at the summit of the pile. If we then remove the jar, it will produce the sensation, corresponding to this degree of tension; and this is confirmed by experiment.

440. Such must be the state of things, if we neglect, as very small, the proper action of the water upon the metals, and suppose, 1. That the transmission of the fluid takes place from one couple to

another in the insulated pile, through the pieces of moistened pasteboard which separate them, even when there exists no other communication between the two extremities of the column. 2. That the excess of electricity which the zinc takes from the copper, is constant for these two metals, whether they are in their natural state or not.

Volta established the first proposition by an experiment already referred to, in which the condenser becomes charged, when we touch the collector plate, covered with moistened paper, with the copper extremity of the metallic plate, holding the zinc extremity between the fingers.

The second proposition is the most simple that can be imagined. M. Coulomb made a series of very delicate experiments to verify it, and it appeared to him exact. I have also myself arrived at the same results.

441. Hitherto, for the sake of clearness, we have supposed the pile to be formed of copper and zinc. The same theory would equally apply to any two metals; and the effects of the different arrangements would depend upon the differences of electricity established between them at the moment of contact.

What we have said extends equally to all other bodies between which there exists an analogous action. Thus, although this action appears in general to be very feeble between liquids and metals, yet there are some liquids, as the alkaline sulphurs, between which and metals, the action is very sensible. Accordingly the English have substituted these for one of the metallic elements of the pile; and they were employed at a still earlier date by M. Pfaff in his experiments.

442. Volta discovered between metallic substances a very remarkable relation, which renders it impossible to construct a pile with them alone. We shall state it after his own manner, having never had occasion to verify it. If we arrange the metals in the following order, silver, copper, iron, tin, lead, zinc, each will become positive by contact with that which precedes it, and negative with that which follows it; the electricity will, therefore, pass from the silver to the copper, from the copper to the iron, and so on.

Now the property in question consists in this; that the moving force from the silver to the zinc, is equal to the sum of the moving forces of the metals which are comprehended between them in the series; whence it follows that if we put them in contact in this order or any other we please, the extreme metals will always be in the same state as if they immediately touched each other. Consequently, if we suppose any number of elements thus disposed, the extremes of which are silver and zinc, for example, we should have the same results as if we employed only these two metals; that is, there would be no effect, or it would be the same with that which a single element would produce.

443. As yet it appears that the preceding property extends to all solid bodies; but it does not subsist between them and liquids. Hence it is that we have succeeded in the construction of the pile, by the intervention of liquids. Hence, too, results the division which Volta has made of conductors into two classes; the first comprising solids, the second liquids. No pile has yet been constructed without a suitable mixture of these two classes. It has not been found possible to form it with the first alone; and we do not yet know enough of the mutual action of liquids, to say whether it is the same with respect to them or not.

444. We have supposed that the pieces of moistened pasteboard, placed between the elements of the pile, had imbibed pure water. If we employ, instead of water, a saline solution, the effect becomes very much more powerful; but the tension indicated by the electrometer does not appear to be augmented, at least in the same ratio. Volta has established this fact by means of the *crown of cups*, by filling them successively with pure and acidulated water.

He concludes from this experiment, that the acids and saline solutions favour the action of the pile, chiefly by increasing the conducting power of the water, with which the pasteboard is moistened. As to the oxydation, he regards it as an effect which establishes a closer contact between the elements of the pile, and thus contributes to render its action more sustained and energetic.

I have since verified this opinion by a series of accurate experiments, and have found it to be perfectly correct. Whatever be the substance interposed as a humid body, provided there is the same number of pairs, the condenser is charged to the same degree; only it requires more or less time, according as the substance interposed has a greater or less conducting power.

Such is a brief sketch of Volta's theory of *galvanic* electricity. His aim was to reduce all the phenomena to one, the existence of which is now well established; namely, the developement of electricity by the mutual contact of metals. It appears to be proved by his experiments, that the particular fluid to which, for some time, the muscular contractions and the phenomena of the pile, were attributed, is nothing but common electricity, put in motion by a cause of which we only see the effects, without knowing any thing of its nature.

445. Such is the fate of the sciences, that the most brilliant discoveries only open a field for new researches. After having discovered and estimated, if we may so say, by approximation, the mutual action of the metallic elements, it remains, in order to determine it in a rigorous manner, to see whether it is constant in the same metals, or whether it varies with the quantities of electricity which they contain, and with their temperature. It is necessary to determine with the same precision, the proper action exerted by the liquids upon one another, and upon the metals. When this is done we shall be able to proceed in our calculations upon exact data, and thus ascend to the true law which governs the distribution and motions of electricity in the Voltaic pile, and complete the explanation of all the phenomena which this apparatus presents. But these delicate researches require the use of the most sensible and accurate instruments which have yet been invented, for measuring the force of the electric fluid. Lastly, it remains to examine the chemical effects of the voltaic current, its action upon the animal economy, and its connexion with the electricity of minerals and fishes; these researches cannot fail, from the facts already known, to be very important.

446. When a science, already in an improved state, has received an important accession, new relations are established between the branches which compose it. It is then pleasant to go back to the beginning and retrace the steps by which it has advanced. If we look to the origin of this science, we find it, in the beginning of the last century, reduced to the simple phenomena of attraction and repulsion. Dufay first ascertained the constant laws to which these are subject, and explained their apparent contradictions. His discovery of the two electricities, vitreous and resinous, was the foundation of the science; and Franklin, by presenting it under a new point of view, prepared the way for a theory, to which all the phenomena, even that of the Leyden jar, could be reduced. Epinus perfected this theory by subjecting it to the calculus, and by the aid of analysis arrived at those results which Volta so happily employed in the condenser and electrophorus. The exact law of electric attrac-

tions and repulsions was still wanting. Coulomb proved that it is the same as that of gravity which governs the celestial motions.

At last the phenomena of galvanism presented themselves, apparently differing from all those hitherto observed. In order to explain them, recourse was first had to a particular fluid; but by a course of ingenious experiments, conducted with sagacity, Volta proposed to reduce them all to one single cause, the developement of metallic electricity, made them subservient to the construction of an apparatus which enables us to increase their force at pleasure, and by his results connected them with the most important phenomena of chemistry and the animal economy. [For more minute information upon this subject, the reader is referred to the *Cambridge Course of Natural Philosophy*, vol. ii.]

SECTION VII.

MAGNETISM.

CHAPTER XXXVII.

General Properties of the Magnet.

447. AMONG the different kinds of iron ore that are found in a natural state, there is one in particular which possesses the surprising property of attracting iron by an invisible force. It is true that all the fragments of this kind of ore do not possess this property to the same degree; but it is found in most of them, and even in considerable masses. These are what we call *natural magnets*. We can communicate this property to iron and steel, and thus produce *artificial magnets*. It was formerly thought that the *magnetic force* belonged exclusively to iron; but it is now found to be common to two other metals, nickel and cobalt; and its energy is proportional to the purity of these substances. Yet, as it is difficult to obtain considerable masses of these substances in a state of great purity, all we know of their magnetic properties is, that they are attracted by a magnet. But it would be interesting to inquire, whether, like iron, they are capable of receiving and communicating magnetism.*

---

* I have made this experiment upon fragments of nickel, prepared at Berlin, and given me by M. Berthollet. I formed them into needles by laminating them, and then examined their magnetic force by means of oscillations, a method which will be explained hereafter. I thus found that the magnetic force of nickel was about $\frac{1}{4}$ that of iron of the same weight. It has, like iron, the property of retaining and communicating the magnetic force. But these results are not absolute; since they must vary with the coercive force given to the nickel by hammering.

Relation between the Magnet and Unmagnetized Iron.

448. Iron in the metallic state and in that of black oxyde, attaches itself to the magnet with considerable force. In the last case, however, it must not be strongly oxydated. This force is measured by the weight of iron which the magnet is capable of raising. It does not depend upon the size of the magnet; for there are large magnets which have very little force, and small magnets which have a very great force. Sometimes they will support ten times their own weight. Lastly, experiment shows that the force of the same magnet varies with the positions in which it acts.

449. The magnetic force does not manifest itself with equal intensity at all the points of the surface of a magnet. Ordinarily there are two points of this surface where the action is strongest; sometimes, but rarely, there are more. These places are called the *poles of the magnet.* They are determined by putting the magnet in iron filings. The filings attach themselves much more strongly about the poles, than any where else. We can also discover them by means of a piece of very fine iron wire. At the poles it attaches itself to the magnet by one of its extremities, keeps the other at the greatest distance; and thus remains perpendicular to the surface of the magnet; at any other point it takes an oblique position directed towards the nearest pole. At points equally distant from the two poles, it applies itself longitudinally to the surface.

450. When the two poles are capable of acting at the same time upon the opposite extremities of a piece of iron, the magnetic attraction is augmented. For this reason, we often give to artificial magnets the form of a horse-shoe, of which the two extremities are the poles. We apply to these extremities a piece of soft iron, and load it with as much iron as the magnet is capable of supporting.

451. The magnetic force is exerted, not only in the case of a contact, but also *at a distance.* A common magnet will raise filings without touching them. This force decreases with the distance; but in a magnet of an irregular form, the law of this decrease appears to be very complicated; and although it is easy to determine the intensity of the magnetic force for each distance, by means of a balance, the magnet being placed in it and counterbalanced, yet experiment shows that the law of decrease is so modified by the form, magnitude, and position of the two bodies,

that it becomes very difficult to determine with exactness the proper law and the influence of modifying circumstances.

452. If we place a magnet under a pane of glass, wood, pasteboard, or any other substance, except iron, and cover the surface with iron filings; upon being agitated the filings will arrange themselves in a certain order, and form curved lines extending from one pole to the other, so that we can easily distinguish these points.

This experiment indicates that the magnetic force exerts itself through all bodies, except iron, which according to the manner in which it is placed, increases or diminishes the magnetic effect. We shall find still stronger reasons hereafter, for believing that this force is not at all weakened by the interposition of material bodies. On account of this singular property, it is easy to conceal either the magnet or the iron upon which it acts. And it is in this way that the numerous instruments are contrived, which are used in the tricks of jugglers.

453. We may preserve all the force of a magnet, and even sometimes increase it by taking care to load it with as great a weight as it is capable of supporting. It is also very useful to give the poles their natural situation. If we leave the magnet without being thus loaded, its force gradually diminishes. Very small magnets may be preserved by iron filings. Rust weakens the magnetic virtue; and magnets strongly heated lose entirely their magnetic properties. It has also been observed that a fall, a blow with a stone, or an elecrical discharge, sometimes impairs the magnetic power.

Properties of the Magnet.

454. If by any means whatever, we place a magnet in such a manner that it can move freely in a horizontal direction, it always takes such a position that one of its poles is directed towards the north and the other towards the south. For this reason we call one of these the *north pole* and the other the *south*.

The observation of this property led to the invention of the mariner's compass, which is nothing more than a needle of magnetized steel, placed upon a pivot, and fitted to move freely in a horizontal direction. It is hardly possible to estimate the utility of this simple instrument. Its inventer is not known, and even the time of its invention is uncertain, though it is generally supposed to be between the

12th and 14th century. The ancients, although unacquainted with it, had noticed the attractive property of the magnet.

However little connexion there appears to be, at first view, between the attractive power of the magnet and its polarity, we shall see hereafter that the polarity is simply the effect of the magnetic attraction of the globe.

The Reciprocal Action of Magnets.

455. Two magnets mutually attract each other at determinate points, and this attraction is even greater than that which exists between the magnet and iron. In other points they repel each other; and by means of two magnetized needles, or a magnet and a magnetized needle, we easily verify the following law.

Poles of opposite names attract each other; those of the same name repel each other.

This law furnishes a convenient method of finding the poles of a magnet.

456. As a magnet of considerable force acts at a great distance upon a good magnetized needle, we can easily satisfy ourselves by experiment, that the interposition of bodies does not diminish the magnetic power.

Communication of Magnetism.

457. We can communicate a sensible magnetic force to a small piece of iron, by passing it several times across the pole of a magnet. Only we must take care to pass it always in the same direction; for, by changing the direction, we diminish the magnetism already communicated. One of the best methods of performing this operation is the following. Let ns (*fig.* 56) be a bar of unmagnetized iron, and NS a magnet, of which N is the north pole and S the south pole. We place the magnet upon the iron as indicated in the figure; so that the north pole shall touch the middle of the bar; then pressing it closely to the bar, we move it in the direction NS to the extremity of the bar; this being done, we carry the magnet back to its position, and repeat the operation several times. We next apply the magnet to the other half of the bar, so that the south pole shall touch the middle, and pass it just as many times along this half, in the

direction *SN*. The iron thus acquires a considerable magnetic power.*

This property is communicated rapidly to soft iron, but not durably. Tempered iron receives it less rapidly; but retains it for a much longer time.

When we communicate magnetism with a single magnet we call this operation the *method of single touch*. For the method of *double touch*, the reader must consult more extensive works. [See *Cambridge Nat. Phil.* vol. ii.]

458. It is a general law for all modes of communication, that *the points which are touched last by one of the extremities of the magnet, take poles of the contrary name.* Thus, in the above operation, *n* becomes a north pole, and *s* a south pole.

459. The magnet loses little if any of its force by this process, when it is performed from point to point as we have described, without changing the direction on the same half of the bar. We can, therefore, communicate the magnetic power to any number of iron bars, with the same magnet; and by uniting these, we form a very powerful magnet.

Distribution of Magnetism, and Sphere of Magnetic Activity.

460. As long as a piece of soft iron touches a magnet, or is very near it, it is itself magnetic. But the moment we remove it, the magnetism it had acquired almost entirely disappears.

In this case we say that the iron is not magnetized by communication, but by participation; and the space within which this effect takes place, is called the *sphere of magnetic activity*. Here we discover an analogy between magnetism and electricity.

By means of a magnetized needle we can verify the following law, which holds true in all cases when iron is magnetized by participation.

The iron acquires, in the part near the magnet, a pole of an opposite name, and capable of being attracted by the nearest pole of the magnet; and consequently the other extremity of the iron acquires a pole of the same name with this pole of the magnet, and capable of being repelled by it.

---

* It is better to incline the magnet to the bar 10° or 12°, than to apply it entirely along the surface.

461. This resemblance to electricity has given rise to hypotheses respecting the cause of magnetism, analogous to those of Franklin and Symmer in regard to electricity.*

462. The above law has led to the invention of what is called the *armature* of a natural magnet. It is constructed in the following manner. Let *A s n* (*fig.* 57) be a natural magnet, of which *s* is the south pole and *n* the north pole. A piece of soft iron *BC* is shaped so as to apply itself exactly to the surface, and touch the two poles. Just below these two poles, the iron must have two prominences *S*, *N*. We cover the rest of the magnet with an envelope of copper, *DEF*, and attach a ring at *F*, by which to suspend it. We then apply a piece of soft iron to the two prominences *S*, *N*, in order to load the apparatus more conveniently.

By means of this arrangement, the soft iron becomes itself a magnet, of which the south pole is *S*, and the north pole *N*.

Experience has shown that an armed magnet has a much more active and durable force, than a common magnet.

---

* On the supposition of two magnetic fluids, M. Coulomb observed the motions with all the precision necessary for a complete hypothesis. He caused a small magnetized needle to oscillate at different distances from one of the poles of a very long bar, also magnetized, but in a much less considerable degree. The effect of the magnetic force in producing these oscillations, is analogous to that of gravity in the case of the pendulum, and the oscillations may equally serve to measure the intensity of this force. Now by comparing together the rapidity of these oscillations, M. Coulomb remarked that they became more and more slow, as the needle is removed further from the centre of the magnetic force, which proves that this force diminishes as the distance increases; and from the law of this retardation, he proved by the calculus, that magnetic attraction is always inversely proportional to the square of the distance, like electric attraction and terrestrial gravity. The celebrated astronomer, Tobias Mayer, of Göttingen, had arrived at the same results.

CHAPTER XXXVIII.

More Particular Examination of the Phenomena of the Magnetized Needle.

463. If an unmagnetized steel needle be balanced on a sharp pivot, so as to be perfectly horizontal, the equilibrium will be destroyed upon being magnetized; and, what is very remarkable, its inclination to the horizon will be different in different parts of the earth. In the northern hemisphere the north end of the needle is depressed, in the southern hemisphere the south end. From this phenomenon we must infer that the force which influences the direction of the magnetized needle, is not exerted horizontally, but in a direction considerably inclined to the horizon. If we would observe accurately the phenomena of the magnetized needle, two kinds of needles are necessary; one for the purpose of finding its direction in a horizontal plane, and this is called a *declination needle;* the other for ascertaining the angle it makes with the horizon or *inclination*, and this is called a *dipping needle*.

Declination Needle.

464. In a declination needle the downward tendency of the northern extremity is counteracted by a weight on the opposite extremity for the purpose of preserving it in a horizontal position. After it is magnetized we inclose it in a copper box, and attach to it a graduated paper circle. For purposes of navigation, this circle is divided into 32 parts called *points*. A needle constructed in this way takes different names according to the purpose to which it is destined. If it is to be employed in determining with accuracy the direction of the needle, we call it a *declination compass*. Its length varies from 6 to 12 inches. The needle and the division of the circle must be made with great care. If it is to be used in navigation, it takes the name of *mariner's compass*. With some slight modifications it is also employed by surveyors in measuring angles and in running lines.*

---

* The best way of fitting a magnetic needle for exact experiments, is to suspend it by a silk fibre, as it comes from the silkworm, or an assemblage of these fibres united longitudinally. This kind of sus-

465. If we compare the direction of a declination needle with an astronomical meridian, carefully determined, we shall find that at Paris, for example, the needle does not point exactly north, but deviates about $22\frac{1}{2}°$ towards the west. For this reason we call the direction of the needle the *magnetic meridian* to distinguish it from the astronomical meridian.

466. But the declination is different in different places; when we go to the west or east of Europe, we observe the declination to diminish as we depart, remaining always west, however. On the continent of America, we find a line running nearly south-east through the gulf of Mexico and Brazil, to the Atlantic ocean, in which the declination is nothing. Another similar line traverses Asia and all the Southern Ocean, in the same direction. Beyond these two lines the needle deviates towards the east.

467. The declination, moreover, is not constant in the same place. In the 17th century, the line of no declination, which is now found in America, traversed Europe. Since this time it has been continually moving westward, and the same is true of all the lines which have the same declination.

It is obvious that there must result from this motion, changes of declination for every place. It appears that the western declination increases slowly to a certain limit, which, at Paris, is about $22°$ or $23°$, after which it begins to decrease slowly till it becomes 0, and after remaining a short time in this state, the declination becomes east, increases to a certain limit, retrogrades, becomes 0, and so on. But continued observations for several centuries will be necessary to determine with certainty the periods and laws of this motion. From the observations hitherto made, which were not accurate till within a century and a half, this does not appear to be very regular.*

468. Independently of these great variations, we observe also a slight diurnal motion; but it can be perceived only by means of

---

pension producing no friction and no sensible force of torsion, allows the needle perfect freedom. It is similar to that used for the electric balance, and was originally invented by Dr Gilbert, an English physician.

* It is not certain that the motion is oscillatory, as the author here supposes. For it is a long time since the needle reached its western limit, and it has not yet sensibly retrograded.

large and accurate needles. During the forenoon the north end of the needle declines a little towards the west; in the afternoon it returns with a slow motion towards the east. Graham first observed this motion in 1722. Wargertin and Canton repeated and extended the observations. The latter proved also by experiments that heat has an influence upon magnetism which deserves to be examined.

Dipping Needle.

469. A dipping needle consists of a steel plate several inches long, made thin at the two extremities, provided with a short and slender axis passing through the centre of gravity perpendicularly to the plate, the whole being fitted in such a manner as to give the needle a free vertical motion on its axis. Since it moves about its centre of gravity, it must, before being magnetized, remain balanced in any position whatever in which it is placed. But when magnetized, the north pole will be considerably depressed, at least in Europe. Its inclination to the horizon is measured by means of a graduated circle attached to the support. The construction of such an instrument is attended with many difficulties, and a good dipping needle is rarely to be found.

470. Much care also is required in the use of this instrument, since it must be placed exactly in the direction of the magnetic meridian, in order to indicate the exact inclination. In all other positions the inclination will be too great, and it may even amount to 90°. This will be manifest, if we direct the needle in such a manner as to make a considerable angle with the magnetic meridian, and suppose a thread attached to its point, drawing it toward the magnetic direction.*

---

* Observations may be made in any direction, without knowing the magnetic meridian, by means of the following property, which I believe I was the first to recognize.

If we observe the inclination of the needle, reckoned on the vertical, in any two vertical planes, perpendicular to each other, the square of the tangent of the inclination in the magnetic meridian, is equal to the sum of the squares of the tangents of the observed inclinations.

Let H be the horizontal force which draws the needle in the

471. In consequence of the difficulties attending the construction and use of this instrument, few accurate observations have been made upon the dip of the needle. In Prussia it is estimated at about 71°. The result of the observations hitherto made, may be summed up as follows.

472. The dip is subject to greater variation in different places than the declination. Towards the north it increases; and probably there is a place in North America from 14° to 17° from the north pole, where the needle is entirely vertical. Towards the equator, the inclination diminishes; and in the torrid zone, there is a line encompassing the earth, where the needle is horizontal. This line passes above the equator in our hemisphere, and below it in the other. Beyond this line, the south pole of the needle begins to dip, and the dip increases as we go south; probably in New Zealand, about 35° or 40° from the south pole, there is a place where the needle again becomes vertical.*

---

magnetic meridian, V the vertical force, and i the inclination, reckoned from the vertical; we shall have, in the magnetic meridian

$$\tang i = \frac{H}{V}.$$

For another vertical plane, making an angle a with the magnetic meridian, the horizontal force will not be $= H$; but it will be equal to H decomposed in the direction of this plane; that is, $= H \cos a$. The vertical force will still be V; and the inclination in this plane, reckoned from the vertical, being represented by i', we shall have

$$\tang i' = \frac{H \cos a}{V};$$

or, substituting for $\frac{H}{V}$ its value; $\tang i' = \tang i \cos a$. If we call i'' the inclination in the vertical plane perpendicular to the preceding, shall have $\tang i'' = \tang i \sin a$; squaring these two equations, and adding them together, we shall have $\tang^2 i' + \tang^2 i'' = \tang^2 i$; which is the property enunciated above.

* In a memoir written by M. Humboldt and myself, and founded principally upon his observations, a law is made known which connects all the results of inclination in all parts of the earth, and which, with a modification indicated by observation, would also represent the declination, and the variations of intensity, of the magnetic forces in the different regions of the globe. I have since seen, in a manuscript of Tobias Mayer, that he arrived at similar results.

473. The dip is also different at different times; but the laws of these variations are only deduced from hypothesis, and not from exact observations.

Terrestrial Magnetism.

474. The phenomena exhibited by the two needles authorize or rather oblige us to consider the earth itself as a great magnet; since it acts upon the magnetized needle according to the same laws, by which one magnet acts upon another. Euler proved that by giving to the magnetic poles of the earth, the position which is indicated in article 472, the phenomena of declination and inclination may be completely explained. It will be obvious from what has been said respecting the reciprocal relations of two needles, that the magnetic pole situated in North America, must take the name of south pole, and that which is situated in New Zealand, the name of north pole.

475. It is not improbable that there exists in the interior of the earth a great mass of magnetic iron; for this metal is found to be diffused in such abundance, that every portion of earth contains more or less of it.* Moreover, observations made with the pendulum, render it probable that the interior nucleus of the earth, consists rather of a mass of metal, than of a merely earthy matter. If in addition to this, we admit the observations of Canton, with respect to the influence of heat upon magnetism, we are led to believe that the diurnal motion of the sun from east to west, may cause a westerly retrogradation of the magnetic poles, by reason of which the variations of declination and dip may be explained more naturally, than by supposing with some philosophers a particular motion of the magnet in the earth.

---

* It is more simple to consider, as M. Humboldt and myself have done, the magnetic action of the entire earth, as the resultant of the action of all the magnetic particles, disseminated through it. Still all the hypotheses proposed upon the subject, are to be regarded merely as more or less convenient modes of representing the facts and connecting them together.

Excitation of Natural Magnetism.

476. To complete the view which we have given of magnetism, it is necessary to add that iron exposed to the air for some time, becomes magnetized, especially if it is placed in the direction of the magnetic meridian. This observation has given rise to the following experiment. We place a bar of iron in the exact magnetic direction of declination and dip, and in a very little time the bar becomes magnetized. The effect may be accelerated by rubbing or striking.

477. The name of *animal magnetism* has been improperly applied to certain singular phenomena which take place in the human body, but which have no connexion whatever with the subject we are considering.

Addition.

478. I shall here add some remarks upon the analogies which may now be perceived between electricity and magnetism, and upon the greater or less probability, that these phenomena are really produced by the reciprocal attraction and repulsion of imponderable fluids.

A glance at the most simple magnetic phenomena, as the reciprocal action of magnets, their influence upon iron, the communication of their properties by contact, and even at a distance, the developement of new poles which are formed instantaneously in the points where we break them; all this leads at once to the supposition of two invisible and imponderable principles, residing naturally in each infinitely small particle of iron, or other magnetic metal, without the power, in any case, of leaving these particles to enter others. In conformity to this supposition, when the magnetic metals are first strongly heated, and then suffered to cool slowly, without any action being exerted upon them, the two magnetic principles return, in each particle, to the state of neutrality by which they are disguised. But if an action be exerted upon them, in this state of indifference, by the influence of another magnetized body, we observe that they are separated by this influence in each particle, one of them being attracted and the other repelled. We next find, that in this experiment, the repulsion takes place between the magnetic principles of the same name, and the attraction between principles of different names; and that both of these tendencies vary inversely as the square of the distance; so that they are not sensible in the natural state of combination of the two principles, because these principles act with equal and contrary forces at equal distances. Guided by these laws, we are able to measure the comparative quantities of free magnetism, existing in each point of a magnetized body; by compounding these elementary forces, we are able to calculate the direction and intensity of their total resultant; and the effort of this resultant, although exerted between single magnetic elements, being transmitted to the material particles of magnetized bodies, by virtue of the impermeability which retains the two principles in each of them, indicates the cause, the law, and the measure of the motions which are produced in them, when they are presented to each other after being magnetized. In order to establish the preceding propositions, we need not take any thing for granted respecting the physical nature of the two magnetic principles. But if it be asked what this nature is, it may be answered, that there exists the most complete and perfect analogy between the laws of the two magnetic principles and those of the two electric principles, so that the state and reciprocal action of magnetized bodies are exactly similar, so far as it respects the distribution and law of the forces, to those presented by non conducting bodies, electrified by influence, and by the decomposition of their natural electricities. Now, when we examine the effects of the electric principles in the state of separation and freedom in which we can obtain them, we find by calculation that their distribution in conducting bodies, whether free, or influenced one by the other, is rigorously conformable to the laws of hydrostatic equilibrium, which two material fluids would obey, if they had no sensibly gravity, and if their particles were endued with the double property of repelling those of the same kind, and attracting those of the opposite kind, with an energy reciprocally proportional to the square of the distance. If then we attempt to deduce the mathematical consequences of this constitution, for those cases in which it is possible in the present state of analytical science, we obtain, not vaguely, but rigorously and in abstract numbers, all the singular and minute details which are observed when electrified bodies are presented to each other, when they are removed, and even when they are brought so near as to cause an explosion. Finally, in this last case, the great rapidity with which the equilibrium is restored in all parts of the bodies subjected to experiment, every point taking instantaneously the new quantity of each principle required by the new state of the system and by the hydrostatic formulas which express it; this rapidity is itself a new indication, by which the fluid nature of the electric principles is most strongly characterized. It seems, therefore, to me, that in the present state of the theory of electricity, the whole honour of which is due to the beautiful analysis of M. Poisson, this theory itself, by the fidelity with which all the phenomena conform to it, furnishes the strongest probability, that the electric principles are really fluids, constituted as this theory supposes. And accordingly the exact resemblance which we observe between the effects of the electric and magnetic principles, in the cases where the first are subjected to a coercive force, indicates with equal probability that the two magnetic principles have also a similar constitution; although the independence of the two classes of actions does not allow us to suppose them to be of the same nature. Here, then, we have proceeded as far in the study of nature as we are permitted to go, since, by observing the phenomena we have ascended to their experimental laws; and from the laws to the forces by which they are produced. What yet remains to be done for this branch of science, depends upon the future perfection of mathematical analysis, and the application of chemistry to the determination of the coercive forces, by which the magnetic principles are retained in the particles of bodies; or at least to the determination of the degree of these forces most favourable to magnetic energy.

SECTION VIII.

OPTICS.

CHAPTER XXXIX.

Of Light in General; particularly the Phenomena which depend upon its Motion in a Right Line; or First Principles of Optics.

479. The sense of touch makes known different properties of bodies in the most certain manner; but the sense of sight extends to a far greater number of objects. We should have very few ideas if the powers of our minds were restricted to what our hands are capable of reaching. The sense of sight raises our faculties above the limits of the spot to which our bodies are confined, and introduces us into the immensity of creation. It is thus one of the greatest triumphs of the human mind, that we have been able to extend the power of this sense far beyond the limits which nature seems to have marked out for it. And since the eye furnishes the means of knowing almost every thing in nature, this consideration ought to give a strong interest to the investigation of the laws which govern the phenomena of vision.

480. The science of optics, considered as comprehending the whole theory of light, is in a more advanced state than any other branch of physics. Its history is very important to the philosopher; for it clearly points out the course to be pursued in bringing a science to its highest state of improvement. All the hypotheses that have been proposed respecting the nature of light, although proceeding from such profound men as Descartes, Newton, and Euler, have been of no assistance in the advancement of the science; but the experiments of Newton, Dollond, and some others, have led to a full explanation of the phenomena of Optics.

481. There must be between the eye and the object seen, some material communication by which a distant object is capable of exerting an action upon the sight. We do not know what this medium is, and we seem destined to remain ignorant, since we cannot perceive the medium itself, but only the objects which become visible by its influence. Meantime it is of no consequence to us, whether, as some of the ancients thought, this medium proceeds from the eye to the object; or, whether, according to the opinion of Newton, it proceeds from the object to the eye; or, whether, according to the opinion of Descartes and Euler, there is an exceedingly subtile fluid, the motions of which produce the phenomena of vision, in the same manner as the vibrations of the air produce the phenomena of sound. It is of little importance whether any of these hypotheses be true, provided we know the laws of the phenomena; and these laws have actually been developed almost as perfectly as those of gravity.

482. The unknown cause of vision we call *light*. We can prevent the effects of this medium, but not the cause. Light is produced in an infinite variety of ways; for example, under all circumstances, when steel and flint are brought into collision. Even under water, steel gives sparks. Electric light is visible in water; and steel enveloped in oxygen continues to appear red under water. Light must, therefore, be a substance, which cannot be prevented from penetrating into all bodies, and which is capable of being traversed by all. It must be of a nature entirely different from perceptible substances, since, in treating of it, we have occasion for an entirely different system of mechanics and statics. Indeed, we cannot employ in optics any of the laws of motion developed in the preceding sections*. We shall nowhere find any indication of impenetrability,

---

* Here the author appears to me to go too far. If we wish to consider light in its effects only, without any thing hypothetical respecting its nature, we cannot propose to subject its motions to mathematical calculation. But if we consider it as formed of material particles, endowed with a very rapid rectilinear motion, and capable of being attracted by bodies, then these motions are subject to the laws of ordinary mechanics; it is thus that Newton has deduced by calculation, the laws of refraction. Nevertheless, this constitution of light must be regarded only as an hypothesis, to which, hitherto, we have been able to reduce most of the phenomena of light; for, in reality, there is nothing by which we can be assured that light is

gravity, impulse, &c. If we may hope for any more precise knowledge of the nature of this substance, we are to expect it from chemistry; for light undoubtedly possesses very remarkable chemical properties. Almost every where it is found connected with heat, which is the most important chemical agent in nature. Its effects not only manifest themselves in the varied phenomena of combustion, but in most of the electrico-chemical experiments. The chemist also observes in the natural properties of certain substances, several changes which can only be produced by the action of light. Finally, no one can fail to perceive the great and beneficent influence of light upon organized bodies. But the laws of its chemical action are as obscure, as the laws of its motion are simple.

Mechanical Phenomena of Direct Light.

483. The sun, flame, and bodies in a state of combustion, emit light in all directions. Such bodies are said to be *self-luminous*. Other bodies simply send back the light which they receive. These are said to be *illuminated*. Light penetrates through all the gases, most liquids, particularly water, and many solid bodies, among which glass is particularly distinguished. Such bodies are called *transparent*; others retain the light, and are called *opaque*.

484. The first law relating to the motion of light, is the following;
In a transparent homogeneous medium the transmission of light takes place in straight lines.

There is no need of any particular experiment to demonstrate this law. Its truth is evident from the following observation, which may be repeated at pleasure. It is impossible to see an object if an opaque body is interposed in the straight line drawn from this object to the eye; also where a room is shut up so as to admit no light, except through a small aperture, the illuminated particles of dust appear to be arranged in straight lines.

485. By this law the effects of direct light are perfectly represented, and the science of optics is reduced within the province of

---

composed of material particles sent forth from the luminous body, and many analogies tend to represent it as merely the effect of vibrations transmitted in the manner of sound, through an elastic medium.

geometry. A straight line, considered as the path described by light, is called a *ray*.

486. From each point of a luminous body the rays proceed in every direction in which straight lines can be drawn in a transparent medium; and each ray of light passes on in a straight line, until it encounters a medium of different material properties; then the direction changes according to the nature of the body encountered.

487. If the ray enters a transparent medium more rare or more dense, or of which the material properties are different, it undergoes a *refraction*; that is, it is more or less deflected from its rectilinear direction. The laws of these phenomena constitute what is called *dioptrics*.

If the ray encounters the polished surface of an opaque body, it is *reflected* in a determinate direction. The laws of this reflection are comprehended under the part of optics called *catoptrics*. If a ray passes very near a body, it undergoes a feeble *inflection*, the laws of which are not perfectly understood, but this phenomena does not appear to have any very important influence on the phenomena of vision. For this reason it will be sufficient to have merely mentioned the fact in this place.

Lastly, if light falls upon an opaque, unpolished body, it undergoes changes which we must here examine with attention.

488. In the case last supposed, the body is *illuminated*, that is, all its points become luminous, because it reflects the light which it receives, towards all the points to which a straight line can be drawn through the transparent medium.*

489. It is evident that a considerable diminution must always result from this dispersion of light, since each ray is subdivided, as it were, into an infinite number of rays. Accordingly the impression made by this disseminated light is incomparably less strong than the dazzling light of self-luminous bodies.

490. But independently of this dissemination, the light is diminished by another cause. Remarkable changes almost always take place in light, by the contact of bodies. There are some bodies which send off nearly all the light they receive. These appear perfectly white. Others reflect very little or none. These are perfectly black. In all others the light undergoes a particular change,

---

* Some particulars relating to this subject will be found in what is subjoined at the end of the section.

which may be considered as a chemical modification of the luminous matter. Dispersed light makes an impression upon the eye altogether different from that of primitive light. We call this impression colour. The primitive light is always diminished when it is thus modified. This effect is less considerable in bright and lively colours, than in those which are obscure and faint. We shall examine the phenomena of colour more fully in a subsequent chapter. We may, however, remark in this place, that colour does not belong to bodies, but that it is the reflected light itself which is blue, green, red, &c.; since the sensations of different colours cannot be conveyed to the eye without this light.

491. A well known experiment proves that the light which comes from a coloured body, has itself colour. In a darkened room, when the light of an illuminated object passes through an aperture, and falls on a white wall, the objects are represented inverted and indistinct, yet they appear with their natural colours. This phenomenon is easily explained on the supposition of the rectilinear motion and colour of light. Suppose some object, a large straight staff, for example, painted with different colours, and placed at some distance in front of a very dark room, through which the light can penetrate only through one small opening, and suppose this triangular. Let the staff be placed in such a manner, that the light proceeding from it, shall enter the room through this opening, and let there be in the chamber a perfectly white, smooth wall, facing the opening, so that the light which passes through the opening may fall upon this wall. If we first observe the light which comes from the top of the staff, which we suppose red, we remark that this light has the form of a triangular pyramid, of which the most brilliant point is at the vertex, and the sides and angles of which are determined by the form of the opening. The light of this pyramid will strike the white wall towards the bottom, and will illuminate a small space of a triangular form like the opening. This illuminated space is the indeterminate image of the end of the staff, and since this image is red, it follows that the light which produces it must also be red. If we suppose the lower part of the staff to be blue, it will produce towards the top of the wall, a similar triangular blue image, rather confused and indistinct. The same is true of all the points of the staff. Hence we see that an inverted image of the whole staff must be painted on the wall, which is not composed of luminous points, but of small triangles of light. If the opening were quadrangular, the image would

be formed of small luminous squares; if it were round, of small circles, &c. The image will be the more confused, according as the aperture is greater, the object nearer, and the wall which receives the image, more remote.

When the sun appears through a thick foliage, and we receive the image of its light upon a plane perpendicular to the direction of its rays, the illuminated places are all circular, but not defined with precision. These are also indeterminate images of the sun which are formed in the same manner.

492. This single observation, that coloured light is much more feeble than white light, would lead us to suppose that the white light of the sun is a mixture of different coloured lights; and that the surface of each body reflects only some of its constituent principles, that is, only some of its colours, while it absorbs others and renders them ineffectual. This opinion will be entirely confirmed by the theory of dioptric colours.

It is a known fact, that some bodies absorb white light, and afterwards send it out in a dark place.

As to the direct motions of coloured light, they are subject to the same laws as those of white light.

493. Kepler supposed that the transmission of light was instantaneous, that is, that its velocity was too great to be measured. Nevertheless, since his time, astronomers have actually measured this velocity; they have observed that the eclipses of Jupiter's satellites, take place so much the later, according as this planet is further from us. From this phenomenon they have calculated that light passes through the diameter of the earth's orbit, or 190 000 000 miles in about 16 minutes, and that so far as we can judge, this motion is perfectly uniform. Thus in one second, light passes through a space of about 200 000 miles.

494. It is difficult to determine whether the intensity of the same luminous ray decreases or remains constant, when it passes through a vacuum or a perfectly transparent medium. The great intensity, however, of the light of the fixed stars, compared with their immense distance, renders the latter opinion the more probable;* it at least proves beyond a doubt, that in the smaller distances which light describes, it does not suffer any sensible diminution.

---

* According to the opinion of astronomers, light, notwithstanding its prodigious velocity, employs at least three years in coming from the nearest fixed star.

495. But the light which proceeds from a body loses its intensity by diffusing itself, since it is spread over a space the more extended the farther it travels from the body. By means of some well known geometrical theorems, it may be demonstrated, *that the intensity of light is inversely proportional to the square of the distance;* on the supposition that it is not diminished by any other cause, except the divergence of the rays. This is the principal theorem relative to the intensity of light.*

496. But independently of the distance, the brightness of the light is modified by several causes, among which are the following; 1. The intensity of the light of the illuminated body. 2. Its magnitude and position. 3. The situation of the plane which receives the light. 4. The properties of the medium through which the light passes.

We should be careful to distinguish the intensity of *illumination* from the intensity of *the light itself;* for the first depends, as we have already shown, upon the quantity which it absorbs.

497. In the construction of optical instruments, brightness is an object of particular attention, because it is necessary to know, not

---

* Let A (*fig.* 58) be a radiating point, and at the distance AB, suppose a geometrical plane BCD, perpendicular to AB. It is obvious that the light falling from A upon BCD, must have the form of a pyramid, whose vertex is A, and whose base is BCD. If we prolong this pyramid indefinitely, and at some distance AE, taken at pleasure, cut it by a plane EFG, parallel to the former BCD, it is obvious that there must be as much light in one of these planes as in the other. But BCD is smaller than EFG; and consequently, the light must be more concentrated in the former, in the ratio of the two surfaces. Let L be the intensity in BCD, and l that in EFG. Then $L:l :: EFG:BCD$. Now EFG and BCD, being parallel sections of a pyramid, are similar polygons; consequently, they are to each other as the squares of their homologous sides; that is, $EFG:BCD :: EF^2:BC^2$. But AEF and ABC are also similar triangles, since the lines BC, and EF are parallel; we have then

$$EF:BC :: AE:AB, \text{ or } EF^2:BC^2 :: AE^2:AB^2;$$

whence, $EFG:BCD :: AE^2:AB^2$. Therefore, $L:l :: AE^2:AB^2$. If A contain several luminous points, the law of each would be the same; hence the law demonstrated is true generally for all luminous bodies; provided we estimate separately the distance of each point of the body.

only what is the intensity of light out of the eye, but also over what space the light is distributed in the eye, by the refraction of the glasses.

498. The total absence of light is called *darkness*. In an illuminated space, we give the name of *shadow* to places which the light of the luminous body is incapable of reaching directly, in consequence of the interposition of some opaque body. Behind each opaque body there is always a space, upon which the light of the luminous body cannot immediately fall; so that an eye placed there would not be able to perceive the luminous body. We call this space *perfect shadow*. But if the luminous body does not consist of a single luminous point, like the fixed stars; but, like the sun, moon, and flame, is of an apparently sensible magnitude, there will also be, behind the opake illuminated body, a space which will receive only a part of the light. An eye placed there, would see a greater or less portion of the luminous body. We call this space the *penumbra*. It is obvious that the gradations between the perfect shadow and the space entirely illuminated, succeed each other in such a manner that in observing the form of the shadow, we are unable to perceive a well-defined limit. Meantime, as the shadow depends simply on the form of the luminary, on that of the body illuminated, and on the rectilinear motion of light, this theory is susceptible of a rigorous mathematical demonstration; that is, we can demonstate for each case the form of the perfect shadow and of the penumbra, as well as the intensity of the light, at each point of this last. Ordinarily, we understand by the word *shadow*, the configuration of the shaded space, which becomes visible upon a second opaque body placed behind the first.

499. We ought not to close this chapter without saying something of the relations which exist between light and heat. Solar light and terrestrial fire exhibit both combined together. In other circumstances, light appears without heat; or more frequently, heat without light. The more we consider their effects, the more we are induced to regard them as two entirely distinct substances.

CHAPTER XL.

Vision.

500. ALTHOUGH a complete theory of vision includes not only dioptrics, but also a description of the eye, we shall only state briefly what takes place in the eye in the case of vision.

The eye itself is a globe provided with various coatings, and placed in a cavity, in which it can move freely in all directions, by means of the muscles attached to it. The exterior coating is composed of a white, opaque, and horny substance $ABCD$ (*fig.* 59), and is called the *sclerotica*. But in the front part of this coating, between A and D, where its curvature is increased, and where it is perfectly transparent, it takes the name of *cornea*. Within the *sclerotica* we find the *choroid* coat composed of a dark-coloured substance; and under this is the *retina*, which is a white membrane, thin and almost viscous, and which is generally considered as the seat of the sensation. This membrane is formed by the continuation of the medullary part of the optic nerve, which proceeds from the brain, and enters the eye at BC. Behind the cornea AD, the choroid is detached and divided into two parts, one of which is in the shape of a ring, and forms the circular opening called the *pupil*. The membrane which forms this ring has received the name of *iris*, on account of the variety of its colours. It consists of a very delicate tissue of contractile fibres, by which the pupil is diminished when the eye is affected by strong light, and which return to their primitive state when the light is feeble. These operations take place independently of the will, and even without our being sensible of them.

Behind the iris is a body EF, of considerable consistency, transparent, and shaped like a lens, which divides the interior of the eye into two unequal spaces, called the *anterior* and *posterior chambers* of the eye. This body is called the *crystalline*. The anterior chamber contains a transparent liquid like water, called the *aqueous humour*. The posterior chamber is filled with a transparent and gelatinous matter, which is called the *vitreous humour*.

A line GB, which passes through the pupil perpendicular to the two faces of the crystalline, is called the *axis of the eye*. In a well formed eye, this axis is directed to the object at which we look, so that the strongest sensation of vision is produced at B.

501. Vision takes place through the medium of a small, inverted, but very distinct image of the object, on the retina. Let *HI* (*fig*. 59) be the object to which the eye is directed. Each of its points will send forth rays in all directions. Let us take the point *G*. A small part of its rays penetrate through the pupil into the interior of the eye, forming a cone which is indicated by three lines in the figure. The ray in the middle of this cone traverses the eye without deviating from its direction, and marks on the retina the point which represents *G*. The other rays which surround it are refracted, but in such a manner that they all unite at the same point *g*. Now if *G* were blue, for example, *g* would receive only blue light, and would itself be blue. This would, therefore, be an image of the point *G*. The same takes place for all the rays which come from any point of the object, from *H* or *I*, for example.

If then we draw from each luminous point, a straight line, nearly through the middle of the crystalline, we can find the place where this point is represented on the retina. Thus *H* will be painted in *h*, and *I* in *i*. Hence we see how a small inverted image will be painted on the retina.

502. All that is required for the explanation of this phenomenon, will be perfectly deduced from the principles of refraction. But there still remain some important questions in anatomy and physiology to be solved.

Experience shows that we do not see objects distinctly, which are either very near or very distant; and that for all eyes, there is a certain distance, at which vision is most perfect. This is entirely conformable to the laws of dioptrics; for we can demonstrate by the principles of refraction, that the rays of a point too near would not unite exactly at the retina, but a little behind it; the rays of an object too distant, on the contrary, would have their point of meeting a little in front of the retina; and in both cases there would not be a distinct image. But we know by experience, that in the eye, nature has remedied this defect to a certain degree. But there has been much dispute as to the manner in which this is effected. Some think that the crystalline is capable of moving a little backward and forward. But it is more probable that the curvature of its surface admits of slight variations.*

---

* The celebrated anatomist, Home, supposes that the four straight muscles which move the eye, change also the curvature of the cornea, which is very elastic; and that, by this means, we are able to see

The distance of distinct vision is very different in different persons. Ordinarily it is about 8 inches. Those persons with respect to whom it is least, are called *myopes*, or short-sighted. Those in whom it is greatest, are called *presbytes*, or long-sighted. But these peculiarities result more frequently from habit, than from the original structure of the eye.*

---

distinctly objects which are placed at different distances. There are animals which must have the faculty of distinguishing very distant objects, without losing the power of seeing them when they are brought near. Birds of prey, for example, which are able, from a great elevation, to spy out a small animal upon the surface of the earth, and to continue to see it till they are ready to pounce upon it, must necessarily change the form of the eye; and in fact, if we examine the structure of this organ, we observe that the sclerotica, which is thin in the back part, is furnished in front with a bony circle, composed of small pieces which are capable of playing upon each other, and which offer a very firm support for the attachment of muscles. Generally, the organ of vision, in different animals, is necessarily adapted to their mode of life. For example, fishes which live in a medium in which light passes with greater difficulty than in the air, and is in a great measure absorbed, have eyes that differ in their structure from those of land animals. The crystalline is spherical, and more deeply imbedded in the vitreous humour, and sometimes moveable. The cornea is almost always flat; and often the pupil, instead of a circular opening, presents a sort of lattice, by means of notches in the iris, which is moveable. We are ignorant in what manner these modifications are favourable to vision, although it is probable that they are suited to the subject. It may be observed also that the crystalline is round in the cormorant, a bird which dives for fish.

* Short-sighted persons, for the most part, have very large, prominent eyes, in consequence of the great convexity of the cornea. Now this convexity supposes a greater interval for the aqueous humour contained in the anterior chamber of the eye, and therefore a larger space between the anterior convex part of the crystalline and the posterior concave part of the cornea. Hence the object must be nearer the eye, in order that the luminous rays may converge sufficiently. In long-sighted persons, on the contrary, the aqueous humour occupies less space, and this is what we observe in those who are advanced in life. This defect, therefore, results less frequently from habit, than from the structure of the eye, although it is undoubtedly increased by habit.

503. The most unaccountable circumstance in the phenomena of vision is, that the image which produces the sensation is in the eye, while the image which we see is without. The cause of this depends undoubtedly upon the power of the imagination, and consequently belongs to psychology. In the mean time, though this phenomenon is not yet explained, and perhaps never will be, yet the fact is so certain that it may serve as a fundamental principle in the explanation of other phenomena.

504. The sensation and the judgment we form in consequence of it, are so confounded by habit, that we often think we experience a sensation, when we only pass a judgment upon one. This is most frequently the case with respect to the sense of sight. For this reason it is necessary to distinguish carefully in the case of vision, what is a true sensation, unmixed with any inference. To do this, we must take the most simple case, which is undoubtedly that in which a single radiant point sends light to the eye. What we remark in this case, is the colour of the light, and the direction in which the middle ray of the luminous cone, strikes the retina. These are the two most simple elements of the sensation of vision.

505. The unquestionable facts stated in the two preceding articles, are sufficient to solve the question so often discussed, *how it happens that we see objects erect, when the image is inverted on the retina.* If the image of the point H which we see, were at the same place where the sensation is produced in the eye, that is, at h, we should perceive the whole object as a thing situated in the eye, and we should certainly see it in the position which the image takes in the eye, that is, inverted; but as we are sensible of the colour and the direction of the light coming from H, the visible image advances and recedes by an inexplicable effect of the force of our imagination, so that we cannot see the point H any where, except in the part of the line Hh which is without the eye; that is, a point the representation of which is below the axis of the eye, is seen above, and *vice versâ*.

506. If we see objects single, with two eyes, it is because we always see objects with both eyes at the same time, and the two images are confounded.

507. The *apparent magnitude* of an object HI, (*fig.* 59) is properly the magnitude of its image hi on the retina. If we bring the object nearer, its image appears larger; if we remove it, its image appears smaller; the apparent magnitude is therefore entirely differ-

ent from the *real magnitude*, for this is invariable. It is obvious that the apparent magnitude increases or diminishes with the angle *HLI*; consequently, we consider the angle *HLI*, under which we see an object, as the measure of its apparent magnitude; and we call it the *visual angle* or *apparent diameter* of the object.

508. If the visual angle is too small, we are not in a state to discern the object. We generally say, that an object ceases to be visible, when its visual angle is smaller than one minute. This estimate, however, can only be considered as approximate; for the visibility of a point or object, does not depend upon the magnitude of the visual angle alone, but also upon the manner in which the light of the object detaches itself from the light of the ground on which it is seen. If a strongly illuminated object is placed on a dark ground, it may be visible under an angle smaller than a second; this is proved by the observation of the fixed stars, among which there is perhaps no one which has an apparent diameter of one second; but when the light of an object is less detached from the ground upon which it is seen, it may be invisible under a much greater angle.

509. The eye cannot discern immediately the distance of objects; for the impression which is made upon the retina, depends solely upon the direction and intensity of the luminous rays at the instant of contact. Accordingly, the greater or less space described by the ray before reaching the eye, can have no influence upon the sensation produced. Consequently, what is indicated by both eyes as to the distance of an object, is not a sensation but a judgment, which is so confounded by habit with the sensation, that we can hardly distinguish them.

510. But nature has greatly facilitated our estimate of distances; for, although distance is not immediately perceived, there are nevertheless, circumstances connected with the sensation which differ according as the object is nearer or more remote. Among these the following may be mentioned.

(1.) In well formed eyes, the axis of each eye must be directed towards the point which we consider. When this point is near, the two axes must make a much greater angle than when it is distant, and the effort of the muscles which is necessary to produce the motion of the pupil, is in fact something to be felt.

(2.) The degree of distinctness and precision with which we see each point, is different for a near object from what it is in the case of a more remote one.

(3.) The light of a distant object, other things being the same, is more feeble than that of a near one, on account of the light being more diffused; and also on account of the imperfect transparency of the air, especially in the lower regions of the atmosphere.

(4.) The apparent magnitude of an object of which we know the real magnitude, determines our estimate of the distance.

(5.) The position of an object with respect to other objects, the distance and situation of which are known, serves also to assist our judgment.

511. For objects at a small distance, where an exact estimate of the distance is most important to us, all these circumstances are combined in forming our judgment. The greater the distance, the less certain is our estimate, and beyond the region of the atmosphere all these means fail entirely, so that not only elevated meteors, but even the stars appear to be situated in the same surface; that is, attached to the blue vault which the light of the air represents to us. According to the observations in article 510, we are able to explain why this vault appears to have the form of a segment less than a hemisphere, and why the sun, moon, and stars appear larger and more distant from each other when in or near the horizon, than when they are in the more elevated parts of the heavens. There are several circumstances which conspire to give us the impression that objects seen near the horizon, other things being the same, are more distant, many of these circumstances being wanting, when the object is at a great altitude.

512. The two last circumstances mentioned in article 510, as a means of judging of distance, serve also to determine the real magnitude of an object; that is, if we are able to judge of the distance by other means, this distance compared with the apparent magnitude of the object, affords an indication of its real magnitude.

Moreover, if we see an unknown object amongst others which are known, these furnish the means of estimating its real magnitude.

513. In like manner the *apparent form* of a thing is not its *real form*. The image which is painted on the retina, is not a body, but a plane, and consequently each object appears to our eyes as a simple surface. Yet we judge with great exactness of the real form of an object, especially when it is very near, since every thing which enables us to determine the magnitude and distance of an object, helps us also to judge of its form. But the best indications of form are the alternations of light and shade, especially when we are able to consider the object on more than one side.

514. From these observations we may conceive the possibility of representing apparent objects upon a simple surface, as is done in painting. Independently of what the inventive genius of the artist does for the picture, it is necessary that the rules of geometrical and aerial perspective should be observed. The first teaches us how to draw the outlines of objects, as they appear to the eye according to the laws of optics. This part is susceptible of calculation; and accordingly it is considered as a branch of applied mathematics. Aerial perspective consists in the exact adaptation of light and distinctness, according to the distance of the object. It cannot be subjected to mathematical calculation, on account of the imperfection of theoretical and practical photometry.

515. When a body appears to us to move, what we perceive is not its *real* but its *apparent motion*. A body which is situated in the axis of the eye, and which advances or recedes in the direction of this line, appears to us at rest, provided it is not so near that we can perceive the change of its apparant magnitude and distance. In other cases it is always the motion of the image on the retina which we perceive; and this may obviously be very different, from the real motion of the object; for when the eye itself is in motion, the images change their place upon the retina, while the objects which they represent, are at rest. If the observer is not sensible of his own motion, he is apt to suppose that it is the objects themselves which move. If the eye and the object seen are both in motion at the same time, the phenomena become more complicated. This is the case with the apparent course of the planets in the celestial sphere.

516. It is evident from what precedes, that all optical deceptions are not false sensations, but false judgments, to which our sensations often give rise. Our judgments would be much more erroneous, if our sensations themselves could deceive us and present false images. This is what sometimes happens in nervous disorders.

CHAPTER XLI.

Reflection of Light by Mirrors, or First Principles of Catoptrics.

517. PROPERLY speaking, all polished surfaces reflect after the manner of mirrors; even when we look obliquely at a polished sur-

face, we see certain images similar to those which are represented in a mirror; but, for the most part, they are indistinct. Among solid bodies there are only certain simple metals, and certain amalgams of metals, which are susceptible of a perfect polish. Looking-glasses form no exception to this remark; for it is properly the amalgam of mercury and zinc, with which the posterior surface is coated that produces the effect.

518. Looking-glasses have indeed rendered metallic mirrors useless for ordinary purposes; but they cannot be employed for exact optical experiments, because they produce a double reflection on the two surfaces of the glass, and also because the light which arrives at the posterior surface is itself refracted twice in the glass, and consequently the phenomena which we observe, are not produced by reflection alone. These inconveniences are the more to be regretted, since it is difficult to prepare a good composition for metallic mirrors.

519. Among the infinitely varied forms which may be given to the surfaces of mirrors, there are only two of which it is important to speak particularly; these are plane and spherical mirrors. Under the latter denomination we include all those which are portions of a sphere polished on the concave or convex surface. Various attempts have been made, without success, since the time of Descartes, to polish mirrors of elliptic and parabolic curvatures, &c. But independently of the almost insurmountable difficulties to be met with in constructing them, it is demonstrated by theory that they would be inferior to spherical mirrors. Conical and cylindrical mirrors are used only for purposes of amusement.

Fundamental Law of Catoptrics.

520. All the luminous phenomena which are produced by means of mirrors, though infinitely varied, rest upon one extremely simple law, which is the following;

If a ray of light HA (fig. 60) *falls upon any surface* BAC, DAE, *or* FAG, *and if we erect at the point of incidence* A, *the line* AI *perpendicular to the mirror, and suppose a plane passing through this line and the incident ray, the reflected ray will also be in this plane, and will make with the perpendicular* AI, *an angle* IAK *equal to the angle* IAH, *formed by the incident ray with this same perpendicular.*

In a word, the incident ray and reflected ray have, with respect to the perpendicular *AI* and the mirror, an opposite but symmetrical position. We call *AI* the perpendicular, *IAH* the *angle of incidence*, and *IAK* the *angle of reflection*. If a ray falls perpendicularly upon a mirror, the angle of incidence, and consequently that of reflection are zero, that is, the ray is reflected back upon itself.

The exactness of this law may be proved by experiment in different ways; and, in general, it is sufficient for this purpose, to render visible the directions of the incident and reflected rays. One of the most simple methods of doing this, is to cause the light of the sun, after passing through a very small opening, to fall upon the surface of a mirror in a darkened room, where the particles of dust floating in the air, are illuminated by the incident and reflected light.

Plane Mirrors.

521. The well known phenomena of the plane mirror are very easily explained by the above law. Let *AB* (*fig.* 61) be the profile of such a mirror; *C* a radiating point situated before its surface; draw the line *CD* perpendicular to the mirror, and produce it making *DE* equal to *DC*. If now any ray *CF* coming from *C*, falls upon the mirror, we have only to draw through *E* and *F* the line *EFG*, in order to find the position of the reflected ray; for the equality of the triangles *FDC*, *FDE*, being easily demonstrated, it follows that the angles *DFC*, *DFE*, are equal; but *BFG* and *DFE* are equal, being vertical angles; consequently, *DFC* and *BFG* are also equal; therefore, according to the law of catoptrics, *FG* is the reflected ray.

We see, therefore, that all the rays coming from *C* are reflected by the mirror, in such a manner that their directions pass through the same point *E*. Consequently an eye placed before the mirror, in such a position as to receive one of these reflected rays, must see in *E* a representation of the point *C*. But what has been demonstrated for the point *C* is applicable to every other point. Thus we see why the image of an object, given by a plane mirror, always appears to be situated behind the mirror at a distance equal to the distance of the object.

Spherical Mirrors.

522. Let *ADB*, (*fig.* 62) be the profile of a spherical mirror, and *C* the centre of the spherical surface of which this mirror is a part. We call this point the geometric centre; and *D* which is the middle point of the segment itself, is called the optic centre. A straight line drawn indefinitely through *C* and *D*, represents the axis. *CD* is the radius of the mirror, and *DA*, *DB*, are the semi-apertures. If the interior surface is polished, the mirror is *concave* or *converging*; if the exterior surface is polished, it is *convex* or *diverging*.*

Phenomena produced by Concave Mirrors.

523. If we direct the axis of a concave mirror towards the sun, all the rays which meet its surface will be concentrated by reflection

---

* When we do not aim at rigorous exactness, we may produce the phenomena of the two kinds of mirrors, with glass mirrors; but then the luminous ray traversing the anterior surface is reflected before it reaches the posterior surface which reflects it. Accordingly, in this case, we must not judge as before, of the properties of the mirror, by a mere inspection of its anterior surface; it is only when the two faces are parallel, or rather when they are of concentric curvature, a point very difficult to be effected with exactness, that the mirror can be called converging when its anterior surface is concave, and diverging, when its anterior surface is convex. But if, on the contrary, the two faces, as is usually the case, are of different forms and curvatures, we call that a convex or diverging mirror, of which the borders are thinner than the middle; and that a concave or converging mirror of which the borders are thicker than the middle; the anterior surface being indifferently, either plane, convex, or concave, because it contributes to the reflection only in a minute degree, compared with the other surface which is coated. Those who are acquainted with the effect of these two kinds of mirrors, know that the converging mirror magnifies an object placed between *C* and *D*, (*fig.* 63) and that the diverging mirror diminishes it. Regard being paid to this observation, we can perform the experiments indicated in articles 522, 523, 524, 525, with glass mirrors.

into a small space *F*, which is exactly in the middle between *C* and *D*. Hence there is at this point not only a dazzling light, but also an intense heat, which may be increased almost indefinitely. For this reason we call this point the *focus* of the mirror, and *DF* its *focal distance*. To render this effect as great as possible, the mirror should be very large, and its focal distance less than the breadth of the mirror, or at least not exceeding it; for the greater the focal distance is, compared with the surface of the mirror, the less will be the effect produced at the focus. A body which we wish to expose to the heat of the focus of a mirror, should be smaller than this focal space, in order to be surrounded on all sides by the heat which is there concentrated. A concave mirror fitted for this purpose, is called a *burning mirror*.

524. If we place a flame in the focus of a concave mirror, all the light which falls upon the surface will be reflected nearly parallel to the axis. And as parallel light always preserves an equal force, except when it is weakened by the absorbing power of the medium through which it passes, we may thus propagate a vivid light to a considerable distance.

525. The images of objects represented by a concave mirror, present phenomena much more varied than those of a plane mirror. If we place a lighted candle before the mirror, in a dark room, the following phenomena become perfectly manifest.

(1.) If the flame is between the focus and the mirror, we see a vertical magnified image of it, which appears to be a little further behind the mirror, than the flame is before it. As we bring the light towards the focus, the image increases in magnitude and distance.

(2.) If we place it at the focus, the image disappears, and we see only the luminous reflection described in the preceding article, which consists almost entirely of parallel rays.

(3.) If we place the light beyond the focus, we no longer perceive its image in the mirror; but when it is at a certain distance, a large inverted image is painted on a white screen or wall opposite the mirror; if we remove the light still further, this image is brought nearer and becomes smaller. When the distance of the flame becomes double the focal distance, the image and object coincide, since in this case, the flame is at the centre of curvature of the mirror. If we remove it still further, the image now smaller than the flame, approaches the focus, and at length, when the light is removed to an infinite distance, the image coincides with the focus. Hence we see that, in a burning mirror, the violent heat which we observe at the focus, is produced by an image of the sun which is there represented.

526. It is only by the calculus that we can give a complete explanation of these phenomena. Yet there is a very simple and ingenious method of determining by geometrical construction, what the phenomenon must be in any given case; it supposes, however, some mathematical analyses of which we shall here state only the results. At the end of the chapter rigorous demonstrations may be found. The propositions are the following.

(1.) Each ray directed parallel to the axis, is reflected to the focus.

(2.) All the rays which come from any point in the direction of the axis, or very nearly in this direction, are reflected in such a manner that their directions all cut each other in one point, and consequently produce there an image of the radiating point; but this image is sometimes before and sometimes behind the mirror; it may even be at an infinite distance, and then the reflected rays are parallel.

The consequence of this principle is, that if we only know the direction, which two rays from the same point take, when reflected, we know also the direction of all the rest.

(3.) When several points are at equal distances from the mirror, their images are also equally distant from the mirror. It is in consequence of this, that, when we place an object before a mirror, the reflected rays must always produce an image, either before or behind the mirror.

527. If we admit the truth of these propositions, it may be demonstrated that we can, in each case, determine all the conditions of the formation of images, if we know only the two rays which come from the extreme points of an object. For this purpose, let *ACB*, (*figs.* 63, 64, 65) be the section of a mirror *CD*, its axis, and *E* its focus. Let the straight line *FG*, perpendicular to the axis, represent the radiating object. This line should be neither less nor greater than the altitude of the mirror, and should extend to equal distances on each side of the axis. From the highest point *F* of this object, we draw two rays, *FA* and *FC*, to the mirror; *FA* parallel to the axis, is reflected to the focus *E*; *FC* directed to the optic centre *C* of the mirror, will be reflected towards the lowest point of the object, according to the law of catoptrics. Produce the

directions of these two reflected rays till they cut each other. The point of their intersection f, is the image of the point F of the object. If we draw from this point f a line fg, passing perpendicularly through the axis, making gh equal to fh, this line will represent the image reflected by the mirror in the circumstances supposed.

Figure 63 represents the case in which the object FG is within the focal distance CE. The two reflected rays AE and CG, which come originally from F, here diverge, and we consequently produce them behind the mirror to find their point of intersection f, which is the image of the point F, as also fg, which is the image of the entire object. This is an illustration of the phenomenon mentioned in article 526, (1.)

In figure 64, the object FG is itself at the focus E. Here the two reflected rays AE and CG become parallel; for since, according to the remark made at the end of article 525, the mirror must have only a small curvature to produce a distinct image, we may consider $CAFE$ as a parallelogram; but then $CAEG$ is also a parallelogram, since CA and EG are equal. In this case, there will be no image formed, or rather we may say, there will be one at an infinite distance behind or before the mirror. This explains the second phenomenon mentioned in article 525.

Figure 65 represents the object FG, beyond the focal distance. The two reflected rays Af and Cf are here sensibly convergent, and produced sufficiently far, they would cut each other below the axis in f, so that in this case the mirror produces in the air an image fg of the object. This explains the third phenomenon of article 525.

We may treat in the same manner all other cases which present themselves. The reader may here examine the changes which take place in the last of these phenomena, according as the object is placed between the geometric centre and the focus, or at the geometric centre. These are mentioned at the end of article 525.

Phenomena produced by Convex Mirrors.

528. The phenomena presented by a convex mirror, when the light of an object falls upon it, are much more simple than the preceding. Whenever we place an object before the mirror, we perceive an image smaller than the object itself, and situated vertically behind the mirror. When we direct the axis of a convex mirror

towards the sun, instead of concentrating, it disperses the light. But it may be proved as well by experiment as by calculation, that the small image of the sun, from which this dispersion of light proceeds, is placed at an equal distance between the optic and geometric centre, and consequently behind the mirror. Hence we call this point the *negative focus of the mirror,* and its distance from the mirror, the *negative focal distance.*

529. The theoretical propositions stated in article 526, may be applied to convex mirrors, as well as to concave ones; only the expression of the first must be changed thus. A ray parallel to the axis must be reflected as if it came from the negative focus. With this modification the construction described in article 527, may serve also for convex mirrors.

Let *ACB* (*fig.* 66) be the profile of such a mirror, *ED* its axis, and *E* its negative focus. Let *FG* be the object; from *F* draw the ray *FA*, parallel to the axis. It will be reflected in the direction *AK*, as if it came from *E*. The ray *FC* is reflected toward *G*. The two reflected rays obviously diverge, and consequently we must produce them behind the mirror in order to find their point of intersection *f*, and represent the entire image *fg* of the object *FG*.

530. It is necessary to know perfectly the focal distance of a spherical mirror, when we wish to employ it in exact experiments.

In the case of a concave mirror, there are several ways of determining the focal distance. For example, we present the mirror to the rays of the sun in such a manner that their direction shall be parallel to its axis, and measure the distance of the image from the mirror. Or we cut a piece of paper of the shape and size of the mirror, draw a diameter across it, and in the diameter make two round holes at equal distances from the centre. This we place upon the mirror and then expose it to the light of the sun. The rays reflected through the two holes will converge; we find their point of meeting and measure its distance from the mirror.

A third method will be given among the additions at the end of the chapter.

For a convex mirror, we can only make use of the second method. When we have attached the paper to the mirror, we perceive that reflected rays diverge, and we are to seek the points where they are at a distance from each other equal to double that which they had upon the mirror. We measure the distance of these points from the mirror, and thus we have the negative focal distance.

Mathematical Additions.

531. The propositions enunciated in articles 526 and 529, are not rigorously but conditionally exact. This condition is, that they approach the more nearly to the truth, in proportion as the extent of the mirror is less compared with its focal distance, or with the radius of the sphere upon which the mirror is constructed. Yet it may be proved by a more extended analysis, that the inaccuracy of which we speak, is scarcely perceptible, even when the spherical segment which forms the mirror, is one of several degrees. In order that mirrors may afford clear and distinct images, the diameter of the mirror should never, at most, exceed half the focal distance, and in certain cases it ought to be much less.

This remark justifies the approximations to which we shall confine ourselves in the following demonstrations.

532. *Theorem.* A luminous ray EA (*fig.* 67), which falls parallel to the axis upon a concave mirror, is reflected between the optic centre D, and the geometric centre C, and the nearer to the focus F, the nearer it passes to the axis.

Demonstration. If we draw from A to C, the straight line AC, it will be a radius of the sphere ADB, and consequently perpendicular at A, to the surface of the mirror. If we take the angle $CAF = CAE$, AE being the incident ray, AF will the reflected ray.

If now we consider the triangle AFC, it will be readily perceived that $AF = FC$, since the angles FAC and FCA are equal; for each is equal to the angle EAC; the first by construction, and the second, because AE being parallel to FC, FCA and CAE are alternate internal angles. Now if we had $AF = DF$, we should also have DF equal to FC, and thus the point F would be exactly in the middle of the line DC. This does not exactly take place for all rays; but the difference between the shortest line DF, and the longest AF, evidently becomes smaller, according as AD is small compared with DF or DC. If the arc AD, or the angle AFD, comprehends only a few degrees, we may, without material error, suppose $DF = AF$. Then $DF = FC$. Thus the first proposition of article 526 is demonstrated.

533. *Theorem.* *In a convex mirror* ADB (fig. 68), *the ray* EA *parallel to the axis, will be reflected in the direction* AH, *as if it had*

come from the middle of the radius CD. The demonstration is similar to the preceding. The line CAG is perpendicular to the arc ADB in A. If, therefore, we make $GAH = GAE$, AH is the reflected ray, which, being produced, will cut the axis in F. Now in the triangle CAF, we have $CF = AF$, since $CAF = ACF$; for $CAF = HAG$, being vertical angles, and $ACF = GAE$, being internal external angles. But $HAG = GAE$ on account of the fundamental law of reflection; consequently CAF must be equal to ACF. But FA and FD are not strictly equal; they only approach to an equality under certain conditions; that is, CF is more nearly equal to FD, according as the incident ray passes nearer the axis. Thus the principle supposed in article 529 is demonstrated.

534. *Problem. In the axis* ED *of the spherical mirror* ADB (fig. 69), *there is a radiating point* E. *A ray* EA *emanating from this point, falls upon the mirror in* A *and is reflected towards* F. *It is proposed to find an equation between the focal distance of the mirror* $= \frac{1}{2}$ DC $=$ p, *the distance of the luminous point* DE $=$ a, *and the distance* DF $= \alpha$, *at which the reflected ray cuts the axis.*

Solution. Let C be the geometric centre of the mirror; CA will be perpendicular to its surface at A. Consequently, from the law of catoptrics, $CAF = CAE$. But AFD, being the exterior angle is equal to the two opposite interior angles, FAC, ACF. Whence $FAC = AFD - ACF$; also $CAE = ACF - AEC$; consequently, $AFD - ACF = ACF - AEC$, or

$$2 ACF = AFD + AEC.$$

Moreover, it is shown in treatises on trigonometry, that when a right-angled triangle has one of the acute angles very small, this angle is nearly proportional to the side opposite divided by the side adjacent, and this proposition approaches so much nearer the truth according as the opposite side is less. Now, if we wish to obtain distinct images, we must regard the arc AD as very small compared with DF, DC, and DE; we may, therefore, consider it as a straight line perpendicular to the axis DE, and consequently the triangles ADF, ADC, ADE, as right-angled triangles, having very small angles at the base, F, C, E. Consequently, the angle ACF is proportional to $\dfrac{AD}{DC}$

. . . . AFD . . . . . $\dfrac{AD}{DF}$

. . . . AEC . . . . . $\dfrac{AD}{DE}$.

If in the above equation $2\,ACF = AEC + AFD$, we substitute for these angles the values which are proportional to them, we shall have

$$\frac{2\,AD}{DC} = \frac{AD}{DE} + \frac{AD}{DF};$$

or, dividing the whole by AD,

$$\frac{2}{DC} = \frac{1}{DE} + \frac{1}{DF}.$$

Finally, if we substitute $2p$ for DC, a for DE, and α for DF, we shall have

$$\frac{1}{p} = \frac{1}{a} + \frac{1}{\alpha};$$

which is the equation sought between p, a, and α.

535. *Remark.* The formula which we have investigated has a very extensive application; and we shall show that all possible phenomena which take place in mirrors and spherical glasses, may be represented by it, and that consequently it may be regarded as the basis of all optical calculations. It is desirable to give a simple enunciation to a proposition so important.

For this purpose, we observe that it is common to call the quotient arising from dividing unity by any quantity, the reciprocal value of that quantity. Thus $\dfrac{1}{p}$ is the reciprocal value of p, and so of the rest. A quantity and its reciprocal value have such a ratio to each other, that if we know one, we always find the other by dividing unity by that which is known. Thus 1 divided by $\dfrac{1}{p}$ gives p. As we find one of these values so easily from the other, we may indifferently consider one or the other as the quantity known or sought. It is advantageous, therefore, to keep the above equation in its present form, and not to eliminate the divisors, because it would lose much of its simplicity and utility.

If we call $DE = a$, and $DF = \alpha$, *the two distances at which the rays meet*, the above formula expresses the following theorem;

The reciprocal value of the focal distance is equal to the sum of the reciprocal values of the two distances at which the rays meet.

536. *Additions.* (1.) It is an essential property of every algebraic formula, that it is not only applicable to the particular case taken as the basis of the calculation, but that it serves also for all imaginable cases of the same kind. We must remark, however, that when we apply it to other cases, it is sometimes necessary to change the sign of one of the quantities. In the case upon which this formula is founded, we have considered all the quantities p, a, α, as positive, by supposing them placed with respect to one another, as represented in figure 69. But if one of these lines, in another case, has a contrary situation, we must give it the negative sign. With this modification, our formula is applicable to all imaginable cases, in which an incident ray EA (*fig.* 69) cuts the axis in any point E. As long as the point E is before the mirror, the quantity a has the positive sign. But if the ray does not come from a point of the axis, but, on the contrary, is directed towards one of these points, as GA (*fig.* 70) is directed towards E, the distance DE, which was before the mirror in figure 69, is now behind it; so that we must represent DE by $-a$, and the formula will then become for a concave mirror $\frac{1}{p} = -\frac{1}{a} + \frac{1}{\alpha}$. If, moreover, the mirror in question is convex, the ray and the focal distance have a position opposite to those represented in figures 69, 70; we must, therefore, represent the focal distance by $-p$. In this case, when the radiant point is before the mirror, as in figure 69, a remains positive; and the formula is $-\frac{1}{p} = \frac{1}{a} + \frac{1}{\alpha}$. But if the intersection of the axis CD, by the incident ray, were behind the mirror as in figure 70, a would be also negative, and consequently we should have $-\frac{1}{p} = -\frac{1}{a} + \frac{1}{\alpha}$. And so on.

What has been said can be applied only to quantities considered in a particular case, as given quantities. But it is obvious that each of the three quantities may be considered as unknown, when the other two are known. Thus the formula serves generally to find one of these quantities by means of the other two, and it determines, at the same time, the sign to be given to it.

(2.) Since AD (*fig.* 69) is entirely eliminated from the calculation, this is a proof that the magnitude of this arc does not sensibly influence the position of the point F, where the reflected ray cuts the axis, provided that AD is in general a very small arc, as the whole calculation supposes. It follows then, that not only the ray EA, but all the rays coming from the same point E, will unite after reflection, nearly in the same point F, and there produce an image of the point E, which will be visible to an eye placed in such a manner as to receive, at some distance, the divergent rays coming from F.

(3.) As the formula applies to all positions of the point E in the axis, it is demonstrated that for each radiant point situated in the axis, there is always produced by reflection a new image of this point, situated in this same axis. This image is before the mirror, if the formula gives a positive value for α; behind it, when this value is negative; and at an infinite distance if this value is infinite, or which amounts to the same thing, if $\frac{1}{\alpha} = 0$. This is the case with a concave mirror, when we suppose $a = p$, for then we have

$$\frac{1}{p} = \frac{1}{p} - \frac{1}{a}, \text{ that is, } \frac{1}{\alpha} = 0.$$

Hence we see when the rays proceed from the focus, they are reflected parallel to the axis; in other words, their point of union is at an infinite distance.

537. Problem. *To determine the circumstances of reflection when the radiant point is without the axis, but at a small distance from it.*

Solution. Let G (*fig.* 71) be a radiant point near the axis. Draw the straight line GCH through the geometrical centre, and produce it till it meets the mirror. It is evident that this line may be considered absolutely as an axis, since KDB is spherical. If therefore, a ray GK falls upon the mirror, and is reflected towards GL, by making $HG = a$, and $HL = \alpha$, we shall have as above

$$\frac{1}{p} = \frac{1}{a} + \frac{1}{\alpha}.$$

And all the consequences which we have deduced with respect to the axis are true with respect to the line GH. Hence it follows that *each radiant point situated in the line GH, produces an image somewhere in this line.* This image may be according to circumstances, sometimes before the mirror, sometimes behind it, and sometimes at an infinite distance.

Thus the second supposition of article 526 is demonstrated.

538. *Additions.* (1.) As we suppose the size of the mirror very small compared with the focal distance, and the radiant point G to be near the axis, it is evident that all the lines drawn from G to the mirror, will be nearly equal in length. The same is true of all the lines drawn from L to the mirror. Hence it follows that the formula

$$\frac{1}{p} = \frac{1}{a} + \frac{1}{\alpha},$$

will vary but little from the truth, even when we do not measure the distances a and α, but substitute their perpendicular distance from the mirror. It follows also that if several radiant points are situated below G, at equal distances from the mirror, their images above L would also all be at equal distances from its surface. For since a is the same for all these points, the formula would give equal values for α. Thus the third supposition of article 526 is sufficiently evident.

(2.) If we represent the object, as we have done above, by a straight line perpendicular to the axis, the image will also be a straight line perpendicular to the axis. Then we may call a the distance of the *entire object*, and not merely that of a radiant point; and, in like manner, α will be the distance of the entire image. For this value of the letters a and α, the formula $\frac{1}{p} = \frac{1}{a} + \frac{1}{\alpha}$, remains always exact.

539. *Remarks.* (1.) The last observation furnishes a convenient method of finding the focal distance of a concave mirror. We place before the mirror the flame of a candle at such a distance, that a distinct image may be formed on a white screen or wall properly placed. Then we measure the distance of the image and object from the mirror, and obtain a and α, from which p may be found by means of the formula.

(2.) All the calculations in optics become difficult and complicated, when we undertake to make them with strict accuracy. But in practice this exactness is not necessary, when the question relates to instruments which are to afford very distinct images. For, in order to obtain this distinctness, mirrors must have a very small surface compared with their focal distance, which consideration justifies all the approximations we have employed; and as to instruments where great precision is not sought, this circumstance of itself justifies them.

CHAPTER XLII.

Refraction of Light in Transparent Bodies; or First Principles of Dioptrics.

540. ALL aeriform fluids, most liquids, and many solid bodies, are transparent. Perhaps there is no one which may not be traversed by light to a certain degree; since gold itself, which in large masses is opaque and dense, appears to have a kind of transparency when reduced to thin leaves. Most transparent bodies permit light to traverse them, without altering it, that is, without changing the colour, which it had before penetrating them. But many only transmit certain colours, and hence appear coloured. There are also bodies which reflect one colour and transmit another, as gold leaf, tincture of turnsol, &c.

541. In order to perfect transparency, the surfaces both of solids and liquids must be perfectly polished. This condition is fulfilled naturally in liquids, by the simple effect of gravity which renders their surfaces perfectly plane. It is also fulfilled to a certain degree, in crystallized bodies. In general, however, the assistance of art is necessary for a sufficiently exact polish. When a transparent body is not polished, it suffers the light to pass; but then it disperses it irregularly in all directions, and we cannot see distinctly through it. Among transparent bodies, the greater number refract light *simply*; that is, the collections of luminous rays are not separated in traversing them; but there are other bodies which separate the rays into two distinct portions. To this class belong all crystallized bodies, the primitive form of which is neither a cube nor a regular octaedron. This phenomenon is called *double refraction*. We shall here consider only simple refraction as being the most common and most simple in its theory.

Law of Dioptrics.

542. All the phenomena observed by means of transparent bodies which refract light simply, may be explained by the following law.

When a luminous ray passes obliquely from one transparent medium into another, it undergoes a refraction, or deviates from its primitive direction. If, through the point of incidence, where the ray meets the second medium, we suppose a line drawn perpendicular to the refracting surface, the refracted ray will approach this perpendicular, when the medium which it enters is more dense than that which it leaves; and, on the contrary, will diverge from it, when it is more rare.

In order to demonstrate this law, let A (*fig.* 72) be the point where the ray passes from one medium into another; let the surface which separates the two media be plane as BC, convex as DE, or concave as FG. Suppose the rarer medium to be above and the denser one below; let the incident ray be HA. If at A we erect the perpendicular IAK at the point of incidence, and suppose a plane passing through IAK and AH, the refracted ray will also be in this plane, but in such a manner that the angle KAL, which is in the denser medium, will be smaller than the angle HAI, which is in the rarer. With A for a centre and a radius taken at pleasure, we describe the circle $HILK$. From the points H and L where the incident and refracted rays cut the circumference, we draw the lines HM and LN, perpendicular to the vertical IAK. It is proved by experiment, that these two lines HM and LN, have always invariable ratios, for all directions of incidence, the two media in which the light moves remaining the same.

In a right-angled triangle, of which the hypothenuse is supposed equal to unity, the two other sides, expressed in numbers, that is, in parts of the hypothenuse, are called the sines of the opposite angles. Since the magnitude of the radius AK is arbitrary, we may here consider it as unity; then HM will be the sine of the angle HAI, or the *sine of incidence*, and LN the sine of LAK, or the sine of refraction; and the law of refraction may be briefly expressed as follows;

When a ray passes from one medium into another, it is refracted in such a manner that the sine of incidence and the sine of refraction are in a constant ratio to each other. This ratio is called the *ratio of refraction*. It is customary to call the angles *HAI* and *LAK*, by the name of the media in which they are situated; as the angle in the air, in the water, &c.

543. Among experiments made in conformity to this law, the one most easily comprehended, if not the most exact, is the following. A glass cube *ABCD* (*fig.* 73) is placed upon two boards joined at right angles, as represented by *EC* and *CF*. They should be longer than the side of the cube. If we expose this apparatus to the light of the sun, so that the luminous ray shall fall in the direction *GH*, this ray *GH* will be refracted to *HK* in the glass; but, on the outside it will pursue its primitive direction to *F*. The shadow of the board *CE* will, therefore, reach to *K* in the glass, and to *F* without it. Now if we draw through *H* the incident vertical *LHM*, it will be easily seen that the angle *FHM* is equal to the angle in the air *GHL*, and that *KHM* is the angle in the glass. If we measure the length of the shadow within and without the glass, we can determine the two angles, either by calculation or by construction. Then if we cause the light to fall under different angles, and trace a figure for each case, we may mark the sines of the angles, and find their ratio by means of an exact scale; and these will verify the law enunciated.

The experiments may be made more accurately with a glass prism; but they could not, in this case, be comprehended without a more perfect knowledge of the theory than we can here suppose.

544. Before the middle of the seventeenth century, it was believed that the angles themselves, and not their sines, were in a constant ratio to each other. Snellius of Holland corrected this idea, and made known the exact principle. Yet when the angles *HAI* and *LAK*, (*fig.* 72) are very small, we may without inconvenience take this ratio for the angles, since they are sensibly proportional to their *sines*; and since we never make use of great angles in exact dioptric instruments, we may admit the ratio of the angles as constant in the calculations relative to these instruments.

545. With respect to the particulars of the preceding law, we are to observe the following circumstances.

(1.) If a ray falls perpendicularly, as *AI* (*fig.* 72) it passes without being refracted; in all other cases it is refracted, and the quantity of refraction is greater in proportion to the obliquity of the incidence.

(2.) A ray of light takes the same direction between two media, whether it be considered as entering or emerging, other circumstances being the same; that is, if *LA* were an incident ray, *AH* would be the refracted ray.

(3.) At each refraction there is always a reflection at the polished surface, whether the ray passes from the denser into the rarer medium, or the reverse; that is, if the ray is broken at *A*, a part is reflected according to the law of catoptrics, and the other part is refracted according to the law of dioptrics. The more obliquely the ray falls, the greater is the portion reflected, and the less, consequently, the portion refracted; for all polished surfaces reflect light much more strongly in oblique directions, than when it falls perpendicularly upon them. Even when the ray is directed from a denser to a rarer medium, there is a limit beyond which there can be no angle of refraction in the other medium, since the sine of this angle would be greater than unity, which is impossible; and then all the light is reflected. In a glass filled with water, it will be easily seen that not only the upper, but also the lower surface, reflects, and that the latter reflects much more than the former, especially if we look very obliquely.

(4.) Moreover, at each refraction, a remarkable change takes place in light. We shall merely mention it here, and afterwards attend to it more particularly. After refraction, the luminous ray is no longer a simple straight line, but enlarges into a pyramidal form, and each point of its breadth exhibits a different colour. Still this expansion is very slight for a single refracted ray, especially near the refracting surface. We shall neglect this circumstance in the present chapter, and represent the refracted ray as a single straight line.

(5.) Dense bodies refract light more strongly, other things being the same, than those which are more rare. Yet the refracting power does not depend upon the density alone, but also upon the chemical composition. Thus, we have observed that combustible bodies refract light more strongly than incombustible. Our knowledge upon this point, however, is so slight, that we can only ascertain the refracting power of each body by direct experiment.*

---

* M. Arago and myself, some years ago, made a variety of experiments on this subject with the repeating circle. We ascertained that hydrogen gives to oils, resins, and other substances which we

(6.) The most interesting ratios of refraction are those which exist between air and glass, and between air and water. That between air and common glass is nearly 3 : 2, or more exactly 17 : 11. Between air and English crown glass, it is 1,55 : 1; between air and flint glass 1,58 : 1. Between air and water, it is nearly 4 : 3.

General Phenomena which depend upon the Refraction of Light.

546. If light were neither refracted nor reflected by transparent bodies, those which are perfectly transparent and colourless would be invisible. We can see them only in consequence of the reflection which takes place at their surfaces, and the difference of direction which refraction produces in the light which traverses them. Thus we can even distinguish two colourless fluids, which exist together in the same vessel without mixing; such as oil and water, or ether and water, &c. The air is invisible in small masses, because the refractions and reflections are insensible. When a visible body is in a different transparent medium from that where the eye is, its apparent position, in most cases, undergoes a change by the refraction of light.

Let A (*fig.* 74) be a visible point at the bottom of a vessel full of water BAC. A ray AD which falls vertically upon the surface of the water, penetrates it without being refracted; but this is the only direction in which we see the point in its actual place. The ray AE which enters the surface of the water under an acute angle, is refracted in the air and diverges still farther from the incident perpendicular, drawn through E. It continues, therefore, through the air as if it came from a more elevated point a; and then an eye which is in the prolongation of the ray EF, must see the point A in the direction EF, that is, in a.

What has been said of A is applicable to all other points at the

---

call combustible, their great refracting power. We also ascertained that the refracting power of the ingredients, is in the ratio of their masses, when the state of aggregation is not changed; so that by means of this law, we can calculate beforehand with considerable accuracy, the refracting force of bodies, and deduce from it some inferences respecting the nature and proportions of their constituent principles.

bottom of the vessel. Thus all this part must appear to be raised to *B a C*. If a straight staff *GHA* is immersed in water, the part below the surface will appear broken, because each of the points which compose it must appear more elevated than it really is.

If the eye were at *A*, and the object observed were in the line *EF*, it would not be seen in its true direction, but in the prolongation of the line *AE*.

We find ourselves in such a situation with respect to the heavenly bodies; and astronomers have long since observed that the heavenly bodies which are not in the zenith, appear more distant from the horizon than they really are. This is called *astronomical refraction*.

Particular Phenomena which are produced by means of Polished Glasses.

547. Polished glasses give rise to phenomena too important to be neglected here. There are two kinds of glasses which we shall examine; those whose faces are plane and parallel, and those whose faces are portions of a sphere. In one of the following chapters we shall speak of glasses whose surfaces are plane, but inclined to each other; that is, of prismatic glasses.

Plane Glasses with Parallel Faces.

548. Let *ABCD* (*fig.* 75) be the profile of a glass of this kind, and *EF* a luminous ray falling upon its anterior surface. At the point of incidence *F*, erect the perpendicular *GH*. The ray will be refracted in the glass at *F*, and will take the direction *FI*. At *I*, the point of emergence, erect a second perpendicular *KL*, which will be parallel to the first. The ray will again be refracted in the air at this point, and will take the direction *IM*. We easily see that *IM* is parallel to *EF*; for since the two angles in the glass, *HFI* and *FIK* are equal, the angles in the air, *EFG* and *LIM* must also be equal.

By refraction in such glasses all the emergent rays remain parallel to the incident rays; thus we must see through such a glass precisely as we should see, if no glass were there. Only when we look very obliquely, the objects must change place a little, yet with-

Spherical Glasses or Lenses.

out changing their magnitude or respective situations. In all other cases, the direction of the ray is so little changed, that we may consider its refraction as nothing.

Spherical Glasses or Lenses.

549. The different kinds of microscopes and telescopes are instruments indispensable to the philosopher. They consist of glasses the faces of which are portions of a sphere. In order to understand the effect of compound optical instruments, it is necessary first to consider the properties of the simple glasses of which they are formed.

550. Although the form of spherical glasses may be varied much more than that of mirrors, we may nevertheless, in considering their essential properties, arrange them in two *classes*; *convex* or *converging glasses*, and *concave* or *diverging glasses*. Each of these two classes are subdivided as follows. The converging glasses are,

(1.) *Double convex*, as in figure 76. The form of this glass is lenticular, and for this reason we usually call it a *lens*; and the term applies not only to glasses of this kind; but also to all spherical glasses, particularly the smallest.

(2.) *Plano-convex*, as in figure 77.

(3.) *Concavo-convex*, as in figure 78. The word *convex* must be placed last, to denote that the convexity here is greater than the concavity. We call such a glass a *meniscus*, on account of the form of its profile.

Diverging glasses are,

(1.) *Double concave*, as in figure 79.

(2.) *Plano-concave*, as in figure 80.

(3.) *Convex-concave*, as in figure 81. It is usual to apply the term *meniscus* to this lens also, the form of which requires that we put the word *concave* last.

551. With respect to all these glasses, we make the following general remarks;

(1.) Their faces are made to take the spherical form, for the same reason that determined us to give this form to mirrors.

(2.) The phrase *radius of curvature* imports the semidiameter of the sphere of which the surface in question is a portion.

(3.) In order to see distinctly through these glasses, it is necessary that their surfaces, like those of mirrors, should not be large portions of a sphere. We may lay this down as the limit of their extent, that the arc of the segment should be at most equal to only half the radius of curvature.

(4.) In the middle of a glass of this kind (*fig.* 76, 81), there is a point C, where the two opposite faces are parallel. This point is called the *optic centre* of the glass. A line DE drawn through this point, perpendicular to the two faces, is called the *axis of the glass*. In this line are situated the *geometric centres* of the two faces, that is, the centres F and G of the two spheres of the surface of which these faces are portions.

When the optic centre and the point of intersection of the axis, are exactly in the middle of the exterior surface, we say that the glass is exactly centred. This is an essential quality for optical purposes. The equal thickness of the exterior circumference indicates this property, but not with all the exactness necessary. The most certain indication is when the objects do not change their apparent position, if we move the glass circularly in a plane perpendicular to its axis.

When we wish to make use of these glasses, it is common to cover a portion of their borders with an opaque ring, and the interior diameter of this ring is called the *aperture* of the glass.

(5.) The *anterior surface* of the glass is always that which is turned towards the object, and the *posterior surface*, that which is turned towards the eye.

(6.) All converging glasses produce phenomena essentially similar. The same is true of all diverging glasses compared with one another. The advantages of the different kinds, depend upon circumstances, and these advantages cannot be determined or even understood clearly without a knowledge of mathematics. In general, double convex or double concave glasses are perferred, especially if their curvatures are symmetrical, because they admit of the greatest apertures.

(7.) Experience has proved that common mirror glass of a slightly greenish colour, is the best for all optical instruments. English flint glass is used only for particular purposes.

Phenomena produced by Converging Glasses.

552. When we expose a converging glass to the sun, and receive the light transmitted through it, on a white surface, this light is collected in a certain space, the extent of which varies with the position of the surface. If it is first very near the glass, and we gradually remove it, the luminous space becomes smaller. Hence the term *converging*. At length we reach a point where the light occupies the least possible space, and beyond that it becomes divergent. This point is called the *focus*, and its distance from the nearest surface of the glass is called the *focal distance*. If we turn the glass and expose the other surface, the same phenomenon takes place. A converging glass has therefore two foci, and they are equally distant from the two surfaces, if these have the same radius. In glasses whose surfaces are not symmetrical, especially *meniscuses*, these distances differ, but by a quantity scarcely perceptible.

553. A burning glass is a convex glass of considerable extent, as two or three feet, and having its focal distance equal to the *aperture*; or at least very little exceeding it. The effects of such a glass become more intense, according to the extent of the surface, and the smallness of the space in which the rays are concentrated. If the focus is very distant, this space is extended, and consequently the effect is small. In this case it is common to place at some distance another convex glass, called a *collector*, which causes the rays to converge into a smaller space. The effects of burning glasses are as remarkable as those of burning mirrors.

554. The focal distance of a symmetrically *double convex* glass, is equal to the radius of either surface, or rather to $1\frac{2}{11}$ of this radius. For a *plano-convex* glass, it is equal to double the radius, or more exactly to $\frac{1}{8}^{1}$. We shall demonstrate in the mathematical additions at the end of the chapter, what is its value with respect to the radii of glasses not symmetrical.

555. The other properties of convex glasses have the closest resemblance to those of converging mirrors, and may be exhibited with even greater facility, by means of a lighted candle in a dark room.

(1.) When we place the candle before the glass and within the focal distance, the eye placed on the other side of the glass sees the image magnified, erect, and very distant, the magnitude and distance increasing as we remove the light.

(2.) If we place the candle at the focus, we do not see any distinct image of it, but only a vivid light which consists principally of parallel rays, and continues behind the lens, so as to illuminate distant objects.

(3.) If we place the candle at a certain distance beyond the focus, we see a magnified and inverted image on the opposite wall. If we continue to move it still farther, this image approaches the posterior focus of the glass, and becomes smaller. If the flame is placed at double the focal distance, the image is at the same distance, and has the same dimensions as the flame itself. If we remove the flame still more, the image approaches and becomes smaller, and if the object be very distant, it falls at length in the focus. Accordingly the *caustic* space within which a burning glass burns, is nothing more than the small image of the sun formed at the focus. If we do not receive the image formed under the preceding circumstances, upon a white screen or ground glass, an eye placed at a proper distance will see it formed in the air. But for reasons which are easily conceived, the imagination represents it not where it really is, but in the glass itself, or rather on the opposite face.

556. So far as we can understand these phenomena without the aid of mathematics, it will be perceived that they do not differ essentially from those described in articles 526, 527. In this case, as before, if we take some principles for granted, we can determine by an easy construction, what phenomena will be exhibited in a given case. To facilitate this construction, it is to be remarked that a ray which passes through the optic centre C (*fig.* 76, 81), must be considered as not refracted. For the rays which make small angles with the axis, this is clear from the position of the surfaces at C; for, since they are here parallel, the ray which passes through must be refracted as in a plane glass with parallel faces.

557. After these preliminary observations, figures 82, 84, do not require much explanation. AB is the section of a convex glass; C is the optic centre, DE the axis, D the anterior focus, E the posterior focus, FHG the radiant object.

(1.) In figure 82 the object is at the middle of the anterior focal distance DC; from its most elevated point F, a ray FA falls upon the glass parallel to the axis, and is refracted towards the posterior focus E. A second ray FCI passes through the optic centre without being refracted. The rays AE and CI diverge after their passage; and if produced in the opposite direction, they will cut each other in f; accordingly all the rays from F, appear to come from this point f. An eye placed behind the glass sees in f the image of the point F; and instead of the object GF, it will see the image fg.

(2.) Figure 83 represents the object FG placed at the anterior focus D; the parallel ray FA is refracted towards E, the ray FC passes without being refracted; but as the lines CE and FA are equal and parallel, since $CE = CD = FA$, it follows that $CFAE$ is a parallelogram, and the rays AE, CI, are parallel after passing through the glass. The same is true of all the rays which proceed from the point F.

(3.) In figure 84 the object FG is placed beyond the anterior focal distance DC; the parallel ray FA is refracted toward E; the ray FCf passes without being refracted; AE and Cf converge after their passage, and their prolongations cut each other in f; all the rays coming from F unite at this point, and an inverted image of the object is formed in fg.

After these explanations it will not be difficult to construct the figures peculiar to the third case, according as the object is at the centre of curvature, or at a much greater distance before the glass.

558. A very extensive and varied use may be made of a single converging glass.

(1.) The effect of the common kind of *spectacles* is explained by the construction of figure 82. These are used to remedy one of the defects of sight common to aged persons, by which the distance of distinct vision becomes so great that the objects with which we are more immediately concerned, are seen only in a confused manner. By the help of spectacles we are able to see objects at a convenient distance. To determine the proper focal distance for spectacles, regard must be paid; 1. To the distance of distinct vision; 2. To the distance at which we are accustomed to read, or to place small objects in order to see them conveniently. For this reason different eyes require different focal distances. There are spectacles which have their focus at the distance of from 16 to 20 inches. It is prudent to begin with using these, and to pass very slowly to shorter focal distances, in order to preserve the sight as long as possible.

An important remark suggests itself, which is applicable to all kinds of simple glasses and compound optical instruments. When we look through a glass, the eye experiences, almost always, an extraordinary tension, which may become very injurious to this organ.

We have already observed that we do not perceive immediately the distance of objects, but use our judgment in estimating it according to circumstances. When we see by the aid of glasses, we want almost all the means which serve to guide us in estimating the magnitude and distance of the image, and commonly the imagination places the image at a false distance. The eye accordingly adapts itself to this false distance; and from this contradiction between the true distance from which the refracted rays come, and that which is supposed by the imagination, there must result a certain state unnatural to the eye. This observation explains many singular phenomena which result from the use of glasses, and also the difference of the judgment which different persons form respecting the magnitude and distance of objects seen through an optical instrument; but, on account of the limits which we have proposed to ourselves, we cannot treat this subject more at length; and shall only observe, that in order to avoid injuring the sight by using glasses, we must first *learn* to see with the aid of these instruments.

559. (2.) The effects of simple magnifying glasses depend upon the same principles; we shall easily be convinced of this, if we consider that in figure 82 the image fg is greater and more distant when the focal distance is smaller, and consequently, that a glass magnifies the more, as its focal distance is less. Magnifying glasses whose focal distance is from half an inch to several inches, are called *magnifiers*. When this distance is less than half an inch, they are called *simple microscopes*, or *microscopic lenses*.

As it is always necessary that the image should be at the distance of distinct vision, that is, about 8 inches before the glass, it is obvious from a mere inspection of figure 82, that the object FG must always be very near the focus D, if the image fg is to be removed from the glass 16 times its real distance or more. In using the microscope, the object must be nearly in the focus. According to this remark it is easy to estimate the magnifying power of a microscope. For, on account of the similarity of the triangles FHC and fhC, the object FH is to the image fh, as the distance of the object HC, is to the distance of the image hC. In a microscope, HC must be only a little smaller than the focal distance, and then hC is nearly 8 inches; thus the focal distance is to 8 inches as unity is to the number which expresses the degree of enlargement or magnifying power.

560. There are still two things to be observed with respect to the magnifying power.

(1.) Since the distance of distinct vision is different for different eyes, and since, moreover, according to the remark made in the preceding article, many optical illusions combine to influence our estimate of distance, there must be a great difference in the magnitude ascribed by different persons to the same object.

(2.) The number which expresses the magnifying power according to the above rule, only indicates the enlargement of the *diameter* of the object. To obtain the enlargement of the *surface*, we must square this number; to obtain that of the *volume*, we must cube it. A microscope whose focal distance is 0,1 inch, magnifies

> The diameter 80 times,
> The surface 6400 times,
> The volume 512000 times.

The last number being the greatest, is that commonly used to indicate the magnifying power of a microscope; but one is astonished that, with a microscope which magnifies half a million of times, the diameter should only appear 80 times greater. When we speak of *telescopes*, we make use of the more just denomination, which expresses the enlargement of the diameter.

561. (3.) The effect of the *solar microscope* may be explained by figure 84. If we place FG near the focus D, we observe that the image fg is removed and becomes greater; indeed there is no degree of enlargement which this image is not capable of attaining. Consequently, if we fix a small glass lens to the shutter of a very dark room, and place a small inverted object a little beyond the focal distance DC, an image is produced at a certain distance behind the glass, which may be received upon a white screen or upon the wall. This image is erect, and magnified, but it is obvious that the solar light which colours it must be extremely feeble, and the more so, according as the image is greater, if the object is not illuminated by all possible means. It is not sufficient to illuminate it directly by the simple light of the sun; this light must be collected nearly to a point by means of a convex lens. Then the size of the object is to that of the image, as CH to Ch, that is, as the focal distance of the lens is to the distance of the screen. The solar microscope has this advantage, that many persons can see the image at the same time; and also that, by means of the image, the figure of the object may be very easily delineated. But this instrument does not admit of the precision that belongs to the simple micro-

scope; and the image loses in distinctness as much as it gains in magnitude, when we increase the distance of the screen.

562. In the *camera obscura* the images of distant objects are formed by a converging glass, as represented in figure 84, and are received directly upon a white screen or upon ground glass; or they are reflected upward or downward by a plane mirror placed at some distance behind the glass, and making with it an angle of 45°; so that these images may be received upon a horizontal plane. Landscapes are represented in a very agreeable manner in the camera obscura, and the painter may advantageously make use of one.

563. We shall now speak of some instruments composed of two converging glasses, but otherwise analogous to the preceding.

(3.) The *camera lucida* consists of a quadrangular box, before which is placed a convex glass of considerable extent; behind this, in the box, is a plane mirror, placed at an angle of 45°, which reflects towards the cover the images of distant objects, which, without it would have been painted on the posterior side. In front of the mirror an opening is made to which a second converging glass is fitted, and through which we view the object as with a simple glass.

(4.) In the *magic lantern*, there are two large convex glasses at a little distance from each other. Before the first, as in FG (*fig.* 82), we pass a figure painted upon glass, placed within the focal distance, and illuminated as strongly as possible, by means of a lamp and a reflecting mirror placed behind. As the figure moves within the focal distance of the first glass, the rays after their passage through this glass, continue as if they came from a distant and inverted image, fg (*fig.* 82). The second glass must be placed beyond the first AB, to receive the transmitted rays, and its situation must be such, that the image fg shall extend a little beyond its focal distance. Then the rays are refracted in this second glass, so as to produce, as in figure 81, a distant image fg, which may be received upon a white screen. This image is erect, because that of which it is the representation is inverted.

(5.) We also make *compound magnifiers* consisting of two convex glasses. The object FG is placed close in front of the first glass, and the rays are refracted as if they came from the distant image fg (*fig.* 82.) Close behind this glass, there is a second whose anterior focal distance extends a little beyond the image fg. Through this last we see the image just as we should see the real object with the simple magnifier.

(6.) There are instruments which consist of a large convex glass, the focal distance of which is from $1\frac{1}{2}$ to 2 feet; these are peculiarly fitted for viewing large designs in perspective. The design being well illuminated, must be placed within the focal distance, but not very far from the focus. Then we see a distant magnified image, rather indistinct, it is true, but for this very reason more true to nature.

564. It is obvious from what precedes, that we must first know the focal distance of a converging glass, in order to judge of its effects. It is found in the same manner as that of mirrors.

We expose the glass to the light of the sun or moon, and measure the distance from its surface to the image produced at its focus; or we cover the glass with a paper circle having two holes made in it, and ascertain the point where the rays which pass through these holes meet.

Much address is required in this operation, when we wish to determine with accuracy very near or very distant foci.

Phenomena produced by Diverging Glasses.

565. The phenomena produced by diverging glasses, are entirely analogous to those which we obtain by means of convex mirrors.

If we direct one of these glasses towards the sun, and receive upon a white surface the light which it transmits, it will be seen that this light diverges as if it came from a point situated in the concavity of the glass. We call this point the *negative focus*, and its distance from the anterior surface, the *negative focal distance*. If we reverse the faces, the phenomena are the same; a diverging glass has, therefore, two negative foci.

The luminous rays transmitted through a diverging glass, form erect images, which are nearer and smaller than the objects themselves. The distance of the object occasions no other modification in these phenomena, except to make the image appear a little farther from the glass, according as we remove the object. But the utmost limit to which the image can be removed is the anterior focus, and this is attained when the object is at a very great distance.

566. Let *AB* (*fig.* 85) be a diverging glass, *HD* its axis, and *E* and *D* the two negative foci. Let the object *FG* be at *H*; the phenomenon which takes place under these circumstances, may be

determined by the same method which was made use of for mirrors and converging glasses. From the most elevated point F, draw the ray FA parallel to the axis; this is refracted in the direction AK, and then seems to come from the focus E; a second ray FCL passes through the optic centre without being refracted. The rays AK and CL diverge, therefore, after passing through the glass, as if they come from the point f; this then is the point from which all the rays from F seem to come. Thus if we draw fg perpendicular to the axis, we shall have the magnitude and position of the image seen through the glass.

567. It is only for *spectacles* that we employ diverging glasses separately. They bring distant objects near, so that short-sighted persons can see them, in the same manner as convex spectacles remove those which are too near, and place them at a convenient distance for long-sighted persons.

The remark made at the end of article 558, applies particularly to concave spectacles. When we see, for example, with a concave glass, the focal distance of which is 10 inches, the imagination cannot easily conceive that the whole extent of a wide prospect is contained in a space of 10 inches radius; and yet all the images which we see, are actually within this space. For this reason, the imagination always removes them too far, and thus the eye experiences an unnatural tension. When, therefore, we are obliged to use this kind of spectacles, we should begin with those lenses whose focal distances are considerable, and pass gradually to those which are shorter.

Mathematical Additions.

568. The essential theory of all spherical glasses, or at least, what is necessary for understanding all the phenomena which we have described, is deduced from two theorems, one of which relates to the refraction of a ray coming from any point of the axis; and the other to the refraction of a ray which comes from a point situated very near the axis.

Figure 86 illustrates the first of these principles. Let ABC be the upper half of the profile of a converging glass. Let D be the geometric centre of the anterior surface AC; E the geometric centre of the posterior surface. Let us suppose that the plane of the profile passes through these two points. A line *FI* drawn through *D* and *E* must be perpendicular to *A* and *B*; consequently it will be the axis of the glass. From the point *F* of the axis, the ray *FG* falls upon the glass. Through *G* and *D*, therefore, draw the normal *KGD*; we shall find, according to the fundamental law of dioptrics, that the refracted ray remains in the plane of the figure, and that it makes with the normal *GD* a smaller angle in the glass than in the air. Let *GH* be its direction. If through the point *H* where it reaches the posterior surface, we draw to this surface the normal *EHL*, the ray, after passing, will still remain in the plane of the figure; but it will diverge from *HL* downward, and consequently will cut the axis in some point. Let *I* be this point; then the problem will be expressed as follows; *To find the position of the point* I, *when the radii of the surfaces, the positions of the centres and those of the points* F *and* G, *are known.*

If we wish to solve this problem with the utmost rigour, we must employ long and complicated calculations. But it is easy to obtain such an approximation as is entirely sufficient for all practical purposes. This is done by means of a relation which exists between the two radii *DA* and *EB*, the *two distances of meeting AF* and *BI*, and the ratio of refraction which we suppose to be known.

The circumstance which facilitates this approximation is, that the arcs must have a very slight curvature, in order that the glasses may produce distinct images. Consequently, the acute angles at *D* and *E* are always very small; but then the acute angles *F*, *I*, *G*, *H*, are always small also, and the arcs *GA*, *HB*, may be considered nearly as lines perpendicular to the axis, and also as equal and parallel lines, on account of the thinness of the glass.

569. *Problem.* Conformably to the above considerations, let $AD = f$, $EB = g$, $AF = a$, $BI = \alpha$, and let the ratio of refraction between air and glass be $n : 1$. To find an approximate equation between f, g, a, α, and n.

Solution. Since the angles *KGF*, *HGD*, *GHE*, *LHI*, are small, we may attribute to them the constant ratio of incidence and refraction, which exists between their sines. Thus we have,

$$KGF : HGD :: n : 1$$
$$LHI : GHE :: n : 1;$$

consequently,

$$KGF + LHI : HGD + GHE :: n : 1.$$

Now if we designate the acute angles by the letters at their vertices F, E, D, I, we have

$$KGF = F + D. \quad LHI = E + I,$$

because the first is the exterior angle of the triangle FGD, and the second of the triangle EHI. From this we have

$$KGF + LHI = F + D + E + I.$$

We shall have by the same principle

$$HGD + GHE = GME = E + D;$$

so that from these values the preceding proportion becomes

$$F + D + E + I : E + D :: n : 1;$$

or, by composition,

$$F + I : E + D :: n - 1 : 1;$$

which gives the equation

$$(n - 1) E + (n - 1) D = F + I.$$

Now, on account of the smallness of all these angles, we shall have, without sensible error,

$$E \text{ proportional to } \frac{BH}{EB} = \frac{BH}{g},$$

$$D \ldots \ldots \frac{AG}{AD} = \frac{AG}{f},$$

$$F \ldots \ldots \frac{AG}{AF} = \frac{AG}{a},$$

$$I \ldots \ldots \frac{BH}{BI} = \frac{BH}{\alpha}.$$

Substituting these values in the preceding equation,

$$\frac{(n-1) BH}{g} + \frac{(n-1) AG}{f} = \frac{AG}{a} + \frac{BH}{\alpha}.$$

But, on account of the small thickness of the glass, the points G and H are nearly coincident; and as, besides, the lines FG, GH, HI, make small angles with the axis, it follows that $AG = BH$ nearly; we may, therefore, divide the whole equation by AG or BH, and then we shall have

$$\frac{n-1}{f} + \frac{n-1}{g} = \frac{1}{a} + \frac{1}{\alpha},$$

which is the approximate formula sought.

570. *Additions.* (1.) Each of the 5 quantities, n, f, g, a, α, may be considered as unknown, the other being given. This gives rise to 5 propositions capable of many important applications.

(2.) The formula is applicable to all the positions of the points F and I upon the axis, provided that in each case, regard be paid to the position of the *part* which is considered as given. According to the form and thickness of the glass, this position may be the same as in the figure, or it may be the opposite. If the glass, for example, were *double concave*, we should have to make f and g negative. If the anterior surface were plane, and the posterior surface concave, we should have to make $f = \infty$, which would give $\frac{n-1}{f} = 0$; and g would be negative. If the ray FG did not come from a point of the axis before the glass, but on the contrary were directed towards a point of the axis, behind the glass, we should have a negative. If the ray FG were parallel to the axis, we should have $a = \infty$, and $\frac{1}{a} = 0$.

The consequences, therefore, deduced from the formula, may serve for all spherical glasses and for all cases in which they can be used.

(3.) Since AG and BH are eliminated from the equation, this is a proof that all rays coming from the point F, and falling on the glass, will unite in the same point I, and consequently produce there an image of F. But in certain cases, this image of F may be before the glass, which happens when the formula gives a negative value for α; it may be at an infinite distance, if $\frac{1}{\alpha} = 0$, that is, $\alpha = \infty$.

(4.) Putting together the consequences above obtained, we find, *that in each kind of spherical glasses, a radiant point, placed in the axis, always produces by refraction an image situated in this same axis, but sometimes before the glass, sometimes behind it, and sometimes at an infinite distance;* all which was taken for granted in our method of construction.

(5.) Let α be the quantity sought, and $a = \infty$, that is, suppose the incident ray parallel to the axis; we shall have $\frac{1}{a} = 0$; consequently,

$$\frac{1}{\alpha} = \frac{n-1}{f} + \frac{n-1}{g}.$$

By means of this formula, we determine the distance where the rays parallel to the axis, cut each other after refraction.

This distance is called the *focal distance* of the glass, and if we represent it by p, we shall have,

$$\frac{1}{p} = \frac{n-1}{f} + \frac{n-1}{g},$$

which is one of the principle formulas of dioptrics. By means of this formula we can find, in each case, the focal distance of a glass, by knowing the radius of its surface, and the ratio of refraction. Many other useful questions may be resolved in the same manner, since if of 4 quantities p, n, f, g, three are given, the fourth may be easily obtained from the formula.

If the glass is symmetrically double convex, $f = g$; consequently,

$$\frac{1}{p} = \frac{2(n-1)}{f}, \text{ or } p = \frac{f}{2(n-1)}.$$

Let the ratio of refraction be 17 : 11. Then we have

$$n = \frac{17}{11};\ n-1 = \frac{6}{11};\ 2(n-1) = \frac{12}{11};$$

consequently, $p = \frac{11}{12}f$; that is, $p = f$, wanting $\frac{1}{12}$.

If the glass is double concave, and symmetrical, we have, in the same manner, $p = -\frac{11}{12}f$.

If the glass is plano-convex, one of the radii g, for example, becomes infinite; consequently,

$$\frac{n-1}{g} = 0, \text{ and } \frac{1}{p} = \frac{n-1}{f} \text{ or } p = \frac{f}{n-1}.$$

If now we make as above, $n-1 = \frac{6}{11}$, we have $p = \frac{11}{6}f$, or nearly $2f$.

When we understand how to employ algebraic formulas, we easily see how the calculation is to be made in all other cases. The following example may serve to indicate the most convenient form of calculation. Let us suppose that the glass is a meniscus, and that its anterior surface is concave. In this case let

$$f = -10;\ g = +\tfrac{1}{5};\ n-1 = \tfrac{6}{11};$$

we shall have

$$\frac{1}{p} = -\tfrac{6}{110} + \tfrac{30}{11} = \tfrac{300}{110} - \tfrac{6}{110} = +\tfrac{294}{110};$$

consequently, $p = + \frac{110}{294}$. Performing the division, we have
$$p = + 0{,}374.$$

(6.) Since in general, according to what precedes,
$$\frac{n-1}{f} + \frac{n-1}{g} = \frac{1}{a} + \frac{1}{\alpha},$$
the first member of this equation being equal to $\frac{1}{p}$, the second member also must be equal to $\frac{1}{p}$; and we shall have generally
$$\frac{1}{p} = \frac{1}{a} + \frac{1}{\alpha};$$
which is the formula obtained in catoptrics, for comparing the focal distance of a mirror, with the *two distances of meeting of the rays*. And in this case, as before, the formula is applicable to almost all optical calculations.

571. It still remains for us to consider the refraction of rays coming from a point placed without the axis. It may be proved as well by theory as experiment, that the radiant points which are near the axis, give distinct images. This is a sufficient reason for directing our attention to them.

The line *AB* (*fig.* 87) represents the profile of any glass whatever, whose optic centre is *C*, and whose axis is *DE*. *F* is a radiant point, from which one of the rays *FG*, is refracted in the direction *GH*. If from the point *F*, we draw the line *FCH* through the optic centre *C*, the refracted ray will cut it in some point, which we shall call *H*. And consequently the distances *CF* and *CH* are connected together by a certain law.

572. *Theorem.* If we call p the focal distance, and if the radiant point is very near the axis, we shall have (570)
$$\frac{1}{p} = \frac{1}{CF} + \frac{1}{CH}.$$

Demonstration. Produce *HG* towards *I*, and *GF* to the axis in *D*. If we designate the acute angles by *D*, *K*, *F*, *H*, we shall have $F + H = D + K$, because each of these two sums is equal to *IGF*. But as *F* is near the axis, the angle *GFC* is very small, and *GC* is nearly perpendicular to *FC*; we may, therefore, consider, without any material error,

Elem.

F proportional to $\dfrac{CG}{FG}$,

H .... $\dfrac{CG}{CH}$,

D .... $\dfrac{CG}{CD}$,

K .... $\dfrac{CG}{CK}$.

If we substitute these values in the equation $F + H = D + K$, we shall have

$$\frac{CG}{FC} + \frac{CG}{CH} = \frac{CG}{CD} + \frac{CG}{CK};$$

or, dividing the whole by CG,

$$\frac{1}{FC} + \frac{1}{CH} = \frac{1}{CD} + \frac{1}{CK}.$$

Suppose that the ray does not come from F, but from D, which cannot make any change in the refracted ray; we have, according to article 571, (5,)

$$\frac{1}{p} = \frac{1}{DC} + \frac{1}{CK},$$

and consequently,

$$\frac{1}{p} = \frac{1}{FC} + \frac{1}{CH};$$

which is the formula sought.

573. *Addition.* It is obvious from this formula, that the results obtained for a radiant point within the axis, may also be applied to points without the axis. Hence, 1. Each radiant point F, placed without the axis, produces after refraction an image H always situated in a straight line drawn from the radiant point to the optic centre. 2. If through the points F and H we draw the lines FL and HM perpendicular to the axis, since F and M are very near the axis, we may suppose, without sensible error, that $CF = CL$, and $CH = CM$; so that the formula will be changed to

$$\frac{1}{p} = \frac{1}{CL} + \frac{1}{CM}.$$

But it hence follows that if FL is a radiant object, each of its points will have its image in HM, and that the image of each of them will be found exactly in the straight line drawn from this point to the centre.

This is the second supposition made in our method of construction. And thus all which was then admitted without proof, is now rigorously demonstrated.

CHAPTER XLIII.

Compound Optical Instruments.

A. *Refracting Telescope.*

574. By means of spherical glasses, we can form a variety of different combinations, which make objects appear larger and nearer than they really are. Such a combination constitutes what is called a *telescope*. When it is composed of glasses alone, it is called a *refracting telescope*; when spherical mirrors are used, a *reflecting telescope*. The glass or mirror which immediately receives the light of the object, is called *object glass*, or *object mirror*. The others are called *eye glasses*, and are designated by first, second, &c., beginning with that nearest the object and reckoning towards the eye.

575. To render the effect of a telescope as perfect as possible, each glass must be exactly centred; the axes of all the glasses must be in the same straight line; each glass must have its focal distance exactly determined by fixed rules, and especially an exactly proportionate aperture. Between the glasses we place *diaphragms*, which are opaque circles having a hole at the centre, and of which it is very important to determine the position and diameter. Lastly, all the glasses must be placed at distances prescribed before hand; and even the eye must have its place exactly determined. Sometimes the last eye-glass only is moveable; but more frequently all the eye-glasses are enclosed in a tube, for the purpose of varying their distance from the object-glass so as to suit the eye.

576. With telescopes we see distant objects under a much greater angle than with the naked eye. The number which expresses how many times this angle is augmented is called the *magnifying power*.

The space which we perceive through the whole system of gasses is circular, and is called the *field of view*. The measure of this field is the angle under which the eye would see, without the telescope, the whole space which it embraces by means of the telescope.

These several particulars are susceptible of mathematical determination; but all that can be expected in an elementary work, is to deduce and explain the effects of telescopes from the properties of spherical glasses and mirrors.

577. To instruments composed of several glasses, the following general remarks are applicable. We have shown in the preceding chapters, that each spherical glass produces an image of the object whose rays fall upon it, but that this image may be sometimes before the glass, sometimes behind it, and sometimes at an infinite distance. If now we place a second glass behind the first, so that their axes shall correspond, the image produced by the first, will serve as an object to the second; but the image produced by the second, may be before, behind, or at an infinite distance. This image will serve as an object for the third glass, and so on. Hence we see that whatever be the number of glasses arranged upon a common axis, and whatever be their distance, each glass will produce a particular image of the object.

Some of these images are actually formed, because the rays which belong to a determinate point of the object, actually unite in the same point after refraction. Such are the images produced by a convex glass in the *camera obscura*. These are called *real* or *physical images*. Others do not actually exist, either because the light is only propagated as if it came from such an image, as is the case in opera-glasses, and in *magnifiers*; or because the rays which would produce an image, are received by a new glass, before the image has been completed. These are called *geometric* images. But cases are presented in compound instruments, which have not been considered in the preceding chapter, where the object was always effective.

A *real* object, for example, is always before the glass. An image which serves as an object to the following glass, may be behind this glass. This case would happen, for example, if instead of letting the image fg be actually formed (*fig.* 84), we should receive the light upon another glass placed somewhere between AB and fg. This case, therefore, gives rise to a particular series of phenomena; but they may be explained by the same method of construction which was employed in the preceding chapter.

Phenomena produced by means of Converging Glasses when the Object is behind the Glass.

578. When the object is behind a converging glass, there is always produced a small real image placed very near the glass.

Let FG (*fig.* 88) be the image which would be produced by a glass placed in D, if the light were not collected by the glass AB, before this image could be formed. We know that this image is produced by the convergent rays which unite to form the point F, for example. Among these convergent rays, there may be one LC, which passes through the optic centre C, and which consequently continues, without being refracted, in the direction CF. There may also be one of these rays KA, which is parallel to the axis. This is refracted towards the principal focus E; the rays CF and AE cut each other in the point f; and there all the rays must meet, which would have met at F, without the interposition of the glass AB; that is, if f is an image of F. Accordingly, if we draw the line fgh perpendicular to the axis, we find that fg is the image of FG. Meantime, we see that the two rays KA and LC need not actually exist. The rays which must represent a point F, are always comprehended in a small angle; and it may happen that within this angle, there is no ray parallel to the axis, and none which passes through the optic centre. But since all the rays which go towards F, have one and the same point of coincidence in f, it is indifferent whether the rays made use of to find the situation of f, exist or not.

We see by the figure that the phenomenon continues always the same in its essential parts. In whatever place the object FG is behind the glass, there is always formed between the glass and the principal focus, a reduced image, which is erect or inverted, according as the object FG is inverted or erect. Only the magnitude and distance of this image change with the distance of the object.

Upon this is founded the effects of a collector placed behind a burning glass which were described, article 553.

Phenomena produced by means of Diverging Glasses, when the Object is behind the Glass.

579. The phenomena produced under these circumstances are very various; yet they may be easily conceived from what has been said above.

(1.) Figure 89 represents the case where the image *FG*, which takes the place of the object, is within the posterior focal distance *CE*; the two rays *KA* and *LC*, which would cut each other in *F*, were it not for the glass *AB*, after their passage take the convergent directions *Af* and *Cf*; accordingly a larger and more distant image *fg*, is produced behind the glass, which has a position similar to *FG*.

(2.) Figure 90 represents the case where the image *FG* is in the posterior focus *E*. Here the two rays *KA* and *LC*, which in the glass, would cut each other in *F*, have, after passing the glass, the parallel directions *AM* and *CF*, so that an image is nowhere formed; or, we may say, it is formed at an infinite distance.

(3.) Figure 91 represents the case where the image *FG* is placed without the posterior focal distance *CE*. In this case, the two rays *KA* and *LC*, after their passage, have the divergent directions *AM*, *CF*; if the lines *AM*, *CF*, are produced before the glass sufficiently far, they will cut each other below the axis in *f*.

The rays continue, therefore, after their passage through the glass, as if they came from an image *fg*, placed without the anterior focal distance, and having an inverted situation with respect to *FG*. But the magnitude and distance of this image may be very different, according as *FG* is more or less distant from *E*. If *FG* is very near *E*, *fg* is very distant and large. If *EH* = *CE*, the two images are equally large and equally distant; but if *FG* is more distant, *fg* is smaller, and nearer the focus *D*.

B. *The most Important Kinds of Refracting Telescopes.*

580. The first instrument of this kind was invented twice near the beginning of the seventeenth century. Accident led Jansen, a spectacle-maker of Middleburg, to the invention; and Galileo, who had heard of this invention, succeeded, by the force of his own genius, and a profound knowledge of the theory, in constructing similar in-

struments. Hence we call this instrument the *Holland telescope*, or *Galileo's telescope*. The object-glass, is a converging lens, and the eye-glass is a diverging lens of a very short focal distance. The latter is disposed in such a manner, that the inverted image of distant objects, produced by the object-glass, does not quite reach the posterior focus of the eye-glass, which refers itself to the case represented in figure 91. An eye placed very close behind AB, will see, instead of FG, the image fg; but as in the telescope, FG is inverted, fg appears erect. The telescope magnifies the apparent diameter as many times as the focal distance of the eye-glass is contained in the focal distance of the object-glass. It cannot be used for very great magnifying powers, because the field of view is too small; accordingly it is now employed only as a pocket telescope or opera-glass.

581. In Kepler's telescope, the inverted image produced by the object-glass, is seen through a convex glass of a very short focal distance, just as we look at a real object through a magnifier. As this last glass does not invert objects, it follows that with such a telescope, which is the best yet known, we see the objects inverted; but in astronomical observations this is unimportant. We ascertain the magnifying power in the same manner as in the Galilean telescope. If we would obtain a great magnifying power it is necessary to give the instrument an inconvenient length.

582. The field of view of a telescope will be much enlarged, if instead of allowing the image, produced by the object-glass, to be actually formed, we receive the light upon a pretty large glass collector. Then a small image is produced behind the glass, which is seen through the last eye-glass, as through a single lens. By this arrangement we lose nothing as to the magnifying power, for the image is magnified as much more, as it is rendered less, by the interposition of the glass collector.

Instruments constructed in this manner, which magnify little, but embrace a wide field of view and much light, are called *night glasses*.

583. It was at the beginning of the seventeenth century, that a Jesuit, named Rheita, invented the terrestrial telescope, in which there are, beside the object-glass, three converging glasses, the focal distances of which are short but equal. The three eye-glasses are generally enclosed in one tube; so that the porterior focus of each of them shall coincide exactly with the anterior focus of the following one. When we wish to use this instrument, it is necessary to push the tube, con-

taining the eye-glasses, into the other tube, so far that the image produced by the object-glass, may be a little within the anterior focal distance of the first eye-glass, that is, the one farthest from the eye. In this position, an eye situated behind the first eye-glass, would see the image of the object considerably distant, but magnified and inverted. This inverted image is therefore considerably in advance of the focal distance of the second eye-glass, and consequently it produces behind the posterior focus of this glass, an erect image of the object. Lastly, since this image is within the anterior focal distance of the third eye-glass, it is seen through this as through a simple lens. The magnifying power, in this case, is measured as in the two preceding, by dividing the focal distance of the object glass, by the focal distance of one of the eye-glasses. To obtain a great magnifying power this instrument also must have an inconvenient length.

584. We may obtain a wider field, without impairing the distinctness and magnifying power, if we add a fourth eye-glass, and employ eye-glasses of unequal focal distances. But this construction has lost much of its importance since the invention of achromatic telescopes.

585. There are several kinds of telescopes which were invented in the seventeenth century. In the 45th chapter, we shall describe the reflecting telescope of Newton, and the various achromatic telescopes.

586. When the focal distances of the glasses of a telescope are determined, together with their positions and apertures, the magnifying power, field of view, and degrees of distinctness, may be calculated. The mathematical process cannot here be made known. But as it is important to know the magnifying power and field of view of a telescope, we shall briefly describe a method of finding them mechanically.

587. The magnifying power may be determined very nearly, by viewing the same object at the same time, through the telescope and with the naked eye, and comparing the apparent magnitude of the two images.

It may be determined very accurately by a small instrument invented by Ramsden, the nature of which is briefly as follows.

When we direct towards the heavens, any telescope except that of Galileo, and hold a strip of paper behind the last eye-glass, at the point where the eye should be placed we see a luminous circle exactly defined. The point most favourable for the distinctness of the circle is found by trial. We measure its diameter with the greatest care; then we measure the aperture of the object-glass, and divide this aperture by the diameter; and thus we find how much the instrument magnifies. Instead of paper, Ramsden used a thin plate of horn. He marked a very exact scale of divisions upon it, and attached it to a tube which could be joined to the telescope, and thus he measured, in a most convenient and exact manner, the diameter of the luminous circle.

The theory of this ingenious instrument cannot be here explained. We shall only observe that the luminous circle is itself an image of the object-glass; hence we may conclude that this image is contained in the diameter of the object-glass, as many times as the telescope magnifies distant objects.*

588. The field of view of a telescope may be estimated by comparing its diameter with the apparent diameter of an object viewed through the tube, this diameter being supposed to be known from other experiments. The diameters of the sun and moon are principally used for this purpose. These diameters are about half a degree. Their exact values may be found in treatises on astronomy.

We may find the field of view of a telescope exactly, by directing it towards a star which is near the equator. We cause the star to pass across the middle of the field, and observe how many seconds elapse during the passage. Four seconds of time always represent an angle of a minute.

C. Compound Microscope.

589. The compound microscope was known soon after the invention of the telescope, but its inventer is unknown.

With respect to the magnifying power, the compound miscroscope has no advantage over the simple microscope; but it has a greater field, more light, and is more conveniently used for small objects.

It may be made with two, three, or more glasses. The object-glass is always a small converging lens, whose focal distance is never more than half an inch. Ordinarily we have several of these

---

* M. Arago has recently invented a method of measuring the magnifying power, which is very ingenious, and which is founded on double refraction. See *Cambridge Optics*.

lenses, whose focal distances gradually decrease, because here, as in the simple microscope, the magnifying power is always greater in proportion as the focal distance of the object-lens is less.

We place the object just before the anterior focus of the object lens; consequently a magnified and inverted image of the object is formed at a considerable distance behind the lens. We can see this image through a convex glass of one or two inches, as through a common magnifier. Such is the construction of the microscope with two glasses.

But the combination of three glasses is preferable. Instead of allowing the image to be formed by the object-lens, as in the case just described, we receive the light, before its formation, upon a large glass of about 3 inches; so that, according to what is said, article 578, a small image of the object is produced behind this glass, which may be seen through a second eye-glass, whose focal distance is about one inch.

It is not expedient to employ a greater number of glasses, because the light is enfeebled by them. Moreover great care must be used in arranging them; otherwise the effect is indistinct.

590. In a compound microscope the magnifying power, field of view, &c., are calculated in the same manner as for a telescope; by the focal distances of the glasses, and their distances from each other; but we have not room to consider this subject.

The magnifying power may be estimated by the following experiment. We put in the microscope a small object of exactly known dimensions; we look into the instrument with one eye; and with the other, towards the points of a pair of compasses held at the distance of distinct vision. We open the points of the compasses, until their distance appears to be equal to the diameter of the object seen through the microscope. We measure this distance upon a scale of equal parts, and divide it by the true diameter of the object. We employ also for the same purpose the measure of the magnifying power described in article 586, and in exactly the same manner as for a telescope; only, for the number that gives the measure of the magnifying power, which in this case will be unity or a fraction, must be multiplied by the distance of distinct vision, that is, by about 8 inches, and divided by the focal distance of the object-lens.

CHAPTER XLIV.

Theory of Dioptric Colours, or the Decomposition of Light.

The Glass Prism.

591. We now proceed to a careful examination of the phenomena of the dispersion of colours, which are produced in every case of refraction.

The very simple apparatus by means of which Newton clearly demonstrated the laws of these phenomena, is a glass prism, of which *ABC* (*fig.* 92) represents a vertical section. Ordinarily the prisms which are used in these experiments are symmetrical, and each of their three angles *BAC, ABC, ACB*, contains 60 degrees. Yet we sometimes use irregular ones. Most frequently they are 5 or 6 inches in length, so that we can look through them with both eyes at once. When the light passes through these prisms, each ray is refracted twice ; namely, at the anterior surface *BA*, and at the posterior one *CA*; by this double effect the refraction and dispersion of the colours are much increased, and we may then easily examine the refracted light, at such a distance as we please behind the prism. The angle *BAC*, formed by the two surfaces *BA* and *CA* of the prism, is called the *refracting angle*.

592. Suppose that we hold a prism of this kind before both eyes in a horizontal position, so that one of the angles, *BAC*, for example, as in figure 92, is at the bottom. If we then view objects through one of the refracting surfaces, *CA*, for example, we see them much lower than they really are, and all the objects which are situated towards the sides, change place still more sensibly, so that a horizontal line appears as an arc concave on the upper side. At the same time the borders of all objects appear to be surrounded with the colours of the rainbow ; but for this very reason they are indistinct.

593. The experiments made with a prism in a dark room are still more remarkable and decisive. We cause a small cone of solar rays *DE* (*fig.* 92) to pass through a small opening *D*, made in a window shutter, and fall upon the face *BA* of the prism. This light is refracted twice at *E* and *F*, and always upward. After refraction it spreads wider, the farther it extends. If this light is received

upon a white screen *VG*, opposite the opening *D*, we observe in *VR*, where the light strikes, the most beautiful phenomenon which colours are capable of producing; that is, an elongated image *VR*, as represented in figure 93. It is nowhere exactly defined; yet the two lateral lines *AB* and *DC* are easily distinguished; nor is it difficult to perceive that the upper and lower parts terminate in a semicircle, although their contour, and especially that of *V* are very indistinct. The entire image is about 5 times as long as it is wide, and each point of its height is marked by different and very lively colours. The order in which these colours are disposed, as well as the space they generally occupy, are indicated approximately by the lines which cut figure 93, and by the words which are placed against them. Yet the determination of the space which each colour fills, cannot be exact, since they run into each other by insensible gradations; so that, in fact, the whole space from *V* to *R* is only a constant variation of colours, in which we can only distinguish the 7 predominant shades indicated above. The image must be received at a considerable distance from the prism, at least 12 feet, since nearer the posterior surface of the prism, the image is perfectly white in the middle, and only coloured towards the top and bottom; whereas, the more the light is dilated by distance, the more distinct are the colours. This image of colours is called the *solar spectrum*.

594. In order to comprehend easily the formation of the solar spectrum, we must examine with care the refraction which a single ray experiences in the prism. Let *BAC* (*fig.* 94) be the refracting angle of a prism with vertical sections. Let the ray *DE* fall upon the anterior face *AB*. At *E* erect the incident perpendicular *IH*. It is evident, from what has been said, that the ray is refracted upward in the glass. Let *EF*, therefore, be the refracted ray. At *F*, where it reaches the posterior surface, erect the perpendicular *LK*. It will be seen that at its emergence from the glass it is again refracted upward. Let *FG*, therefore, be the emergent ray. If we produce the incident ray *DE* indefinitely towards *N*, and the emergent ray until it meets *DN* in *M*, the acute angle *GMN* is the quantity by which the ray *DE* is turned from its primitive direction, by the two refractions which it successively experiences. It is demonstrated by the calculus, that when the refracting angle of the prism is not very large, this angle *GMN*, at whatever place the ray *DE* falls, has a nearly constant ratio with the refracting angle *BAC*.

For example, let the ratio of refraction between air and glass be $n : 1$. We have almost exactly $GMN = (n - 1) BAC$; and as we find that the ratio of refraction in common glass is about $3 : 2$, we have $n = \frac{3}{2}$; consequently, $n - 1 = \frac{1}{2}$; therefore,
$$GMN = \tfrac{1}{2} BAC;$$
that is, by the effect of the glass prism, the ray DE is turned from its primitive direction by a quantity nearly equal to half the refracting angle, and always towards the opening of the angle.*

---

* *Demonstration.* The formula $GMN = (n - 1) BAC$, would be rigorously exact, if the angles themselves, instead of their sines, were as $n : 1$. Upon this supposition, and observing that $DEH = LEM$, we have
$$LEM : LEF :: n : 1;$$
whence we obtain
$$MEF : LEF :: n - 1 : 1;$$
also at the other surface
$$GFK = LFM,$$
and we have
$$LFM : LFE :: n : 1;$$
consequently,
$$MFE : LFE :: n - 1 : 1.$$
From the second and fourth proportion we deduce
$$MEF + MFE : LEF + LFE :: n - 1 : 1.$$
We have, moreover,
$$MEF + MFE = GMN,$$
$$LEF + LFE = ILF,$$
consequently,
$$GMN : ILF :: n - 1 : 1;$$
Now ILF is the supplement of ELF; and as the quadrilateral $AELF$ has two of its angles E and F right angles, ELF is the supplement of EAF; consequently, ILF is equal to EAF, or to the refracting angle of the prism. Thus the preceding proportion is changed into the following;
$$GMN : BAC :: n - 1 : 1,$$
whence we obtain
$$GMN = (n - 1) BAC.$$

595. We here remark also, that the use of the prism is the most convenient mechanical means of finding exactly the ratio of refraction $n:1$; for from the formula $GMN = (n-1) BAC$, it follows that

$$n = \frac{GMN}{BAC} + 1.$$

We have only, therefore, to measure these two angles, which operation is attended with no difficulty; yet, if we wish to determine their ratio with extraordinary precision, we must employ for the value of n a more rigorous formula.

596. The preceding remarks upon the phenomena of the prism must be sufficient to give a clear idea of it.

Let us suppose, then, an observer having his eye placed at G (*fig.* 94.) The point D, from which the ray $DEFG$ proceeds, will appear to him in the direction GF, lower than it is. Yet if each ray which passes through the prism were only to experience a deviation equal to $\frac{1}{2} BAC$, from its primitive direction, it is clear that all the effect of the prism would consist merely in causing all objects to appear out of their place, by a quantity equal to the angle indicated. But our theorem is only applicable to the rays which pass in a plane perpendicular to the prism. Those rays, on the contrary, which, when we look through the prism in the manner directed in article 590, come from the objects placed at the sides, are more strongly refracted, since they describe a greater space in the prism, and since, by meeting the surface obliquely, they must make, in the interior, a greater angle of refraction. Thus when we view, through a prism, a straight horizontal line, parallel to the edge of the prism, it must appear arched and with its extremities directed downward, since the light which comes from these extremities, is turned more from its primitive direction.

After what has been said of the phenomena observed in a dark room, the formation of the spectrum will be easily understood.

597. If we take away the prism BAC (*fig.* 92) and let the light which enters through the opening D, fall directly upon the screen, we only see a round, white, and ill-defined image of the sun. Now, if there were no dispersion of colours by refraction, the whole effect of the prism would consist in making the image appear in VR with the same colour, and with a very slight change in the form and magnitude. The elongated figure of the image VR shows, then, unquestionably, *that the refracted light* FVR *has an ununiform refrac-*

tion, since the part which is carried to *V* by refraction, is turned further from its primitive direction than the part which arrives at *R*. Moreover, since the image exhibits a different colour at each successive point, we infer *that the whole light of the sun is divided by refraction, into rays of different colours, and that the light of each of the colours has a ratio of refraction peculiar to itself.*

In the glass of which Newton's prism was made, the ratio of refraction,

For violet light was . . 1,56 : 1
For the intermediate green 1,55 : 1
For the extreme red . . 1,54 : 1.*

598. If all the light which passes through the prism were violet, and of an equal refrangibility, we should see in *V* only a round and violet image of the sun. If this light were red, we should see in *R* a red image, and so of the rest. Hence we conclude that the elongated image *VR* (*fig*. 93) consists properly of an infinite number of round solar images placed one above the other, so that each of them is a little higher than that which precedes it. In figure 95 we have by way of illustration, represented only the images which the 7 principal colours produce; but it is obvious that the solar spectrum (*fig*. 93) cannot be formed simply of seven such circles, but of an

---

* The green rays which are placed in the middle of the spectrum, have, as their situation shows, an intermediate refrangibility; and consequently it is to these only that the denomination mean refrangibility would seem to belong. Yet it is common to apply it to the lowest yellow, because the light is more feeble towards *V* than it is towards *R*. The yellow rays are, then, really the mean rays, not with respect to their situation, but as to their brightness. Newton found for their ratio of refraction in glass 17 : 11; or 1,5454 : 1; and this is the ratio of refraction usually employed in questions where no regard is paid to the dispersion of light.

Indeed we employ the ratio given by yellow light, in estimating refracting powers, without any error; for if we use prisms of a small refracting angle, and which do not consequently produce a sensible dispersion, we find precisely the same result, as I have proved by experiment.

infinite number, since otherwise, the lateral lines *AB* and *CD*, would not appear straight.*

599. These principles are confirmed by a multitude of experiments. If at some distance from the prism, we receive the coloured light with a pretty large converging glass, we find *white* light at the focus; beyond the focus the different colours appear in an inverted order. If we place a second prism near the first, but in a contrary situation, all the light is again refracted downward in the same ratio as it was refracted upward by the first, and the light emerges white from the second prism. We can examine each of the colours separately, by placing at some distance behind the prism a black surface, having a narrow horizontal aperture, through which only a thin uniform section of the solar spectrum can pass. Each colour may be separated still better by placing a second surface perforated horizontally at some distance behind the first, so as to transmit a still narrower line of light than the first. In this way we are enabled to examine any colour we please. Having separated it from the rest we can cause it again to pass through a prism and determine its ratio of refraction. We are thus able to separate two or more colours from the rest, and afterwards to unite them with a converging glass, or metallic mirror, &c.

600. The following question has been much agitated. Into how many colours is the white light of the sun divided by the prism? Newton in his Optics, has affirmed that there are innumerable shades from the darkest violet to the brightest red, and that each of these, however feeble, has a particular ratio of refraction. This is the only tenable opinion.

601. The observations of Newton prove that the bodies which appear white, reflect equally all the colours of the spectrum, while those which appear coloured, are so, because they reflect certain rays and absorb the rest. Bodies which appear black, are those which absorb nearly all the light which they receive. These remarks are not hypothetical, but rest upon well established facts.

---

* The straight line is the common tangent of all the circles, because they have an equal diameter, and it is produced by their continual intersections.

Colours produced by Thin Laminæ.

602. The prism is not the only means of decomposing the solar light into different colours. Thin laminæ of transparent bodies, as soap bubbles, produce similar effects.* Newton made many experiments upon this subject, and ascertained that the effect in question is common to thin laminæ of all transparent bodies, not excepting air. He showed that under all circumstances the colour has a constant relation to the thickness of the lamina; and that, consequently, for each different thickness there is a determinate order in the situation of the colours. But neither he, nor any of those who have followed him, has been able to reduce the formation of these colours to a theory so simple as that of the formation of the colours of the prism. Consequently, we must be contented, as to this phenomenon, with the following general consideration; namely, that there must be, in a thin, transparent lamina, very various refractions and reflections; and this enables us to understand why we perceive a decomposition of colours.

603. Newton deduced from these observations an hypothesis respecting colours. He supposed each body to be composed of very thin transparent laminæ, and each of these laminæ to give a particular colour suited to its thickness. And it is true that there are phenomena which cannot be otherwise explained. The changing colours of mother of pearl, Labrador stone, &c., must be referred to such a cause. Glass and all other transparent colourless bodies, appear white when they are very finely pulverised because each of the particles sends off decomposed light, and white light is produced by their mixture. Yet, there are many obstacles when we undertake to generalize the applications of this hypothesis. According to all appearances there is a kind of chemical affinity, by means of which each body attracts certain constituent principles of light, and

---

* Some explanation is here necessary. It is true, that thin laminæ decompose the light, but not into its simple rays. The prism alone has this power. The colours reflected by thin laminæ are *compound*, and may be divided by the prism. Some remarks on Newton's theory of colours may be found at the end of the chapter.

combines them with itself, so that only the others can be reflected in conformity to the mechanical laws of optics.*

General Observations upon Newton's Theory of Colours.

604. The essential part of this theory consists in incontestible facts and in the consequences which are naturally deduced from them. Accordingly, what is important in it remains invariable. But it has often been ill understood and falsely applied.

In particular, men have confounded the colours produced by the decomposition of solar light, with those of material substances, and applied to these what Newton has advanced respecting the other. It is true, that the colours of all colouring matter are produced by the reflection of differently coloured light; but as it is probable that no body, and consequently no colouring substance, reflects light of one simple, fundamental colour, we cannot expect that the colours of these substances should observe the same laws as those of the solar spectrum. Yet it may be demonstrated that the purest artificial colours resemble, to a certain point, the colours of solar light. For this purpose we use a plate containing 7 divisions, in which the colours of the solar spectrum are imitated as nearly as possible. When we turn the plate with great rapidity, it appears perfectly white. This is explained in the following manner. The successive impressions made upon the retina continue for a certain time. Consequently, we experience nearly the same effect, when colours succeed each other very rapidly, as when their rays come simultaneously to the eye and are actually confounded.

Another remark which must not be omitted in considering the prismatic colours, is the following. When we view a large surface of one single colour, through the prism, this surface appears uniformly coloured in the middle, although this uniform colour is actually compound, according to the sense in which we have considered that term in article 599. This is easily explained. Each ray coming from the surface is in fact decomposed by the prism into different colours; but these different colours, which come from different

---

* It is true, that this mode of representing the phenomena seems more simple at first view; but when we examine the subject more thoroughly, we find it infinitely less probable than that of Newton.

neighbouring points, again combine together, being partially superposed upon each other, so as to form in these points a single colour. Only at the extremities of the surface, where two compound colours, blue and red, for example, touch each other, we see the colours of the rainbow; and this is not produced by the decomposition of one of the colours which fall upon the surface, but by a mixture of simple colours, arising from the decomposition of the two colours which touch each other.

In the same manner, we can explain the formation of all the colours seen through the prism.

Effects of the Dispersion of Colours in Optical Glasses.

605. Let AB (*fig.* 96) be a converging glass; at a great distance before it, let there be an object CD, the white light of which falls upon the glass; in this case, according to art. 556, 557, an inverted image KH is produced at the posterior focus of the glass. But it is obvious, without calculation, that the focal distance of a glass depends upon the ratio of refraction, and that it becomes shorter as the refracting power becomes greater. Moreover, we have seen that the violet rays are refracted more than the red; it is clear, then, that the different colours which compose the light, cannot have the same focus. Let V, therefore, be the focus of the violet rays, and R that of the red rays; it is obvious that the white light of the object CD, will produce in V a violet image FG of this object, and in R a red image LM of the same object; and between these two, images of the intermediate colours of the spectrum; so that between FG and LM, there will be a great number of images placed one upon the other and variously coloured. Accordingly, if the eye of the observer is placed beyond LM, and views this image, he will not see it exactly defined in any of its parts; the indistinctness will increase from the centre to the borders; the red will pass beyond all the rest, and the entire image will appear to be fringed with the hues of the rainbow. This effect must take place in all the images produced by spherical glasses, and it becomes more striking, in proportion as the light is more refracted; that is, according as the object is more magnified.

606. We know, therefore, now two causes of the indistinctness which takes place in all optical instruments.

(1.) The first consists in this, that there is no curvature in which all the rays that come from one point, are, under all circumstances, exactly united again in a single point; and that especially the spherical curvature which we give to glasses, can never perfectly effect such a union of rays of the same nature. This imperfection is common to lenses and mirrors; it is called the *aberration of sphericity*.

(2.) The second cause of confusion depends upon the circumstance above considered. It consists in this, that instead of a single image, there is an infinite number of images differently coloured and placed nearly behind one another. This last cause of indistinctness is of much greater importance than the other; but it exists only in glasses, and not in metallic mirrors; it is called the *aberration of refrangibility*.

607. Experience shows, however, that the eye is capable of bearing very great aberrations of each kind, with less inconvenience as to distinctness, than we should expect from theoretic principles. Nevertheless, in the construction of optical instruments, we pay so much regard to these defects, as always to preserve certain ratios between the focal distance and the aperture of the object-glass; nor can we neglect this, without essentially impairing the distinctness of the image. Hence the making of a good compound optical instrument, is a difficult work, and requires a thorough acquaintance with the science.

CHAPTER XLV.

Reflecting Telescope and Achromatic Lenses.

608. The history of optics is so instructive and interesting to those who would observe the progress of the human mind, that in what remains of this treatise, we shall adopt the historical form, and only intersperse such theoretical remarks as may be necessary for the understanding of the subject.

State of Optics before Newton's Time.

609. Before the exact law of refraction was known, men were ignorant of the causes of indistinctness in optical instruments. When

Snellius had discovered this law, Descartes remarked the aberration of sphericity, which is the slightest cause of indistinctness. But he was deceived in supposing that he could remedy this defect, by employing other than spherical curvatures; and this mistake continued till our times.

Errors of Newton in the Theory of Colours.

610. Newton ascertained that the dispersion of colours is the most important cause of indistinctness in optical instruments; and so long as mankind appreciate the sciences, his researches in optics will be regarded as models of accuracy and sagacity. Unfortunately he did not bring them to a complete termination, and by only bestowing a passing glance upon one circumstance, of which he did not suspect the importance, he fell into some remarkable errors, which have been productive of numerous evil consequences.

611. Newton made all his experiments upon the dispersion of colours, with prisms of a single kind of glass. To complete his researches, he should also have observed the dispersion of colours through other transparent media. In the second part of the first book of his Optics, he touched lightly upon this subject; but he was deceived in respect to three circumstances.

(1.) He made an erroneous assertion. He says, that he caused light to pass through water and glass, varying in many ways the refracting surface; and that he found the emergent light to be always coloured when it was not parallel to the incident light; and that, on the contrary, it was always uncoloured when restored to parallelism. The incorrectness of this remark has since been ascertained.

(2.) He tacitly supposed, without an experimental examination, that the dispersion of colours is subject to the same laws in all transparent media; and consequently, he thought, that since he had observed with so much precision, the dispersion of colours, in ordinary mirror glass, it was only necessary for other transparent media, to examine the ratio of refraction for the mean rays, and then, by comparing this ratio with that of the glass which he had used, he might deduce, by proportion, the ratio of refraction for the other colours of the spectrum. Subsequent inquiry has proved this reasoning to be incorrect.

(3.) He deduced from the experiment mentioned at the beginning of this article, a law, by which the dispersion of colours in two different media might be compared. He considered this law as universally true; but it has since been ascertained that it only approaches the truth, for very small angles of refraction; and that even granting the experiment were precise, no principles regulating the dispersion of colours could be deduced from it.

612. If these ideas of Newton had been conformable to truth, it would have followed as a necessary consequence, that the effect of dispersion in optical instruments, could not by any means be remedied; for, in order to remedy this effect, it would be necessary to dispose the instrument in such a manner, that each ray when it emerged from the last glass, should be parallel to the direction which it had before it entered the object glass. But this would frustrate the design of the instrument, for we could see an object only as far as with the naked eye, and with much less clearness. Newton, therefore, abandoned refracting telescopes, because he supposed them incapable of a high degree of improvement. But the errors of this great man have been attended with one good effect; namely, that of leading him to the invention of a reflecting telescope, commonly called the *Newtonian telescope*.

Reflecting Telescope.

613. The essential part of Newton's reflecting telescope is a converging metallic mirror, which takes the place of an object-glass; it is attached to the bottom of a tube, the length of which is equal to the focal distance of the mirror, in such way that the polished surface is turned towards the opening, and thus toward external objects. If the common axis of this mirror and of the tube is directed towards a distant object, a small inverted image of the object is formed at the focus. But instead of allowing this image to be actually formed, we receive the light at a distance from the focus nearly equal to the radius of the tube, upon a small plane mirror, attached by a thin support, to the middle of the axis of the tube, and making with this axis an angle of 45 degrees. This small mirror, therefore, reflects the light which it receives from the large mirror; and thus the image which the large mirror would have produced, is formed by the small one on the side of the tube, which has an opening at this place, so

that we can view the image with a microscopic lens, as in Kepler's telescope.

As no dispersion is produced by the reflection of metallic mirrors, and as the aberration of sphericity is very small, the image presented by such a mirror is incomparably more distinct than the image produced by an object-glass. This instrument, therefore, admits of a much greater magnifying power, and experience has proved, that with a reflecting telescope of only a few feet in length, we can see as far as with a refracting telescope of a hundred feet in length.

614. Gregory improved the Newtonian telescope, by introducing instead of a small plane mirror placed obliquely to the axis, a small converging mirror having its polished surface turned towards that of the large one. This small mirror is so disposed that its surface is a little without the focal distance of the great mirror. Accordingly, if we consider the inverted image produced by the object mirror, as an object throwing its light upon the small mirror, it is obvious (*fig.* 65) that the latter will produce a second image, a little larger and inverted. The small mirror may be so placed, that this image would fall behind the great mirror, if the light could pass through it. To effect the formation of this image, we make a circular aperture at the centre of the great mirror of nearly the same dimensions with the small mirror, through which the light, reflected by it, is perceived. There would, therefore, be produced behind the great mirror, an image of distant objects; but before it is formed we receive the light by means of a convex glass. In this way the rays are concentrated into a smaller image, which is seen through a microscopic lens. The principal advantage of this ingenious instrument over that of Newton, is, that it exhibits the objects erect and in the direction in which they are actually situated.

615. To obtain the greatest possible magnifying power, and to remedy the want of light which is common to all reflecting telescopes, the celebrated Herschel added to the Newtonian telescope a modification which is applicable only to very large instruments. He entirely dispensed with the small mirror, and directed the tube of the telescope towards an object not in the axis, but a little above it. Let the object, for example, be a star, and conceive a ray coming from this star to the centre of the mirror. In this case the tube must be so placed, that this ray shall pass very near its upper edge; but then this ray must manifestly be reflected towards the lower edge of the opening in the tube; and the length being equal to the focal distance

of the mirror, an image of the star will be formed near the lower edge of this opening. Accordingly, we can view this image directly with a lens, provided the diameter of the tube is so large that the part which the head of the observer occupies, is inconsiderable compared with the whole opening. This arrangement is favourable to distinctness, brightness, and magnifying power.

Ingenious Researches of Euler; his Errors.—Dollond.—Klingenstiern.

616. The errors of Newton passed unobserved for 50 years; and even the great Euler, the most profound analyst of the last century, seemed not to have known the experiment of Newton and the consequences which are deduced from it, when in 1747, he came to the conclusion, from the mere inspection of the human eye, that it would be possible to remedy the dispersion of colours produced by refraction, since this defect does not exist in our eyes. His sagacity led him to perceive, in the combination of many transparent substances, the means employed by nature to produce this effect. He thought it possible to imitate such an arrangement by placing one upon the other two convex-concave glasses, and filling the interval between them with water. For this important object he employed all the resources of analysis; but in order to succeed, it would be necessary that the force with which water disperses colours, should have been determined with as much exactness as that of the glass had been by the experiments of Newton.

Two methods suggested themselves to Euler; experiment and theoretical considerations. He chose the latter. He supposed with Newton, that the dispersion of colours is subject to the same law in all refracting media; he strove to discover this law; he found one which satisfied all the conditions that could be required, and proved it to be the only one that had this advantage. This law was entirely different from that of Newton, but it appears that Euler had no knowledge of the latter. He calculated, therefore, according to his own law, how the two faces of an object-glass, composed of glass and water, ought to be disposed, in order to give uncoloured images.

617. The inquiries of Euler created a great sensation. The most skilful artists attempted to execute object-glasses according to his principles, but without success. The elder Dollond, an excel-

lent English artist, first perceived the contradiction which existed between the laws of Newton and Euler; and as those of Euler did not appear to be confirmed by experiment, he thought that the truth was on the side of Newton. Euler, without examining the experiments and calculations of Newton, contented himself with demonstrating by a rigorous course of reasoning, that his law was the only possible one, and attributed the failure of practical attempts to the great difficulty of execution.

618. Klingenstiern, a Swedish geometer, subjected the assertion of Newton to a rigorous examination, and found that he deduced from Newton's experiments not one single law, but a multitude of contradictory laws. Hence he concluded that there must be some error in this experiment.

619. This induced Dollond to repeat the experiment of Newton. He found it to be incorrect, but at the same time satisfied himself that the law of Euler was not exact, since the results of his experiment did not conform to it. Yet as the opinion of Euler respecting the impossibility of uncoloured refraction, deduced from the structure of the eye, appeared plausible, he undertook a new course of experiments to verify it. He found that the union of glass and water would not be adapted to such a purpose. He examined different kinds of glass, and found some which refract light and disperse the colours much more than ordinary glass. After repeated trials, he obtained from two prisms which were placed one against the other, with opposite refracting angles, an emergent ray which was uncoloured, although the refraction was very considerable. One of these prisms was English crown glass, which is a kind of mirror glass of a greenish colour; this had a refracting angle of 30°. The other was flint glass, a kind of white glass, containing much oxyde of lead. The refracting angle of this was 19°.

620. This experiment convinced Dollond of the possibility of obtaining an object-glass which should give uncoloured images, by employing these two kinds of glass. He effected this object by uniting a convex lens of crown glass and a concave one of flint glass. Thus he became the inventor of *achromatic telescopes*, or refracting telescopes that represent the object without colour; that is, with its natural colour.

621. Euler completely atoned for his error, which led to this interesting discovery, by executing a task, which he would not perhaps otherwise have undertaken. He reduced to general and very

simple formulas, not only the whole theory of the aberration of refrangibility, but also the much more difficult one of the aberration of sphericity. Accordingly, we can now calculate, without difficulty, the effect of these two causes of confusion, for each position of the glass. He showed, moreover, that a triple object-glass, composed of two convex lenses of crown glass, separated by a double concave one of flint glass, would have a great advantage over that of Dollond. He ascertained what would be the best arrangement of the eye-glass, if such an object-glass were used; and above all, he gave such a generality to all his researches, that they may now be applied to all optical instruments. Finally, he showed that though theory might sometimes err, yet when properly directed it extended much farther than the method of simple experiment.

To those who would be farther acquainted with this part of the subject, we recommend Priestley's History of Optics; a work which is at once interesting to the profound inquirer, and yet adapted to the humblest capacity.

622. Strictly speaking, the error of Euler consisted in having sought a law where there is none. For it is manifest from the examination of several kinds of glasses, that the different ratios which are found between the refraction of light and the dispersion of colours, do not depend upon any general law, but simply upon the particular properties of refracting substances; and consequently, that we can only ascertain them in each particular case, by direct experiment. Nothing can better evince the justness of this opinion, than the interesting experiments made by Professor Zeiher of Petersburgh, upon the different kinds of glass. He ascertained that an addition of oxyde of lead, would considerably affect the dispersive power, while the mean refraction remained very nearly the same. The contrary effect is produced by the addition of alkali.

623. The construction of achromatic telescopes is not without difficulty; and although they are made in many places besides England, yet the English alone possess the flint glass which is employed in them. Hitherto no artist has been able to make large instruments of this kind; and this is the reason why Herschel, as we before observed, had recourse to the reflecting telescope to obtain very great magnifying powers. For instruments of the ordinary dimensions, those which are made according to these principles have very decided advantages, not only over common refracting tele-

scopes, but also over reflecting telescopes; as to distinctness, degree of light, and extent of the field of view.*

In compound microscopes it is not possible to make the object-lens achromatic, because the glasses of which it must be composed, would be so small that they could not be executed with exactness.

Mathematical Additions.

624. We now proceed to add some mathematical reasonings, which will aid us in forming precise ideas respecting the theory of colours, and the possibility of producing achromatic images.

625. *Experiment.* Let there be any two media, *ABCD*, *CDEF*, (*fig.* 97) terminated by plane surfaces; and let there be above *AB* and below *EF*, a medium whose refracting power is different. If we suppose a ray *GH*, which is refracted at the points *H*, *I*, *K*, the emergent ray *KL*, is always parallel to the incident ray *GH*, and consequently uncoloured.

626. *Theorem.* Let $n : 1$ be the ratio of refraction between air and any medium *A*; and let $m : 1$ be the ratio of refraction between air and another medium *B*; the ratio of refraction between *A* and *B*, will be $\frac{m}{n}$.

Demonstration. Suppose that there is air above *AB* and below *EF* (*fig.* 97); between *AB* and *CD* let there be the medium *A*, and between *CD* and *EF* the medium *B*; through *I*, *K*, draw the perpendiculars *MN*, *OP*, *QR*; and call the ratio of refraction between *A* and *B*, $\frac{x}{y}$; we have,

$$\sin GHM : \sin NHI :: n : 1,$$
$$\sin HIO : \sin PIK :: x : y,$$
$$\sin IKQ : \sin RKL :: 1 : m.$$

Now $NHI = HIO$, and $PIK = IKQ$; also, (article 625) $GHM = RKL$; we have then, compounding these three propositions;

---

* Since the publication of this work the best kind of flint glass has been made in France and Germany.

$$1 : 1 :: nx : my;$$

consequently, $nx = my$; whence

$$x : y :: m : n.$$

627. *Theorem.* Let CAB and ABD (*fig.* 98) be the *perpendicular* sections of two prisms of different refracting powers, placed one against the other. Let the ratio of refraction of the first be $n : 1$; that of the second $m : 1$. Let a ray $EFGHI$ be refracted by these prisms, as in the figure. Produce the incident ray EF, and the emergent ray HI, till they cut each other in Q. Let us suppose, moreover, that the constancy of the ratios of refraction is true of the angles themselves considered as very small. Then the angle by which the ray is turned from its course by these refractions, will be

$$IQR = (n-1)\, CAB - (m-1)\, ABD.$$

Demonstration. At F, G, H, erect the incident perpendiculars KL, SM, NO, and produce them till the first cuts the second in L, and the second cuts the third in N. For the sake of abreviation let

$$CAB = A;\ ABD = B;\ EFK = F.$$

We first remark that the angles formed by the two incident perpendiculars, which fall upon each prism, are equal to the refracting angle of each of the prisms; consequently,

$$SLF = CAB = A;\ HNG = ABD = B.$$

This has already been demonstrated, article 594. Accordingly we have

$$LFP : LFG :: n : 1;\ \text{then}\ LFG = \frac{1}{n} F;$$

$$LGF = SLF - LFG = A - \frac{1}{n} F;$$

moreover, according to article 626.

$$LGF : HGM :: m : n;$$

whence we obtain

$$HGM = \frac{n}{m} LGF = \frac{n}{m} A - \frac{1}{m} F;$$

$$NHG = HGM - HNG = \frac{n}{m} A - \frac{1}{m} F - B;$$

and, as

$$NHG : IHO :: 1 : m,$$

we have
$$IHO = mNHG = nA - F - mB.$$
But
$$IQR = QHP + HPQ = QHP + FGP + PFG.$$
We have also from what precedes,

(1.) $QHP = IHO - NHG = +nA - F - mB - \dfrac{n}{m}A + \dfrac{1}{m}F + B;$

(2.) $FGP = HGM - LGF = +\dfrac{n}{m}A - \dfrac{1}{m}F - A + \dfrac{1}{n}F;$

(3.) $PFG = EFK - LFG = +F - \dfrac{1}{n}F.$

Consequently,
$$IQR = (n-1)A - (m-1)B.$$

628. *Addition.* The ratios of refraction $n:1$, $m:1$, may belong to the mean rays. For the most refrangible violet rays, these ratios may be $N:1$ and $M:1$; and then the angle by which the violet ray is turned from its primitive direction, after all the refractons, will be
$$IQR = (N-1)A - (M-1)B.$$

Now if the emergent light is uncoloured, the rays of different colours are parallel to one another after refraction. Consequently, the angle IQR is the same for all. Accordingly, if we make its value equal to that which the mean rays give, we shall have the equation
$$(n-1)A - (m-1)B = (N-1)A - (M-1)B;$$
whence
$$(N-n)A = (M-m)B,$$
or
$$M-m : N-n :: A : B.$$

According to the experiments of Dollond, article 619, crown glass and flint glass produce an uncoloured refraction, when $A = 30$, and $B = 19$. We have, then, with respect to these two substances,
$$N-n : M-m :: 19 : 30,$$
or, very nearly,
$$N-n : M-n :: 2 : 3.$$

We call the values $N-n$ and $M-m$, *the measure of the dispersion of colours.* This ratio has not been hitherto determined by any general law. It can only be ascertained in each particular case by direct experiments, similar to those of Dollond.

629. *Remark.* If the experiments of Newton, article 611, were exact, IQR must be equal to 0, as well for the mean rays as for the violet, when the emergent light is uncoloured. Then we should have

$$(n-1)A = (m-1)B,$$

or

$$m-1 : n-1 :: A : B.$$

Moreover,

$$(N-1)A = (M-1)B;$$

consequently,

$$M-1 : N-1 :: A : B.$$

Whence it would follow

$$M-1 : m-1 :: N-1 : n-1.$$

Now the difference between the 1st and 2d term is to the 3d, as the difference between the 3d and 4th, is to the 4th; that is,

$$M-m : m-1 :: N-n : n-1,$$

or

$$M-m : N-n :: m-1 : n-1.$$

Such was the law of Newton; it was erroneous; 1. Because it was founded upon inexact observations; 2. Because it supposed that the ratio of refraction belongs to the angle itself, which only approaches the truth when the angles are very small. When we make the calculation exactly, without neglecting any thing, the experiment of Newton gives no determinate ratio (618.)

630. The first law of Euler was very different from this; he thought that M must depend upon m, in the same manner as N upon n; and he showed that this could only be possible in the case where we have,

$$\log M : \log m :: \log N : \log n.$$

631. *Problem.* In A (*fig.* 99) let there be a spherical glass, for which the mean ratio of refraction is $n : 1$. Let a second glass of another substance, for which the mean ratio of refraction is $m : 1$, be placed so near against the other, that their distance AB may be considered as nothing. These two glasses must be disposed so as to

have the same axis AD. By this arrangement the images of distant objects, seen by refraction, will be formed at a certain determinate distance which will depend upon the preceding data.

Let the focal distance of the first glass be p, that of the second q; whatever be their signs, f and g are the radii of the two surfaces of the first glass, h and i, the radii of the two surfaces of the second. According to article 570, (5), if, for the sake of abridgment, we make

$$\frac{1}{f} + \frac{1}{g} = F, \text{ and } \frac{1}{h} + \frac{1}{i} = H,$$

we shall have

$$\frac{1}{p} = (n-1) F,$$

$$\frac{1}{q} = (m-1) H.$$

Now let C be the focus of the first glass, which we have designated by A; the image of an object at an infinite distance, formed by this glass, will be in C.

This image serves as an object to the second glass, and the image produced by this second glass B is in D; thus BD is the quantity upon which all the effects depend.

In the general formula, $\frac{1}{p} = \frac{1}{a} + \frac{1}{\alpha}$ (570), we must, for the case in question, write q instead of p, and $-BC$ instead of α, since the object is at the distance BC behind the glass; but as we suppose $AB = 0$, we have $BC = -AC = -p$; and we find

$$\frac{1}{q} = -\frac{1}{p} + \frac{1}{BD}, \text{ or } \frac{1}{BD} = \frac{1}{p} + \frac{1}{q};$$

or, if we put for $\frac{1}{p}$ and $\frac{1}{q}$ their values found above,

$$\frac{1}{BD} = (n-1) F + (m-1) H.$$

Consequently,

$$BD = \frac{1}{(n-1) F + (M-1) H}.$$

632. *Addition.* Let the ratio of refraction for the most refrangible rays be $N:1$ in the first glass, and $M:1$ in the second. Then if E is the place where the image is produced by the most refrangible rays, according to article 630, we shall have

$$BE = \frac{1}{(N-1)F + (M-1)H}.$$

Now, if the combination is to be achromatic, the images of all the the colours must be united in one. Consequently, we shall have $BE = BD$; whence it follows that

$$(n-1)F + (m-1)H = (N-1)F + (M-1)H,$$

or

$$(N-n)F + (M-m)H = 0.$$

Now, as we have

$$\frac{1}{p} = (n-1)F, \text{ whence } F = \frac{1}{(n-1)p};$$

and

$$\frac{1}{q} = (m-1)H, \text{ whence } H = \frac{1}{(m-1)q};$$

we obtain

$$\frac{(N-n)}{(n-1)p} + \frac{(M-m)}{(m-1)q} = 0;$$

or, multiplying by pq, and transposing the second terms,

$$\frac{(N-n)}{(n-1)}q = -\frac{M-m}{(m-1)}p.$$

Whence

$$p : q :: \frac{N-n}{n-1} : -\frac{M-m}{m-1}.$$

These focal distances of the two glasses must, therefore, be in this ratio, in order to produce a single uncoloured image.

633. *Addition.* According to the experiments of Dollond, the ratio of refraction of the mean rays in crown glass is 1,55 : 1; consequently $n - 1 = 0,55$. In flint glass this ratio is 1,58 : 1; consequently $m - 1 = 0,58$. The dispersion of colours in the two glasses being as 19 : 30; we shall have

$$N - n : M - m :: 19 : 30;$$

consequently,

$$p : b :: \frac{19}{0,55} : -\frac{30}{0,58};$$

that is,

$$p : q :: 1 : -1,497\ldots\ldots$$

The last term of this proportion being negative, it follows that the lens, which is of flint glass, must be diverging.

Although this result is very exact in theory, it might not be very certain in practice, since Dollond only gives the ratio of dispersion 19 : 30, as an approximate one.

In practice it would be necessary to enter into a more difficult calculation; that is, to ascertain the most advantageous dimensions of the radii f, g, h, i. At the same time it is obvious from the formula

$$\frac{1}{p} = \frac{n-1}{f} + \frac{n-1}{g}; \frac{1}{q} = \frac{m-1}{h} + \frac{m-1}{i},$$

that these radii admit of infinite variation for the same focal distance. By selecting the most suitable values, the aberration of sphericity also may, according to the theory of Euler, be made entirely to disappear, or at least become very much diminished; so that object-glasses, calculated exactly in this manner, are exempt from two causes of confusion.

It is in the correction of this aberration of sphericity, that we have the means of giving proportionally a greater aperture to these object-glasses, than to any simple lenses or mirrors. This is moreover the cause of the perfect light in achromatic telescopes. As to the extent of the field of view it depends upon the disposition of the eye-glass.

APPENDIX TO OPTICS.

Many optical phenomena relating to the physical properties of light, having of late years acquired some importance, we will here give, not a detailed account of them, which would not suit the plan of this work, but a sketch which will indicate the principal results.

Coloured Rings.

When two plates of glass whose surfaces are not quite plane, are placed one on the other, the lamina of air naturally adhering to these surfaces has usually thickness enough to exercise a complete action on light, that is, it reflects and refracts all the coloured rays in the same manner as if it were of considerable depth. If, however, one of the glasses be rubbed on the other, and forcibly pressed to it, to exclude a part of the intermediate air, there will soon be perceived a degree of adhesion, which is generally greater in some parts than in others, either because the surfaces are always a little curved, or because they invariably bend under strong pressure; in this manner there is obtained a lamina of air, thinner than the preceding, and the depth of which increases gradually in all directions from the point in which the surfaces are most closely in contact. If now these glasses be turned so that the eye may receive the light of the clouds, reflected by the lamina of air, there will be perceived a number of concentric coloured rings, which, when the glasses are pressed sufficiently, surround a dark spot, at the point of contact.

These coloured rings may be formed by pressing together transparent plates of any other substance, besides glass; they may be observed, when a glass lens is placed on a plane surface of resin, of metal, of metallic glass, or any other polished body. These rings subsist, moreover, in the most perfect vacuum that can be produced. Neither is it necessary for their formation, that the interposed lamina be of air, nor that it be contained between two solid substances; a layer of water, of alcohol, of ether, or any other evaporable liquid, spread on a black glass, produces similar colours, when sufficiently attenuated; they may be observed also on soap bubbles, and on blown glass, when thin enough.*

In whatever manner, and under whatever circumstances these rings are formed, the succession of their colours from the central dark spot is invariably the same; the only difference perceptible is in their brightness, which varies with the refracting power of the lamina, and in their form, which depends on the law by which the thickness of the lamina is regulated in different parts. In fact, for any one substance, the colour reflected at any point depends on the thickness of the lamina, and the incidence under which the reflection takes place.

So far we have supposed the colours of the lamina to be seen only by reflection; if it be placed between the eye and the light, concentric rings will again be observed similar to the others in form, but not in colour, and fainter, surrounding a *bright* spot.

This might naturally be expected, for when the incident light is decomposed, so as to give coloured rays in the reflection, those transmitted must of course be also coloured, and the one set must, in fact, be complementary to the other, that is, both together would produce *white*.

It follows from all this, that to discover the laws of these phenomena, the best method is to study them in cases where the variation of thickness is regular and known. This is what Newton did; and he conducted his researches with a careful nicety, which could be owing only to the importance which he foresaw would be attached to the consequences of them.

He formed the rings by placing a convex glass of small curvature on a piece of perfectly plane glass; then the thickness of the lamina of air increasing symmetrically in all directions from the point of contact, the rings were perfectly circular round the dark spot formed at that point.

He measured the diameters of these rings, in a particular case, and thence, knowing the curvature of the surface, he was able to calculate the thickness of the lamina at each ring.

Repeating this observation under different angles of incidence, he

---

* Of the same nature are the coloured stripes often seen in cracked ice, in transparent calcareous spar, selenite, and other substances.

remarked the variations produced in the rings; he found that they grew wider as the obliquity increased, and by measuring their diameters, he calculated the different thicknesses at which the same colour appeared.

He made similar experiments on thin plates of water, contained between two glasses, and on thin soap bubbles, blown with a pipe. These bubbles being placed on a plane glass, became perfectly hemispherical, and being covered over with a bell-glass, they lasted long enough for him to observe at leisure their brilliant tints. He thus found that the thicknesses, at which the same colours appeared were less than in air, in the ratio of 3 to 4, which is, in fact, that of refraction between these two substances. Other trials with laminæ of glass, led him to generalize this remark, which many other experiments afterwards confirmed. He collected all his results into empiric tables, which express the laws of them in numbers.

These laws were, however, still complicated in consequence of the unequal refrangibilities of the different rays, by which the rings were illuminated. To reduce the phenomenon to its greatest simplicity, Newton formed rings with *simple* light, by looking, in a dark room at a white paper, which received in turns all the simple colours of the prismatic spectrum. This paper thus enlightened, and seen by reflection on the thin laminæ, became like a kind of sky, coloured by that tint alone, which was thrown on it. In this manner the following results were obtained;

(1.) Each kind of simple light produced rings *of its own colour*, both by reflection and by transmission.

(2.) In each case, the rings were separated by dark intervals, which made them much more distinct than in the original experiment, and caused many more to be discerned. They were more and more crowded together as their distance increased from the central spot.

(3.) The dark intervals which separated the bright rings, seen by the reflected light, were bright rings themselves by the transmitted rays, and they were separated by dark intervals answering to the former rings. However, those intervals were not exactly *black*, because the reflection on a thin lamina of air is far from being perfect, even in the most brilliant part of the reflected rings; and the same thing may be observed of all thin transparent plates of any substance whatever.

(4.) In observing the luminous reflected rings, Newton remarked, that they were not simple geometrical lines, but that each of them occupied a certain space, in which the brightness diminished gradually each way from the middle.

(5.) Measuring the diameters of the reflected rings at their brightest part, he found that for each particular kind of rays, the squares of the diameters followed the arithmetical progression of the numbers 1, 3, 5, 7, &c.; consequently, the thicknesses of the lamina, which are as the squares of their diameters, were in that same progression.

When the glasses were illuminated by the brightest part of the *spectrum*, which is between the *orange* and *yellow*, the diameter of the sixth ring was found to be the same as that of the brightest part of the corresponding ring in the experiment made in full day-light.

(6.) The diameters of the dark rings being likewise measured, he found that their squares, and consequently, the thicknesses of the air below them, followed in the progression, 2, 4, 6, 8, &c.

(7.) By other measurements, he discovered that the brightest parts of the *transmitted* rings answered to the darkest parts of the intervals in *reflection*, and *vice versâ*, the darkest parts here were the brightest in the other case, so that the thicknesses of air which transmitted the bright rings, and those which gave dark intervals, were respectively as 2, 4, 6, 8, &c., and as 1, 3, 5, 7, &c.

(8.) The absolute diameters of corresponding rings of different colours were different, as were also their breadths, both these dimensions being greatest for the extreme red rays, and least for the violet.

(9.) The simple rings of each colour were least when the rays passed perpendicularly through the lamina of air, and increased with the angle of incidence.

These observations explain completely the more complicated phenomenon of the rings formed by the natural light; for this light, consisting of different coloured rays mixed together in definite proportions, when a beam of this mixture falls on the thin lamina of air between the glasses, each kind of simple light forms its own rings by itself, according to its own peculiar laws, and as the diameters of these rings are different for the various kinds of light, they are sufficiently separated from each other to be distinguished. However, this separation is by no means so perfect as in observations made with simple rings, because the rings of different colours encroach a little on each other, so as to produce that infinite diversity of tints that the experiment shows. But, though this successive superposition of the simple rings is really the key of the phenomena, one cannot be very sure of the fact without having measured exactly the absolute magnitudes of the diameters and breadths of the rings, formed by the different coloured rays; for when these results are once known, it can only be a simple arithmetical problem to find the species and the quantity of each colour that may be reflected or transmitted at each determinate thickness; and consequently, if the effects of the composition of all these colours be calculated by the rules which Newton has given in his Optics, it will be easy to deduce with perfect accuracy, the numerical expressions of the tint and intensity of colour that must exist at each point of the compound rings, which may then be compared with experiment. In a word, we have as yet only a suspicion, a probable one no doubt, of the cause of our phenomena; accurate measurements are necessary to convert that probability into certainty.

This is just what Newton did. He measured the diameters of the simple rings *of the same order*, both at their inner and outer edges, taking successively the various colours of the spectrum, from the extreme violet to the deepest red; afterwards, according to his usual method, he took care to connect these results by a mathematical law, which might represent them with sufficient accuracy. Then comparing the squares of the diameters, he deduced the proportional thickness of the lamina of air at each edge of the observed rings. Similar measurements, effected with respect to the different orders of rings, formed by one simple colour, proved to him, that the intervals of thickness, throughout which reflection took place, were sensibly equal to those which allowed transmission, at least when the light was incident perpendicularly. Thus, designating generally by t the thickness of the air at the beginning of the first lucid ring, for any simple colour, that ring ended at the thickness $3t$, and therefore occupied an interval of thickness equal to $2t$. Then came the first dark ring, occupying an equal interval $2t$; then a second lucid ring from $5t$ to $7t$, and so on.

Combining this law of succession for the different orders, with that of the distribution of the various tints of the same order, one easily conceives that a single absolute thickness, measured at the beginning, the middle, or the end of any ring, formed by a simple colour, is sufficient to calculate the value of the first thickness t, relatively to that colour, and thus all the thicknesses of the several rings of each colour may be determined.

In this manner Newton, measuring the thickness represented by $2t$ for the different simple rays, in vacuo, in air, in water, and in common glass, found their values as shown in the following table, where they are expressed in ten thousandth parts of an inch.

	Values of $2t$.			
Colours.	In Vacuo.	In Air.	In Water.	In Glass
Extreme violet............	3,99816	3,99698	2,99773	2,57870
Limit of { violet and indigo....	4,32436	4,32308	3,24231	2,78908
indigo and blue......	4,51475	4,51342	3,38507	2,91188
blue and green......	4,84284	4,84142	3,63107	3,12350
green and yellow...	5,23886	5,23732	3,92799	3,37891
yellow and orange..	5,61963	5,61798	4,21349	3,62450
orange and red......	5,86586	5,86414	4,39811	3,78331
Extreme red..............	6,34628	6,34441	4,75831	4,09317

In this table the values relating to air were alone immediately obtained by observation; the others were calculated from them by means of the several ratios of refraction, that is, by multiplying them by $\frac{3389}{3388}$ for the vacuum, $\frac{3}{4}$ for water, and $\frac{20}{31}$ for glass. It must be remembered, that these values all suppose the incidence to be perpendicular.

Applying to these results a rule that he had found to determine the nature of the compound colour resulting from any given mixture of simple colours, Newton deduced the following table, which shows the thickness at which the brightest tints of each ring appear, when seen under the perpendicular incidence. This table is calculated only for air, water, and common glass, but may of course be extended to all other substances, by the method above mentioned.

The unit is the thousandth part of an inch. By the side of different colours are put the names of certain flowers or metallic substances, just to give more distinct ideas of them.

Colours reflected.	Thicknesses in thousandth parts of an inch.			Names of the Colours, or substances having them.
	In air.	In water.	In glass.	
1st Order.				
Very black	$\frac{1}{2}$	$\frac{3}{8}$	$\frac{10}{31}$	
Black	1	$\frac{3}{4}$	$\frac{20}{31}$	
Beginning of black	2	$1\frac{1}{2}$	$1\frac{2}{7}$	
Blue	$2\frac{2}{5}$	$1\frac{4}{5}$	$1\frac{11}{20}$	Whitish sky-blue.
White	$5\frac{1}{4}$	$3\frac{7}{8}$	$3\frac{2}{5}$	Tarnished silver.
Yellow	$7\frac{1}{9}$	$5\frac{1}{3}$	$4\frac{3}{5}$	Straw colour.
Orange	8	6	$5\frac{1}{6}$	Dried orange-peel.
Red	9	$6\frac{3}{4}$	$5\frac{4}{5}$	Geranium Sanguineum.
2d Order.				
Violet	$11\frac{1}{6}$	$8\frac{3}{8}$	$7\frac{1}{5}$	Iodine.
Indigo	$12\frac{5}{6}$	$9\frac{5}{8}$	$8\frac{2}{11}$	Indigo.
Blue	14	$10\frac{1}{2}$	9	Cobalt blue.
Green	$15\frac{1}{8}$	$11\frac{1}{3}$	$9\frac{5}{7}$	Water, aquamarine.
Yellow	$16\frac{2}{7}$	$12\frac{1}{5}$	$10\frac{2}{5}$	Lemon.
Orange	$17\frac{2}{9}$	13	$11\frac{1}{9}$	Orange.
Bright red	$18\frac{1}{3}$	$13\frac{3}{4}$	$11\frac{5}{6}$	Bright May-pink.
Scarlet	$19\frac{2}{3}$	$14\frac{3}{4}$	$12\frac{2}{3}$	
3rd Order.				
Purple	21	$15\frac{3}{4}$	$13\frac{11}{20}$	Flax-blossom.
Indigo	$22\frac{1}{10}$	$16\frac{4}{7}$	$14\frac{1}{4}$	Indigo.
Blue	$23\frac{2}{5}$	$17\frac{11}{20}$	$15\frac{1}{10}$	Prussian blue.
Green	$25\frac{1}{5}$	$18\frac{9}{10}$	$16\frac{1}{4}$	Bright meadow green.
Yellow	$27\frac{1}{7}$	$20\frac{1}{3}$	$17\frac{1}{2}$	White wood.
Red	29	$21\frac{3}{4}$	$18\frac{5}{7}$	Rose.
Bluish red	32	24	$20\frac{2}{3}$	
4th Order.				
Bluish green	34	$25\frac{1}{2}$	22	
Green	$35\frac{2}{7}$	$26\frac{1}{2}$	$22\frac{3}{4}$	Emerald.
Yellowish green	36	27	$23\frac{2}{9}$	
Red	$40\frac{1}{3}$	$30\frac{1}{4}$	26	Pale pink.
5th Order.				
Greenish blue	46	$34\frac{1}{2}$	$29\frac{2}{3}$	Sea-green.
Red	$52\frac{1}{2}$	$39\frac{3}{8}$	34	Pale pink.
6th Order.				
Greenish blue	$58\frac{3}{4}$	44	38	Light sea-green.
Red	65	$48\frac{3}{4}$	42	Paler red.
7th Order.				
Greenish blue	71	$53\frac{1}{4}$	$45\frac{4}{5}$	Very faint.
Ruddy white	77	$57\frac{3}{4}$	$49\frac{2}{3}$	Ditto.

Reduction of the phenomena of the rings to a physical property of light, called fits of easy reflection and transmission.

The phenomena of the rings being reduced to laws extremely exact and well adapted to calculation, Newton concentrated them all in a still simpler expression, making them depend on a physical property, which he attributed to light, and of which he defined all the particulars conformably to their laws.

Considering light as a matter composed of small molecules emitted by luminous bodies with very great velocities, he concluded, that since they were reflected within the lamina of air, at the several thicknesses t, $3t$, $5t$, $7t$, &c., and transmitted at the intermediate thicknesses 0, $2t$, $4t$, $6t$, &c., the molecules must have some peculiar modification of a periodical nature, such as to incline them alternately to be reflected and refracted after passing through certain spaces. Yet this modification could not be *necessary*, since the intensity of the reflection at the second surface varies with the medium contiguous to that surface, so that a given molecule arriving at it, at a given epoch of its period, may be either reflected or transmitted, according to the exterior circumstances which act on it. Newton, therefore, characterized this property of the luminous molecules as a simple *tendency*, and designated it appropriately enough by the phrase, *fit of easy reflection*, or *transmission*.

According to this idea of the *fits*, their duration must evidently be proportional to the thickness t, which regulates, in each substance, the alternations of reflection and transmission. Thus, in the first table given, we find the measure of it for a vacuum, for air, water, and glass, in the case of perpendicular incidence. In other substances, the duration of the fits must vary as the quantity t, that is, inversely as the refracting power; it will vary also, by parity of reason, with the obliquity of incidence, and the nature of the light; but the laws of these variations are exactly those which regulate the rings themselves; so that, these last being known, it remains only to apply them; this Newton did, and after having defined completely all the characters of the fits, he employed them as a simple property, not only to unite under one point of view the phenomena of the colours produced by thin plates, but also to foresee and to calculate beforehand, both as to their general tenor, and their minutest details, a crowd of analogous phenomena observed to attend reflection in thick plates, which, in fact, in his experiments, exceeded by as much as twenty or thirty thousand times those on which the calculations had been founded; moreover, applying the same reasoning to the integrant particles of material substances, which all chemical and physical phenomena show to be very minute, and to be separated, even in the most solid bodies, by spaces immense in comparison of their absolute dimensions, he was able to deduce naturally from the same principles, the theory of the different colours they present to us, a theory which adapts itself with a surprising facility to all the observations to which those colours can be submitted. The number and importance of those applications account sufficiently for the care which Newton took with his experiments on the rings; I am sorry to be obliged to confine myself here to the bare indication of those fine discoveries.

Another Explanation of the Coloured Rings on the Hypothesis of Undulations.—Dr Young's principle of Interferences.

If light be really a material substance, Newton's *fits* are a necessary property, because they are only a literal enunciation of the alternations of reflection and transmission which coloured rings present; but if light be otherwise constituted, these alternations may be accounted for differently.

Descartes, and after him Huygens, and a great number of natural philosophers, have supposed that the sensation of light was produced in us by undulations excited in a very elastic medium, and propagated to our eye, which they affect in the same manner as undulations excited in the proper medium of the air, and propagated to the ear, produce in it the sensation of sound. This medium, if it does exist, must fill all the expanse of the heavens, since it is through this expanse that the light of the stars comes to our eyes; it must also be extremely elastic, since the transmission of light takes place with such extraordinary velocity; and at the same time its density must be almost infinitely small, since the most exact discussion of ancient and modern astronomical observations, does not indicate the least trace of resistance in the planetary motions. As to the relations of this medium with earthly bodies, it is plain that it must pervade them all, for they all transmit light when sufficiently attenuated; moreover, its density must probably differ in them according to the nature of the substances, since unequal refractions appear to prove that the propagation of light takes place in different media with various velosities. But what ought to be the proportions of the densities for these different substances? How is the luminiferous ether brought to, or kept in, the proper state for each? How is it inclosed and contained so as to be incapable of spreading out of them? Moreover, how is this medium, so non-resisting, so rare, so intangible, agitated by the molecules of bodies which appear to us luminous? These are so many characters which it would be necessary to know well, or at least to define well, to have an exact idea of the conditions according to which the undulations are formed and propagated; but hitherto they have never been distinctly established.

At any rate, if a body be conceived to have the faculty of exciting an instantaneous agitation in a point of such a medium, supposed at first equally dense in all its extent, this agitation will be propagated in concentric spherical waves, in the same manner as in air, except that the velocity will be much more considerable. Each molecule of the medium will then be agitated in its turn, and afterwards return to a state of rest.

If these agitations are repeated at the same point, there will result, as in air, a series of undulations analogous to those producing sound; and as in these there are observed successive and periodical alternations of condensation and rarefaction, corresponding to the alternations of direction which constitute the vibrations of a sonorous body, in like manner, it will be easily conceived that the successive and periodical vibrations of luminous bodies might produce similar effects in luminous undulations; and again, as the succession of sonorous waves, when sufficiently rapid, produces on our ear the sensation of a continuous sound, the quality of which depends on the rapidity of the opposite vibrations, and on the laws of condensation and velocity that the nature of these vibrations excites in each sonorous wave; in like manner, under analogous conditions, the ethereal waves may produce sensations of light in our eyes, and different sensations in consequence of the variety of the conditions. Hence the differences of colour. In this system, the length of the luminous waves correspond to Newton's *fits*, and their length is, as will be seen hereafter, exactly quadruple; the rapidity of their propagation depends, as in air, on the relation between the elastic force of the fluid and its density.

When a sonorous wave excited in air arrives at the surface of a solid body, its impact produces in the parts of that body a motion, insensible indeed, but nevertheless real, which sends it back. If the body, instead of being solid, is of a gaseous form, the reflection takes place equally, but there is produced in the gas a sensible undulation depending on the impression that its surface has received.* Luminous undulations ought to produce a similar effect when the medium in which they are excited is terminated by a body in which the density of the ethereal fluid is different; that is to say, there must be produced a reflected wave and one transmitted; which is, in fact, what we call reflection and refraction. In this system, the intensities of rays of light must be measured by the *vis viva* of the fluid in motion, that is, by the product of the density of the fluid by the square of the proper velocity of its particles.

To confirm these analogies, already very remarkable, it would be necessary to follow up their consequences further with calculations; but unfortunately this cannot be done rigorously. The subject of undulations thus sent back or transmitted in oblique motions, is beyond the existing powers of analysis. In the case of perpendicular incidence the phenomenon becomes accessible, but then it teaches nothing as to the general direction of the motion communicated, as the propagation must be continued in a straight line, if for no other reason, on account of there being no cause why it should deviate from it; nevertheless in this case theory indicates the proportions of intensity for the incident and reflected waves, which appear, in fact, tolerably conformable to experiments on light, which is, at any rate, a *verification* as far as it goes.

When the ear receives at once two regular and sustained sounds, it distinguishes, besides those sounds, certain epochs at which undulations of the same nature arrive together or separate. If the periods of these returns are very rapid, a third sound is heard, the tone of which may be calculated *à priori* from the epochs of coincidence; but if these happen so seldom as to be heard distinctly, and counted, the effect is a series of beats which succeed each other more or less rapidly. The mixture of two rays, which arrive together at the eye, under proper circumstances, produces an effect of the same kind,

---

* This phenomenon may be observed in the sounds produced by organ-pipes when filled with successive strata of gases of unequal densities, for instance, with atmospheric air and hydrogen. The sounds which should be produced under such circumstances, have been calculated by Mr Poisson, and his results agree perfectly with experiment.

which Grimaldi remarked long ago, but of which Dr Young first showed the numerous applications. The neatest way of exhibiting this phenomenon is the following, which is due to M. Fresnel.

A beam of sun-light, reflected into a fixed direction by a heliostat, is introduced into a darkened room; it is transmitted through a very powerful lens, which collects it almost into a single point at its focus. The rays diverging from thence form a cone of light within which there are placed, at the distance of two or three yards, two metallic mirrors inclined to each other at a very small angle, so that they receive the rays almost under the same angle; the observer places himself at a certain distance, so as to observe the reflection of the luminous point in both the mirrors. There are thus seen two images separated by an angular interval which depends on the inclination of the two mirrors, their distances from the radiating point, and the place of the observer; but besides these, which is the essential point of the phenomenon, there may be seen, by the help of a strong magnifying lens, between the places of the two images, a series of luminous coloured fringes parallel to each other, and perpendicular to the line joining the images; if the incident light is simple, the fringes are of the colour of that light, and separated by dark intervals. Their direction depends solely on those of the mirrors, and not at all on any influence of the edges of those mirrors, as each of them may be turned round in its own plane without producing the slightest alteration in the phenomenon.

Let us confine our attention, for the sake of greater simplicity, to the case in which the incident light is homogeneous; this case may be easily exhibited in practice by observing the fringes through a coloured glass which will transmit only the rays of a particular tint. In this case if we select any one of the brilliant fringes formed between the two images, we may calculate the directions and paths of the luminous rays which form that fringe, coming from each of the mirrors. Now in making this calculation, we find the following results.

(1.) The middle of the space comprised between the two luminous points, is occupied by a band of colour formed by rays the lengths of whose paths from the luminous point to the eye are equal.

(2.) The first fringe on each side of this is formed by rays for which the difference of length is constant, and equal for instance to l.

(3.) The second coloured fringe arises from the rays having $2l$ for the difference of the distances they pass over.

(4.) In general, for each fringe this difference is one of the terms of the series $0, l, 2l, 3l, 4l$, &c.

(5.) The intermediate dark spaces are formed by rays for which the differences are $\frac{1}{2}l, \frac{3}{2}l, \frac{5}{2}l$, &c.

(6.) Lastly, the numerical value of l is exactly four times that of the length which Newton assigns to the *fit* for the particular kind of light considered.

The analogy between these laws and those of the rings is evident. The following is the explanation given of them in the system of undulations; the interval l is precisely equal to the length of a luminous wave, that is, to the distance of those points in the luminiferous ether, which, in the succession of the waves, are at the same moment in similar situations as to their motion. When the paths of two rays which interfere with one another, differ exactly by half this quantity at the place where they cross, they bring together contrary motions of which the phases are exactly alike. Moreover, the motions produced by these partial undulations take place almost along the same line, as the mutual inclination of the mirrors is supposed to be very small. Consequently, the two motions destroy one another, the point of ether at which they meet remains at rest, and the eye receives no sensation of light. The same thing must occur at those points where the differences of the spaces passed over by the rays is $\frac{3}{2}l, \frac{5}{2}l$, or any other such number; whereas at points where the difference is $l, 2l, 3l$, or any other multiple of l, the undulating motions coincide, and assist each other, so that the appearance of light is produced.

This way of considering the combination of luminous waves and the alternations of light and darkness which result from it, has been called by Dr Young, the *principle of interferences*.

The phenomenon of the alternations of light and darkness is *certain*; if, reasoning *à priori*, it appeared to be *possible, only* on the hypothesis of undulations, it would reduce the probability of that hypothesis to a certainty, and completely set aside the theory of emission. It does not, however, appear to offer that character of necessary truth which would be so valuable, whichever argument it favoured, because it would be decisive. One may, without violating any rule of logic, conceive equally the principle of interferences in the system of emissions, making the result which it expresses a condition of vision.

In fact, the phenomenon of the fringes does not prove that the rays of light really do affect each other under certain circumstances, it only shows that the eye does, or does not receive the sensation of light, when placed at a point where the rays coincide with those circumstances; it proves also that an unpolished surface placed at such a point, and seen from a distance, appears either bright or dark; now in the former case it is possible that vision may cease when the retina receives simultaneously rays which are at different epochs of their fits; and in the latter, when such rays arrive together at an unpolished surface, and are afterwards dispersed by radiation in all directions, it is clear, that having the same distance to pass over from each of the surfaces to the eye, they will have, on arriving at it, the same relative phases that they had when at the surface; if, therefore, they were then in opposite states, they will be so likewise in arriving at the retina, and thus there will be no vision produced. I do not pretend that this explanation is the true one, or even that it bears the character of necessity; it is both true and necessary if light be material, for it is but the statement of a phenomenon; but if only it implies no physical contradiction, that is quite sufficient to prevent the phenomenon from which it is derived from being decisive against the system of emission.

Dr Young has with equal success applied the principle of interferences to the explanation of the coloured rings, both reflected and transmitted, of thin plates. When such a plate is seen by reflection, the light coming from the first surface to the eye interferes with that from the second; this interference either does or does not produce the sensation of light, according as the different distances that the rays have to pass over, place them in similar or opposite phases of their undulations; but then, at the point where the thickness is nothing, this difference is nothing, and consequently one would expect to see a bright spot instead of a dark one. To get over this difficulty Dr Young introduces a new principle, namely, that the reflection within the plate makes the rays lose an interval $\frac{1}{2} l$, exactly equal to half the length of a wave. By means of this modification, the rays reflected from the two surfaces at the point where the thickness is nothing, acquire opposite dispositions, and therefore produce together no sensation of light in the eye; then in the surrounding places, the law of the periods of the undulations gives that of the succession of bright and dark rings; this law, thus modified, agrees with the measurements of the coloured rings observed in the case of perpendicular incidence; but for oblique incidences it is not quite consistent with Newton's statement. Is it possible that the laws which Newton established upon experiments may be inexact, or must we introduce in the case of oblique waves some modification depending on their impact on the surfaces? This point is yet to be decided.

We have hitherto considered only the rings observed by reflected light; the others are formed, according to the *undulation* system, by the interference of waves transmitted directly, with those which, being reflected at first at the second surface of the thin plate, are again reflected on returning to the first, and are thus sent to the eye, at which they arrive without any farther modification. In this case the point where the surfaces touch should give a bright spot, as we find by experience that it does, so that here we have no additional principle to introduce as in reflection; but this is quite necessary in many other cases.

According to this system, the thicknesses at which the rings are formed indicate the length of the oscillations in any substance. Now for one given mode of vibration of the luminous body, the length of the waves must be equal to the distance that the light passes over whilst the vibration takes place; since, therefore, the waves are found to be shorter in the more strongly refracting substances, this velocity of transmission must be less in them according to the same law; that is to say, it must be inversely as the ratio of refraction.

By considering the alternations of light and darkness as produced by the superposition of luminous waves of the same or of a different nature, we give to the phenomenon a physical character, and it is thus that Dr Young first announced the principle of interferences; but we may detach it, as he has done, from all extraneous considerations, and present it as an experimental law; it may then be expressed as follows;

(1.) *When two equal portions of light, in exactly similar circumstances, have been separated, and coincide again nearly in the same direction, they either are added together, or destroy one another, according as the difference of the times, occupied in their separate passages, is an even or odd multiple of a certain half interval which is different for the different kinds of light, but constant for each kind.*

(2.) *In the application of this law to different media, the velocities of light must be supposed to be inversely proportional to the ratios of refraction for those media, so that the rays move more slowly in the more strongly refracting medium.*

(3.) *In the reflections at the surface of a rarer medium, on some metals, and in some other cases, half an interval is lost.*

(4.) Lastly, it may be added, that *the length of this interval, for a given kind of light, is exactly four times that of the fits attributed by Newton to the same light.*

To give an instance of these laws, suppose that when two simple homogeneous rays interfere and form fringes in the experiment with the two mirrors, you interpose across the path of one of these a very thin plate of glass that that ray alone is to pass through. According to the second condition, its motion through the glass must be slower than through the air in proportion as the refracting power is greater. Thus, when after leaving the glass, and continuing its motion, it meets the ray with which it before interfered, its relations with this as to intervals will have been altered; and if the intervals are ever found to be the same, it must be when the ray is so refracted by the glass that the diminution of its velocity be compensated by shortening its path; in this case the fringes will be formed in different places, and their displacement may be calculated from the thickness of the glass and its refracting power; now this is confirmed by experiment with incredible exactness, as M. Arago observes, to whom we are indebted for this ingenious experiment.

By the same rule, if the displacement of the fringes thus produced by a given plate be observed, which may be done with extreme precision, we may evidently find the refracting power of that plate; we may also compare the refractions of various substances by interposing plates of them successively on the directions of the interfering rays. MM. Arago and Fresnel tried this method, and found it so exact that they were able to use it to measure differences of refraction that no other method would have given.

Diffraction of Light.

When a beam of light is introduced into a dark room, if you place on its direction the edge of some opaque body, and afterwards receive on a white surface placed at a certain distance that portion of the light which is not intercepted, the border of the shadow will be observed to be edged with a bright line; and on increasing the distance, several alternations of coloured fringes are thus seen to be formed. This phenomenon constitutes what is called the *diffraction* of light.

To give it all the exactness of which it is capable, it is advisable to use the same disposition as in the experiment with the two mirrors, that is, to take a sunbeam directed by a heliostat and concentrated by a lens almost in a geometrical point; an opaque body is then to be placed in the cone of rays diverging from that point. To fix our ideas, suppose we use an opaque lamina with straight edges, and about a tenth of an inch broad; if then the rays be received on a piece of ground glass placed at a certain distance, and the eye be placed beyond this glass, there will be observed on each side of the shadow of the lamina a numerous series of brilliant fringes parallel to the edges, and separated from each other by dark intervals; the brightness of these fringes diminishes as they recede from the shadow; and the shadow itself is not quite dark, but is formed also of luminous and dark fringes all parallel to the edges of the lamina. Moreover, the ground glass is not necessary to exhibit these fringes, for they are formed in the air, and may be seen in it, either with the naked eye or by the assistance of a lens placed exactly on their direction. If then a lens be fixed to a firm stand which can be moved horizontally, by means of a screw, along a scale divided into equal parts, its axis may be brought successively opposite each bright and dark fringe; the position of one of these may be determined precisely by referring it to a fine thread stretched in front of the lens, and thus the intervals of the fringes may be measured, on the graduated scale, by the distance through which the lens is moved to set it opposite to each; this advantageous arrangement was devised by M. Fresnel, who made use of it to measure all the particulars of the phenomenon with extreme precision.

Now these particulars, as Dr Young first announced, may be represented pretty exactly by supposing that the light which falls on the edges of the lamina, spreads over them radiating in all directions from those edges, and interferes both with itself and with the rays transmitted directly.

The first kind of interference forms the interior fringes; the light radiating from one edge interfering with that from the other, these two sets of rays are exactly in the same predicament as the two luminous reflected points in the experiment of the mirrors; thus also the disposition of the interior fringes both bright and dark, and the ratios of their intervals are exactly similar. If you determine in your mind the series of points in space at which the same kind of interference takes place at different distances behind the lamina, which gives the succession of the places at which the same fringe appears, you will find that those points are, to all appearance, on a straight line; and their intervals, when measured, are very exactly conformable to what the calculation of the interferences indicates.

As to the exterior fringes, they may be considered as formed by the interference of the light transmitted directly with that radiating from each edge; but we must here, as in the reflected rings, suppose a loss of an interval $\frac{1}{2} l$. It thus appears that the points at which each fringe appears at different distances from the lamina, are not placed on a straight line, but on a hyperbola of the second order which experiment confirms completely.

We must not conclude from this that diffracted light does not move in straight lines, for it is not the same ray that forms a fringe of a given order at different distances. That the ray changes, as the distance is altered, may be concluded from this alone, that the fringes may be observed in space either with the naked eye or with a lens; for then it is evident that the rays which form them must converge, and afterwards diverge; otherwise they could not be collected by the lens so as to afford a visible image of their point of concourse.

Very remarkable phenomena of diffraction are again produced, when the cone of light, instead of being intercepted by an opaque lamina, is transmitted between two bodies terminated by straight parallel edges. In this case, the diffracted fringes may, with great appearance of truth, be attributed to the interference of the two portions of light which fall on the opposite edges.

Nevertheless, there are many physical particulars in the phenomenon, which it is difficult to explain on this hypothesis. M. Fresnel has even found that it is not quite consistent with the measurements of the fringes when they are very exact; he has been convinced that the small portion of light which the edges may reflect is not sufficient to produce the observed intensities of the fringes; and that it is necessary to suppose that other rays assist which do not touch the edges. He has thus been induced to consider all the parts of the direct luminous wave as so many distinct centres of undulations, the effects of which must be extended spherically to all the points of space to which they can be propagated; according to which supposition, the particular effect at each point would result from the interferences of all the partial undulations that arrive at it. This consideration, applied to the free propagation of a spherical wave in a homogeneous medium, makes the loss of light proportional to the square of the distance, conformably to observation; but when a part of the light is intercepted, it indicates, in the different points of space towards which it is afterwards propagated, alternations of light and darkness, which, in point of disposition and intensity, agree most minutely with those observed in diffracted light.

The introduction of this principle has enabled M. Fresnel to embrace all the cases of diffraction with extraordinary precision; but an exposition of his results, though very interesting, would lead us farther than the plan of this work would allow.

Double Refraction.

The rays of light, in passing through most crystallized substances, are generally divided into two parcels, one of which, containing what are called the *ordinary* rays, follows the usual mode of refraction; but the other, consisting of what are termed the *extraordinary* rays, obeys entirely different laws.

This phenomenon takes place in all transparent crystals, except those which cleave in planes parallel to the sides of a cube, or a regular octaedron. The separation of the rays is more or less strong, according to the nature of the crystal, and the direction which the light takes in passing through it. Of all known substances, the most powerfully double-refracting, is the clear carbonate of lime, commonly called *Iceland spar*. As this is a comparatively common substance, and may easily be made the subject of experiment, we take it as a first instance.

The crystals of this variety of carbonate of lime are of a rhomboidal form, as represented in figure 100. This rhomboid has six acute angles, and two obtuse; these last are formed by three equal plane angles; in the acute diedral angles, the inclination of the faces is $74° 55'$, and consequently, in the others, it is $105° 5'$. Malus and Dr. Wollaston have both found these values by the reflection of light.

If a rhomboid of this description be placed on a printed book, or a paper marked with black lines, every thing seen through it will appear to be double, so that each point under the crystal must send two images to the eye, and consequently, two pencils of rays. This indicates that each simple pencil must be separated into two in its passage through the rhomboid; and this may be easily shown to be the case, by presenting the crystal to a sunbeam, when it will give two distinct emergent beams. To measure the deviation of these rays, and determine their paths, Malus invented the following simple method; on the paper on which you place the rhomboid, draw with very black ink, a right-angled triangle ABC (*fig.* 101), of which let the least side BC be, for instance, one-tenth of AC. If this triangle be observed through the rhomboid, it will appear double, wherever the eye be placed; and for each position of the eye there will be found a point T, where the line $A'C'$, the extraordinary image of AC, will cut the line AB, which I suppose to belong to the ordinary image. Take then on the triangle itself a length AF' equal to $A'F$, and the point F' will be that of which the extraordinary image coincides with the ordinary one of F. The ordinary pencil proceeding from F, and the extraordinary one from F', are therefore confounded together, on emerging from the crystal, and produce only one single pencil which meets the eye; hence, conversely, a natural pencil proceeding from where the eye is placed to the crystal, would be separated by the refraction into two pencils, one of which would go to F, and the other to F'. This may indeed be easily confirmed by experiment with the heliostat. If then the lines AB, AC, be divided each into a thousand parts, for instance, and the divisions be numbered as represented in the figure, a simple inspection will suffice to determine the points of AB and AC, of which the images coincide; consequently, if the position of these lines and the triangle be known, relatively to the edges of the base of the crystal, it will be known in any case to what points of the base F and F' correspond, so that to construct the refracted rays, it will only remain to determine on the upper surface, the position of their common point of emergence (*fig.* 102). This might be done by marking on that surface the point I, where the images of AB and AC intersect; but as it is useful also to know the direction of the emergent pencil, it is better to make the observation with a graduated circle placed vertically in the plane of emergence IOV. The sights of this circle must be directed to the point I, and if the precaution has been taken of levelling the plane on which the crystal lies, the same observation will determine at once the angle of emergence IOV, or NIO, measured from the normal, and the position of the point I on the rhomboid. The positions of the points F, F', are also known *à priori*, so that the directions FI, $F'I$, may be constructed; whereupon we may remark, that in many cases the extraordinarily refracted pencil $F'I$ does not lie in the plane of emergence NIO.

Such is the process devised by Malus; if we admit it, we may admit also all his observations, and consider them as data to be satisfied, but I will shortly indicate a more simple method, which would allow us to repeat these same measurements with equal facility and accuracy.

Among all the positions that may be given to the crystal, resting always on the same face, there is one which deserves particularly to be remarked, because the extraordinary refraction takes place, like the ordinary, in the plane of emergence. To find this position, it is necessary to conceive a vertical plane to pass through the side BC of the triangle, to place the eye in this plane, and slowly turn the crystal round on its base, till the two images of BC coincide; then, as the ordinary image is always in the plane of emergence, the extraordinary must in that case be in it likewise. The particular plane for which this takes place is called the *principal section of the rhomboid*. If the crystal used in the experiment be of the *primitive* form, for the carbonate of lime, the bases of the rhomboid will be perfect rhombs, and the principal section will be that containing the shorter diagonals of the upper and lower faces. This section of the rhomboid will be a parallelogram $ABA'B'$ (*fig.* 103), in which AB, $A'B'$, are the diagonals just mentioned, and AB', $A'B$, edges of the rhomboid. The line AA' is called the axis of the crystal; it is equally inclined to all the faces, forming with them angles of 45° 23′ 25″. It is to this line that all the phenomena of double refraction are referred.

Let us examine at first the manner of this refraction in the principal section. All its general phenomena are exhibited in figure 104, in which SI represents an incident ray, IO the ordinary refracted ray, IE the extraordinary; IN is the normal. When the incidence is perpendicular, the ordinary ray is confounded with the normal, and passes through the crystal without deviation; but the extraordinary is refracted at the point of incidence, and is more or less deflected towards the lesser solid angle B'. A similar effect is observed in every other case, as shown in the figure, the extraordinary ray lying always on the same side of the ordinary.

The inference to be drawn from this is, that there exists in the crystal some peculiar force which abstracts from the incident pencil a part of its molecules, and repels them towards B'. But what is this force? We shall soon see that it emanates, or seems to emanate from the axis of the crystal; that is, that if through each point of incidence there be drawn a line IA' parallel to that axis, and representing its position in the first strata in which the pencil is divided, all the phenomena take place just as if there emanated from that line a repulsive force, which acted only on a certain number of luminous particles, and tended to drive them from its direction. This force always throws the rays towards B', because they are always found on that side of the axis, under whatever angle of incidence they may have entered.

Let us follow up this idea, which does not appear repugnant to the few observations that have been made, and to verify it by a direct experiment, let us divide the crystal by two planes perpendicular to its axis (*fig.* 105), so as to form two new faces abc, $a'b'c'$, parallel to each other. Now if we direct a ray SI perpendicularly to those faces, it will penetrate them in a direction parallel to the primitive axis of the crystal. Supposing then that the repulsive force emanates from that axis, it will be nothing in this case, and the incident rays will not be separated. This is, in fact, what takes place; there is in this case but one image.

It is even found, in making the experiment, that the image remains single when the second face of the plate is inclined to the axis, provided that the first be perpendicular to it, and to the incident rays. This would happen, for instance, if only the first solid angle A of the primitive rhomboid were taken off. The incident ray SI would continue its progress parallel to the axis, as before, and on emerging from the second surface, it would be refracted in one single direction, according to the law of ordinary refraction. Hence, we may conclude, conversely, that an incident ray $R'I'$, which passed out of air into such a prism under the proper angle of incidence, would be refracted in one single ray parallel to the axis, and emerge at I in the same manner. This again is confirmed by experiment. If, after having cut a rhomboid in the manner described, the eye be applied to the face which is perpendicular to the axis, so as to receive only the rays which arrive in that direction, all the images of external objects will be single; they only undergo at their edges the diffusion which belongs to the general phenomenon of the decomposition of light by the unequal refractions.

But if the repulsive force which produces the extraordinary refraction, really emanates from the axis, as the phenomena seem to indicate, it cannot disappear, except when the incident ray is parallel to the axis. The section, then, which we have described, is the only one in which a crystal prism can give a single image; this again is confirmed by experiment, and we might avail ourselves of this character, to find the position of the axis in any piece of Iceland spar, not in the primitive form.

To return to our plate with parallel faces, cut perpendicularly to the axis. We have seen that the rays are not separated when they are incident perpendicularly; but when they enter obliquely, they ought to be separated, since they then form a certain angle with the axis, from which the repulsive force emanates. This is really what takes place; and, moreover, for equal angles of incidence, the extraordinary refraction is the same on all sides of the axis, which shows that the repulsive force acts from the axis equally in all directions.

Many other crystallized substances, very different from the Iceland spar, exhibit like it a certain single line or axis, round which their double refraction is exerted symmetrically, being insensible for rays parallel to that axis, and increasing with their inclination to it, so as to be strongest for those which are at right angles to the axis. Crystals thus constituted are called *crystals with one axis*. For instance, quartz, commonly called rock crystal, has an axis parallel to the edges of the hexaedral prism, under the form of which it is generally found. But there is between its double refraction and that of the spar, this capital difference, observed by M. Biot, that in the spar the deviation of the extraordinary rays from the axis, is *greater* than that of the ordinary, whereas in quartz crystals it is *less*. All crystals with one axis, that he has examined, have been found to possess one or other of these modes of action, which has occasioned their distinction, by him, into *crystals of attractive* and *repulsive double refraction;* these denominations, which express at once the phenomena, are useful in innumerable cases, to indicate how the extraordinary ray is disposed with respect to the other, since it is only necessary afterwards to know the direction of the axis at the point where the refraction and separation of the rays take place. The progressive and increasing separation of the rays, as their direction deviates more and more from the axis in each of these classes of crystals, may also be conveniently expressed by saying, that the phenomena take place as if there emanated from the axis a force attractive in the one class, and repulsive in the other; which does not, however, imply a belief that such forces do actually exist, or are immediately exerted.

There are, however, other crystals in great number, in which the double refraction disappears in two distinct directions, forming an angle more or less considerable, so that rays are singly refracted along those two lines, but are separated more and more widely as their incident direction deviates from them; crystals of this kind have been called *crystals with two axes*. In those which have hitherto been examined, it has been found that one of the refractions is always of the *ordinary* kind, as if the substance was not crystallized, whilst the other follows a law analogous to that of the crystals with one axis, but more complex, which will be afterwards explained. There are here, as in the simpler case, two classes distinguished by attractive and repulsive double refraction. No crystals have as yet been discovered, possessing more than two directions of single refraction, except indeed those in which it is single in all directions, which is the case with those of which the primitive form is either a cube, or a regular octaedron.*

The general circumstances which characterize the phenomenon of double refraction, being thus recognised, its effects must be exactly measured in each class of crystals, in order to try and discover the laws of it. In order to this, there is no better plan to be pursued, than to cut them into plates, or prisms in different directions, relatively to the axis, to observe the extraordinary refractions, under different incidences, and endeavour to comprise them in one general law. This Huygens has done for Iceland spar. The empiric law inferred by him, has been since verified by Dr Wollaston, and subsequently by Malus, by means of direct experiments, which have confirmed the exactness of it. M. Biot has made similar experiments with other crystals of both classes, by means of a very simple apparatus, which affords very exact measurements of the deviations of the rays, even in cases where the double refraction is very weak. As observations of this kind are indispensable, as the foundations of

---

* This important remark of the connexion between the primitive form of a crystal, and its single or double refraction, is due to Dufay, who was likewise the discoverer of the distinction between the vitreous and resinous electricities.

all theory, it will be as well to give here a detailed description of the apparatus.

It consists principally of two ivory rulers AX, AZ, (*fig.* 106) divided into equal parts, and fixed at a right angle. The former, AX, is placed on a table; the other becomes vertical. A little pillar Hh, of which the top and bottom are parallel planes, is moveable along AX, and may therefore be placed at any required distance from AZ.

This disposition is sufficient, when the extraordinary refraction to be observed takes place in the same plane as the ordinary, which we have seen to be the case under particular circumstances. As this is the simplest case, and is all that is necessary to understand the method, I will explain it first.

If the substance to be observed, had a very strong refracting power, it would be sufficient to form a plate of it with parallel surfaces, upon which experiments might be made in the manner about to be described; but this case being of rare occurrence, we will suppose, in general, that the crystal is cut into a prismatic form, to make its refraction more sensible; it is even advisable to give the prism a very large refracting angle, a right angle, for instance, (*fig.* 107) which has the particular advantage of simplifying calculations. As, however, the rays of light cannot pass through both sides of such a prism, of any ordinary solid substance placed in air, being reflected at the second surface, there must be fixed to this surface, represented by CD in figure 108, another prism, or parallelopiped of glass $CFED$, of which the refracting angle D, is nearly equal to the angle C of the crystal prism, so that the faces CB, DE, of the crystal and glass, may be nearly parallel. The two prisms are to be joined together, by heating them, and melting between them a few grains of very pure gum-mastic, which on being pressed, will spread into a very thin transparent layer. This, when cooled, will be quite sufficient to make the prisms cohere together very strongly, and to let the rays pass from one into the other.

The double prism is to be placed on the pillar Hh, as in the figure, and the observer is to look through it at the vertical scale AZ. This scale will appear double, the ordinary and extraordinary image being, in the simple case here considered, in the same vertical line. Now whatever be the law of the two refractions, the corresponding lines of the two scales seen, are never equally separated in all places, so that if in one part the separation amounts to half a degree of the scale, a little further on it will be a whole degree, in another place a degree and a half, two degrees, and so on. If, for instance, number 451 of the extraordinary division, which we will represent by 451_e, coincides with number 450, of the ordinary (450_o), so that here the separation of the images is of one degree, it will perhaps be found that 502_e falls on 500_o. This shows that the extraordinary rays coming from 502, enter the eye together with the ordinary from 500, and since the glass prism can produce no effect beyond simple refraction on these rays, it is certain that the rays from 500_o and 502_e, must coincide at their emergence from the crystal. This condition furnishes a very accurate method to verify the law followed by the extraordinary rays in the crystal. In fact, the directions of incidence of the two pencils may be determined, since one of them EI, proceeds from the point E of the scale, of which the place is known from the graduation, and arrives at the point of incidence I, the position of which is also determined by the known height of the pillar Hh, and its position on the horizontal scale. There are similar data for the other Oi, which undergoes only the ordinary refraction, whether its point of incidence be supposed the same as that for EI, or whether the small distance of those points be estimated by calculation, taking into account the thickness of the crystal prism, as will be hereafter mentioned.

Now if the ordinary refracted pencil OI be followed through the crystal, which may be done by the common law of refraction, it may be traced to its emergence from the second surface CD. Thus it will only remain to calculate the position of the extraordinary pencil, which should enter the crystal by the same surface, accompanying the exterior ray $I''I'$; and following back this pencil through the prism, to the first surface by an assumed law, for the extraordinary refraction, it will be seen whether it coincides, as it ought, with the incident pencil EI. It is not irrelevant to remark that this condition and indeed every part of the observation, is quite independent of the greater or less refracting power of the glass prism $CDEF$, which serves merely to receive the rays refracted into the crystal, and make their emergence possible.

In the above instance, I have supposed the crystal to be cut so that the extraordinary refraction took place in the vertical plane, like the ordinary; that is the simplest case; but when there is a lateral deviation, I place perpendicularly to the vertical division, a divided ruler RR (*fig.* 109), which is fixed at the point from which the refracted rays proceed. Then there are observed certain lateral coincidences on the scale of *RR*, on each of the vertical rods, if the direction of the point or line of incidence be marked on the first surface of the crystal, by a small line drawn on it, or by means of a little strip of paper stuck to it, to limit the incidence of the rays of which the common incidence is observed.

Similar means are used to fix the heights of the points of incidence on the crystal, when the coincidences are observed on the vertical scale, but then the edge of the strip of paper must be put horizontal.

One may even observe the coincidences on the horizontal scale *AX*, on which the pillar stands. Then the places of incidence on the crystal must be limited as before.

One of the data of the calculation must be the ordinary refracting power of the crystal. This may be measured by observing on what line of the horizontal, or vertical scale another line falls, which is observed by ordinary refraction through the double prism, or through a crystal prism of a smaller angle, without a glass one. One may even see whether the ordinary refraction follows, in all cases, the law of the proportionality of the sines.

It is necessary to make the edge of the crystal prism as sharp as possible, in order that the corrections made for its thickness be inconsiderable. In fact, the best way of making the observation, when it can be done, is to let the rays pass actually through the edge, for then the two refracted pencils have but an infinitely small space to pass through, before they emerge together. For a similar reason, the pillar should, in the experiments, not be placed very near the vertical scale, on which the coincidences are observed, because the corrections for thickness, which are nearly insensible at moderate distances, might become more considerable.

Besides these precautions, the faces of the prisms should be ground very smooth and plane, and their inclinations should be accurately determined, by the reflecting goniometer. Moreover, it is necessary that the direction in which the prism is cut, relatively to the axis or axes of the crystal, should be accurately known; in order to which these axes should be previously determined, either by immediate observation of the directions in which the reflection is single, or by inferences drawn from the experiments themselves, or by other processes that will be hereafter detailed. By following these rules, the observer will be, I believe, perfectly satisfied as to the nicety and accuracy of the mode of experiment. These advantages are derived from the multiplicity of the coincidences, seen on the doubly-refracted scale. The alternate superpositions and separations of the lines of division produce, if I may so express myself, the effect of verniers, and enable one to judge with extreme precision, of the point where the coincidence is most perfect.

Suppose then, that by this, or some analogous process, we have determined for some given crystal, the deviation of the rays in different directions round the axis, it remains to find out the general law, which regulates the phenomenon in all cases. This Huygens has done, as has been before mentioned, for crystals with one single axis, by means of a remarkable law that he connected with the system of undulations; but this same law has since been deduced by M. Laplace, from the principle of material attraction.

If light is to be considered as a material substance, the refraction of its rays must be produced by attractive forces, exerted by the particles of other bodies on the luminous molecules, forces which can be sensible only at very minute distances, and which are therefore quite analogous to those which are exerted in chemical affinities. It follows, that when particles of light are at a sensible distance from a refracting body, the effect they experience from it is quite inappreciable, so that their natural rectilinear direction is not altered; they begin to deviate from this direction only at the moment when they are in the immediate vicinity of the refracting surface, and the action takes place only for an infinitely short period of time; for as soon as the particles have penetrated within the surface to a distance ever so small, the forces exerted on them by the molecules of the medium become sensibly equal in all directions, so that the path of the light becomes again a straight line, though different from the preceding. It is, therefore, clear that the curved portion of the path being infinitely small, it must appear to consist, on the whole, of two straight lines forming an angle, which in fact, is conformable to experience. But for the very reason that the *curve* is not perceptible, it is useless to seek, from experiment, any notions of its form that might lead to a knowledge of the laws which produce it, as observations on the orbits of the planets have led to a knowledge of the laws of gravitation. We must, therefore, have recourse to some other characters derived from experiment.

Newton has succeeded in the case of ordinary refraction, by considering each luminous molecule passing through a refracting surface, as acted on before, during, and after its passage, by attractive forces sensible only at very small distances, and emanating from all parts of the refracting medium. This definition specifies nothing as to the law of the attracting forces; it allows us only to calculate their resultant for any distance, and to suppose that they become evanescent when the distance is of sensible magnitude. Now these data are sufficient to calculate, not indeed the velocity of the molecules in their curvilinear motion, nor the nature of that motion, but only the relations of the final velocities and directions, which ensue, either in the medium or out of it, when the distance of the luminous molecules from the refracting surface is become so considerable that the trajectory is sensibly rectilinear, which will comprehend all distances that we can observe.

For extraordinary refraction, we have not the advantage of being able to define the origin of the molecular force, nor the manner in which it emanates individually from each particle of the crystal; for what we have said about accounting for the phenomena by the supposition of attractive and repulsive forces, emanating from the axes, is only the indication of a complicated result, and not the expression of a molecular action. What is known then, in this case, or at least what may be supposed, when the idea of the materiality of light is adopted, is that the forces, whatever they may be, which act on the rays of light, in these as in other circumstances, are attractive or repulsive, or both, and emanate from the axes of the crystal. Now in all cases when a material particle is subjected to the action of such forces, its motion is subjected to a general mechanical condition called the *principle of least action*. Applying this principle here, and joining the particular condition that the forces are sensible only at insensible distances, M. Laplace has deduced two equations which determine completely and generally the direction of the refracted ray for each given direction of incidence, when you know the law of the final velocity of the luminous molecules in the interior of the medium, at a sensible distance from the refracting surface.

In the case of ordinary refraction the final velocity is constant, for the deviation of the ordinary ray is the same in a given substance in whatever direction the experiment be made, provided the angle of incidence and the nature of the ambient medium be unchanged. Accordingly, if the interior velocity is supposed to be constant, the equations deduced from the principle of least action, show that the refraction takes place in the same plane as the incidence, and that the ratio of the sines is invariable, as it appears to be from all observations hitherto made.

Reasoning from analogy, it appeared natural to suppose that the extraordinary refraction was produced by a velocity varying according to the inclination of the ray to the axes of the crystal. Now taking at first crystals with one axis, we have seen that the extraordinary refraction takes place symmetrically all round the axis, that it disappears when a ray lies along the axis, and is at its maximum when they are at right angles. We must then, in the case of these crystals, limit ourselves to the laws of velocity that satisfy these conditions. M. Laplace has tried the following;

$$V^2 = v^2 + K \sin \vartheta^2,$$

where v represents the ordinary velocity, V the extraordinary, ϑ the angle between the extraordinary ray and the axis, and K is a coefficient which is constant for any one given crystal. Introducing this law of the velocity in the equations of the principle of least action, he obtained immediately Huygens' law. This law had been completely verified only for Iceland spar, but M. Biot has found it true for quartz and beryl; only the coefficient K is positive in crystals of attractive double refraction, and negative in the others. Its absolute value is different in different substances, and it is even found to vary in specimens of the same mineralogical species; but with these modifications it is probable that the law applies equally to all crystals with one axis.

As to those having two axes, it is clear that the extraordinary velocity V must depend on the two angles ϑ and ϑ', made by the refracted ray with the two axes. Analogy leads us to try whether the square of the velocity V cannot be expressed here also by a function of the second degree, but more general, that is, depending on both the angles; now in such crystals the refractions become equal when the ray coincides with one or the other axis. This proves that the extraordinary velocity must then be equal to the ordinary. This condition limits the generality of the function, and reduces it to the following form;

$$V^2 = v^2 + K \sin \vartheta \sin \vartheta'.$$

that is, there must remain only the product of the two sines. Introducing this formula into the equations of the principle of least action, the path and motion of the rays is found for all cases, and it remains only to try whether it is conformable to experiment. M. Biot has done this for the white topaz which has two axes of double refraction, and the formula agreed perfectly with observation. One may, besides, judging by other phenomena that will be hereafter indicated, be convinced that the same law applies to other crystals with two axes on which experiments have not been made; and it is highly probably that it is universally applicable.

It may be remarked that the general law comprises Huygens' as a particular case, for crystals with only one axis, considering these as having two axes which coincide, for then ϑ and ϑ' become equal, and the equation for V contains the square of sin ϑ.

It will be seen farther on, that the same analogy extends also to another species of action that crystallized substances exert on light, which will be explained in the following article.

Polarisation of Light.

The polarisation of light is a property discovered by Malus, which consists in certain affections that the rays of light assume on being reflected by polished surfaces, or refracted by these same surfaces, or transmitted through substances possessing double refraction.

Though it would be impossible here to give a complete exposition of the details of these phenomena, we will at least describe some of the experiments by which they may be exhibited.

The first and principal of these consists in giving to light a modification, such that the rays composing a pencil will all escape reflection when they fall on a reflecting surface under certain circumstances.

As an instance, suppose a beam of sun-light SI (*fig.* 110) falls on the first surface LL of a plate of glass, smooth but not silvered, making with the surface an angle of 35° 25′; it will be reflected in the direction II', making the angle of reflection equal to that of incidence. Let it then be received on another plate of glass, smooth but unsilvered, like the former; generally speaking, it will be again reflected with a partial loss. But the reflection will cease altogether if the second glass be placed like the first, at an angle of 35° 25′ to the line II', provided also it be so turned that the second reflection take place in a plane $I'L'$ perpendicular to that of the first, SIL.

In order to make this disposition of the glasses more clearly intelligible, we may imagine that II' is a vertical line, that IS lies north and south, and $I'L$ east and west.

Before we enter upon the inferences to be drawn from this remarkable experiment, I will make a few observations on the manner of performing it conveniently and accurately.

Many kinds of apparatus may be devised to attain this end. That which M. Biot usually employs, is represented in figure 111. It is very simple, and is sufficient for all experiments on polarisation. It consists of a tube TT', to the ends of which are fixed two collars which turn with sufficient friction to keep them fast in any position. Each of them bears a circular division which marks degrees. From two opposite points of their circumference proceed two brass stems TV, $T'V'$, parallel to the axis of the tube, and between them is suspended a brass ring AA, which can turn about an axis XX perpendicular to the common direction of the stems. The motion of the ring is likewise measured by a circular graduation, and it may be confined in any position by screws. When a plate of glass is to be exposed to the light, it must be fixed on the surface of the ring; then it may be placed in any situation whatever with respect to the rays of light which pass through the tube; for the collar, turning circularly round the tube, brings the reflecting plane into all possible directions, preserving a constant inclination to the axis, and this inclination may be varied by means of the proper motion of the ring round its axis XX. The graduated circle which regulates this motion should mark zero when the plane of the ring is perpendicular to the axis of the tube, and the divisions on the two collars should have their zeros on the same straight line parallel to the axis. In constructing the apparatus one should take care that these conditions are fulfilled; but it is of no great consequence that they be so exactly, as any error may be compensated by repeating each observation on both sides of the axis, and taking the mean of the numbers of degrees found in the two opposite positions.

If it be desired, for instance, to repeat Malus's experiment described above, a plate of glass must be placed on each ring, and they must be disposed so as to be inclined to the axis at angles of 35° 25′. Then the graduated circle of one of the collars must be brought to mark zero, and the other 90°, that the planes of reflection may be perpendicular to each other. The tube must then be secured, and a candle placed at some distance in such a position that its rays may be reflected by the glass along the axis TT'. This will happen when on looking through the tube the reflection of the candle is seen in the first glass. Every thing being thus arranged, the reflected rays will meet the second glass at the same angle of 35° 25′; then according to the different positions given to the collar $T'T'$ which carries this glass, the light proceeding from the second reflection will be more or less intense, and there will be two particular positions in which there will be no rays reflected at all, of those at least which are regularly reflected by the first glass. Care must be taken to put a dark object behind the glass $L'L'$ on the side opposite to the reflected light, in order to intercept the extraneous rays which might be sent on this side from exterior objects, and which, passing through the glass, and arriving at the eye, would mix with the reflected rays that are the subject of the observation. The same precaution should be taken for the glass LL; and, indeed, as this is never used except to reflect light at its first surface, the back of it may be blackened once for all with Indian ink, or smoked over a lamp; it would not do to silver it for a reason that will be given hereafter.

For the light of the candle mentioned above, may be substituted that coming from the atmosphere, which may be received into the tube when reflected by the first glass LL; but in this case to preserve to the rays the precise inclination required for the phenomenon the field of the tube should be limited by some diaphragms, with very small apertures, placed within it. The first glass should be blackened or smoked, as before mentioned, to intercept any rays that might come by refraction from objects situated under it. In this manner, on looking through the tube, when the glass LL is turned towards the sky, a small brilliant white speck will be seen, on which all the experiments may be made. The perfect whiteness of this spot is a great advantage; it is an indispensable qualification in many cases, where different tints are to be observed and compared; it is impossible to succeed so well with the flame of a candle or any other inflamed substance, as none of these flames are perfectly white. Lastly, the brightness of the incident light must be modified, so that the portion irregularly reflected by the two glasses may not be sensible; for this portion, being after such reflection in the state of radiant light, cannot be polarised in one single direction; the other part which is regularly reflected, alone undergoes polarisation, and therefore alone escapes reflection at the second glass.

Whatever be the nature of the apparatus employed, the process will always be the same, and the same phenomena of reflection will be observed on the second glasss. To exhibit them in a methodical manner, which will allow us easily to take them all in at one view, we will suppose, as above, that *SIL*, the plane of incidence of the light on the first glass, coincides with that of the meridian, and that the reflected ray *II'* is vertical. Then if the collar $T^v T^v$ which bears the second glass be turned round, this glass will also turn all round the reflected ray, making always the same angle with it, and the second reflection will be directed successively to all the different points of the horizon; this being premised, the phenomena that will be observed are as follows;

When the second or lower glass is placed so that the second reflection takes place in the plane of the meridian like the first, the intensity of the light finally reflected is at its maximum. As this glass is turned round, it reflects less and less of the light thrown on it.

Finally, when the lower glass faces the east or west point, the light passes altogether through it without being reflected at either surface.

If the collar be turned still farther round, the same phenomena recur in an inverse order, that is, the intensity of the light reflected increase, by the same degrees as it diminished before, and attains the same maximum state when directed towards the meridian, and so on through the whole circle.

It appears then, that during a whole revolution of the glass the intensity of the reflected light has two *maxima* answering to the *azimuths* 0 and 180°, and two *minima* answering to 90° and 270°. Moreover, the variations are quite similar on different sides of these positions. These conditions will be completely satisfied by supposing, as Malus does, that the intensity varies as the square of the cosine of the angle between the first and second planes of reflection.

The results of this interesting observation being thus collected into one point of view, we may draw this general consequence from them, that a ray reflected by the first surface is not reflected by the second, (under a particular incidence) when it presents its *east* or *west side* to the surface, but that in all other positions it is more or less reflected. Now if light be a matter emitted, a ray of light can be nothing else but the rapid succession of a series of molecules, and the *sides* of it are only the different sides of these molecules. We must, therefore, necessarily conclude that these have faces endowed with different physical properties, and that in the present case the first reflection turns towards the same point of space, faces, if not similar, at least endowed with similar properties. This arrangement of the molecules Malus denominated the *polarisation of light*, assimilating the operation of the first glass to that of a magnet which turns the poles of a number of needles all in the same direction.

Hitherto we have supposed that the incident and reflected rays made angles of 35° 25′ with the glasses; it is indeed only under that angle that the phenomenon takes place completely. If while the first glass remains fixed, the inclination of the second to the ray be ever so little altered, it will be found that the second reflection will not be entirely destroyed in any position, though it will still be at a minimum in the east and west plane. If again, the inclination of the ray to the second glass being preserved, that on the first be changed, it will be seen that the ray will never pass entirely through the second glass, but the partial reflections which take place at its surfaces are at a minimum in the above mentioned position.

Similar phenomena may be produced by means of most transparent substances besides glass. The two planes of reflection must always be at right angles, but the angle of incidence varies with the substance. According as the refracting power of this is greater or less than that of the ambient medium, the angle of polarisation, measured from the surface, is greater or less than half a right angle. We have seen that for glass this angle is 35° 25′; for sulphate of barytes it is only 32°, and for diamond only 23°. If glass plates be placed in essential oil of turpentine which has a refracting power almost exactly equal to that of glass, the angle of polarisation will be found to differ very little indeed from 45°. The reflection at the second surface is supposed to take place on the ambient medium which bounds the glass. In general, according to an ingenious remark of Dr Brewster's, the angle of polarisation is characterized by the reflected ray being perpendicular to the refracted. The angles calculated on this hypothesis agree singularly well with experiment, and also confirm the rule given above for the different magnitudes of them, as will easily appear from figures 112, 113, and 114, in which the refracting power is supposed to be respectively greater than unity, equal to that number, and less than it.

This law applies equally well to substances which, like the diamond and sulphur, never produce more than an incomplete polarisation, for the quantity of light reflected is invariably a minimum for the angle so determined.

If the mode of observation which we have applied to smooth glass plates be universally employed, it may serve to show that polarisation when complete is always a modification exactly of the same kind for all substances; for when a beam of light has been once polarised, it will equally pass through all substances, with the exception mentioned above, provided each be presented to it under its proper angle; and whatever be the nature of the first or second substance employed, the variation of intensity in the light after the second reflection is always subject to the same laws.

To represent these circumstances geometrically, let us consider a a ray II' (*fig.* 115) polarised by reflection on a glass plate LL, and through any one of the molecules composing it, let there be drawn three rectangular axes cz, cx, cy, the first coinciding with the ray, the second in the plane of reflection SIC, the third perpendicular to both the others. Then when the ray II' meets a second glass $L'L'$ placed so as to produce no reflection, the reflecting forces which emanate perpendicularly from the glass, must be perpendicular to the axis cx; moreover they must act equally on molecules lying towards cx, and towards cx', for if the glass be turned a little from the position of no reflection, the effects are found to be symmetrical on all sides of that position. The action, therefore, of these reflecting forces, in this position, cannot make the axis xcx' turn either to the right or left, any more than the force of gravity can turn a horizontal lever with equal arms. They cannot bring the axis into their own plane, in which we see it was in the first reflection, by which the polarisation took place on the glass LL. This proves that it is on that axis that the properties of the luminous molecules depend. We will for that reason call it the *axis of polarisation*, and suppose its direction similar and invariably determined for each molecule. Farther, for the sake of conciseness, we will call cz the *axis of translation*; but we do not suppose this invariable in each molecule, and we will consider it only as relative to its actual direction, in order to leave each molecule at liberty to turn round its axis of polarisation. According to these definitions all the results that we have hitherto obtained may be enounced very simply and clearly in the following manner;

When a ray of light is reflected by a polished surface, under the angle which produces complete polarisation, the axis of polarisation of every reflected molecule is situated in the plane of reflection, and perpendicular to the actual axis of translation of that molecule.

If the incident molecules are turned so that this condition cannot possibly be fulfilled, they will not be reflected *at least under the angle of complete polarisation*. This happens when the axis of polarisation of an incident molecule is perpendicular to the plane of incidence, the angle of incidence being properly determined *à priori*.

Generally speaking, when a polished surface receives a polarised ray under the angle at which it would itself produce polarisation, if it be made to turn round the ray without changing that angle, the quantity of light reflected in different positions varies as the square of the cosine of the angle between the plane of incidence, and the axis of polarisation.

When a ray of light has undergone polarisation in a certain direction, by the process above described, it carries that property with it, and preserves it without sensible alteration, when made to pass perpendicularly through even considerable thicknesses of air, water, and in general, any substance that exerts only single refraction; but double-refracting media alter, in general, the polarisation of a ray, and in a manner, to all appearance, sudden, communicating to it a new polarisation of the same nature in a different direction. It is only when crystals are held in certain directions, that the ray can escape this disturbing influence. Let us endeavour to compare more closely these two kinds of action.

That of single-axed crystals has been studied by Malus, who has comprised its effects in the following law. When a pencil of light naturally emanating from a luminous body, passes through a single-axed crystal, and is divided into two pencils having different directions, each of these pencils is polarised in one single direction; the ordinary one in the plane passing through its direction and a line parallel to the axis of the crystal, the extraordinary one perpendicularly to a plane similarly situated with respect to its direction. Either of these rays, when received on a plate of glass after its emergence, shows all the characters of polarisation that we have described.

This law subsists equally, when the ray has been polarised by reflection before its passage through the crystal. The two refracted pencils are always polarised, as if they had been composed of direct rays, but their relative intensities differ according to the direction of the primitive polarisation given to them; this direction must therefore have predisposed the particles to undergo in preference one or other of the refractions.

These two laws were discovered by Malus. The analogy remarked above between the single-axed and double-axed crystals, indicates sufficiently how it is to be extended to the latter; to find the direction of polarisation for the ordinary pencil, draw a plane through its direction, and through each of the axes of the crystal. If either of these axes existed alone, the ordinary pencil would be polarised in the plane belonging to it. Now it is really found polarised in a plane intermediate to those two, and the extraordinary pencil perpendicularly to the analogous plane drawn through its direction between the two planes containing the axes. If the angle between these be equal to nothing, the crystal is single-axed, and the direction of polarisation is conformable to Malus's indications; this law has been directly verified on the two pencils refracted by the topaz; as for other crystals in which it has not been possible to verify it directly, we may, by the consideration of some other phenomena that will shortly be mentioned, judge that it applies to them also.

These laws of polarisation are applicable in all cases where the two pencils transmitted by a crystal are observed separately, but when they are received simultaneously, and in nearly the same direction, that of their apparent polarisation is found to be modified, and at the same time their coincidence produces certain colours, which M. Arago first observed, and of which M. Biot determined the experimental laws. The most simple arrangement to exhibit these colours, is to place a thin lamina of some crystallized substance, in the direction of a white ray, previously polarised by reflection, and to analyze the transmitted light by means of a double-refracting prism. The light is thus separated into two portions, of which the colours are complementary to each other, and identical with those of the rings between two glasses. One of these portions appears to have preserved its primitive polarisation, whilst the other exhibits a new polarisation, of which the direction depends on that given to the axes of the crystal by turning the lamina round in its own plane.

Following gradually in this manner the direction of the polarisation given to a molecule of light, transmitted through different thicknesses of a crystalline medium, it will be found to undergo periodical alternations, which, if light be a matter emitted, indicate an oscillatory motion of the axes of the molecules accompanying their progressive motion. M. Biot has designated the fact by the name of *moveable polarisation*, which is merely the expression of results observed.

If the system of undulations be adopted, the colours of the two images may be attributed to the interference of the two pencils into which the incident polarised light separates in passing through the lamina. This is what Dr Young does, and it is remarkable that calculations founded on this principle gave him the nature of the tints, and the periods after which they recur, precisely as M. Biot had determined them by experiment. As to the alternations of polarisation, they become, in the undulation system, a compound result produced by the mutual influence of the interfering rays, and it is easy to deduce from observation the conditions to which the mixture of the waves must be subjected to produce the new direction of apparent polarisation. M. Fresnel has done this, and the indications of his formula have been found conformable in all respects to the laws deduced by M. Biot from observation.

These interferences of the rays may be produced without the assistance of crystalline laminæ; we may equally employ thick plates, provided the rays pass through them at very small inclinations to their crystalline axes. If the experiment be made with a conical pencil of light, large enough to give the various rays composing its inclinations sensibly different to the axes, so that they experience double refractions sensibly unequal, these rays, analyzed after they emerge, offer different colours united in the same system of polarisation; and the union of these colours forms round the axes coloured zones, the configuration of which indicates the system of polarising action exerted by the substance under consideration. This kind of experiment is, therefore, very proper to exhibit the axes and to indicate the mode of polarisation with which any given substance affects the rays.

Upon the whole, the interferences of polarised rays offer very remarkable properties, many of which have been discovered and analyzed by MM. Arago and Fresnel, with great ingenuity and considerable success, but as the limits of this work do not allow of a full exposition of them, I will only cite one, which is, that rays polarised at right angles do not affect each other when they are made to interfere, whereas they preserve that power when they are polarised in the same direction. It is not only crystalline bodies that modify polarisation impressed on the rays of light; MM. Malus and Biot found by different experiments made about the same time, that if a ray be refracted successively by several glass plates placed parallel to each other, it will at length be polarised in one single direction perpendicular to the plane of refraction. Malus, by a very ingenious analysis of this phenomenon, has moreover shown that it is progressive, the first glass polarising a small portion of the incident light, the second a part of that which had escaped the action of the first, and so on. M. Arago, measuring the successive intensities by a method of his own invention, has shown that they are exactly equal to the quantity of light polarised in contrary directions at each reflection. A phenomenon analogous to this is produced naturally in prisms of tourmaline, which appear to be composed of a multitude of smaller prisms, united together, but without any immediate contact. All light passing through one of these prisms perpendicularly, is found to be polarised in a direction perpendicular to the edges, so that if two such prisms be placed at right angles, on looking through them a dark spot is seen where they cross. This property of the tourmaline affords a very convenient method to impress on a pencil of rays a polarisation in any required direction, or to discover such polarisation when it exists.

Moreover, M. Biot has discovered that certain solid bodies, and even certain fluids, possess the faculty of changing progressively the polarisation previously impressed on rays passing through them; and, by an analysis of the phenomena produced by those substances, he has shown that the same faculty resides in their smallest molecules, so that they preserve it in all states, solid, liquid, and aeriform, and even in all combinations into which they may happen to enter. M. Fresnel has found certain analogies between these phenomena and those of double refraction, which seem to connect the two together most intimately through the mediation of total reflection.

Since reflection and refraction, even of the ordinary kind, modify the polarisation of light, we may expect to find this effect produced when rays of light are made to pass through media of regularly varying density. It is accordingly found that all transparent bodies which are sufficiently elastic to admit of different positions of their particles round a given state of equilibrium, as glass, crystals, animal jellies, horn, &c. produce phenomena of polarisation when they are compressed or expanded, or made unequally dense by being considerably heated, and then cooled suddenly and unequally. These phenomena, discovered originally by Dr Seebeck, have been since studied and considerably extended by Dr Brewster, who has moreover remarked, that successive reflections of light on metallic plates produced phenomena of colours in which both M. Biot and he have recognised all the characters of alternate polarisation.

Knowing, by what has preceded, the experimental laws, according to which light is decomposed in crystals endued with double refraction, we may consider these effects as proofs proper to characterize the mode of intimate aggregation of the particles of such bodies, and to give some insight into the nature of their crystalline structure. Light becomes thus, as it were, a delicate sounding instrument with which we probe the substance of matter, and which, insinuating itself between their minutest parts, permits us to study their arrangement, at which mineralogists previously guessed only by inspection of their external forms. M. Biot has shown the use of this method, applying it to a numerous class of minerals designated by the general name of *mica*, and he thinks he has decisive reasons to believe that several substances of natures extremely different as to their composition and structure have been improperly comprised under that name. He has also made use of the phenomena of alternate polarisation, to construct an instrument which he calls a *colorigrade*, which, producing in all cases the same series of colours in exactly the same order, merely by the nature of its construction, affords a mode of designation just as convenient for comparison as that furnished by the thermometer for temperatures.

Many other experiments have been made, and are daily making; many other properties have been discovered in polarised light; but the limits of this work do not allow us to give any detailed account of them, so that we have been obliged to confine ourselves to the results, which are, perhaps not the most important part of the subject, but the easiest to explain; our aim in this rapid sketch being rather to stimulate than satisfy the desire of knowledge on this branch of science, which presents so vast a field for research both in theory and experiment, and which, though so lately discovered, has already furnished some useful applications to physics and mineralogy.

TABLE

Of the Refractive and Dispersive Powers of different Substances, with their Densities compared with that of Water, which is taken as the Unit.

The substances marked (*) are combustible.

The refraction is supposed to take place between the given substance and a vacuum.

Substances.	Ratio of refraction.	Dispersive power.	Density.
Chromate of lead (strongest)	2,974	0,4	5,8
Realgar	2,549	0,267	3,4
Chromate of lead (weakest)	2,503	0,262	5,8
*Diamond	2,45	0,038	3,521
*Sulphur (native)	2,115		2,033
Carbonate of lead (strongest)	2,084	} 0,091	6,071
—— weakest	1,813		4,000
Garnet	1,815	0,033	3,213
Axinite	1,735	0,030	
Calcareous Spar (strongest)	1,665	0,04	} 2,715
—— weakest	1,519		
*Oil of Cassia	1,641	0,139	
Flint glass	1,616	0,048	3,329
—— another kind	1,590		
Rock crystal	1,562	0,026	2,653
Rock salt	1,557	0,053	2,130
Canada balsam	1,549	0,045	
Crown glass	1,544	0,036	2,642
Selenite	1,536	0,037	2,322
Plate glass	1,527	0,032	2,488
Gum arabic	1,512	0,036	1,452
*Oil of almonds	1,483		0,917
*Oil of turpentine	1,475	0,042	0,869
Borax	1,475	0,030	1,718
Sulphuric acid	1,440	0,031	1,850
Fluor spar	1,436	0,022	3,168
Nitric acid	1,406	0,045	1,217
Muriatic acid	1,374	0,043	1,194
*Alcohol	1,374	0,029	0,825
White of egg	1,361	0,037	1,090
Salt water	1.343		1,026
Water	1,336	0,035	1,000
Ice	1,307		0,930
Air	1,00029		0,0013
Oxygen	1,00028		0,0014
*Hydrogen	1,00014		0,0001
Nitrogen	1,00029		0,0012
Carbonic acid gas	1,00045		0,0018

THE END.

Elements of Nat. Phil. Pl. I

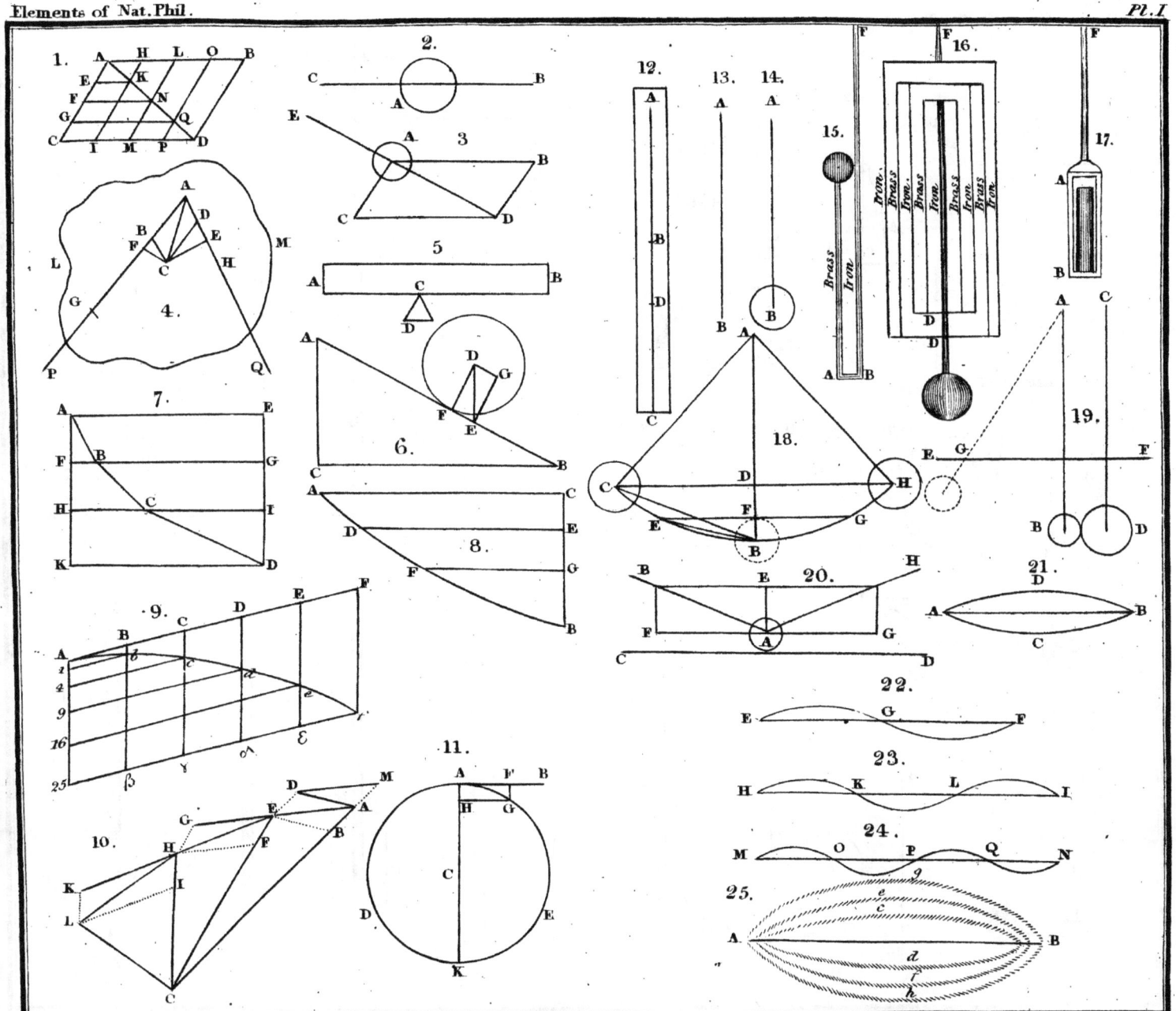

Elements of Nat. Phil.   Pl. II.

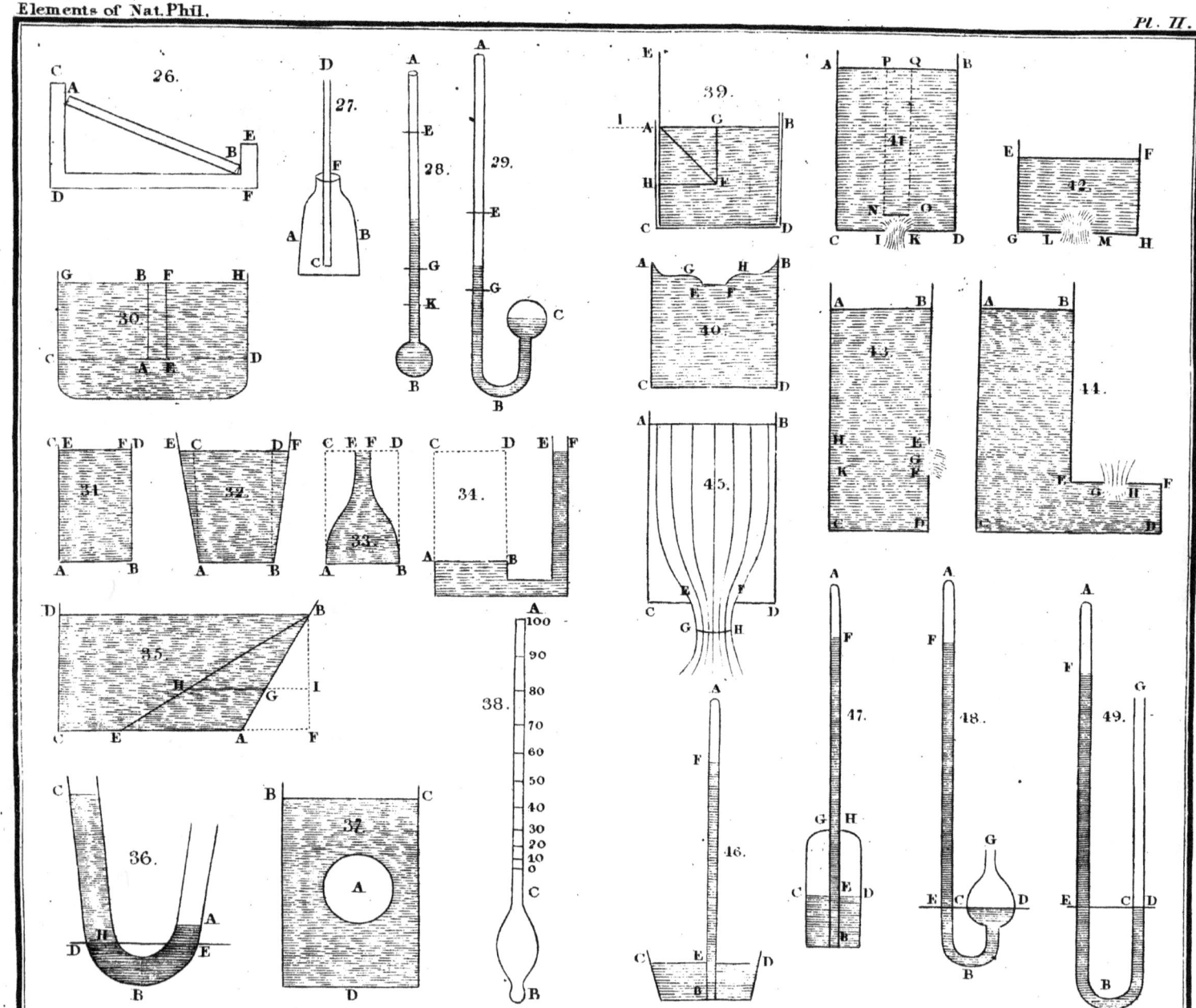

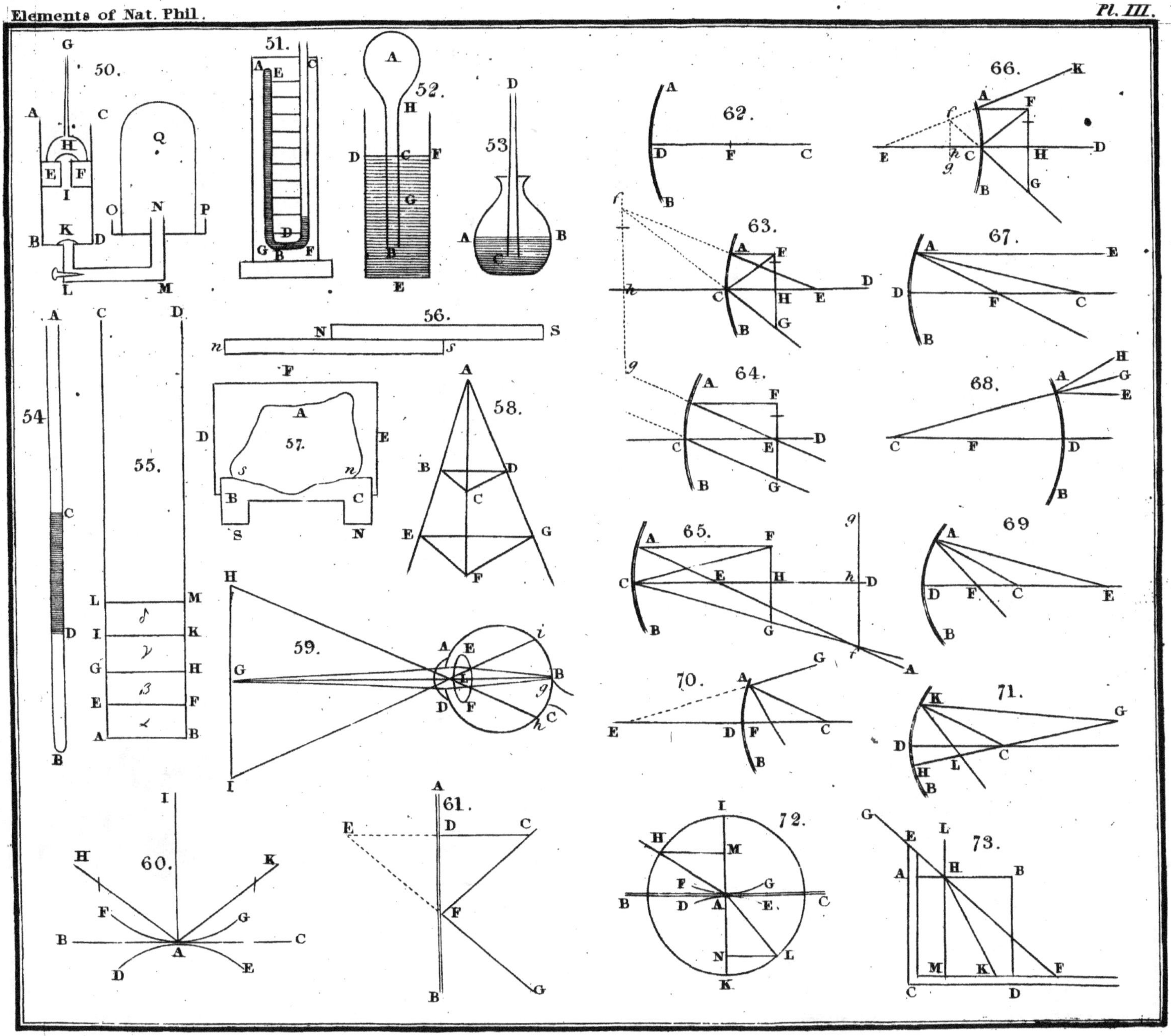

Elements of Nat. Phil.

Pl. III.

Elements of Nat. Phil.
Pl. IV.

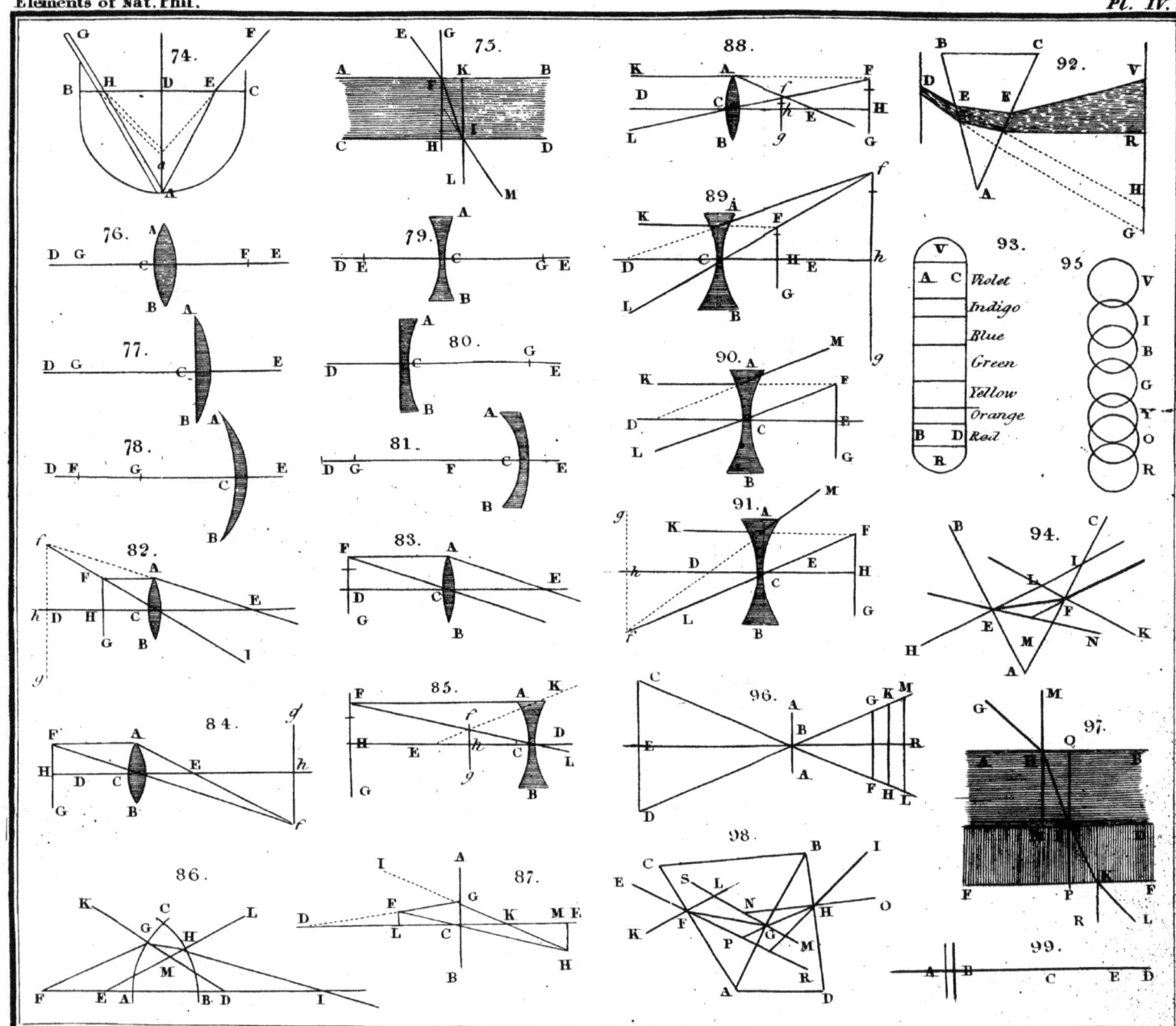

Elements of Nat. Phil.   Pl. V.

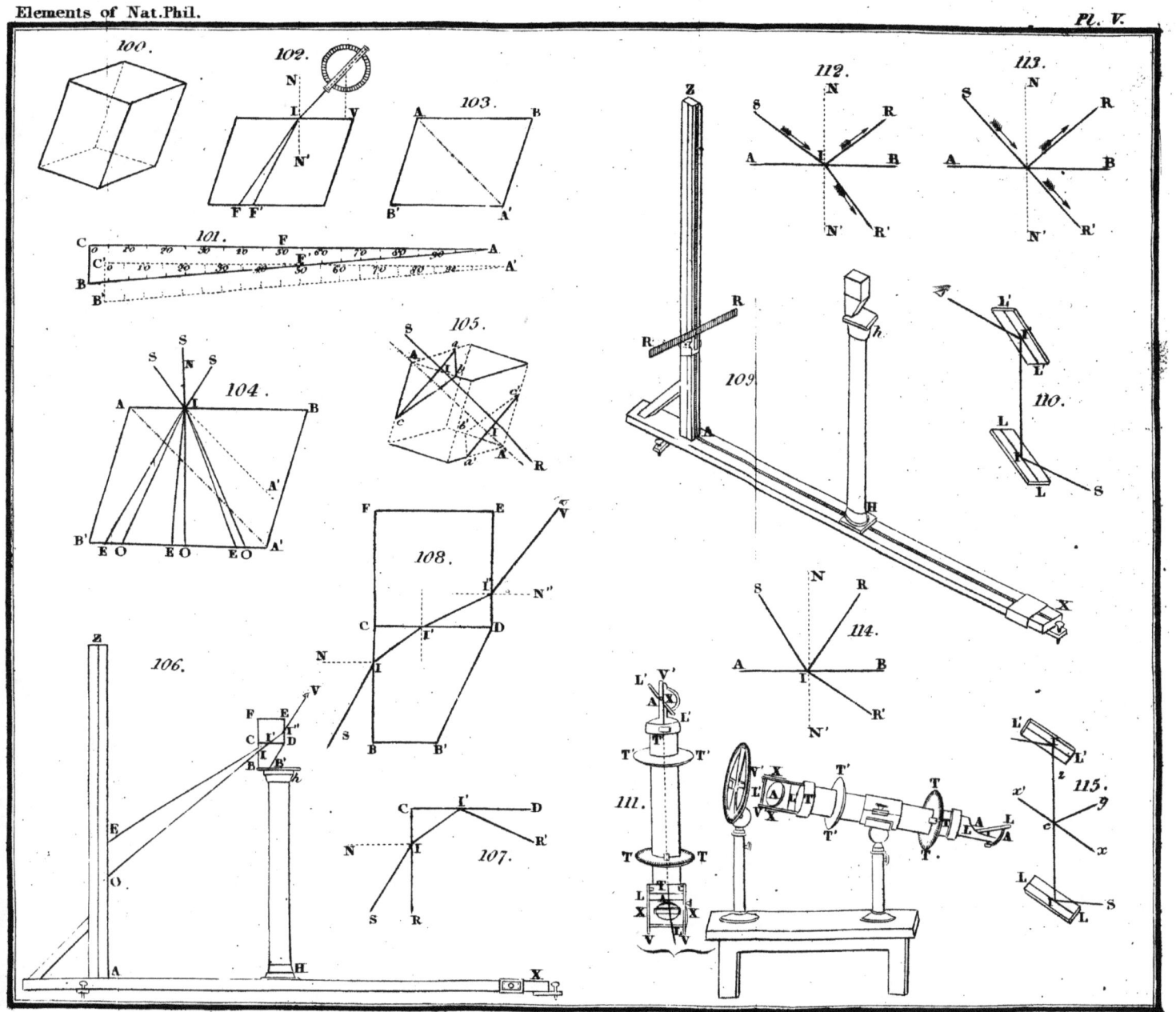

www.ingramcontent.com/pod-product-compliance
Lightning Source LLC
Chambersburg PA
CBHW081215170426
43198CB00017B/2617